Rock Gardening

Rock Gardening

A GUIDE TO GROWING ALPINES AND OTHER
WILDFLOWERS IN THE AMERICAN GARDEN

by H. Lincoln Foster
with drawings by Laura Louise Foster

 TIMBER PRESS *Portland, Oregon · 1982*

Library of Congress Cataloging in Publication Data

Foster, H. Lincoln
  Rock gardening.

  (Timber Press horticultural reprint series)
  Reprint. Originally published: Boston: Houghton
Mifflin, 1968.
  Bibliography: p.
  Includes index.
  1. Rock gardens. 2. Rock gardens—United States.
3. Rock plants. I. Title. II. Series.
SB459.F6   1982   635.9'672   82-16994
ISBN 0-917304-29-2

To

Dorothy Haven

Though she will not be fascinated by
the content of this book, it was through
her that I met my wife and through her
generosity that we have been privileged
to live and garden together at
Millstream House.

Contents

ii   Contents

Foreword

At long last, Linc and Timmy Foster's *Rock Gardening* is to be reprinted. American enthusiasts have long depended on this book for clues as to how to satisfy the exquisite wildflowers of the world's uplands and woodlands in a variety of often inhospitable garden environments on this continent. Now, 14 years after publication, copies are quite literally wearing out (the prudent bought two copies — one for the study and one for outdoor use by muddy fingers). Meanwhile, a whole new audience for *Rock Gardening* has emerged from the milions of young Americans who have embraced America's burgeoning Green Revolution.

But *Rock Gardening* is more than a syllabus of alpines and wildflowers for American gardens. It is also an encouraging, literate and optimistic definition of the art and horticulture of rock gardening, an enterprise once only practiced by the adventurous or wealthy few. The chief source of data for Linc's words and Timmy's illustrations is the Foster's six acre garden of woodland, rocky outcrop and streamside at Millstream House in northern Connecticut. From their observations here, from "botanizing" travels on several continents, and from their constant contact with fellow enthusiasts (Linc is a past president of the American Rock Garden Society, while Timmy is currently Editor of the Society's quarterly BULLETIN), this couple have honed their talents of plantsmanship and garden design. Their experience, distilled in *Rock Gardening*, has enlightened, delighted and persuaded thousands of gardeners to know and grow a host of interesting plants and dwarf shrubs usually seen only in the wild or in botanical collections.

Rock gardeners old and new are deeply in debt to the Fosters. Their book has set a standard for literacy and horticultural excellence rendered with energy, joy and love.

Robert L. Means, *President*
American Rock Garden Society

Preface to the Timber Press Edition

The original edition of this work was published in 1968 followed by a Garden Book Club edition and a reprint. But it has been out of print for a number of years now.

The growing number of new rock gardeners has created a demand for a general book on construction, on soils, on propagation techniques with a description of the plants suitable for the variety of sites in an American rock garden. There have been a few new books since 1968 with an English or a German background, but no one has come forward, as I hoped he or she would, to write a modern replacement for the American rock gardener.

I will admit that I contemplated, almost as soon as I had finished my original composition of the work, a revised edition, with slight shifts of emphasis, with additions to the plant dictionary, a few updated name changes and a reflection of new enthusiasms.

Because I was far too busy just gardening and hybridizing, I took some comfort in the fact that the pages of the *Bulletin of the American Rock Garden Society* were keeping abreast of name changes, describing new plants being introduced, and adequately reporting all kinds of experiments in rock garden construction and propagation schemes.

When people telephoned to ask where they could get hold of a copy of my book, I felt embarrassed to report that it was out of print. A publisher did approach me with the idea of a revised edition. I did study the matter and, in fact, actually reread from front to back my own copy of the book. I could not frankly see any reason to revise the basic text. To be sure I would like to include more information on the use of tufa and devote a section to the sand bed. There might be more emphasis on the reconstruction, after five to ten years, of tired segments of the garden. I would certainly have to consider carefully the new plants that have been introduced since 1968 by the numerous recent expeditions into the Middle East, South America and the newly opened Asian reaches. But at this point very few new plants have proved themselves, except as specialist's plants.

There have been name changes fairly generally accepted since the book was first published. For instance: some **Asarums** are also called *Hexastylis; Cyclamen europeum* is now *C. purpurascens* and *C. neopolitanum* is now *C. hederafolium; Gentiana prophyrio* is now *G. autumnalis; Saxifraga aizoon* is now *S. paniculata.* And there are other name changes accepted or proposed, such as absorbing the American Douglasias into the genus *Androsace,* and putting *Douglasia vitaliana* into a separate genus *Vitaliana* with a species epithet *primulaeflora.*

These taxonomic revisions are important, but I don't think it is necessary to revise the Descriptive Catalogue of Plants here because these changes are either so recent or so tentative that any modern writing about the plants will refer to the alternative names.

Furthermore, there have been new works written since the publication of the Descriptive Bibliography at the rear of the book and many of those listed have gone out of print, but I still think it lists a basic library of valuable rock garden literature.

I would certainly like to expand the catalogue of plants. Since writing the original draft of the work, I have experimented with hundreds of plants not listed. Reflecting my changing enthusiasms, I'm sure I would be tempted to say more about Arisaemas, about Cassiope hybrids, about Saxifrage hybrids and many others. As it stands, the catalogue of plants includes most of the really garden worthy. For those who would like to experiment further, and I would encourage that with all my heart, I would strongly recommend the third edition of *The Seedlist Handbook* by Bernard Harkness, published by Kashong Publications, Box 90, Bellona, N.Y. 14415. Here is an alphabetical listing of literally thousands of plants offered in rock garden society seed exchanges during the 1970's. Though there are no illustrations and no cultural directions there is considerable coded information about each plant. This work is essential for all rock gardeners, beginners or experts.

I have been gratified by the number of rock gardeners who have reported to me that this book, *Rock Gardening,* is used by them as a frequent reference. In fact not a few have complained that their volume is breaking down and tattered by such constant use. I'm pleased that those devoted ones will have a chance to get a fresh copy and I hope that this book will prove useful to many new rock gardeners also.

H. Lincoln Foster
Falls Village, Connecticut

Preface

THIS WORK has a modest purpose, which was difficult to keep before me because my enthusiasms carried me out of bounds. Primarily it is a guide to growing a wide range of rock garden plants under American conditions, chiefly those of the northeastern United States, where I have done my gardening over a period of years in a variety of soils and sites.

From personal experience I know that most books of this sort are read through rapidly by those who already have a rock garden or are contemplating one. Very quickly the reader decides whether the book will gather dust on the shelf or be kept at hand as a day-to-day reference guide. Most rock gardeners are experimenters. They want to try all kinds of plants from the high places and faraway regions of the world. They want clues, however: what soil, what exposure, what secret formula for success.

An effort has been made to suggest a variety of landscape effects, adaptable to different sites and suitable for growing alpine plants and also for those which, because they prefer a stony habitat, are called saxatile plants. The problems of construction, planting, maintenance, proper soils, and propagation have been briefly delineated. Whatever value the work may have as a reference guide, for the beginner or the experienced, is principally in the description and cultural directions for specific plants to be found in Part II. Here is the heart of the book, and here is where I kept running over the margins.

This book cannot possibly give the answers for all the plants that readers may acquire by gift, purchase, exchange, and by growing from seed. It does not pretend to list, describe, and prescribe for all the plants suitable for rock gardens and similar growing sites. Nor does it pretend to have all the answers for growing even those that are described. Under each genus most of the species likely to be available to American gardeners are discussed, along with a few that are still uncommon. The list is based almost entirely on those plants I have personally grown or have seen growing.

Almost all the literature dealing with rock gardening has been written by gardeners whose experience has been in England, where climatic conditions are not only more favorable in general but also more uniform from one section to another. Warnings given about avoiding the drip from trees and advice about seeeking the driest and sunniest sites for most high alpines apply in England, but they lead American gardeners astray. Conditions of climate in the northeastern United States are not ideal for alpine plants. Rapid changes of temperature, periods of alternate freezing and thawing in winter, frequently without snow cover, days of hot, humid weather under a cooking sun in summer, extended spells of withering drought followed by sudden battering thunderstorms—these are not ideal conditions for growing alpines. But it is possible to succeed with almost all rock garden plants even under these adversities; so, the following suggestions will certainly fit more nearly ideal regions, like the Northwest Coast.

There are, it is true, no sure-fire prescriptions, no foolproof guidelines; yet with a willingness to experiment, based on the best available previous experience, a devoted gardener can successfully grow most of even the challenging alpine plants. I do not mean that rock gardening is easier than vegetable gardening or growing annuals in a windowbox, but I do suggest that it is no more difficult and that the creative pleasure derived from it is greater in every respect.

Of great value to me, as I am sure they are to every rock gardener, have been visits to gardens in various parts of this country and in Europe. Of equal, if not greater, importance have been trips to the Swiss and French Alps, the Pyrenees, the mountains of Great Britain and Canada, and the principal ranges in the United States to learn as much as possible by seeing plants in their wild habitat. From these trips I have brought back not only inspiration and lore but seeds and plants. Many of them still thrive here at Millstream House as reminders of these field trips. Some have been propagated and disseminated to other gardens. Many unfortunately have not survived. But all rock gardeners are optimists, just because they are dealing with plants that wax and wane, renew themselves year after year, and create moments of excruciating pleasure.

From rock gardeners and botanists too numerous to name I have acquired generous gifts of plants and seeds and a store of valued information and advice. I have learned much and enjoyed myself thoroughly by reading and rereading the journals published by the Alpine Garden Society of England, the Scottish Rock Garden Club, and the American Rock Garden Society. Above all, it is to my wife that I am most deeply grateful. Together we have built the rock garden here at Millstream House, together we have made garden visits and field trips, and together we have written this book. If reading this book gives anyone a fraction of the pleasure and inspiration that my wife and I have shared in building and tending our garden and in writing this guide, we shall feel rewarded.

H. LINCOLN FOSTER

Millstream House
Falls Village, Connecticut

Glossary

1

Acid soil. *See* pH.

Acute. Terminating in a sharp point; as of a leaf, bud, or other portion of a plant.

Alkaline soil. *See* pH.

Alpine. Above treeline in mountainous areas.

Alpine-house. A well-ventilated, cool greenhouse where winter temperatures may go as low as 20°F.

Alpine lawn. An area planted to resemble a flowery mountain meadow.

Alpine plants. Plants native to mountainous areas, usually above treeline.

— 2

Alternate leaves. Leaves placed at regular intervals along a stem with none springing from the same point (1).

Anther. The pollen-bearing portion of the stamen (2).

3

Awl-shaped. Tapering rather abruptly to a sharp point (3).

Axil, axillary. The angle between a stem and a leaf or another stem (4).

4

Basal leaves. Leaves growing directly from the crown of a plant or from the lowest section of the stem (5).

Batter. The slight backward slope of a wall.

5

Bedding-plane. The angle of the layers (strata) in sedimentary rock.

Bipinnate. Characterizing a leaf deeply cut into segments or leaflets, which are in turn cut into subleaflets (6).

Bluestone. A hard bluish-gray stone frequently crushed to surface driveways.

Bonsai. An artificially dwarfed and shaped tree or shrub grown in a pot; originally an oriental art.

Borage-like. Resembling plants of the Borage Family; hairy-leaved herbs with 5-petaled flowers like forget-me-nots.

Boulder field. An area formed primarily of loose rocks of all sizes, whether broken and angular or weatherworn and smooth, among which fine particles of decayed vegetable, animal, and mineral matter have been deposited.

Bract. A leafy structure, usually green but sometimes brightly colored and petal-like, closely connected with the flowering part of a plant, occasionally large enough nearly to conceal the flower (7).

Bulb, bulbous. A swollen underground leaf bud made up of fleshy scales which remains dormant until favorable conditions urge it to spring into growth (8).

Bulblet. A small bulblike structure usually borne in leaf axils on the stem.

Calcicole. Found growing only in limestone soils.

Calyx (pl. calyces). The outer section of a flower, made up of sepals that are usually green and frequently joined together at the base to form a lobed tube (9).

Campanulate. Bell-shaped or cup-shaped.

Cartilaginous. Hard and tough but flexible.

Ciliate. Fringed with hairs along the margin (10).

Clasping leaf. A leaf whose base partially surrounds the plant stem (11).

Clone. A group of plants all of which have been derived by vegetative propagation from a single individual.

Composite, Compositae. A plant belonging to the Compositae Family, the flowers of which are densely packed into a head resembling a single flower. For example, aster, daisy, dandelion, goldenrod.

Compound leaf. A leaf divided into several separate leaflets (12).

Conifer. A cone-bearing tree, such as pine.

Cordate. Heart-shaped (13).

Coriaceous. Leathery in texture.

Corm. A solid fleshy enlargement formed underground at the base of the stem (14).

Cottonseed meal. A fertilizer made of cottonseed pulp from which the oil has been extracted; particularly good for conifers and acid-loving plants.

Course. In wall construction, a continuous band of stones or blocks laid side-by-side.

Crenate. With rounded teeth along the margin (15).

Crenulate. Finely crenate.

Crosier. A shape like a bishop's staff or shepherd's crook (16).

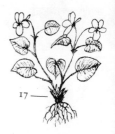

Crown. The thickened junction of stem and root (17).

Crucifer. A plant belonging to the Mustard Family, the flowers bearing four petals and four sepals in the form of a cross (18).

Cuneate. Wedge-shaped, with the narrow angle at the stem end (19).

Cutting. A part taken from a plant for propagation purposes.

Cutting-frame. An enclosed container into which light may penetrate, filled with a special soil-mix in which cuttings are inserted for propagation.

Cylindrical. Shaped like a cylinder (20).

Cyme. A broad, more or less flat-topped flower cluster in which the central flowers open first (21).

Damping-off. Collapse and death of seedlings due to parasitic fungi encouraged by wet conditions and over-crowding.

Deciduous. Losing its leaves for a portion of the year; opposite of evergreen.

Decumbent. Reclining but with the tip ascending.

Deflexed. Bent downward.

Dentate. Sharp-pointed teeth, as along the margin of a leaf, usually pointing outward (22).

Die-back. The death of young shoots due to disease or other adverse conditions.

Disk. An enlargement of the receptacle of a flower which surrounds the ovary. In composite flowers, the central part of the flower head (23).

Division. Separating a plant to form two or more plants, each complete in itself.

Dry wall. A wall in which the stones are fitted together without the use of mortar.

Dry well. An excavation filled with loose rock into which water is drained and from which it then seeps into the soil.

Duff. The layer of partly decayed vegetable matter found on the floor of a forest.

Edging. The removal of weeds and grasses that grow into the edge of a flowerbed by slicing down through the top growth and roots with an implement such as a sharp spade and entirely digging out all weed growth within this cut edge.

Elliptical. Oval in shape, rounded about equally at both ends (24).

Encrusted. Coated with a hard, limy crust on the edges.

Endemic. Native to a particular region.

Equisetum-like. Resembling *Equisetum*–horsetail (25).

Ericaceous. Belonging to the Heath Family (usually requiring acid soil), as do blueberry, heather, laurel, rhododendron.

25

Farina, farinose. A meal-like powder; thus a farinose stem is powdered.

Fastigiate. Of an erect plant whose branches are upright and close together, producing a narrow column (26).

Fibrous-rooted. Characterized by coarse threadlike roots growing directly from the crown.

Fiddlehead. An unfurling fern frond, shaped like the head of a fiddle. *See* Crosier.

26

Flowers of sulphur. Finely powdered pure sulphur used to control mildews and red spider mites.

Flower stalk. The stalk that carries the flower above the leaves (27).

Form. As used in horticulture, a term loosely synonymous with "variety" but more properly applied to the original plant of a clone.

27

Fracture line. The angle at which rock cracks naturally under stress.

Frond. The expanded leaf of a fern. Fertile fronds bear spores, usually on the back; sterile fronds bear no spores.

Fruiting-stalk. A stalk bearing the sporing bodies of certain ferns, different from the leafy frond (28).

Garden hybrid. A hybrid plant produced under garden conditions.

28

Genus (pl. genera). A category of classification for a group of closely related species. Groups of closely related genera form a family. The generic name of a plant is the first part of the Latin binomial, thus: *Allium* (genus) *flavum* (species) belongs to the Liliaceae (or Lily Family).

Glabrous. Not hairy and hence smooth.

Glandular. Bearing glands, usually on the tips of hairs (29).

Glaucous. Covered with a whitish bloom, giving a grayish or bluish color to the leaf or stem.

Globular. Round and solid (30).

Gravel. Small fragments of rock either rounded as in pebbles or with sharp angles as in crushed or broken rock.

Grit. A very fine gravel or very coarse sand.

Ground-pine-like. Resembling ground pine. *See* Lycopodium-like.

Grow-on. To place young plants in a controlled environment following propagation and prior to setting in permanent sites.

Half-block. A term used in this book to describe the dimensions of half a 16-inch cement block, 8 x 8 x 8 inches.

Half-ripened wood. A shoot of this year's growth which is no longer soft but is beginning to become firm and mature.

Hand Pollination. A process used in hybridizing plants in which the pollen taken from the anthers of one plant is placed on the stigma of another plant, usually by means of a small watercolor brush.

Harden-off. To introduce more light and a drier atmosphere by gradual degrees to plants that have been grown under moist and shaded conditions.

Hardpan. A compacted, sometimes almost cemented lower layer in certain soils virtually impervious to plant roots and water.

Heath. A site of acid sandy-peaty soil suitable for growing ericaceous plants.

Herbaceous. Characterizing a plant that dies down to the ground at the end of the growing season.

Horsetail-like. *See* Equisetum-like.

Humus. A dark brown organic material formed of partially decayed vegetable and animal matter.

Hybrid. A plant having parents of different species, occasionally of different genera.

Inflorescence. A complete flower head.

Involucre, involucrate. A collection of bracts or leafy structures surrounding a flower cluster or single flower (31).

Kidney-shaped. Shaped like a kidney (32).

Kill-back. Death of a portion or the whole upper part of a plant, the roots remaining alive and sending up new growth.

Labiate. Lipped; having one portion lip shaped (33).

Lanceolate. Shaped like a lance head; much longer than broad, with a narrow pointed tip, broadest toward the base but somewhat tapering toward the stem (34).

Layer. A branch or shoot that develops roots where it contacts the soil. Also used as a verb to describe the process of making a branch develop roots in this manner.

Leaf axil. *See* Axil.

Leaf-cutting. A leaf that is induced to send out roots and a growing point so that it becomes a complete plant.

Leaflet. A single division of a compound leaf, usually having its own stem (35).

Leaf mold. Partially decayed leaves.

Leaf node. *See* Node.

Leafy-bracted. Bearing leafy bracts at intervals throughout the length of a flower stalk.

Lime-pitted. Having deposits of lime on a leaf, usually along the edge. *See* Encrusted.

36

37

Linear. Long and narrow, with almost parallel edges (36).

Linear-oblong. A narrow oval with almost parallel edges (37).

Loam. The upper layer of soil; a mixture of mineral particles and decayed organic material.

Lobed. Partially divided into segments; deeply indented but not completely separated (38).

Lycopodium-like. Resembling *Lycopodium* (ground pine), finely branched and densely clothed with scale-like leaves (39).

38

Medium-acid. Somewhat acid (referring to soil). A pH of about 6.

Monocarpic. Flowering only once and then dying.

Moraine. A site where a deep layer of rock particles has been deposited by moving water and through which water still flows, with a small amount of partially decayed vegetable matter washed between the rocks.

39

Mound layering. A method of propagation in which soil is piled over the base of a plant in an attempt to make the partially buried shoots develop roots.

Muggs. A colloquial term to describe both weather conditions of high temperature and high humidity and also the resulting damage, especially to cushion plants.

Mulch. Any substance such as straw, leaves, gravel, ground bark, etc., spread upon the surface of the ground as insulation, for moisture retention, or to prevent mud-splash.

40

Natural hybrid. A hybrid plant produced by natural causes in the native habitat of its parents.

Neutral soil. *See* pH.

Node. The point on a stem from which leaves or other stems rise, usually somewhat thickened (40).

Offset. A short lateral rosette or leafy shoot, primarily propagative, which arises near the base of a plant (41).

41

Opposite. Springing from the same point on a stem but on opposite sides; describing leaves or branches (42).

Orbicular. Circular (43).

Outcrop. A section of underlying rock stratum that is exposed on the surface of the ground.

Ovate. Egg-shaped, broadest at the stem end (44).

Ovoid. A solid with an ovate outline (45).

Palmate. Radially lobed or divided (46).

Panicle. A loosely branched flower cluster, longer than wide, the basal flowers opening first (47).

Pappus (pl. pappae). The hairs or bristles attached to the dry, hard, one-seeded fruit of many of the composite plants, replacing the calyx (48).

Peastone. Gravel, either rounded or broken, with a diameter of about ⅜ inch.

Peat. Semicarbonized vegetable matter that has partially decomposed in water. Michigan peat is a name generally applied to sedge peat, which is almost black and is formed of rather thoroughly decomposed grasses and sedges. It is less acid than peat from sphagnum moss, which is light brown and more fibrous because it is not as thoroughly decomposed.

Peat block. Peat originally removed from a bog in blocks that when dried are hard and tough. These are then processed to make the crumbly material used horticulturally.

Pedicel. The stalk of a single flower in a cluster of flowers (49).

Peduncle. The primary flower stalk, springing from a leafy stem, which bears either a cluster or a solitary flower (50).

Perfoliate leaf. A leaf having a stem that appears to pass through it (51).

Petal. A single segment of the corolla which surrounds the sexual parts of the flower; usually brightly colored and conspicuous (52).

Petiole. The stem of a leaf (53).

pH. A symbol indicating the degree of alkalinity or acidity. Acid soil has a pH below 6; neutral soil has a pH of 7; alkaline soil has a pH of 7 and above.

Pine barren. A site where an acid sandy soil is kept moist from below by a high water table, located almost exclusively on the East Coast of North America, inhabited by stunted pines and containing certain endemic plants.

Pinnate. Composed of leaflets arranged on either side of a central stalk and referring to a compound leaf (54).

Pistil, pistillate. The female organ of a flower; when complete consisting of ovary, style, and stigma. The adjective usually applies to flowers having no stamens.

Pit house. A greenhouse; the top is translucent, the walls are underground.

Planted wall. An uncemented wall of stone or cement block containing soil so plants will grow in its sides and top.

Planting pocket. A hole filled with soil, usually among rocks, deep enough and sufficiently well drained to accommodate comfortably one or more plants.

Plunge. To insert a flowerpot to its rim in water or in a quick-draining but moisture-retaining substance such as sand, which had been placed in a bed in a greenhouse or in a sheltered position out-of-doors.

Pouch. A swollen, hollow, sack-shaped petal (55).

Procumbent. Prostrate or trailing but not naturally rooting at the nodes.

Pubescent. Covered with hairs, especially if soft, short, and downy.

Raceme. An unbranched, long, slender flower head (56).

Raised bed. A freestanding flowerbed, enclosed and raised off the ground by built-up walls of stone or similar material on all four sides. The walls as well as the top may be planted.

Ray flowers. The conspicuous flowers with a single strap-like petal around the margin of some composite flower heads, such as daisies (57).

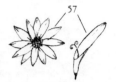

Rhizome, rhizomatous. A swollen, prostrate, usually subterranean and horizontal stem producing roots on its lower side and leaf-shoots on its upper side. A plant having stems of this nature is called rhizomatous (58).

Rhombic. Having a diamond shape (59).

Rockery. Rocks placed in a close-set group and planted with material generally unsuitable to such a site.

Rogue. To weed out inferior individual plants, leaving only those with desirable qualities.

Root-cutting. A section of root which is to be used to produce a complete plant.

Rooting medium. A material into which cuttings are inserted in an effort to make them grow into a complete plant.

Rootlets. The fine roots that branch out from the main root or rootstock (60).

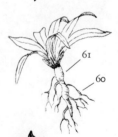

Rootstock. An upright rhizome from which roots and rootlets spring (61).

Rosette. A cluster of leaves arranged in a circular form, frequently arising directly from the crown of a plant at ground level (62).

Rue-like. Resembling rue, usually referring to the shape of the leaf, which is broadly triangular and bipinnate, the leaflets deeply cut into many spatulate or wedge-shaped lobes; almost feathery in general effect (63).

Rugose. Wrinkled.

Sagittate. Shaped like an arrowhead, as of a leaf, with basal lobes toward the stem.

Sand frame. An area, usually enclosed by sides and preferably shaded, filled with sand or a very sandy soil mixture.

Saxatile. Growing among rocks.

Scape. A flower stem bearing one or more flowers, growing directly from the crown of a plant, either leafless or with bracts only (64).

Scree. A site consisting mostly of rock particles of various sizes, usually broken from and accumulated at the base of large rock masses. A small amount of decayed vegetable matter is admixed with the broken rock.

Sedimentary rock. Rock originally formed by the deposition of sediment in water. For example, sandstone, shale, limestone.

Sepal. A single segment of the calyx (the outer section of a flower) usually green but occasionally brightly colored and petal-like.

Serrate. Having sharp teeth that point forward (65).

Sessile. Without a stalk of any kind.

Sharp sand. Sand with grains that are angular rather than rounded.

Shoot-wood. A newly grown stem with its leaves.

Spadix. A fleshy spike bearing flowers (66).

Spathe. A single large bract enclosing a flower head (67).

Spatulate. Spoon- or paddle-shaped (68).

Species. A closely related group of individuals with similar characteristics which may interbreed. A group of related species form a genus. The specific name is the second part of the Latin binomial, thus: *Allium* (genus) *flavum* (species).

Sphagnum. A particular genus of moss which grows in very moist sites. It is porous, will absorb great quan-

tities of moisture, and is almost surgically sterile. When partially decayed it forms an acid peat.

Sphagnum soup. Pulverized sphagnum moss kept saturated with water, used for germinating some types of seed.

Spike. An elongated flower head of stalkless or nearly stalkless individual flowers (69).

Spiral. An arrangement of branches, leaves, or flowers in a coil around the stem (70).

Spore. The one-celled, sexless reproductive germ of ferns and their relatives which grows into an organism containing both male and female functions.

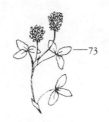

Spring-cutting. A cutting, usually a soft stem-cutting, removed from the parent plant during the period of active growth.

Stamen, staminate. A male pollen-bearing organ of flowering plants, consisting of the anther and a supporting filament (71). The adjective is usually applied to a flower bearing no pistils.

Stellate. Star-shaped; usually applied to branching hairs (72).

Stem-cutting. A section of the stem of a plant which is induced to grow roots and become a complete plant.

Stem-leaves. Leaves that grow from the stem of a plant (73).

Stemless. Characterizing flower and leafstalks that spring directly from the crown (74).

Stemmed. Characterizing flower and leafstalks that branch out from a stem ascending from the crown (75).

Sterile frond. *See* Frond.

Stigma. The part of the female organ (pistil) which receives the pollen; normally sticky when ripe and situated at the top of the pistil (76, see next page).

Stolon. A runner or basal shoot that develops roots.

Stoloniferous plants are those commonly producing stolons (77). Root-stolons run out underground from the crown of a plant and send leafy stems to the surface, sometimes at considerable distance from the parent plant.

Stone chips. Gravel; small particles of rock ranging from about ⅜ inch to 2 inches in diameter, either rounded or angular.

Straplike. Shaped like a strap; long and wide, with nearly parallel sides.

Strata. The layers in sedimentary rock, sometimes differing from each other in texture and composition. Stratified rock is that which is formed in layers.

Strike. A horticultural term to describe the forming of new roots on a cutting.

Strip. To remove unwanted leaves from the basal part of a stem-cutting.

Style. The usually thin portion of the pistil which holds the stigma above the ovary (78). This will occasionally persist in some plants after the seed matures and will develop into an organ for disseminating the seed (79).

Succulent. A fleshy and juicy plant.

Summer-cutting. A cutting, usually a stem-cutting (which may be termed summer-wood), removed from the parent plant shortly after the period of most active growth.

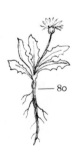

Talus slope. An unstable area of broken rock sloping away from the base of a cliff.

Taproot. A long, descending main root (80).

Taxonomy. The technical classification of plants and animals into groups.

Tender perennial. A plant that would live several years in a warm climate but is unable to survive frost; but because it blooms the first year from seed it may be grown as an annual in colder climates.

Thong-root. One of several thick roots descending from the crown.

Tip-cutting. The tip of a stem with its terminal growth-bud which is induced to develop roots and become a complete plant.

Tomentose. Densely covered with matted woolly hair.

Tongue-shaped. Long and broad, widest near the tip and ending in a rounded point (81).

81

Toothed. With a jagged margin.

Topdressing. A very thin layer of such ingredients as soil, gravel, humus, and fertilizer spread over and around plants most commonly as nutriment.

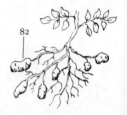

82

Top-spit. The top layer of soil in which decayed organic matter is mixed with the mineral soil; usually about a spade depth.

Tuber. A short thickened subterranean stem or root serving for food storage and having buds (82).

Tubular. Shaped like a tube; long, slender, and entire, with very little or no spread at the top (83).

83

Type species. The specimen or group of nearly identical specimens from which the original description of the species was made.

Umbel, umbellate. A flower head in which all the individual pedicels spring from the same level (84).

Unstratified rock. Rock that has no distinct layers.

Urn-shaped. Shaped like a bell with a narrowed mouth (85).

84

Variety (abbreviated var.). A group of plants within a species with one or more characteristics different from those of the type, such as size, growth habit, an obvious flower color variation, or marked difference in shape or color of leaf. Variety may be indicated by a third Latin adjective following the plant's binomial name, thus: *Juniperus* (genus) *squamata* (species) *prostrata* (variety).

85

86

Viable. A seed capable of sprouting and growing.

Viscid, viscous. Sticky.

Water table. The upper limit of ground continually moistened by underground water.

Wedge-shaped. Narrowest at the point of attachment and widening regularly to the apex (86).

87

Whorl. A circle of leaves, stems, branches, or flowers all rising from the same level (87).

Winged petiole. A leaf stem with lobes of leafy material extending from it (88).

88

Woody plant. A plant with hard stems that do not die to the ground at the end of the growing season; opposite of herbaceous.

PART I

*Alpines and Wildflowers
in Your Garden*

1

What Is Rock Gardening?

THERE ARE many reasons why people become charmed by rock gardening. The reason may be a remote and tenuous recollection of plants combined magically with rock in a childhood experience when the ineffable perfection of a natural creation took on some special meaning now forgotten but haunting. Or it may be a glimpse of the way the Japanese create serenity with strength in a composition of plant form and rock form, leaf texture with rock texture. Or it may be a glorious day in the rugged beauty of alpine uplands in Italy, Greece, the Rockies, or wherever the earth has thrust toward the sky, and brilliant dwarf plants have edged and laced the rocks and embroidered the turf under a blue sky in a clear, heady atmosphere. Or it may be as prosaic as this: you find yourself living in a region where the bones of the earth show through a shallow soil and you long for flowers but the terrain says no to a conventional garden, and you come to terms with it.

There was a time when to come to terms with the structure of your own landscape, or with your memories, was to hire a landscape specialist who could build for you a miniature alp or compose your rocky outcrops into a mountain gorge or design a full-blown Japanese garden with water and bridges and stepping-stones and stone lanterns. Some people still do it this way, but most of us

nowadays have to make compromises. The Japanese garden becomes a bonsai dish, the cascade becomes a rill created by a water
pump, the alp becomes a single outcropping ledge. These are not
compromises in the tawdry sense. They are a recognition that the
scale of living for most of us today is modest. Our acreage has
shrunk; our grounds-staff is one man, one day a week, if that; rock
and labor are expensive, and we *would* rather do, it ourselves.

It is time to think in different terms and consider possible and
pleasant ways of bringing into our modest landscape some of the
magic of alpine and saxatile plants. There are among them some
of the easiest and most abundantly flowering garden plants, and also
those challenging haunters of remote places, which by the very
difficulty of their taming lure us year after year to discover the
secret of their adoption.

Alpine and Saxatile Plants

Strictly speaking, true alpines live in high mountain conditions
above the treeline and are mostly of dwarf stature. At these lofty
elevations, however, there is a wide variety of terrain: craggy cliffs,
rocky pastures, screes, moraines, and even bogs and meadows. Saxatile plants, on the other hand, are all those that do best and look
most natural growing among rocks—though for a considerable
number large rocks are not absolutely essential. Many thrive in
nature among gravels and relatively small fragments of stone.
These saxatile plants may be found at lower elevations in either sun
or shade. Both these types of plants can include dwarf shrubs and
trees and ferns as well as flowering herbaceous material.

Some of these denizens of the high mountains and of the crags
and broken rock may be tamed and grown in a soil bed without
a trace of rock and will, in fact, flourish there more magnificently
than they do in the wild. Most of the saxatile plants, however,
particularly those of alpine places, may have a shorter life in a

sybaritic setting. Nor can it be denied that a spartan diet induces the compactness and flowery proportion we associate with the classic model of the alpine. Sometimes it is suggested that this dwarf compactness is a response to the high winds and short growing season at lofty elevations, but there are many sites in nature where these facts alone do not explain the classic proportions of the plants growing there.

In such places—where the surface is basically stony and fine soil is only at the deeper root levels, on outcrops of fractured rock, in crannies, and among broken fragments of stone—grow the true alpines. A few yards away, where the exposure is identical but where deeper, finer-grained soil has accumulated, grow heavier turfs and taller meadow plants. Thus it appears that the rocky substrate is the controlling factor. It is possible to suggest that the plants we classify as typical rock garden plants are found where they are not only because they will grow only among rocks but also because they are relegated to these bleak aspects by a constitutional fragility that will not permit them to compete with the stronger vegetation needing better soil. When we move these plants into the garden, we provide them with a situation where, by weeding, we remove the competition; hence we can grow some of the alpines in nonrocky soil. But for many of them, rocks *are* essential for continued health.

First, many of the true alpines, especially those with downy gray leaves, cannot endure to have their foliage resting on a moisture-retentive soil of humus or clay; hence a stone mulch is necessary. A number spread their cushion of foliage and flower from a heavy, rather succulent taproot, which appears to demand rapid drainage to prevent rot at the crown; drainage is quick in a surface of rock fragments or in a crevice. Furthermore, most alpines by nature are deep-rooted and find essential cool moisture at considerable depth beneath and among rocks. Even those saxatile plants that apparently cling to the bare surface of sheer cliffs have in fact forced hairlike roots deep into microscopic fissures in the rock. These various factors would indicate that a rock garden is basically a *rock* garden.

The true rock garden, nevertheless, small or large, is to be distinguished from the "rockery," a bank or mound studded with stones and planted to bearded iris and other herbaceous border plants intermingled with petunias and other annual bedding plants. Such a planting may have its place in some settings, but this type of rockery is not a true rock garden. My purpose in this book is to suggest a number of ways that alpines, saxatile plants, and other wildflowers can be grown successfully and in harmony with a variety of sites.

Sites Suitable for the Rock Garden

Where you grow the alpine and saxatile plants will of course depend largely on the lie of your own land. There once was a rather strict rule: a rock garden should never be located within view of the house. It should be, thought the lawgivers, at the end of an excursion about the grounds of the estate, at least beyond the hedge or over the hill. It was something to come on by accident, like an adventure in nature, when suddenly on a mountain climb or horseback ride in the hills you come upon a secluded valley or open slope where the carpet of blossoms on the close turf among the ledges and boulders fairly takes your breath away. There is much to be said for this notion. Dwarf dianthus and minute campanulas are certainly not the same as petunias in a windowbox or a round bed of Scarlet Sage and fancy-leaved caladiums. Each has its place, but this is not to say that alpines must always have a natural setting. The setting can be either formal or informal.

There are certain general principles to keep in mind for the successful growing of these specialized plants, but before you consider these—or, rather, while you are considering these—you might well think of the total picture you are creating. Do not be in a hurry. Better to live in a new location without a garden for a year or two before you commit yourself than to lay out the grounds hastily in the light of some preconceived notions of landscape design and live with it in regret afterward. Let the setting of your plants be in terms of their immediate surroundings and especially in terms of the total picture that your particular parcel of land is expressing. Remember that this is *your* garden and *your* land. You will live intimately with it. You will work in it. If it pleases you, there is little doubt that it will please your visitors, because it will be consonant with your land and with yourself.

How often we hear apologies for the garden as it is, with phrases such as, "If only I had it all to do again, I would—" Not that any garden is in static perfection. Every gardener is constantly, in his mind at least, revising sections of it. And let me warn you, rock gardeners are particularly prone to this creative urge, not solely to enhance the visual impact but to improve the site as a home for more demanding alpines as well. They forever long to grow more perfectly the gems they have or to try others that they merely dream of.

In spite of future revisions, it is essential to commence with an overall conception of the way you will mold your landscape so that it is pleasing and convenient to live with. This means thinking about the location and proportion of various units from a number of points of view, both aesthetic and utilitarian. In your enthusiasm you must not forget that your land will be used for other things than a garden: a play space if you have children, outdoor living, and areas for daily housekeeping. In locating your garden avoid conflict with these necessary sections. Of course, once your children have grown up, you can always transform the sandbox into a moraine. In addition, it is well to keep in mind that as your gardening activities progress you will want convenient access to tools and supplies. You will probably also decide that you want a seed frame and compost pile. All these things must be fitted into your overall design.

Once having allowed for these, consider how the garden fits into the total picture. From where do you view the garden? This may be from your second-floor window, from the dining room, from the terrace, the driveway approach, or from a combination of several aspects. Think about it from all of these, remembering especially that once you have a rock garden you want to enjoy it for it's own sake also. If it is to be large and splashy, with sweeps of color created by only a few species of plants, then a distant prospect from window or terrace is your aim. If it is to be a small, specialist's garden of rare saxifrages and androsaces, and other minute treasures from the lofty, rocky peaks, then you want to be able to approach close, to gaze in wonder and to cosset and study. You must decide.

There are some general principles that may be laid down about conditions under which alpine and saxatile plants live happily away from their mountain homes and in our fickle lowland climate. It is well to remember that many of them, alpines in particular, do not like cramped and airless quarters. In general they are not content when hemmed in by buildings and boardings. Yet it is true that air moves up and down as well as across; on a slope or vertical planting site, the atmosphere does not stagnate as it might on a flat surface. It must also be remembered that though high mountains are fully exposed to sun as well as wind, the temperature is many degrees cooler than it is in the lowlands. These are probably the two most important facts in selecting the site for your garden, at least in the northeastern United States, where summer temperatures combined with humidity can reach a condition approaching the interior of a pressure cooker. Alpine and most saxatile plants, exposed to full summer sun and humidity, literally cook and turn to a sodden, mildewed mass. Defend them against the full blast of the sun, since you cannot lower the humidity short of outdoor air-conditioning.

This suggests some kind of shading. Many good saxatile plants will stand exposure to the fullest sun, but there are others that cannot take it. The latter, along with the true alpines, need in addition to plenty of light and air some shading from the full rage of the sun. A north-facing slope in the open is ideal. A dwarf shrub or a bold rock will provide enough shade to guard the health of a small number of plants. Tall trees with the lower branches trimmed up are fine, unless, like maple and elm, they have a thick mat of feeding roots close to the surface; in this case the competition for moisture and nourishment can be worse than blazing sun. On the whole it is better to keep large trees to the south as distant sources of high shade.

The composition of the soil and its moisture-holding capacity play a major role in the health of the plants and should be carefully considered in relation to the other environmental factors. These matters will be considered at greater length in Chapter 3 in the section about soils.

Such basic requirements of free air circulation, protection from the blazing rays of the summer sun, and a proper soil can be combined in a variety of sites: the planted wall, raised bed, rocky ledge, sunken valley, planted bank, and alpine lawn, the bog garden, woodland glade, and pine barren, or various combinations of these.

These can be large or small. One great advantage of alpine and saxatile plants in today's reduced landscapes is their size. It would be difficult to accommodate more than a dozen border perennials in a space 6 x 6 feet, but this same area will easily absorb fifty alpines and still allow room to include a miniature evergreen and some rocks, to say nothing of fifty or so of the small bulbous plants that can be tucked in between the tuffets and buns and planted beneath the mats of herbaceous material.

A single dogwood can shade a woodland planting; a pine barren can be accommodated beneath a single pine. A pool and stream, complete with waterfalls, can bring to a corner of your terrace the cool trickle of water on a hot summer day, the delight of delicate ferns such as the aspleniums, and the jewel-like brilliance of diminutive streamside plants such as *Primula frondosa,* with its silvery rosettes of mealy foliage and fragile pink blossoms. A ledge or outcrop of only three rocks, encrusted with saxifrage or sempervivum, makes a delightful accent by the doorstep and one more original than the ubiquitous yew and juniper. Or it could be used as a decorative feature thrusting up from the flagstones or gravel of the outdoor living space.

The patch of ground enclosed by a circling driveway can become an alpine lawn or rocky pasture, textured and enameled with flowering carpeters such as sedum, *Phlox subulata,* thyme, and heather, underplanted with drifts of the smaller spring bulbs: scilla, the wild type of crocus and narcissus, and the blue-and-white-striped chimes of puschkinia. An occasional rock or group of rocks rising from the mats of flower and foliage will lend interest and a dwarf conifer or two can be used for dark accents.

Or, in lieu of the usual foundation planting of shrubs, try a narrow bed with groups of rocks and an occasional dwarf tree or shrub to break the rigid line between house and ground. To the south and west grow the sun lovers, which thrive on heat and scorching light. Plant those needing some shade in the east-facing bed and on the north side of the house, if it is not overhung with dense-leaved trees. Where the sun seldom reaches, plant the woodlanders: hepaticas, ferns, Foamflower, the miniature *Iris verna,* and others requiring little sun; *Primula acaulis* and *P. polyanthus* for early bloom, the ferny-leaved epimediums, which send out sprays of delicate flowers in late spring, the wood anemones, astilbes for summer flowers, and the dainty *Cyclamen neapolitanum* and *C. europeum,* which send their butterfly-like flowers above the marbled leaves from late summer to frost —if you are lucky! The small bulbs will thrive at the foot of the rocks and in the flat spaces between. The groups of stone could rise like green and flowery islands from a graveled, unplanted surface, or could be surrounded by mats of creeping plants. The possibilities are endless.

If you live in an area where the underlying rock is close beneath the surface and in places breaks through, take advantage of this stony foundation. Why try uselessly to keep turf green and lush where rock lies so near the thin layer of soil that grass turns sere in summer drought? Strip off the sod and soil and you will probably find an outcrop ready-made for planting. When you do this it is a good plan to clear an area large enough to permit an easy and natural grade around the exposed rock as well as to expose the substrate. That ledgy place—at present an unsightly tangle of weeds and brush— might become, if cleaned and suitably planted, a focal point in your landscape, a natural sculpture shaped with textured foliage and high- lighted with flowers.

The preparation of natural ledges and outcrops is covered more thoroughly in Chapter 2, but a word of advice should perhaps be included here. Do not, in your enthusiasm, clear and plant more than you can take care of without drudgery. Newly cleared soil is usually full of weed seeds and will need considerable attention for a year or two. Once the young plants you have set in are well estab- lished and cover the bare soil fairly thoroughly, weed seeds will have difficulty in competing with them. It is also well to concentrate your attention on one area at a time rather than clear and plant small patches everywhere. Not only will a single well-organized and pre- pared planting be more effective than small, scattered plots; it will be much easier to take care of. The boundary where your garden comes in contact with the surrounding area is the easiest point for unwanted growth to infiltrate your planting; a single bed has less boundary susceptible to such invasion than the same area divided into several small beds.

There is not such a thing, however, as a garden that requires *no* work, though some types of gardens need more attention than others to keep them looking really well. An herbaceous border and a vegetable garden probably take more time than any other type of planting. A shrubbery probably requires the least attention, but it takes up a comparatively large area and the initial cost is likely to be high—and even bushes need pruning, fertilizing, and usually spraying. The so-called wild garden is also hardly care free. The indigenous plants will everlastingly try to take over, be they trees that seed and sprout, grasses that creep in from the edges, or the local weedy growth of fields or woods, which, if permitted to do so, will swamp out desirable plants.

Once you have your first planting under control you can always enlarge it, and will probably want to, as your plants grow and fatten and offer you the possibility of progeny through division, cuttings, or seeds. Keep this possibility in mind, therefore, in planning your first planting so that it will blend harmoniously with both your present and future landscape.

These prescriptions and warnings are not intended to make rock gardening sound terribly difficult and demanding of time and energy; rather, they aim to provide a few suggestions that may prevent later discouragement and enhance your enjoyment. For the amount of energy and money you expend in planning and constructing your rock garden you could possibly purchase a larger area of ready-made alpine flowering sward in the Rockies or the Pyrenees. Yet much of your pleasure will be in the very handiwork: and your deep delight will come when you rise early and saunter along the path, stopping for close inspection of old familiar faces and the unexpected loveliness of some new plant just opening a flower which before had been for you only a name in a catalogue. And again on a May evening to traverse the same paths and find still new wonders. These may be simple pleasures, but there is a quiet serenity nurtured in the soul when you stand in the midst of the garden among the plants that through your love and care have come to grace your world.

2

Making and Planting a Variety of Sites

As ALREADY INDICATED, there are several types of sites suitable for growing alpine and saxatile material. Plants vary in their needs: some require shade, others sun; their soil preferences differ; some prefer moist or even wet conditions, and others thrive on drought. Your taste in landscaping, your choice of plants, and your particular property will all help determine what kind of garden you end up with. Different types of sites can be combined to provide homes for plants with differing requirements and also a variety of outlooks; or you may choose to concentrate on one type site and grow only those plants that are happy in it. Either arrangement can be accomplished on a very small plot of land.

The Planted Wall and Raised Bed

For sheer economy of space and adaptability to a wide miscellany of sites and plants, nothing can compare to the planted wall and the raised bed. Both have the advantage of providing a range of ideal sites for alpine and saxatile plants, combined with an admitted architectural functionalism that avoids many of the awkward problems of a conventional rock garden in a limited area. Moreover, small, choice flowers growing in such positions are brought close to the eye of the viewer for minute inspection and admiration.

Either the planted wall or the raised bed may be happily related to existing natural features and man-made structures. The former is in essence a retaining wall built against a bank of earth, constructed of stone or cement blocks according to availability and the effect you want. Of course a construction of cement block is by nature more formal than one of stone and is more completely artificial. A special soil mixture is sandwiched between the rocks or used to fill the holes in the cement blocks of a planted wall. Alpine and saxatile plants delight in such a situation. Planted in the soil between the rocks where their roots can cling to the cool moist surfaces of stone, their crowns receive perfect drainage and their foliage and flowers can spray out over the dry, rocky face, safe from mud-splash. The planted wall is well suited to the short steep bank that so frequently and awkwardly results where a house site has been clumsily graded or where a driveway is lower than the abutting land. An ugly retaining wall, against which it is impossible to grow vines and shrubs, could be replaced with a planted wall or concealed behind one. A planted wall is an excellent way of masking an exposed house foundation.

Let me warn you at this point that it is not possible successfully to plant an already constructed cemented wall by bashing holes in the cement and stuffing in handfuls of soil and a plant. Nor is it satisfactory to try to poke soil into the interstices of even a dry stone wall for planting purposes. The reasons for this become obvious when you consider the needs of the plants that are to live in your wall. They must have a deep root-run between the rocks and into a mass of soil behind the wall in order to obtain the nourishment and moisture necessary for healthy growth. If, therefore, you wish to plant a dry wall, take it apart and rebuild it as described below, into either a planted retaining wall or a raised bed. If you are building against a cemented wall, have a 2- to 3-foot thickness of good soil mixture between it and your planted wall.

The raised bed is a freestanding wall planted on all exposed surfaces. In addition to the sides and ends, which are built of stone or
cement blocks in the same manner as the planted retaining wall,
there is enclosed by the sides a bed of soil into which rock and other
rubble has been mixed. This makes an excellent site for the kind of
material that looks better planted on a horizontal rather than a vertical surface. It has all the advantages of the planted wall in addition
to a greater number of planting exposures. Such a bed can be used as
a divider between one section of the garden and another and makes
a charming surround for the patio. It creates a more definite
boundary than a ground-level flowerbed. Because it is raised it is less
likely to be overrun by playing children and dogs, which can be a
real hazard to both small plants and a gardener's nervous system. A
small raised bed, about 3 feet square, could be used to create a
flowery mound wherever such a feature might be an attractive accent.
A raised bed also is the ideal way of providing a site for plants requiring a special soil. Ericaceous plants like heathers can be grown in
such a bed even in a limy district, if the rocks of which it is built are
nonlimy and the bed is filled with acid soil; lime from the surrounding area cannot leach in to raise the pH.

The building of both planted wall and raised bed is basically the
same. Start by laying out with stakes the actual area to be covered
by the construction. In the case of a retaining wall, this involves a
preliminary excavation of the bank which should be cut back to the
top of the slope in order to present a vertical face. Save the good soil
from this excavation. In locating the foot of a planted wall it is important to place it far enough from the foot of the vertical cut to
allow for a slight backward slope of the wall from bottom to top,
and when possible to allow for a good width of planting area on the
top behind the finished wall.

Next, for either the planted retaining wall or the free-standing
raised bed, excavate inside your stake line to the depth of about
6 inches to 1 foot below the natural soil level in order to prevent

frost heaving. You need not go below frost line, as necessary when building a brick or mortared wall. The soil between your stones will have considerable "give"; there are dry walls in New England which have stood for centuries, despite Robert Frost's "frozen-ground-swell," and though laid on the surface of the earth without foundations they have merely settled more deeply into the soil as the freezing and thawing ground has yielded to their weight.

It is wise to establish a work area nearby where you can pile the soil you dig out of the excavation and the rocks you will need for building. The soil should be separated into topsoil and the unusable nether material. Have a wheelbarrow beside you as you dig, and carry the top spit of soil from the whole length of your excavation to the work area for future use. The top spit of a good soil is generally about a spade depth (4 inches), unless, of course, the area has been disturbed by grading. All soil except this top spit may just as well be trundled off right away to fill some low spot or to be combined with the vegetable material in your compost pile. Do not utterly discard it, if you are a serious gardener. It is good mineral soil that can be made usable by the incorporation of composted material.

Now you are ready to build. You need rocks! If you do not have them on your own property, explore your local area for sources. From northern New Jersey northward the glacial ice of a few thousand years ago left quantities that it plucked from the mountains in its path and left scattered throughout the land for future farmers to gather up and make into stone walls. Nowadays, with all farm work done by machine, a wire fence is preferred to a stone wall. For enough money to buy wire for a fence most farmers will willingly let you cart away their rocks. Or you may prefer to have your local contractor make the negotiations, because you will probably need his truck for hauling.

Explain to him carefully what you intend to do with the stone. What you want are "one-man" rocks, flat enough so they will rest on one another with a thin layer of soil in between. Some variation in size will give the finished wall a more natural look and make it easier to space the planting pockets irregularly on the face of the wall. It is best to use rock all of one sort and to avoid polished or brilliantly colored stone. If sandstone and limestone are available these are best, because their porous surfaces make a more congenial home for the roots of plants than do quartz and granite. Shales and schists are satisfactory if they are not crumbly. A strong sandstone is probably best of all, because in it you can grow both acid-loving plants and those that want a neutral soil. Some of the finest alpines do their best, however, among limestone rocks, and if you are willing to forgo the few that demand acid conditions, limestone is excellent. A bed built of nonlimy rock can, however, be made limy by adding agricultural lime or ground limestone to the soil. It is far easier to make a neutral soil limy than it is to acidify a limestone soil. This question is taken up in greater detail in Chapter 3, the section on soils.

If in lieu of rock you plan to use cement blocks for your construction you can ignore the foregoing. In general, the construction with either cement block or natural rock is the same. Special instruction for making planted walls and raised beds of cement blocks will be found at the end of this section (see p. 26). If you have decided on natural stone and have located a good supply of desirable rock—and it is worth spending time and money on this, because your wall is going to stand a long time—be sure that you have an adequate supply delivered before you begin. You will need roughly a ton of rock for 30 square feet of wall face. As you work you perhaps will wish that you had even more than a ton, so that you could be selective, reserving the best stones for the face and using the awkward ones in the soil root-run behind the wall.

Now, for the actual construction. If when you excavated your site you found a stiff clay or impervious hardpan at the bottom, place a layer of broken rock or coarse gravel in the bottom of your hole, filling it up to very nearly ground level. Under any conditions your foundation hole should be half filled with coarse gravel to prevent waterlogging during wet periods of the year. Slope this fill down from the lip of the excavation so that your first course of rocks will tip inward. This tilt, which will be repeated in every course of your wall or raised bed, serves a double purpose: it prevents the wall from toppling forward because of freezing or gravitational thrust of the soil behind it, and it carries rainfall back into the root-run behind the wall. In addition to the inward tilt of each course, and for the same reasons, the entire wall will have a backward slope, known as the "batter." This need not be precisely measured, but in general a 2- to 3-inch batter per foot is adequate; the higher the wall the greater the batter. To obtain this, place the front edge of each successive course of stones slightly farther back than that of the course beneath it; not too much, or the wall will look like a flight of steps. A stout string tied to the stakes outlining your construction will keep the first course, and consequently the wall, from weaving in and out. For this kind of construction a reasonably straight line does look better. You may also wish to use a level for your first course and occasionally during the building; but this is by no means essential unless you wish your wall or bed to be absolutely horizontal. In many cases it is better to compromise the level somewhat to make it fit into the slope of your land. You will want to select the flattest and largest of your rocks for the first course to give an even and stable base. Be sure they do not teeter. They do not have to be all the same thickness, though too great a disparity will present some problems in laying the second course.

When you have laid the first course of stones you are ready for the soil and your first planting. It is convenient to have a good supply of soil mixed; you will be surprised how much will be gobbled up by the space between the wall and the bank or by the enclosed rectangle of your raised bed. Some of this space should be taken up by loose rock (the poorly shaped bits you do not want to use on the face), but be sure the soil-mix is well packed around them so that there are no air pockets. This rubble buried in the soil behind the wall not only takes up space, so that the soil-mix will go further, it also provides cool, deep pockets for the roots of your alpines. The soil mixture that fills the interstices between these loose rocks and also acts as mortar between the stones of the face should be composed of roughly ⅓ topsoil (the spit of soil you saved from the excavation sifted through ½-inch-mesh hardware-cloth to remove all weed roots), ⅓ leaf mold or peat, and ⅓ stone chips or gravel. This is the standard rock garden soil-mix as described in more detail in the section on soils, Chapter 3, where you will also find directions for various methods of mixing the ingredients.

Work this soil mixture in back of the first course of rocks and into the spaces between them; *pack it firm.* To avoid scraping your knuckles against the rock, use the rounded end of a sawed-off broomstick as a poker. Tramp down the soil among the fill-rocks you have tossed into the trench behind the rock wall. In order to allow for the gentle inward tilt of the next course, do not let any of the fill-rocks project higher than the back edge of the first course. Otherwise, when you start placing the next row of rocks you may find that one will tip forward as its back edge rests on a high point in the fill. Now spread a thin layer of soil, about ½ inch, on the upper surface of your first row of stones.

Next comes planting. Almost all alpine and saxatile plants will thrive in the face of the wall. Many will flow down over the rock in sheets and mounds and spread out on the ground below the wall. This is to be desired, since it blends the vertical with the horizontal in uneven billows of foliage and flowers. Other of these plants will tend to grow upward and some will stay tight in the crevices, merely advancing with increased growth along the thin fissure between the rocks. Do not overplant. Allow for the natural increase in size and for the overflow of plants in higher niches. Leave some pockets for plants you acquire or propagate in the future and remember that there will be natural seeding; self-sown plants have a way of locating themselves in crevices in more fitting array than one can possibly devise.

You will, nevertheless, want to have an adequate number of plants available as you build the wall, because you will not find it easy to work in anything except the tiniest seedling or division between the rocks later on. Potted material is perhaps best; but plants growing in flats and dug from the nursery frame, and even divisions of established plants from other parts of your garden, will take hold. Losses are surprisingly few in this sort of planting. The roots are well protected, keep moist under and against the rocks, and except for those on the directly south-facing wall are shaded for part of the day.

When planting, spread the roots out over the surface of the thin layer of soil on the rock, with the crown where the front edge of the next course of stones will come, about an inch back from the front edge of the rocks already placed. Cover the roots with a layer of soil-mix, about ½ inch thick, and then place on it the stone for your second course. Be sure that this rock is resting firmly on the soil beneath it and has a proper backward pitch, though you will be filling in behind it later and can poke soil in from behind. It may on occasion be wise to do this right away, to cover long roots extending from a plant you have just sandwiched between the rocks.

Work your way down the whole reach of the first course of stones, planting as you go. It is important that the joints between the stones in the second course do not come directly above a joint in the first course, or else a gully will wash out when rain or water from the hose runs down the face of the wall. It is not essential that the joint come precisely in the middle of the rock below; in fact, variation in this respect adds charm. In building the next course you may have to compensate for unevenness in the one below by spreading a thicker layer of soil upon the low stones. If this has to be as much as 2 inches thick, you should place in it a couple of thin shims of rock to help carry the weight of the upper stone. This will prevent soil from being squeezed out and thereby upsetting the pitch of the

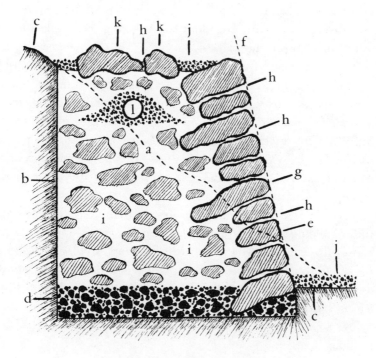

CROSS SECTION OF PLANTED RETAINING WALL

a. Original slope of bank
b. Vertical cut in bank
c. Ground level
d. 6 inches of drainage material
e. Rocks on face tilted back into bed
f. Backward slope of wall, 2 to 3 inches per vertical foot
g. Anchor rock
h. Planting pockets
i. Fill consisting of rubble and special soil-mix
j. 2 inches of gravel mulch
k. Rocks set in top of bed (optional)
l. Perforated pipe laid in gravel for underground watering
   (optional)

upper rock. It is also foresighted, as you work along a course, to place a few rocks with their long axis running well back into the soil to help anchor the wall.

By the time you have finished the second course you will probably want to stop for refreshment and rest. This is a good time to survey your handiwork from all angles, and make a mental note of methods to improve your procedures. You might also at this time water the soil around the rocks and roots of the plants you have already placed; use the fine spray of the hose to do this. If you have plants waiting around for you to go on to the next course, be sure they are all in the shade, and you might give them a bit of water too.

Having rested and admired the job thus far along, you can continue building and planting and filling in behind the completed part of the wall until you have reached the top. In placing plants in the upper courses, be sure that you do not put one that will spread down in a billowing mat too close to smaller plants below it. Plant strong spreaders above the vacant spots you have left in the course below, so that they may foam freely without smothering small and precious items.

The procedures for making a raised bed are identical with those for building a dry wall except that you will have four corners to contend with and in staking out the area of the bed you will have to consider carefully the proportion of width to height. Because all four sides of the raised bed slope inward it will be slightly wider at the bottom than at the top, which should certainly be no more than 6 feet wide, and you can easily reach to the middle without climbing. The height is somewhat a matter of taste and site, but in general should be no greater than 3 feet. If it is higher than this it will be awkward to work at the bed on the top, and the drainage will be excessive. A planted wall can be made much higher, since the soil bank against which it is built helps keep it moister. Remember, though, that with the raised bed you can reach the top from either side, whereas for the wall your approach will be mostly from the front, unless the bed on the top can be reached easily from behind and above the wall. So do not build your wall too high if you do not plan to use a ladder to work on the upper reaches, and do not plant so heavily at the base that you will not have any place to put your feet while working above.

Since the topmost course of either the wall or the raised bed should be fairly level, it is well to save a number of thin flat pieces of rock to use as boosters under shallow stones. Before you fill in with soil behind the top course you will want to decide whether or not you wish to have in the top bed rocks that project above the soil. Stones chosen for their surface beauty and carefully placed frequently enhance the appearance of the upper bed. Two or three small rocks placed close together with the thin fissures between filled with soil will furnish an excellent planting site for minute tuffets that like to get their roots deep under rock and have their crowns resting on stone. Whether you use projecting rocks or not, you should allow for a good 2 inches of stone chips over the whole surface of the top bed. Because of the backward tilt of the rocks in the face you can generally fill with soil to the level of the back edge of the top course of rocks and still have room for about 2 inches of chips, which will spread out toward the edge of the wall.

This mulch of stone chips, preferably neutral in color, not only provides a pleasing background for foliage and blossom but is essential for the health of the plants. The importance of the gravel mulch cannot be too strongly emphasized. It keeps the susceptible crown of the plant dry. By furnishing a dry surface for the foliage to rest upon, it prevents rotting of leaves and the splashing of mud during heavy rain, which for low-growing plants is not only unsightly but can be fatally smothering; it keeps the soil cooler in hot weather and helps conserve moisture; and to a large extent it really does keep windblown weed seed from germinating.

Though you may wish to use the top surface of either the wall or the raised bed for the same kind of plants that you used on the vertical face, here is a perfect location for miniature trees and shrubs and for such diminutive charmers as saxifrages, androsaces, and others. Here is a deep root-run, a quick-draining surface, and a position where their miniature beauty may be enjoyed without your getting down on hands and knees. In a section of raised bed, 3 feet wide by 15 feet long, even with the inclusion of some projecting rocks you can grow hundreds of the small bun and cushion alpines. It is a fine showcase for the specialist.

When you see the vigor and beauty of your collection of alpine and saxatile plants, even the first spring after planting, it is safe to predict that you will be tempted to expand it. You will wish your wall or raised bed were many feet larger, or that you had not planted it with so many sprawly easy-doers. The latter can be remedied by steeling yourself to a program of replacement as your skill and enthusiasm develop. You may also wish that you had provided for an underground watering system for the difficult and lovely things that flourish in the high-alpine rocky moraines where snow melt-water keeps the roots perpetually moist and cool.

Though many prized plants do not demand these moist moraine conditions, few will refuse them. Therefore, as you erect your wall or raised bed you may wish to anticipate what is likely to happen to your ambitions and appetites. It is rather difficult to add an underground watering system after the bed is made and planted but fairly easy to put it in at the time of building.

When you are about a foot below the top of your construction, spread an inch-thick layer of stone chips over the soil behind the rock face as a foundation on which to lay the pipe for your under-ground watering. This pipe will be located in the center of the bed, halfway between wall and bank, or between wall and wall in a raised bed, and should run the full length. Excellent for this pur-pose is 4-inch sewer pipe, of fiber or plastic. This is a black, un-crushable septic tank field-pipe, light in weight and easily handled. It is better not to use the type in which holes have already been bored, because these are too large for your purpose. Get the solid pipe and drill your own holes, a double row, ⅜₆ inch in diameter, about 1 inch apart along the bottom of the pipe. This can easily be done with a hand drill.

Close one end of the pipe with a watertight cap by forcing over the end of the pipe a round, flexible plastic refrigerator container of the correct diameter or by fastening over the open end a sheet of the heaviest-gauge flexible plastic. Several turns of rustproof wire will hold it in place. Put a 90-degree elbow joint at the other end, and, if necessary, insert into the slip joint of the elbow the amount of solid unperforated pipe needed to reach the upper surface of the bed. You can easily saw off the unwanted length of pipe with a coarse-toothed saw. When the bed is completed you may conceal the yawning black hole with a small, attractive stone when it is not open for filling.

Place the pipe, hole side down, on the gravel bed you have prepared and level it so that water will not settle in either end; then cover it with a generous mound of gravel before adding the soil layer. During dry weather a daily filling of this reservoir will allow water to seep slowly into the soil mass, and by mere evaporation at the surface will cool the foliage without sopping it. During a real drought you may want to leave your hose trickling into the open end to give your bed a good soaking.

The same beneficent effect may be achieved by employing (instead of sewer pipe) a length of semirigid plastic waterpipe, ½ to 1 inch in diameter. You can make holes in this pipe with a drill or, during warm weather when the plastic is more yielding, with an old-fashioned icepick or a common nail and a hammer. Make enough small holes all around the pipe so that the water will seep steadily into the ground without flooding the lower levels of the bed or surging back to the hose fitting that you will attach to one end. The set of your faucet for this type of watering will require experiment on your part; if you leave the connection between hose and pipe slightly loose you can soon determine how great a flow of water is needed to fill the pipe without its backing up. This pipe too should be covered with a generous mound of gravel, to prevent soil from clogging the holes, and its terminus capped. The inlet end of the watering system can be fitted with a hose adapter that will come to the surface in or near the bed. You can, however, extend the pipe (unperforated after it has left the bed you wish to water) underground until it has reached a more inconspicuous spot before bringing it to the surface and attaching the hose adapter—a method that obviates the sprawl of unsightly hose across your terrace or lawn.

If for utilitarian reasons you decide to use concrete blocks instead of rocks for your retaining wall or raised bed, there are certain differences of construction to be observed. Since the blocks are perfectly rectangular it is impossible to pitch them back toward the fill soil without running into problems at the corners; nor is a tilt necessary, because of the free exposure of the planting holes on the upper surface of each block, where they will catch the rainfall, and because you have no soil for planting purposes between the blocks. A raised bed or planted retaining wall of concrete blocks *must be laid level.* Also because a construction of cement blocks must remain level and neat in appearance, it is important to build a more solid footing than you would for a rock construction. A poured concrete footing, preferably reenforced with a strip of chicken wire, should be made to prevent heaving of the bottom course and consequent disalignment of upper courses. An 8-inch-wide trench at least a foot deep should be dug around the periphery of your proposed construction site. If your soil is firm no additional forms will be needed. Into this trench pour the concrete, allowing it to harden thoroughly before digging out behind it for the drainage layer of gravel. On this firm foundation you will lay your first course.

Use 16 x 8 x 8-inch blocks that are flush at both ends and have three holes through them. As explained above, these blocks are placed level, tightly end to end, with no soil between them, the holes facing up and filled with soil-mix. Fill behind the blocks to the top of each course as it is laid with well-tamped soil and rubble. This firming of the fill behind the blocks is essential to keep the successive courses from tilting forward or back. Each course is set back so that the front half of each of the three holes in the blocks below is exposed. Continue in this manner to the top of your construction.

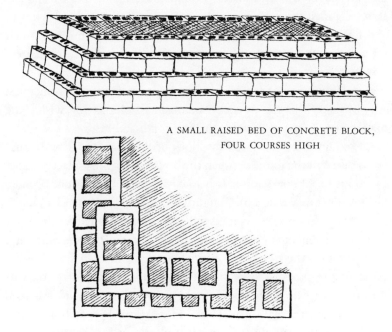

A SMALL RAISED BED OF CONCRETE BLOCK,
FOUR COURSES HIGH

Detail of corner of concrete-block bed, showing how
upper course is set back half the width of the blocks
in the course below

For the raised bed, five courses are the maximum height (40 inches) for weeding without climbing; lower beds are preferable from this point of view. Also, since each course is set back 4 inches a raised bed of cement blocks narrows more abruptly than one built of stone; by laying your bed nine half-blocks wide in a comfortable base of 6 feet, five courses would narrow the top bed to 20 inches of free soil. Nevertheless, there is no reason why the bed could not taper to a top of one block's width with only the holes for a planting area on the top of the bed. Moreover, as the drainage in a cement-block bed is not as acute as in a raised bed built of rocks, it is conceivable to make it high enough to serve as a wall along a property line, for example. By using a combination of 8-inch-thick and the thinner 4-inch-thick blocks at the corners, a flush vertical back wall and flush end walls can be achieved while still retaining the 4-inch setback on the front face. Flush vertical walls have to be cemented, however, for stability.

A retaining wall of cement block is built on these same principles. Any of these beds can of course be made as long as you wish. The matter of proportion depends on site, need, and taste.

Be certain in building cement-block beds and retaining walls that in no case will the joints between the blocks in a course exactly match the joints in the course directly below it. If your bed has one or more flush walls it may take a bit of figuring to discover what size of block and what position at the corners will achieve the desired result. Even in laying a regular raised bed the pattern at the corners will vary, depending on the number of blocks you have in each side; but because of the proportion of the blocks things work out. You will notice in a previous paragraph that the term "half-block" was used for describing the width of a bed. This is merely a matter of convenience in measurement—nine half-blocks is the length of four 16-inch cement blocks laid end-to-end plus the width (8 inches) of the block that starts the contiguous side at the corner.

The finished construction of a raised bed built of cement blocks will rather resemble a truncated step-pyramid, but when the numerous holes and the top of the bed are planted with billowing and sprawling plants the sharpness will be pleasingly softened. Moreover, such a bed would be used only where its severity and functionalism would fit with its surroundings. As a planting site it is not unlike the troughs and sinks popular in England for growing alpines. One major advantage of this type of construction is that you can change the planting nearly as easily as you would fill a flowerpot. Cement, nonetheless, does not give the natural effect of rocks, no matter how used.

Walls and raised beds of peat blocks were first developed at the Royal Botanic Garden, Edinburgh, and proved so satisfactory as sites for very difficult acid-loving plants that they have become popular throughout the British Isles, where these blocks are easily available. They have not proved eminently satisfactory in this country; first, because firm block-peat is almost impossible to obtain, and secondly, the severity of our climate—at least in the Northeast—

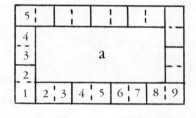

ARRANGEMENT OF CONCRETE BLOCKS FOR RAISED BED

a. A course having four sides with an uneven number of half-blocks
b. A course having two sides with an even and two sides with an uneven number of half-blocks
c. A course having all four sides with an even number of half-blocks

soon breaks down the blocks. Where available, they are well suited for a one-block-high edging to an acid bed.

It is quite possible to make a raised bed or planted retaining wall of peeled logs or billets of wood; old telephone poles or railroad ties, preferably not creosoted, are excellent for this purpose. In time these will decay; but cedar, locust, and hemlock have a fairly long life. They can be treated with a wood preservative that delays the rot; be sure to get a wood preservative containing no ingredients injurious to plants, and follow the directions for its use. Suitable mixtures are those made for greenhouse benches and cold frames.

In building a wall or bed of logs, the construction is similar to that used for log cabins except that each successive log is set back slightly and the notches in the ends, where two logs are overlapped to form a corner, are not so deeply cut, thus creating a wider space for planting purposes. Such beds are best suited to a woodland setting.

It is wise to have a paved, graveled, or tanbarked area about 2 feet wide at the base of any type of planted wall or raised bed. Not only is this in keeping with the formality of the structure, it also provides an easily maintained walk area and a pleasing background for the plants that will sprawl down from the lower levels of your bed onto its surface. It also simplifies maintenance. Grass at the foot of a wall cannot be mowed and therefore hand-clipping becomes necessary; in addition it has a nasty habit of sending out stolons to invade the face of the wall. My wife and I have found that a gravel walk at the foot is an ideal seedbed from which we are able to transplant numerous self-sown items.

Planting on the top of a retaining wall is a matter of taste and site. Grass, even when mowed, makes for eventual trouble. The roots will invariably work their way down into the rich fill and produce irremovable tuffets among the plants on the face. It is best, therefore, when planting the top of the retaining wall, to avoid all rootstoloniferous plants.

The near-vertical faces of either a wall or raised bed make a fine home for those plants that cannot stand water soaking their crowns: haberleas, ramondas, and some lewisias, to name a few. Here also will thrive such plants as aubrietia; in our climate it must have a steep, rocky slope for tumbling its gray leaves and brilliant blossoms or they will rot and die in muggy weather.

No verbal instructions will answer in advance all the questions that will arise as you build your retaining wall or raised bed. Your own adaptions of the general principles outlined here will meet the needs of your specific situation, and you may discover improvements that can be shared with others in a how-I-did-it article for the *Bulletin* of the American Rock Garden Society.

It has been found that in a well-constructed raised bed or planted wall even many of the most difficult alpine and saxatile plants can be grown with success: saxifrages, androsaces, drabas, alpine primulas, and the like. If I could have only one small rock garden, it would be a raised bed.

Outcrop and Ledge

In many parts of the country, rock outcrops and glacial deposits of rock are conspicuous features of the landscape. These sites offer the most natural groundwork for an outcrop or ledge garden. Sometimes these are perfectly situated in your landscape and only need clearing and planting to create a delightful spot. More often, unfortunately, they have not been placed by nature in the location that you would prefer in relation to other existing features. It is almost always possible, though, if you can clear your mind of preconceived notions, to incorporate a natural group of rocks into your garden scheme. A few suggestions have been offered in the opening section, but in the final analysis your garden is the creation *your* imagination produces out of the raw elements of your property.

If you have outcrops, ledges, or boulders already situated on the property, study them carefully from all angles. Try to visualize what they will look like when they become part of a composition of background trees and shrubs and surrounding lawn, of soil pockets filled with bright flowers; perhaps with the existing rocks rearranged or new ones added. Also to be considered are the approach to your garden and the paths around and through the area. These are discussed in some detail in the section about walks, paths, and pavements (p. 69). It is generally not profitable to try to draw a plan in advance. Working on the ground itself is the usual rule in the making of a rock garden.

Most important, whether your garden is to be made on an area where there is already rock or whether stone must be brought in for construction, are the planting sites. These are your first concern; the plants, after all, are what make it a garden. Too often one sees existing ledges and outcrops scraped bare of all but a thin layer of soil, and planted with sedum, sempervivum, and a few phloxes and dianthus leading a miserable existence. Though few alpine and saxatile plants demand a rich soil, most want a generous depth of root-run. Less rock exposure and more good alpine soil may be the answer; or, where the rock conformation makes it impossible to add a good depth of soil without its washing off, the rock should be bared completely and not planted. This does not suggest that you merely scrape off the thin places and pile additional soil on top of that already present in hollows and cracks. It is absolutely essential that the whole area be cleaned thoroughly of all existing grass and weeds. Grass and weed roots wedged in the cracks of your ledge or lurking in the existing soil rise up later to plague you and infest your best plants. The soil itself should probably be improved by the addition of gravel and humus as suggested in the section on soils (p. 83) in order to achieve the approximate proportions of ⅓ loam, ⅓ gravel, and ⅓ humus.

If it is necessary to bring in more rock to supplement your existing outcrops or boulders, try by all means to get ones of similar color and texture. A collection of various types of stones, especially those of bright color or freakish shape, may be geologically amusing, but such rocks are always distracting in a rock garden. The same advice holds where no rock exists on the location and the whole garden is to be constructed of imported stone.

Where rock is not exposed on the surface, irregular contours, slopes, and embankments offer a setting appropriate for the incorporation of rocks into the landscape. Even on level ground a rock garden may be made to blend pleasantly into the land. In any case, the location and dimensions of the garden will be determined largely by the existing natural features, by your sense of proportion, and by the amount of time and money you are willing to expend.

There are certain basic principles to remember in constructing a rock garden. The size, consistency, and arrangement of the rocks and ledges should be pleasing even devoid of planting. Select stone all of a kind, preferably with rather flat but irregular faces so that small blocks may be brought together to form some strong, bold features. A spattering of separate rocks stuck into a bank is restless and unnatural. If the only obtainable rocks are rounded cobbles and boulders, which are impossible to place so that they appear to be all of a piece, it is best not to attempt to form an outcrop or ledge; use them to make a boulder field planted as a rocky pasture or alpine lawn, described in the next section (p. 45, and see drawing, p. 48).

Should your ledge or outcrop have to be built of imported stone, it is of utmost importance to design the arrangement of rocks and planting sites so that the whole composition looks as natural as possible. Time spent studying a variety of situations in nature where rocks and ledges are the principal elements of the landscape will prove most rewarding. To be sure, your garden will be an artificial construction and need not be a slavish imitation of nature; but, in general, a feeling of composure and "rightness" is achieved by providing as natural a setting as possible for rock garden plants, which are essentially wildflowers.

If there is a slope or hill, try to place the stones in such a way that they suggest the surface exposure of rock ledges or masses buried within the slope or hill. Ordinarily it is easiest to work up from the bottom of the slope, though if your plan is to have a rather bold ledge near the top that may be the place to start. As a rule, the steeper the grade, the more rock: on a steep natural ledge more rock is exposed than on a gentle one. Also, plenty of stone on a steep slope will help prevent erosion of the soil.

The frequent tendency, in order to avoid the spatter effect of separate stones dotted here and there on the face of the slope, is to construct a series of terraces with rows of stones of approximately uniform height running the full length of the rise, with flat planting areas above each row. Such a construction, though suitable for plants, tends to be monotonous. It is better to vary levels with groups of rocks, some quite bold, others lower and less conspicuous. Bays of nearly stoneless soil running up to another strong cluster of rocks at the next level will break the face of each rise; a few rocks, almost completely buried, will support the soil and help prevent erosion if the slope is steep.

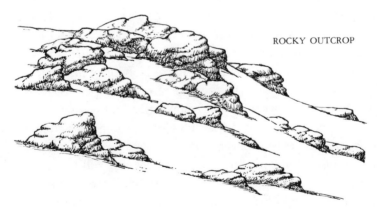

ROCKY OUTCROP

When rocks are placed to imitate an outcrop or ledge they should appear as though they are all connected underground. This effect is enforced when the bedding-plane of each rock and group of rocks lies at the same general angle (slanting gently up and back as in the above drawing). To further strengthen this feeling of cohesion the rocks should be placed so that their side and front edges follow, for the most part, the natural fracture lines as shown in the ground plan for this formation in the next drawing. Note that the fracture lines run at right angles to each other and at a slight diagonal to the general slope (indicated by the dotted contour lines). Placing the rocks so that they lie diagonally back into the slope makes it easier to bury the back corner, since the soil runs out and down in natural contours to cover them. Medium-sized rocks as well as large ones can be used in this manner, stepping them back in a series of uneven zigzags as the slope rises. This helps prevent the "straight terrace" and "stairway" effects that are difficult to avoid if the fracture lines run parallel and at right angles to the slope. The steep concave slope (b) would be an excellent site for a moraine or scree (see p. 36). A few scattered stones could be partially buried at random on this incline to suggest that they were pieces broken away from the ledge above.

The effect of weathered promontories of stone with low soil-filled pockets between them, where the bedrock has eroded away into hollows at the cracks and joints, is furthered by using weathered rock, when obtainable, with rounded faces exposed. Such an outcrop can be a bold one of large rocks, as illustrated in these two drawings, or can be made up of small rocks rising only a few inches above the surface of the soil.

It is possible to create fairly substantial rock formations, though, out of relatively small stones by fitting these together to simulate large rocks seamed and cracked by weathering (see illustrations, pp. 37-42). Many types of rock, unless they have been warped and crushed by heat and pressure after their original formation, tend to break naturally into fairly rectangular blocks. This is particularly true of sedimentary rocks like limestone, sandstone, and shale, which are formed in layers, or strata. Such stratified rock breaks into slabs,

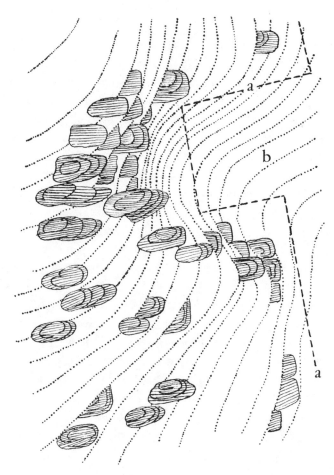

GROUND PLAN OF ROCKY OUTCROP IN PRECEDING DRAWING

a. Fracture lines
b. Concave slope

   Rocks visible in preceding drawing

   Rocks not shown in preceding drawing because concealed
         by curve of the ground or another rock

splitting quite smoothly along the original bedding-planes and frac-
turing less regularly through these layers but more or less at right
angles to the bedding-plane. It is important to keep this fact in mind
when building an outcrop or ledge or when fitting small stones together to create the effect of a single large rock, particularly if
stratified rock is used. Because erosion tends to wear away the
sharply defined surfaces of the cleavage lines it is not necessary to
adhere slavishly to the bedding-planes and fracture lines when placing the rocks. A more natural effect results, however, if these
surfaces are kept at the same general angle.

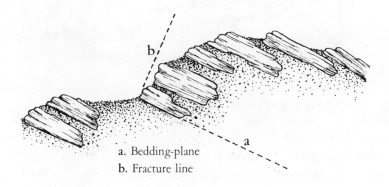

a. Bedding-plane
b. Fracture line

This drawing shows a cross section of rocks sunk into a slope with
the bedding-plane (a) tilted back into the ground. Note that the
stones on the top of the rise keep the same tilt as those in front and
beneath them and continue this angle on the reverse side of the slope.
The front edges of the exposed rocks are worn back by weathering
and therefore no longer follow the original fracture line (b).

Rocks that break into chunky blocks with relatively smooth faces,
such as sandstone, can be used to build up fairly impressive ledges.
In the illustration on page 38, the bedding-plane is horizontal but
could be tilted back into the slope or sidewise, or both. Construction
of such a ledge is very like building a raised bed or planted wall,
except that the joints between the rocks *should* line up to form fis-

An artificial ledge constructed by fitting stratified
stones together, shown before adding more soil to conceal
lower front edges of stones

sures and cracks running down through the bedding-planes to
approximate natural fracture lines. It must also be remembered that
in nature a vertical crack usually starts at the surface of the exposed
rock in each setback in the face and not below a solid rock. Small
stones as well as soil should be used to level rocks which might
otherwise tilt out of the proper plane, and may be wedged into
vertical fissures once in a while to prevent excessive washing of soil.
Plants will soon conceal such "faking."

The soil on the top of each setback may be sloped up toward the
rear before placing the next course of rocks upon it in order to gain
additional height without using so much precious stone (see drawings, pp. 37, 39). Be sure, though, that the lower front edge of each
layer of rocks is concealed by soil; in the ledge illustrated in the
drawing above, more soil must be added for this purpose. Unstratified rock can be used for such a formation, but even in this case it is

best to place the stones so that the exposed faces lie at approximately the same angle throughout the construction.

When building an overhang be certain that enough of the projecting rock is buried to ensure its staying firm if someone stands on the unsupported front edge. In nature an overhang is usually caused when a layer of softer and therefore more easily eroded rock underlies a harder layer of stone. In the illustration below, *b* indicates the fracture line before erosion.

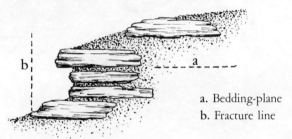

a. Bedding-plane
b. Fracture line

Chunky blocks are easiest to use for creating different effects. If your rock is all in thin flat sections, it might be best to construct a planted wall, but it is possible to arrange thin flat stones in an interesting manner by sinking them into the ground at a vertical or nearly vertical angle. One finds in nature outcrops of stratified rock, originally formed as layers of mud, sand, or lime deposit, where the bedding-planes have been tilted out of the horizontal by some natural cataclysm. At times these planes are vertical, or nearly so. Such formations can be imitated in building a rock garden.

Even fairly small flat slabs can be set in groups of varying size and shape to create a most attractive and natural-looking series of outcrops. In the next drawings, the bedding-plane is nearly vertical and lies flat against the slope. This is an excellent method of using thin slabs of rock, since it exposes their largest surface. When constructing such a formation, the bedding-plane (*a* in the illustration) should be tilted back against the slope to some extent to give stability to the individual rocks. The front slabs in each face should have their lower ends buried deeply enough to keep them from shifting. Smaller flakes can be packed behind these face-rocks to give them an appearance of greater thickness; the top can be quite rough, even jagged, in imitation of a naturally weathered fracture line (*b* in the drawing).

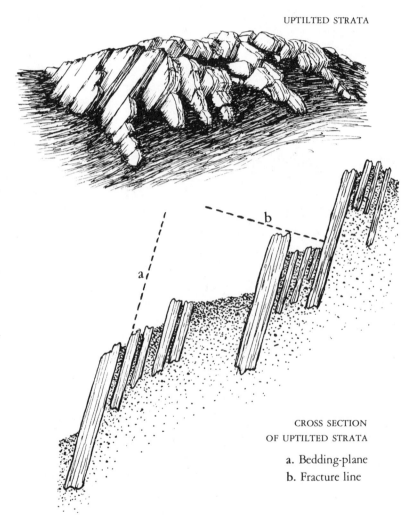

UPTILTED STRATA

CROSS SECTION
OF UPTILTED STRATA

a. Bedding-plane
b. Fracture line

The bedding-plane shown below is also nearly vertical, but runs back, edgewise, into the hillside instead of lying flat against the slope. In such a formation the individual slabs are buried one beside another rather like books in a bookcase. They may be placed upright or given a slight sideways cant. This is a very stable formation, and the individual rocks need not be tilted backward into the slope as much as in the formation illustrated in the two preceding drawings. It takes much more rock, however.

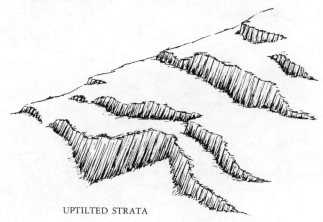

UPTILTED STRATA

Such vertical constructions provide excellent root-run for plants between the stones. They must be carefully made, so that the bedding-planes are running at the same angle throughout the garden as well as in each course.

Quite massive rocks can be constructed out of even fairly small stones if these are of the rough shapes common in tufa and some types of twisted limestone. These pieces can be placed close together and even on top of each other, with soil packed between and under them. The individual stones should be fitted against each other as closely as possible and placed, when feasible, so that the weather-worn faces show. Small stones wedged between the individual rocks will help to make them rest firmly and will also prevent soil from

washing out of the cracks. Such built-up "rocks" have a core of soil
mixture and rubble, as in a raised bed. They should be irregular in
outline and grouped to appear as parts of a natural outcrop.

ROCKY OUTCROP CONSTRUCTED
OF SMALL ROUGH STONES

If the area for your rock garden is flat or nearly so, you may
arrange groups of rocks here and there to suggest outcroppings of
bedrock, with stretches of soil where the bedrock has supposedly
eroded away—thus simulating a frequently occurring condition to be
found in alpine meadows. The rock exposures can be low, barely
rising above ground level, or can be as bold as the size of your rocks
permits. An irregular low hummock or ridge of soil can be paved
completely with rather flat stones of no great size fitted closely
together to resemble the exposed, worn surface of an extensive stony
substrate. A few smaller groups of the same sort near the main rocky
feature will add considerably to the effect. When the cracks of this
pavement are laced with foliage and flowers and the soil between the

outcrops is planted to low-growing material and clusters of small spring bulbs, the effect is not only delightful but closely resembles many rock formations seen in the old pastures in New England. For such a feature the rock you use may be laid flat, or thin plates may be sunk more or less vertically into the soil in close-packed formations to resemble the upthrusting, weather-broken edges of tilted underground strata. These two types of formations should *never* be combined in the same area.

The natural-seeming appearance is greater if a few large groups are used fairly close together surrounded by rockless soil rather than scattering smaller formations over the entire garden. A very slight amount of grading to create gentle knolls and hollows will enhance the effect. If you prefer a greater change of levels on flat land—one of the most attractive features of a rock garden—it is probably wiser to excavate part of the surface to create a valley, rather than heap up soil and rock to form a mound or mounds. The sides of the valley may be furnished with ledges and outcrops as on sloping land. Do not forget, though, if you excavate, that you are apt to get down into subsoil; reserve the topsoil from your excavation and make your hollow deep enough to allow for the addition of good rock garden soil without raising the bottom too high.

If there is a choice, an east exposure is perhaps best for your slope or artificial valley, but almost any site can be made suitable. True alpines want plenty of light to keep the growth tight and firm and to encourage abundant blossoms. Except for those that come from the sunny slopes of the Mediterranean or the parched hills and lowlands of the American West, most rock garden plants do better facing away from the full glare of the sun at noon and in the afternoon.

If the garden is on a slope the drainage will surely be adequate without special provisions; but if you have low-lying pockets and valleys, 4 to 6 inches of broken stone or coarse gravel beneath the soil mixture may prevent excessive standing water at the roots. Of even greater importance is drainage at the crown of the plants, provided by the gravel mulch on the surface—a method explained on page 23.

Before you begin to place your rocks, it is advisable to have on hand a generous supply of well-mixed soil such as described in . Chapter 3, the first section. The placement of the construction stones is of primary importance in the final effect, but a careful preparation of the growing areas will determine the success of the plants. A prerequisite when settling the rocks into position is to pack the soil mixture around them so that no air pockets are left below or between them. At this time it is possible to work ground limestone or limestone chips into the standard soil mixture to create small pockets to accommodate the really calcicole plants. Of considerable value to the successful growing of alpine and saxatile plants is the incorporation of small stones into the soil mixture throughout the garden as well as the generous topdressing of fine stone or gravel. This mulch can be spread over the whole garden before planting, or it can be put on between the plants and worked in around the root-collar and under the foliage at the time of planting. In addition to the previously mentioned value to the plants themselves, this layer of rock chips helps to prevent erosion on the slopes. For the most natural appearance it is advisable, for this purpose, to use gravel of the same color and tone as that of the rocks in your construction.

The problem of how to relate the rock garden to the rest of your landscape has no pat answers. Every situation is different. A surround of evergreen shrubs and dwarf trees as a background is frequently attractive, but, once again, proportion and scale are important. Where it is desirable to block out some unwanted feature in the view, an artificial mound or ridge crowned with dense shrubs and a few selected trees, and planted in whole or in part as a rocky slope, makes an excellent screen. Such a rise in ground could be used around the edge of a small property to give a greater feeling of seclusion and privacy. It is, furthermore, a remarkably effective sound deadener.

Usually it is more effective to have the boundaries of the garden irregular in outline, even where they abut mowed lawn. It is well to remember, however, that grass plots must be edged regularly (see Chapter 3, p. 93) to prevent the disastrous spread of roots among the rocks and cushion plants.

Alpine Lawn and Rocky Pasture

In the uplands and among the mountains on all the continents of the world are extensive flowery sections without conspicuous rocky features. Here in company with grasses and sedges grow some of the loveliest of the alpine flora. Relatively level areas in the garden may be transformed into alpine lawns or rocky pastures where you may grow a wide variety of mountain plants.

Small areas within or adjacent to the rock garden may be constructed to imitate these natural features, or they may be the sole area for growing many alpine plants, especially in level, nonrocky terrain and also where the only stones available are rounded, water-worn cobbles and gravels such as shown and described on pages 48–49. Of course within these areas, if you have suitable rock, you may incorporate a few small outcrops—even a large one—to lend variety and provide additional and different planting sites; but these should be in proportion to the size of the area.

In nature the alpine lawn is found where the meltwater of ancient glaciers has brought down and deposited from the craggy mountains above minute rock particles that over aeons of time have become mixed with the humus of decayed vegetation to form a deep mineral soil of fine texture containing only a few stones. Depending on the parent rock, this soil may be a clay loam, which in dry weather bakes to a bricklike firmness, or a silty or sandy loam, rich in mineral salts. Such sites are the home of tall grasses, and the characteristic meadow flowers strong enough to compete with them. These are the upland hayfields and cattle pastures. In alpine lawns of this sort are found the brilliant flowering bulbs, most of which bloom while the grasses are short in early spring and disappear as summer advances.

In the garden the alpine lawn may be a section, principally planted to grass, where drifts of bulbs that flower early may be combined with a few spring-flowering herbaceous plants such as violets and bluets. The mowing of the grass will have to be delayed until around the middle of June, to allow bulb foliage to mature. Except as a separate area, such an arrangement tends to look rather untidy as the spring advances into summer.

It is quite possible, nevertheless, to plant in lieu of grass a mixture of ground-covering plants that do not require mowing and yet give the general effect of an alpine meadow. All ordinary grasses must be rigorously excluded from such a lawn, since it cannot be mowed without destroying the flowering plants of which it is composed and would therefore become extremely unsightly. Also, in this climate, grasses would soon choke out all but the strongest-growing plants.

This type of flowering alpine lawn, though not the location for slow-growing and small species, is excellent for a wide range of rock garden plants of vigorous growth. If it is thickly populated with plants that are permitted to self-sow, this type of garden requires very little attention after the first two or three years, except to keep out creeping grasses by edging and removing the few weeds able to sow themselves and grow despite the thick carpet of flowering plants and ground covers (which should be allowed to grow into one another). Occasionally it may be necessary to clip back a few that are too aggressive or to rogue out some self-sown seedlings of a species that might otherwise take over. The general effect to be sought is of a solid cover of plants with some variation in height and enough variety of species to ensure a succession of flowers over a long period. The various low-growing phloxes, dwarf iris, veronicas, spring bulbs, aethionema, several types of alyssum, saponaria, geraniums, dianthus, alliums, thymes, oenotheras, heathers (if your soil is acid), helianthemums, campanulas in all their many varieties, sedums, penstemons, dwarf asters, and the small goldenrods will form a foundation planting among which you may put many others.

Though the soil of an alpine lawn is that of a typical grassy meadow, keep it on the lean side to maintain restrained and tight growth. Into a good loamy topsoil should be worked generous amounts of gravel or coarse sand. If your natural site is already very sandy or clayey enough, humus should be added to make a lean, open meadow soil. Of course all sod and weed and grass roots should be thoroughly cleaned from the area before anything else is done. Unless you wish to concentrate on acid-loving plants such as heathers and Bearberry, it is well to work in some ground limestone at this time; a neutral pH will allow you to use the greatest variety of plants.

Such an area can eventually become very extensive by clearing and planting each season only what you can easily keep free of weeds until the introduced material takes over the open soil. In this way, too, you will accumulate enough mature plants to provide divisions and seedlings to fill adjacent areas once they are cleared. Or your alpine lawn can be very small. If you own a city lot with room for only a few square yards of grass and one or two shrubs, why not dispense with both grass and bushes and plant the whole area as a lawn of flowering plants with a few dwarf trees and shrubs as accents?

The rocky pasture is somewhat different from the alpine lawn, though they are both formed in nature by much the same phenomena. In this case, however, the parent rock from which the rock particles have been brought down (usually by glacial action) is of a sort that does not break down as completely as the kind forming the deep, fine soil of the alpine meadow. The top few inches remain a shingle of mixed stones, some quite large, through which the rains and melting snow drain quickly down. The finest particles, sometimes gritty and sandy, sometimes clayey—depending on the composition of the rock from which they came—are carried down by the percolating moisture, along with the debris of decayed plants, to form a nourishing soil at deeper levels, where it fills the interstices between buried stones. Here grow only dwarf grasses and sedges and those plants that have roots able to reach the moisture and food below the rocky surface. These are the pastures that for centuries have been the grazing grounds for sheep and goats.

Such a site, when imitated in the garden, is almost a complete substitute for the sunny outcrop and ledge and, in a sense, is an extensive scree. Except for the few plants requiring a vertical growing situation or those needing considerable underground moisture, even the most sought after alpine and saxatile plants can be made to flourish in a properly constructed rocky pasture. It is important to remember that what you are striving for is a deep root-run with rich nourishment at the lower levels and a stony, quick-draining surface. Stones of varying sizes from 6 inches in diameter to fine grit will give the surface the most natural appearance. Even a few large boulders scattered over the area find a frequent parallel in such sites in nature. The boulders have the advantage of offering in their lea planting situations for plants like saxifrages and androsaces, many of which do not like full exposure to the sun.

For the most natural effect boulders are best placed in scattered groups among gravels and smaller stones of various sizes on either flat or gently sloping or undulating ground. It is important that all

USE OF BOULDERS FOR THE ALPINE LAWN
OR ROCKY PASTURE

the boulders and larger stones be set in the soil with their heaviest side down and sufficiently deep to appear completely and permanently stable. Either rounded waterworn boulders or sharp-angled broken rock can be used successfully in this manner, but the two types should not be combined on the same site if it is to appear natural. Rounded boulders require rounded gravel and stones among them; rocks with sharp edges should be surrounded by crushed gravel and broken rock. The gravel used in either case should match the rocks as closely as possible in texture and color: boulders of mixed sorts of stone should be set among mixed gravels, dark boulders in dark gravels, and white or light-colored boulders in light-colored gravel.

Rocky pastures in the wild are generally open to the full measure of sun and wind. In lowland gardens, on the contrary, high shade on the south or, indeed, high broken shade over the whole area will help to simulate the coolness of mountain pastures that are frequently shrouded in fog or cloud. The parklike areas of our own West are examples of rocky pastures where widely spaced Ponderosa Pine and other trees supply shade for those plants that cannot endure the full blast of the sun all summer.

The building of a rocky pasture is slow but straightforward, and not so arduous as moving great rocks. The area should be excavated to a depth of 10 inches to a foot, and the good topsoil screened of weeds and roots and saved as a component of the soil mixture with which the cavity is to be filled. If the bottom of the excavated site is hardpan, this must be broken with a pick and left rough.

The soil mixture for this area is the standard mix described in Chapter 3, the section on soils (p. 83), except that coarse sand is used instead of gravel. In addition to this soil-mix you will need an equal quantity (in bulk) of mixed stone. River gravels are ideal, though a mixture of various sizes up to 6 inches can generally be supplied at commercial gravel banks or crushed-rock plants. Be sure to get washed stone.

Start by spreading a 2- to 3-inch layer of assorted stones in the bottom of your excavation. On this spread 2 to 3 inches of the soil-mix; then water well with a hose. This will wash the soil down between the stones. Repeat these alternate layers, each time hosing in the soil mixture, until you have filled the depression. Scatter a few larger stones or boulders on the surface.

If the area is extensive it will be necessary to leave an unplanted winding path across the stony shingle. Mark this out with a hose or rope before beginning to plant. It may be necessary when planting, especially with young material that has not yet developed a deep or extensive root system, to put a small amount of the soil mixture in the planting hole around the roots. A hand-fork, an old chisel, or a large screwdriver may prove a better planting tool than a trowel or shovel. All sorts of rock garden plants will thrive in this situation, once established, and therefore slow-growing, easily smothered alpines should be given a section to themselves and not be compelled to compete with more rampant neighbors. Until the roots have had time to grow deeply down into the lower levels, and certainly at the time of planting, generous watering is important.

Such a site, as a narrow bed or a more extensive area, is admirably adapted for foundation plantings, particularly for low houses of modern design. In this case the assorted stones should be selected to present a surface in harmony with the construction material of the house, and the larger rocks and boulders should be carefully placed in relation to the architectural features and each other.

The rocky pasture makes an excellent place for those alpines and saxatile plants that demand perfect drainage and some baking in summer; the hard little tufts of western phloxes will be less likely to succumb to the muggs; here *Douglasia montana* will cover itself with rosy stars; and the beautiful Bitter-root, *Lewisia rediviva,* will be able to aestivate after its wide pink and white blossoms have gone to seed. The gray mounds of lesquerella will delight in such a home, as will the stiff, shrubby little *Leptodactylon pungens* with its needlelike leaves and pink and white bell flowers. Here you can grow the tiny white Desert Lily and *Fritillaria pudica, Dodecatheon cusickii,* and the lovely Mariposa Lilies. The hardy cacti will appreciate such a site and *Sphaeralcea coccinea* will run about among the stones and open its glowing, brick-orange blossoms to the summer sun. If your winters are not too severe and you make a pocket with a little more clayey loam mixed in among the rock, you may succeed in growing *Silene hookeri* so that it will become a mat of furry gray leaves spangled with fringed salmon-pink blossoms.

Moraine and Scree

In many respects the moraine and scree are similar to the rocky pasture in that all three provide a quick-draining site composed largely of broken stone. The difference is mostly one of location and extent. Whereas the rocky pasture in nature is an extensive feature usually at subalpine elevations, screes and moraines are found as accumulations of broken rock in pockets of the mountain itself, frequently at very high elevations.

For garden purposes, screes and moraines are special planting sites, ordinarily quite small, situated within the rock garden to provide homes for demanding plants such as drabas and androsaces and other gemlike favorites that do not thrive in the rock garden itself and cannot compete with the more aggressive plants frequently found there. In contrast, the rocky pasture as a separate area or as a complete substitute for the rock garden itself will be planted with a variety of material, easy and difficult, delicate and pervasive.

The distinction between a scree and a moraine is here a completely arbitrary one, since they are both man-made. In nature a moraine is a gravel formation related to glacial action, while a scree is an accumulation of rock particles that have tumbled together at the base of a cliff with or without the aid of running water. Because the true moraine, in its association with glaciers, is frequently kept moist from beneath by the running water of melting snow and ice, the name is here assigned to an underground-watered area of broken stone.

Both scree and moraine should be located in relation to rock ledges and cliffs, though these need not be large, to suggest the original source of the stony material of which they are formed. The commonest and most natural place is a fan-shaped slope beginning between ledge-like rocky outcrops and spreading down and out to end close to a path. If so located, the small plants are somewhat isolated from invasive neighbors and are brought nearby for close viewing, yet the whole structure is blended naturally into the existing garden features. It is, of course, possible to build a completely artificial site for either the scree or the moraine. A raised bed filled with the correct soil-mix serves the plants as well and can be left dry to serve as a scree or be watered from underneath to imitate the conditions of a moraine.

When constructing either scree or moraine as a natural-appearing part of the rock garden proper, it is important to have a really deep pocket, provided for at the time of construction or subsequently dug out: at least 2 feet deep, 3 is better. The bottom is lined with 6 inches of rather sizable chunks of rock, brick, or old broken cement. This provides drainage at times of heavy rain and during spring thaws, which is its main purpose, and there may be a question as to whether it does not offer, during times of drought, too thorough a draining off of groundwater. Yet, because most gardeners can and will water during prolonged dry periods, it is probably fairly essential. In addition it acts as a kind of concealed cistern into which excessive moisture is drained and stored, encouraging roots to penetrate deeply. Thus they escape the danger of minor drought *and* of too much moisture at the crown. It also creates some cooling effect through evaporation.

For the scree, the soil above the rocky cistern should be composed of 1 part loam and 2 parts of coarse leaf mold or peat, laced with dry sheep manure and bone meal; then this amalgam in turn is mixed thoroughly with ⅛-inch to ¾-inch gravel, the final blend consisting of about 1 part of the loam-humus mixture to 4 parts of the rock chips. To prevent the fine particles from being utterly washed down into the blocky stuff beneath, lay a good 2-inch layer of leaves or salt hay over the rough drainage material before filling the excavation with the soil-mix. An annual topdressing of leaf mold (or peat) and gravel, spiced with dry manure and bone meal as suggested in the section on maintenance (p. 94), should be applied in early spring or late fall.

Many plants will succeed in such sites, but a few demand it; and since most of them are lime-lovers the rock particles should be of limestone, or ground limestone added to the above mixture. For further information about making soil mixtures refer to Chapter 3.

Such a scree, watered only when plants show flagging or wilting in the early morning, is designed to offer a home to rare and difficult plants from similar sites in nature. Typical plants, which come from the sunny rockslides and talus slopes and are happy in the garden scree, are acantholimons, onosmas, some asperulas and drabas, all those already mentioned as being suitable for the rocky pasture, and others that demand absolute drainage at the crown because they are susceptible to mildew and rot during muggy weather and resent soggy conditions in winter.

An eastern or northern slope will allow you to grow a greater range of plants in your scree, including many of the high alpines that cannot take the excessive heating of southern and western slopes by the summer sun in the lowlands. Yet there are many plants, especially those from the Mediterranean basin and sections of our own West and Southwest, that flourish with such baking. Their foliage may tend to become rather crisp in the driest part of the summer, but they generally take on green hues in the fall and will be lush in the spring.

A few very special and fussy plants (probably considered special because they are demanding) want not only the quick drainage and spartan diet of the scree but appear to demand access to constant *moving* water during the growing season. It is for these plants that the moraine is designed.

The construction and ingredients of the moraine are the same as for the scree except that provision is made during the building for watering about a foot beneath the surface. The ideal would be to build the gentle slope of the moraine above an area of either pond or bog, but the underground seepage of water should be of such an amount that the transpiration of the plants and the evaporation from the surface prevents an excess from puddling at the bottom. The water is led into the upper end of the moraine through a hose or ½- to ¾-inch underground pipe connected to the main water supply. This should have its own shutoff valve. Branching out from this water source at the top are perforated pipes of the same small diameter buried approximately 1 foot beneath the entire surface of the moraine about a foot apart. The perforated pipes are sealed at the lower end so that the water will be under pressure and will fill the entire water system, oozing out through the small holes to percolate through the moraine, the excess collecting in the rough drainage material of the rock-filled cistern below.

In nature, the meltwater from snow seeps through the soil only during the spring and summer and is utterly stilled during the winter. It even fluctuates during the growing season, sometimes halting at night, when there is no melting of the glacier above, and moving most rapidly and copiously on warm sunny days. It is not necessary in the garden to manipulate the supply in absolute accordance with the tempo of nature. A slow steady flow during the growing season, with the water supply shut off from October to April, will meet the demands of the plants.

An alternative method for underground watering of a small moraine, where a continuous water supply is not available, is similar to that suggested in the earlier section on raised beds. In this case a series of perforated sewer pipes are laid about 2 feet apart, horizontal and level, across the slope of the moraine. These would have to be filled periodically through elbow sections that come to the surface, the openings concealed by flat stones. The frequency of filling obviously would depend on the weather, the rapidity of drainage, and the local conditions of the slope and surrounding soil. Common sense, a spirit of experimentation, and close observation of the health of the plants will have to set the watering schedule.

If you are fortunate enough to have a stream or pond on your property, this natural water supply can be used to great advantage. You can build the moraine on a slope above the pond and with a circulating pump obtain a continuous flow to the upper end of the system of perforated pipes beneath the bed. If a stream is your water source, you can build the moraine along its banks, but high enough so that there will be no danger of flooding. Remember, though, that the moraine should have no water flowing through the soil in winter when the plants are dormant. It is therefore usually best to lead the water from the stream into the moraine through a pipe that can be shut off in winter. If your brook meanders through fairly flat land, the use of a circulating pump is probably the easiest solution. If, however, the gradient of the brook is a steep one and the banks are fairly high, it may be possible to bring the water into the moraine by gravity, leading it into the upper end of the bed through a pipe that has its inflow end farther upstream. A controlling device is usually necessary where the water passes from the natural stream into the garden, to prevent flooding and to permit shutting off the water during the freezing months. A rampart or dyke of stone or earth high enough to contain the stream when it is in spate can be constructed, and the water for the garden feature led beneath this through a pipe of relatively small diameter. A gate valve installed in this pipe allows you to shut off the water at will, although a board to cover the inflow end of the pipe usually will serve the purpose adequately. This will be held firmly in place by the pressure of the water against it and can be pried loose and removed when you wish water to flow through the pipe. The water thus introduced into the garden can be permitted to seep through perforated pipes underlying the moraine or it can be used to create a small controlled brook with a narrow moraine built along its banks. In the latter case, the necessary underground watering will be supplied naturally by the water seeping into the soil through capillary action.

Such a moraine should have its surface raised about 18 inches above the level of the water in the brooklet. Place large rocks along the edge of your artificial stream to form a buttress, then fill behind these with stone and the gravelly moraine soil-mix. If for some reason the soil itself must slope down to the water's edge, the saturated soil nearest the water can be used as a home for the true streamside plants and only the higher reaches planted as a moraine.

An east or north slope is to be preferred for the moraine unless it is protected by high shade from the sun; good air circulation is also a basic qualification. Given these conditions, there is hardly a plant that will not thrive in such a site. Perhaps it would be wise to keep the moraine for those temperamental little specimens you cannot get to grow anywhere else.

The Heath

The heath is a rather special type of alpine lawn in imitation of those spots in nature where a deep bed of peaty, acid humus has accumulated. Such areas are usually of limited dimension, found in small rock-girt pockets high in the mountains or at the fringe of evergreen groves. Occasionally they are vast areas, such as the upland, poorly drained stretches of Scottish moorland, or old burn sites in the evergreen mountain forests of the American West. The common feature is a deep soil of very acid reaction containing a high proportion of peaty material that holds moisture and yet is open enough to provide an adequate supply of oxygen at root depth. Some of the most beautiful mountain plants thrive in this type of soil: heathers, cassiopes, dwarf rhododendrons, gaultherias, shortias, and many of the difficult primulas of the Himalayas. In fact, a number of the finest plants from the lofty Himalayas succeed nowhere else in the garden.

Because so much of the material suited to the heath is evergreen, in lowland areas the peat bed should be placed on either a north slope or the north side of tall evergreen shrubs and trees to prevent sunscorch during snowless periods in winter; also, though heath plants never want to be parched, they will not endure waterlogged conditions. The heath looks most natural and functions best as a section in the ledgy rock garden when located at the base of outcrops. Should the rock be limestone, however, the alkaline properties would leach down and neutralize the essential acidity of the bed. It is quite possible, if the rock garden is on a slope with a background of tall evergreen shrubs and trees above it, to locate the peaty area between these and the rocky outcrops, whether these are limestone or not. A heath also may be appropriately placed in an opening in the woods garden, or on the higher land surrounding a primrose bog, or in conjunction with a pine-barren area.

The principal ingredient in the heath soil is acid peat, which in itself of course does not contain plant food; therefore some source of fertility should be incorporated. Heath plants are not greedy feeders, fortunately. The nutriment should be supplied as acid leaf mold, cottonseed meal, or other organic materials that will break down slowly; most commercial fertilizers will, in time, alkalinize the soil. To keep the mixture mechanically open, it is wise to mix 1 part of sharp sand (mineral particles with unsmooth edges) by bulk to each 4 or 5 parts of sphagnum peat. Some of the peat content may be replaced by leaf mold, crumbled, rotten wood, ground conifer bark, tea leaves, and coffee grounds. In fact, the incorporation of such substitutes produces a soil more nearly like heath soils in nature. This mixture should be at least a foot deep and may either fill a natural depression in the ground or excavated pockets. Where the soil is limy the heath bed must be raised above ground level. This could be done as a raised bed, as in a woods garden, by placing logs at the edge of a path and filling behind them with a really good depth of peaty soil. Watering during dry periods in summer will probably be essential, and if your water supply is hard you will have difficulty maintaining minimum acidity in the soil.

The Wooded Area

This section might be titled "The Wildflower Area," but purposely the title is phrased to avoid the built-in associations that equate wildflowers with woods. All alpine and saxatile plants suited to the rock garden, whether sunny or shaded, are *wildflowers*. That is above all one of the basic marks of plants admissible to the rock garden ledges, lawns, boulder fields, screes, bogs, and woods in contrast to the domesticated, developed, and bedded plants of the perennial border and the annual bed.

At the alpine heights, in screes, moraines, and rocky pastures, among the ledges and bouldery tumbles are found the dwarf cushion plants of neat foliage and sparkling blossom with which we try to furnish our rock gardens. But in nature, and in every fine rock garden with which I am familiar, there are transition zones—blendings of the lowland meadow plants and those of the seaside, the pine barren, the bogs, woods, and copses. Only a few purists, and they with difficulty, would exclude from the man-made rock garden landscape all but those plants that grow in the ethereal upper regions above timberline—the high, remote, and special haunts of true alpines, of chamois and mountain goats, amid thin pure air.

Just as the mountain climber passes from the lowland meadows, streamsides, swamps, and bogs, through the mountain forests and copses before he reaches the high and barren peaks, so most rock gardens encompass a mixture of sites for growing an array of the vast

and wonderful variety of wildflowers. Unless you live above timberline, your garden will of necessity become a medley. Who would
wish to leave out of his rock garden the meadow primroses, woodland
anemones, the swamp orchids, seaside hudsonias, moorland heathers,
and the dwarf shrubs and trees from the scrubland? That, indeed, is
one of the great charms of the so-called rock garden. It can be made
to include harmoniously, in a way impossible for the perennial border, an almost limitless variety of plants distinguished by the hall-
mark of wildness. This is why all prescriptions for rock gardens are
fundamentally based on an imitation of situations in nature.

The woods garden is therefore but a natural segment of the rock
garden, fittingly associated with true alpines, bog plants, and dwarf
trees. As a rule, most woods gardens are developed in an already
existing woodland, but it is not impossible to plant trees and shrubs
in an open setting to provide the requisite shade for forest plants.
Even in actual woodland rather thorough preparation of the site and
its soil is essential for success. Too commonly it is thought that because "wild" flowers are found in abundance in nature, they may be
thrust at random beneath trees to flourish. In many naturally wooded
sites the shade is too heavy to ensure abundant bloom. Forests vary.
The shade of evergreens, unlike that of deciduous trees, is year-round,
and only some plants are adapted to this kind of condition; others
need spring sunshine for flowering. Frequently there is so much
root competition from certain types of trees that only a limited number of tolerant plants will thrive. Or there may be such a solid
ground cover of matted, weedy native plants that introduced material
is soon driven out by the competition.

Almost all plants native to woodland sites thrive on soil lightened
and nourished by an abundance of leaf-moldy humus, and many
prefer acid or neutral soil; very few require lime. An extremely acid
reaction will limit the species that will grow really well. The duff
beneath oak trees and conifers is acid, and most other tree leaves
break down into a neutral humus. But leaf mold alone, or peat

(sphagnum peat is a good source of acid humus), does not provide all the nourishment needed for vigorous plant growth. Most woodland soils are not rich in fertility, and it is amazing how woodland plants respond to feeding. Old barnyard manure worked into the soil is a wonderful tonic; but, lacking this, you will find that commercially available dried manures, or a balanced chemical fertilizer, will furnish the required nourishment. This, plus some powdered sulphur if the soil needs acidifying, should be worked into the ground at the time of preparation. Or, contrariwise, a small amount of ground limestone will not be amiss if the pH is below 5.

The preparation of the planting sites in the woods garden is just as important as in any other section. The terrain bordering the paths through the woods should be reserved in the main part for the more delicate and special woodlanders. These, therefore, will require the most careful preparation of the soil. Dig the beds deep, removing all weeds and roots, and incorporate additional humus and fertilizer. Sections more remote from the paths may be planted with shrubs and coarser herbaceous plants. Though it may be necessary only to make planting pockets for such material, thorough preparation of the whole area with attractive ground covers among and beneath the shrubs will not only enhance the total effect but will eliminate a source of weed seeds that could contaminate the beds along the paths. This involves thinning out some of the trees where they are too thick and eliminating unwanted brush by digging them up whenever possible. Otherwise cut them off close to the ground. Sprout growth from both tree and brush stumps may be discouraged by annual clipping or by careful but thorough treatment of the stumps with brush-killer. Trimming the remaining trees also improves the general effect, with the extra advantage of letting in more light and air.

Dense planting in large drifts is most desirable, for beauty and also for discouraging weeds. And a woodland garden, like any other, does need weeding. There is nothing more dispiriting than a fine

sweep of hepaticas swamped and crowded by coarse wood asters or
sedges; and tree seedlings are as pernicious as any other weed.

A light annual topdressing of leaf mold and cottonseed meal will
maintain a high degree of fertility, but it is not absolutely necessary
if the natural fall of leaves and pine needles is allowed to rot on the
ground.

If your soil is naturally acid and the area is not too waterlogged,
rhododendrons make attractive evergreen accents beneath the trees.
Azaleas are also excellent shrubs for a woodland setting where the
soil is not limy. Spicebush, *Daphne mezereum,* and the many vibur-
nums are not fussy about pH and will endure shady locations.
Depending on the natural moisture content of the earth beneath the
trees, a variety of herbaceous plants may be drifted along the paths
and farther back among the trees.

Spring comes early to a woodland garden. Ragged remnants of
snow may still linger in shaded hollows when the hepaticas flower,
and after a long winter what is more heartening than the sight of
these delicate blossoms starring a sun-warmed slope above the sere
leaves? Planted thickly a colony of hepaticas is a delight hard to du-
plicate. Pragmatic business tycoons who do not know a phlox from a
begonia wax nostalgic over the sweet-scented Trailing Arbutus, its
white and coral-tipped flowers half concealed beneath the leathery
leaves symbolize spring to everyone who has had a country childhood in the Northeast. Then overnight it seems the woodland
garden is filled with flowers: scillas form rivulets and pools of blue
beside the paths, Dutchman's-breeches tremble in the soft air at the
foot of a rock, trilliums raise their three-petaled flowers on strong
stalks, the English Wood Anemone covers the ground with its wide-
eyed blooms of blue, pink, and white. Trout lilies—both the yellow
variety of the eastern woodlands and the white, yellow, and pale pink
ones from the West—thrust their nodding bells through the dark
leaf mold, and violets of every description jostle each other for living
space. You should not neglect the woodland primroses so suitable

to such a site, or the fragile beauty of the epimediums, even though these are not native to our woods. Ferns, too, are indispensable in the shady garden. In spring their unfurling croisers add architectural accents to the carpet of leaves and flowers; in summer they become the main constituent of the woodland flora, foaming cool and green in a flood of feathery fronds at the foot of trees and against the gray upthrust of rock.

But, though native woodlanders are mainly spring-blooming, a few will flower later, among them the three species of snakeroot with their graceful spires of white blossoms. *Chrysogonum virginianum* covers its low mat of coarse leaves with small yellow sunflowers all season, and *Silene virginica* will add splashes of brilliant red to the summer green. The Wood Lily *Lilium philadelphicum* and *L. canadense* are both summer bloomers, and Cardinal Flower will glow in August. In addition to these there are the berry-bearing herbs *Actaea rubra,* with its clusters of holly-red fruit in midsummer, and *Actaea pachypoda,* whose white "doll's-eyes" ripen in late summer; and do not forget that the "jack" in the Jack-in-the-pulpit becomes a club of scarlet beads in the fall.

In addition you can introduce such foreigners as the astilbe tribe, which in its varieties will bring flowering feathers, from white through pink to red, to your woodland setting for most of the summer. The tall wands of the Willow Gentian will add a note of blue to a moist spot beneath the trees, and the hostas look their best when naturalized in the woods. The yellow and orange "poppy flowers" of the biennial *Meconopsis cambrica* flutter in the shadows from June to frost and will self-sow for the future.

A woodland garden can be a pleasure to wander through at all seasons, but essential to its beauty is the architecture of upright tree trunks and well-placed shrubs. The herbaceous material is only the interior decoration of your woodland domain, whether it be only a few yards square or an acre or two in extent. Therefore, when planting or clearing, always keep in mind the position of the dark boles of the trees rising as columns from the floor to the canopy above; and do not allow scrubby brush, a tangle of low branches, or a thicket of spindly saplings to confuse the effect so that you can no longer see the trees for the woods.

Swamps, Bogs, and Pine Barrens

The finest plants of moist and boggy sites may find a congenial home in the rock garden, since they are as appropriate and as adaptable as the woodland-dwellers. If there are depressions at the foot of slopes and ledges in the rock garden proper or in the wooded area, these may be developed as special sites. The lower edge of the underground-watered moraine is another ideal location.

Essential to all these habitats is a high water table and a moisture-holding soil. A swamp in nature is a low area of rather heavy, moist soil with a high clay or loam content. It may be either in the open or in a forest. A bog, on the other hand, is generally without trees and is more constantly saturated, with soil of almost pure decomposing peat. The pine barren, though it may appear completely dry, is also underwatered by a high water table. Its soil is composed almost entirely of acid sand; the widely scattered and usually dwarfed pines give it its name.

These natural features are distinguished basically by the soil mixture. For the constructed swamp, the soil should be composed of 3 parts clay loam, 1 part humus, and 1 part fine sand. For the bog use either pure peat or 3 parts of peat to 1 part of fine sand. For the pine barren the soil is made up of 5 parts of fine, acid sand to 1 part of acid leaf mold or peat. These are rough proportions and slight modifications in one direction or another can do no harm.

Though swamps and pine barrens tend to become dry at the surface during drought periods and only the bog is constantly saturated, the presence of ample moisture beneath the surface is important for each. This need not be moving water, as in a moraine. Perhaps the simplest way to provide this steady supply of water is to construct the site as a bay or bypass adjacent to an existing stream—if you are fortunate enough to have one flowing through your garden—or on the shore of a pond or lake. Then all that is necessary is to excavate an area in the bank deep enough for the water to back into or pass through. When this is filled with the proper mixture, even to considerable height above the surface of the water, constant moisture will be available at root depth and higher by capillary action.

If a natural source of water is used to create a bog, swamp, or pine barren, the possibility of serious flooding during spring or seasonal cloudbursts must be taken into consideration. A gentle, temporary overflow of water generally does no harm; most bog, swamp, and waterside plants can stand considerable water over their crowns during the growing season. A rushing torrent of floodwater is a different matter, since it may sweep away plants, soil—all. If this is liable to happen, a controlling device such as that suggested on page 55 will be necessary.

Where water must be artificially introduced, an underground perforated pipe (also described in the section on moraines) is ideal. Larger holes and hence more water will be wanted for the bog. The smaller holes will suffice for swamp or pine barren. Small areas can be satisfactorily constructed by burying a watertight container or by lining an excavation with heavy plastic and filling up the hole with special soil. These may be kept sufficiently moist by overhead-watering with a hose or watering can. Such areas have been successfully made by sinking barrels, bathtubs, septic-tank tiles with a bottom of waterproofed cement, and other watertight containers. That they are watertight ensures that the applied moisture does not rapidly leak away, but it does mean that during heavy rainy periods the surface may become too wet. It is important, therefore, to have the lip of the watertight compartment about 2 inches or more below the surrounding soil level so that excess surface water may seep off. The depression above the sunken container is then filled to ground level with the proper soil-mix, covering the rim of the container and hence concealing it completely. A method of making a permanently moist area around an artificial pool is discussed in the next section.

Water in the Garden

Open water adds immeasurable charm to the rock garden, whether running or still, as in a pool. A pool can be made either by constructing a watertight basin of cement or by sinking a container into the ground. The edge can be concealed by rocks that blend into the rockwork of the surrounding garden and by creeping plants that will grow over it. If the rim of the pool is a few inches below the surrounding ground level, it will be easier to hide the edge with overhanging rocks; in nature it is quite normal for the water level in a pool to be considerably lower than the ground level. Any rocks placed on the lip of the pool should be cemented down or so firmly balanced that they will not tip and precipitate someone standing on them into the water.

Another method of making a natural-looking edge to your pool is to construct it with a double rim. The inner, deeper section contains the pool itself, which is surrounded by a shallower depression filled with a soil mixture suitable for bog, swamp, or pine-barren plants. The soil on this shelf slopes down from the surrounding land into the water and is kept from sliding into the pool by a raised lip, low enough to allow the water in the pool to pass over it. The outermost edge of the pool-bog is higher and thus prevents the water from seeping out into the soil beyond the area to be kept saturated. This section of waterlogged soil need not be regular in outline, nor need it completely surround the pool (see p. 66).

A wide range of plants that thrive in boggy conditions can be planted in this saturated area if the soil mixture fulfills the plants' requirements. *Parnassia glauca, Calopogon pulchellus, Pogonia ophioglossoides,* various species of *Sagittaria, Caltha palustris, Menyanthes*

trifoliata, Calla palustris, Trollius laxus, species of *Mimulus,* and the
bog primroses are all suitable for such a site. If your pool is large
enough, some of the taller plants, such as Japanese Iris, *Osmunda
regalis,* and *Lobelia cardinalis,* make handsome waterside plants. A
few well-placed rocks partly in the water and partly exposed will add
to the natural effect.

POOL WITH BOGGY EDGE

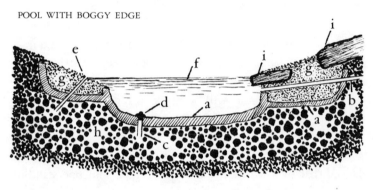

a. Reenforced, waterproofed concrete walls and bottom at least 6 inches thick
b. Inlet pipe (optional) **f.** Water level
c. Drainpipe at low end of pool **g.** Saturated soil
d. Removable plug **h.** Dry well of rock and gravel
e. Screened overflow pipe **i.** Rocks set into boggy edge (optional)

It is important to remember that a pool should be located in a low
hollow in the garden to look natural. Pools, except those formed
as a part of a flowing stream, are seldom seen in nature on top of a
ledge. Turquoise and deep blue may make excellent colors for the
inside of a swimming pool but they are quite unsuitable for a natural-looking garden pool. The inside can be left the neutral color of
cement, which will eventually become stained and coated by algae,
or it may be painted dark brownish green or brown.

A drain with a removable plug in the bottom of the pool, facili-
tating emptying for cleaning or for the winter months, can lead

into a dry well of rock and gravel installed under the pool at the time of construction or into an out-of-the-way section of the property where the runoff will do no damage. It is of course quite possible to empty the pool by siphoning. Regardless of which system is used, a firm base of at least 6 inches of crushed rock should be placed under a permanent pool. An overflow pipe draining into this dry well will prevent excessive flooding of surrounding soil in heavy rains. Strainers, preferably removable for cleaning, in the mouths of both the main and the overflow drains prevent fish, leaves, and other debris from entering and clogging the pipes.

A cement pool should be made with walls and bottom at least 6 inches thick, and these should be reenforced with a layer of wire mesh sandwiched within the cement. A mixture of 1 part Portland cement to 2 parts of clean sharp sand and 3 parts of gravel about ½ inch in diameter is considered suitable for constructing pools. Since concrete is not naturally waterproof, it will have to be painted with waterproofing paint or an appropriate waterproofing agent will have to be added to the amalgam as it is mixed. Such an additive can be obtained at hardware or building-supply stores. Allow the concrete to dry slowly and thoroughly, or it is apt to leak. A covering of burlap bags kept dampened for a week to ten days or a plastic sheet spread over the concrete to retain the moisture will ensure this slow hardening process. The pool should not be filled with water for at least two weeks (better, four weeks). The first water to be put in the pool will absorb the free alkali in the new concrete and will consequently poison plants or fish. Let this first filling remain in the pool for a minimum of two weeks, then drain it off, flush the sides and bottom with a hose, and refill with fresh water before stocking or planting the pool. Such a pool can be kept filled by a hose or bucket or an inflow valve connected to the water supply.

If the topography of your land permits, it is quite possible to construct a small stream or series of cascades in conjunction with your pool. Cascades generally are more satisfactory, because it is difficult to conceal the artificiality of a cement runnel unless the waterflow is copious and continual. A series of small shallow pools with water trickling over the ledges between them make a delightful effect for both eye and ear. Such a stream should be placed above your pool. If its source is neither too high nor too far from the pool, a circulating pump concealed in or beneath the pool will create sufficient flow. Add water to the pool when necessary to compensate for loss by evaporation.

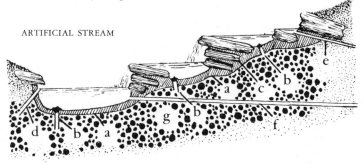

ARTIFICIAL STREAM

a. Reenforced, waterproofed concrete at least 6 inches thick
b. Drainage pipes with removable plugs
c. Rocks set in concrete
d. Overflow pipe
e. Inflow pipe
f. Pipe for returning water to inflow pipe via a circulating pump (optional)
g. Dry well of rock and gravel

If your stream is to be a long one or one with a considerable fall, there must be a separate water source with a shutoff valve. The opening of the inflow—whether connected to a circulating pump or to another water supply—should be concealed beneath and between rocks, so that the flow appears to be coming from a natural source such as a spring. A rise of ground above the source adds considerably to this effect.

You may, perhaps, have on your property a small stream, which during the dry season reduces to the point of very little water between unsightly banks of weedy mud. Such a watercourse can be improved by building several low dams to hold back the water in a series of pools. This can of course be done with cemented rocks, but it is possible to build such dams of firmly wedged stones, the chinks tightly packed with salt hay, particularly on the upstream side. Since salt hay takes a long time to disintegrate, it will catch silt that will gradually fill the interstices to make the dams reasonably watertight. Carefully done, such an arrangement will look completely natural.

Walks, Paths, and Pavements

It is essential to have easy access to all parts of the rock garden, for maintenance as well as for close viewing of plants. It is important, therefore, to plan your walks and paths with great care. The amount of traffic in any section will determine their width and, to some extent, the surface material. Their placement will depend considerably on the logical flow of movement from one section of the garden to another, and how these will lead you most easily and naturally among the rocks and up the steeper slopes. They also should take into consideration the type of planting in the garden. Wide swatches of mass plantings may be viewed with pleasure from a distance, but it is well to provide for access to sections planted with the minute and special species better enjoyed close-up. Be warned, though, not to plant delicate and cherished plants so close to the path that they are liable to be trod upon.

Asphalt, cement, or formal flagstone paths, easy as they are for upkeep, are out of place except in public parks and gardens. Grass paths, unless they are very wide and more like meadow areas, look out of place in the rock garden. Moreover, they are a nuisance to mow, are a source of weed seeds, and must be rigorously edged at least twice a season to prevent the grass roots from creeping in among the rocks and cushion plants. A narrow path mowed through a *grassy* alpine lawn obviously does not present any of these problems. And such a passage through your alpine lawn keeps your visitors from wandering aimlessly among the bulbs and other plants in the grasses.

For most purposes, paths should be no wider than 3 feet; they usually look most appropriate as narrow tracks wending through a wild garden. Three feet will permit passage of a wheelbarrow, probably the largest implement you will need to bring in, once the garden is finished. But it is frequently advisable, if the garden is extensive, to provide also a few larger, flat "standing areas." If groups of people walk through the garden and have to progress in single file, some stopping places for talking and viewing are convenient.

The simplest type of path to construct and maintain is one of gravel to match the stone-chip surface of the garden. At least 3 inches of gravel are necessary to cut down on the weeding, an otherwise tedious chore. Along both edges, where gravel path meets rock garden, you will discover an ideal seedbed, into which will sow all kinds of plants from the garden—unless you are a scrupulously neat gardener and remove all seedheads. From this seedbed along the paths it is possible to dig husky young plants for replenishing the garden or for gifts to your visitors and friends. A few, left to spread into the path, will soften the edges, but unless you are periodically ruthless your passage will become narrower and narrower.

To be sure, the whole path system may be paved with flat stones firmly set in the soil. These should be of irregular outline and of rock similar to that used in the construction of the garden proper. These can be given a natural effect and happily blended with the garden by growing a few carpeting plants between them. Thymes are excellent, since they will withstand considerable trampling. Taller plants, which may self-sow, will have to be weeded out; they can become annoying obstacles. Paths through shady, woodsy gardens are best made of materials like pine needles, tanbark, or woodchips, although stones can be used if the woods garden is naturally stony.

Steps will be needed if the path must ascend a slope. Stone steps are usually most suitable, but log risers supporting earthern treads are quite appropriate for a woodland path. On a really steep grade these may be set one above another, as in a stairway, the treads level with or slightly below the planted areas on each side. It is possible, though, to mount even fairly steep slopes on steps placed at intervals with level or slightly sloping stretches of path between them. In the rock garden proper such alternations of gravelly surface and steplike outcrops are perfectly in keeping, since they are frequent in the mountains.

For several reasons a paved terrace, if it is used as a sitting or dining area, is not a suitable site for planting. To remain level, the flagstones must be set in cement or on a deep bed of sand to prevent frost heaving; otherwise they will tilt and cause furniture placed on them to teeter alarmingly. Obviously no self-respecting alpine or saxatile plant will thrive in a growing medium of cement or sand. Even if you and your guests are willing to put up with uneven paving laid on a bed of soil, plants will form tuffets that can make walking or sitting hazardous. In addition, most plants resent being trodden on and will eventually succumb to this treatment, leaving a space in which weeds may sow. There are a few exceptions to this rule— *Thymus serpyllum* can grow in such a site.

If your terrace is large enough, the stones on the periphery can be set on good alpine soil and the cracks between them planted. In general, though, it is better to construct a low raised bed alongside the terrace or to mound slightly the surrounding soil and set into this bed groups of rough stones simulating outcrops. Here your plants will be safer from the feet of your visitors.

Where it is necessary to cross boggy ground, a raised walk that can be traversed dry-shod is essential. Ordinary steppingstones may be used if the soil is not too squashy to support them. It is also possible to make attractive raised steppingstones by sinking upright sections of round or rectangular tile into the soft ground at convenient intervals and filling these with concrete. A topping of gravel pressed into the concrete while it is still soft makes a pleasant finish for the stepping surface.

A corduroy path of short sections of log laid side by side is quite often satisfactory. A layer of woodchips, sawdust, or tanbark will make the footing less slippery, or boards can be nailed lengthwise to the logs to make a flat boardwalk. If the logs are of cedar, hemlock, or locust they will not disintegrate rapidly; treating them with creosote also will help prevent decay. Where the ground is very wet it may be necessary to sink pilings to support the boardwalk. This need not be raised more than a few inches above the surface of the swampy area. If the walk is narrow, groups of pilings with their upper ends projecting above the boardwalk, set alongside it at short intervals, will add to its charm and will give a sense of greater security to those crossing upon it. Walks such as these can zigzag across the marshy ground, providing both an attractive pattern and a view of more area at close quarters. A thick layer of brush laid crosswise will make a reasonably solid path across soft ground if it is covered with earth. Such a path disintegrates rather rapidly, however, and has to be rebuilt at frequent intervals.

Rock Garden Plants in Containers

The small bog garden, moraine, and scree are in a sense basins of specific soil-mixes as planting areas for particular plants. The idea can be carried a step further by using actual containers of all sorts to make special sites for individual plants or small collections. These may range from a sizable tabletop tray in which is built a miniature rock garden landscape to a clay pot containing a single Kabschia saxifrage. They offer an opportunity for creating a precise environment and also may be used for the intimate display of special plants on the terrace and even, briefly, in the house. Another advantage is that portable containers may be moved about to give individual plants a change of exposures to light and shade and to temperature at various seasons of the year.

Clay and plastic pots with drainage holes in the bottom are available in all sizes and shapes. Extensive collections of alpine and saxatile plants are grown exclusively in such pots by many growers in Great Britain, though the scheme has only recently received much attention in this country. This method is perhaps best suited to the connoisseur, who is more interested in growing and displaying a single perfect specimen of a species than in creating a landscape effect.

With very small containers, careful attention must be given to the proper soil mixture and to frequent watering. For this reason it is easier to handle alpines in large containers in which a collection of plants is established. Clay pots of great size are heavy and unwieldy and will crack if exposed to freezing, but suitable containers may be made of wood or other materials. In Great Britain sinks and troughs of stone are used for housing delightful miniature gardens. These, however, are very cumbersome and in addition are not easily available in the United States. It is quite possible, though, to make planters closely resembling stone which are considerably lighter in weight. These can be cast in different shapes and sizes from a mixture of 1 part Portland cement, to 1½ parts of sphagnum peat and 1½ parts agricultural perlite. Such pots should be reenforced with 1-inch-mesh-chicken-wire netting sandwiched within the concrete. They must also be supplied with drainage holes, made by inserting wooden dowels or short lengths of stiff plastic tubing (diameter about ¾ inch) in the cement while it is still soft; these are easily removed with a slight twisting motion once the cement has set.

Rectangular concrete planters can be shaped by using forms of wood or corrugated cardboard. Round and freeform planters are best made in a sand mold. Wooden forms should be constructed so that they can be dismantled easily in order to extricate the pot once the concrete has set; the main advantage in using cardboard forms is that they can be torn away from the hardened concrete with no difficulty. For the latter method use two cartons of heavy corrugated cardboard, one somewhat smaller than the other. The larger of the two boxes should be trimmed to the depth wanted for the outside dimension of the planter. Strengthen the open side by binding it tightly with several strands of twine. Place this box on a firm, flat, level surface and cover the bottom with a 1½- to 2-inch layer of concrete made with the ingredients described above. A piece of chicken wire, previously cut to fit the bottom of the box, is embedded in the concrete. The dowels used to form the drainage holes are then inserted into the wet concrete with their lower ends firmly pressed against the bottom of the carton and their upper ends protruding from the cement mixture. Next the smaller box is placed *bottom side up* within the first carton, the edges of its open side pressed

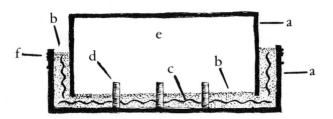

CROSS SECTION OF CARDBOARD CARTONS USED TO
FORM A CONCRETE PLANTER

a. Cardboard cartons
b. Concrete
c. 1-inch-mesh chicken wire embedded in concrete
d. Wooden dowels or stiff plastic tubing
e. Airspace
f. Cord around top edge of outside carton

slightly into the soft concrete. This inside box should be enough smaller than the outer one to allow for a 1½- to 2-inch-thick layer of concrete between the sides of the two boxes. A strip of chicken wire, long enough to encircle loosely the inner box and slightly narrower than the depth of the outer box, is then slipped into the slot between the two cartons, its lower edge pressed firmly down into the concrete bottom. Cut and shape this strip of chicken wire before pouring the concrete bottom, but do not forget to allow for the thickness of the concrete base.

Permit the concrete to harden for about one-half hour, then fill the aperture between the two boxes with enough concrete to conceal the upper edge of the wire netting. Pack the cement mixture down with your fingers or a stick to eliminate the air bubbles. The concrete mixture is most satisfactorily handled if it is about the consistency of rather liquid cottage cheese. The concrete should harden for twelve to twenty-four hours before you peel away the boxes and remove the dowels. At this point the concrete will still be somewhat soft and can be scrubbed with a stiff brush to improve the surface texture. Some buckling of the cardboard is inevitable, but the slight unevenness caused by this will add to the similitude of natural stone.

Where a round or freedom planter is wanted it should be made *upside down* over a mound of damp sand packed into the desired shape over a bowl or group of bowls, also upside down. The armature of chicken wire is then shaped over the mound of sand. A piece of dampened cloth pressed over the sand mold will keep it from being destroyed while you form the armature. Once the armature is shaped it is removed temporarily for later use. The cloth can then be discarded. The mound of sand is next covered with a large sheet of thin flexible plastic and a ½- to 1-inch layer of concrete spread over this mold. The wire armature is pressed into the soft concrete and another ½- to 1-inch layer smeared over it. The edges of the plastic sheet are then brought up around the sides of the planter, but not the bottom, and held in place with more damp sand. Now the dowels can be inserted into the exposed bottom of the pot.

After the cement is partially hardened (in twelve to twenty-four hours) the sand and plastic sheet should be peeled away and the dowels removed. The bottom is leveled by scraping it with a horizontally held pane of glass or a board and the surface brushed. If carefully done the planter may be removed completely from the mold at this point, so that the upper edge and inside surface can also be shaped and brushed. It can be left in place to dry completely, though, as the plastic will peel off the cement even when dry. In either case it is necessary to clear out the drainage holes with a sharp implement, since these are blocked with a thin film of concrete.

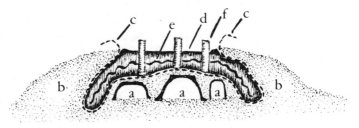

CROSS SECTION OF CONCRETE FREEFORM
PLANTER IN MOLD

a. Empty bowls
b. Hard-packed moist sand
c. Sheet of flexible plastic
d. Concrete
e. 1-inch-mesh chicken wire embedded in concrete
f. Wooden dowels or stiff plastic tubing

The rather dead gray of concrete can be altered by tinting it with lime-proof cement-coloring powders added to the dry amalgam in the proportion of about ½ cup of powder to each quart of Portland cement. These coloring powders are obtainable at hardware or building-supply stores.

Cement pots, like cement pools, must be allowed to harden slowly and should then be weathered out of doors for several weeks so that the free lime will be leached out by rain; however, soaking the hardened planter in a solution of potassium permanganate for two or three days will help neutralize the alkali more rapidly.

Such pots, like plastic pots, are relatively light in weight and do not crack if exposed to freezing as clay pots do. They have proved ideal for growing a wide assortment of rock garden plants and can be used as a decorative feature on top of a wall or on the terrace. They do not require plunging, but should in winter be set directly on the ground.

The expert management of difficult alpines in pots requires such careful attention to soil, drainage, watering, and shading that a whole volume of experience would go into directions for specific plants and particular sites. Suffice it to say that common sense in these matters and an adventuresome and experimental spirit will produce success in most instances.

The consistency of the soil in the containers is perhaps more important than any other single factor. For most alpines a freely draining yet moisture-retentive mixture is best. The magic formula of 1 part leaf mold, 1 part loam, 1 part sharp sand or fine gravel is standard; but this will vary from 3 parts of leaf mold and 1 of sand for gentians, to 3 parts of fine gravel and 1 of leaf mold for *Douglasia montana*. If a free-draining soil mixture is used, clay pots and planters of wood or concrete may be filled completely with it; plastic pots, however, because they are not porous, need considerable extra drainage in the form of a layer of coarse gravel beneath the growing medium. When a community of various plants are grown in a single container it is important that these should all like the same environment: type of soil, amount of moisture, sun or shade.

If you grow alpines in clay or plastic pots it is important, even in summer, to have some place where they may be properly watered, shaded, and stored, in a sense, until they are ready for display. This can be a frame filled with plunge material and shaded with lath, snow-fencing, or plastic or cotton shading-cloth. Sinking clay pots in plunge material is particularly necessary in hot dry weather to prevent rapid evaporation through the sides of the pot; even though plastic pots neither lose nor take in moisture through the sides, there is an advantage in also sinking them to prevent rapid fluctuations in temperature at the roots. The plunge medium should be free-draining but moisture-retentive: fine ashes from industrial furnaces, when available, are ideal, but just as satisfactory are pure sand or a half-and-half mixture of sharp sand and peat.

This is placed in the frame over a 2- to 4-inch base of coarse drainage. The plunge material itself should be deep enough to take your deepest pots sunk nearly to the rim. Frames may be made of wood, poured concrete, or concrete blocks. Though they may be of any length, they should be narrow enough to reach across so that it is not necessary to step into the frame to get at a pot in the rear. If the frame is for summer plunging only, the sides may be level and just high enough to contain the plunge material. Supports for shade covers should rise above the frame to allow as free a circulation of air as possible across the plants in hot, muggy weather. If the frames are to be covered by glass or plastic sash in winter, they must be built with a higher back and sloping sides so the sash will lie at a sufficient angle to provide runoff. Enough height is also necessary to allow adequate air space above the growing plants.

The location of the frames will depend on your available space, but if there is a choice, a north or east exposure with access to free movement of air, particularly in summer, is important. For convenience, they should be located near a source of water, because alpines in pots need frequent watering during the growing season. Since plants in plastic pots do not need watering as often as those in clay pots, it is expedient to segregate the plastic from the clay. It is also a help, when feasible, to keep together plants requiring approximately the same amount of moisture.

Very few rock garden plants will succeed as "house plants," because they do not like the dry atmosphere and the pallid light of most house interiors. Nevertheless, one can grow them in a cool enclosed sunporch, where, because of the protection against the extremes of our winters, they will flower early, and frequently with a perfection of blossom and for a longer period than if exposed to the rains and winds of spring. As much fresh air as possible on frost-free days and a careful program of watering encourage compact, healthy growth.

A frame covered with weatherproof, translucent sash makes an excellent winter home for potted alpines. Better, though, than any sunporch or frame is an alpine-house. This is a greenhouse operated at really cool temperatures and to which is admitted as much air as possible on sunny days. In areas where the winter temperatures do not go below 10°F. except for brief periods, no supplementary heat is needed. If lower temperatures or prolonged cold periods are the rule, some form of heat should be provided, just enough to keep the alpine-house from going below 20°F.; of course if you use a hot-water system the temperatures will have to be maintained above freezing. For a small alpine-house a vented gas or kerosene heater, preferably with a thermostatic control, is adequate. A ventilator fan, also worked on a thermostat, is a great convenience and of real benefit because of the extreme fluctuations of temperature on sunny days even in winter; it may, in fact, reach so high a temperature within the house if the ventilation is not adequate as to be damaging to plants that want coolness during dormancy.

During dormancy they also want very little water. In an unheated alpine-house or one consistently kept really cool, plants will generally want no more than one watering a month. But observation will have to set the schedule. Setting pots into a plunge medium in the benches will prevent drying of the soil in the pots and will tend to moderate rapid temperature changes at the root level.

Though whole books have been written on the management of the alpine-house in Great Britain, only within the last few years has this method been tried in the United States. Conditions vary so widely in this country that no short set of prescriptions can fit all regions and there is still much to be learned by experiment. There is no doubt, however, that many rare and beautiful plants flourish in an alpine-house, where they may be enjoyed in all their fragile loveliness at close hand and out of wind and storm. Moreover, in the alpine-house can be grown those rock garden plants not quite hardy when exposed to variable winters without snow cover and with sudden plunges into subzero temperature.

The pit-house type of greenhouse, dug into the ground with only the glass or plastic roof aboveground, does much, even with no heat, to provide equable temperatures in severest weather. The natural warmth of the earth is the main factor involved, but protection from the wind plays its part, as does also the warmth from the sun, which, trapped during the day, is retained to a considerable extent in a pit house. The ridge of the roof should run parallel to the direction from which come the most severe winds of winter; therefore, in our climate one side of the glass or plastic roof usually slopes toward the south. It is well, if your winters are extremely cold, to cover the northerly slope with some kind of insulation: hay or fiber-glass batting, covered with a plastic sheet and weighted down with boards, will serve the purpose. The covers can be removed as soon as the sun becomes stronger and the nights less frigid, to allow the plants as much light as possible when they start active growth.

To take full advantage of the warmth engendered by the earth, carve your benches directly out of the soil, facing them with boards or cement block, rather than have them freestanding as is the case in the more conventional greenhouse. It is best to have all four walls of the pit house underground; sometimes it is more convenient to have the house dug into a slope with a ground-level door in one gable end. If this is the arrangement the door must be double and the exposed wall should be well insulated, either with commercial

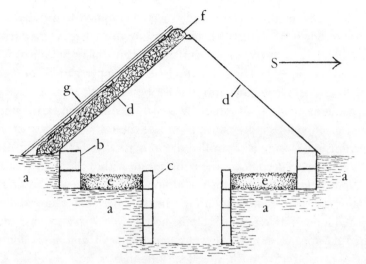

A PIT HOUSE IN CROSS SECTION

a. Native soil
b. Cement-block wall around periphery of pit
c. Retaining wall of boards or cement block to support front edge of earthern benches
d. Roof of glass, plastic sheeting, or fiber glass
e. Sand or special soil-mix
f. Insulation material against very cold weather
g. Board frame to weight down insulation
"S" indicates south

The end walls, not shown in this cross section, should be of board or cement block from ground level to the peak of the roof and should be insulated. These walls contain the entrance and the ventilating fan. The roof could be hinged or made with removable panels to increase ventilation in warm weather.

insulating material or soil mounded against it. If insulation with earth is necessary for one or more walls, this can be kept in place with planted retaining walls of stone or cement block.

It is possible, of course, to build a planted wall either of cement block or stone inside the alpine-house, whether it is above- or below-ground; a large alpine-house could even accommodate a raised bed running down the center. If the plants are to be left *in situ* during the summer, however, more ventilation than can be supplied by a fan will be needed. Hinged sections in the upper part of the roof which can be opened in warm weather best provide this. These can be hand-operated, or an especially constructed roof can be obtained from greenhouse supply houses; some of these are so made that the opening and closing is controlled thermostatically. Shading will also be necessary to keep down the temperature within the alpine-house.

Nonetheless, all plants in the alpine-house, at least in most climates, are best removed during the summer and plunged into shaded frames. If kept in the alpine-house, even if shaded and ventilated during the summer, they are demanding of time for watering and very subject to attack by leaf-sucking insects.

For the collector and connoisseur, the alpine-house or alpine frame expands his gardening season and enlarges his scope. Here rare and difficult bulbs, cyclamen, saxifrages, androsaces, lewisias, alpine primroses and many other charming dwarf plants flower earlier and more perfectly than in the rough and tumble of outdoor weather.

3

Planting and Maintenance

Soils

IT IS certainly true that the quality of the soil in which you grow your rock garden plants is the primary factor determining success or failure. Yet, it is safe to say that most plants desirable for the rock garden have considerable tolerance of variations in soil. If you were to take samples of soil from quite different sites in the wild where alpines are growing naturally, you would find a wide range of color, texture, and acidity of the soil. But all would contain, except in extreme cases, some proportion of fine-particled clay or loam, humus, and broken-down stone or mineral matter. Rarely in nature will these be in equal proportion, because factors of slope, type of parent rock, amount of rainfall, the land use, summer and winter temperatures, and other subtle influences will play a part in providing or altering various ingredients.

What you should strive for in your rock garden is a basic soil suitable for the largest possible selection of worthwhile plants. Then modify certain sections for growing those demanding special conditions. Rock garden plants in general want an open, quick-draining but moisture-retentive soil of a neutral pH, with only a moderate fertility. These soil characteristics are most easily supplied by mixing together sharp sand or fine gravel for drainage, with loam and leaf mold for moisture-holding and fertility. One part of each of these three ingredients by volume is a rough guide. Variations in the direction of more drainage material will suggest a screelike soil; in the direction of more loam, an alpine-lawn soil; whereas a greater proportion of leaf mold will approach the soils of wooded sites. Suggestions for specific mixtures for differing sites will be found in the sections of Chapter 2 describing the preparation of the raised bed, alpine lawn, rocky pasture, and other special growing areas. Prescriptions of soil for specific plants are included in the Descriptive Catalogue of Plants.

Sand and gravel in themselves do not vary a great deal, no matter where they are procured. Generally they are composed of particles of hard mineral, such as quartz. The shape and size of these grains may differ, depending on the forces that have worked on them and deposited them. Some sea sands and wind-deposited sands are too fine to provide much drainage. Some glacial sands and gravels are so mixed with clay particles that they must be washed before use as a drainage material. In a few areas, sands and gravels are so high in lime content that they cannot be used in mixtures for growing acid-loving plants like heathers and rhododendrons.

The terms gravel, stone chips, crushed stone, and peastone are synonymous for garden purposes. In some localities natural deposits are available. In other parts of the country gravel is manufactured by crushing rock into small particles; bluestone, widely used for driveways, is an example. Gravel, whether of natural origin or man made, if procured commercially, is usually graded in size by sieving and subsequently washed to remove fine particles of clay and silt. Either crushed stone or naturally deposited gravel is suitable for growing purposes, and the choice of one or the other depends largely on availability and cost and—if these are offered—on texture and color. Ideally, the gravel used in a rock garden should resemble as closely as possible the type of rock used for construction.

For the standard rock garden soil-mix, ⅜- to ¾-inch gravel provides the best type of drainage. Coarse sand may be substituted, though gravel provides a more open texture to the soil than does sand and is more nearly like the accumulation of broken-down rock, which, mixed with decayed vegetable matter, is the natural home of alpines. Some larger-sized stones in the mixture do no harm, and when scattered on the surface of the bed give it a natural appearance.

For some purposes (seed frames, cutting beds, heaths, and pine barrens), sharp sand is suggested rather than gravel. The term sharp sand describes mineral particles that have not been worn smooth by prolonged wind or water action. It is usually coarse and gritty-feeling and if examined under a hand lens will look like pieces of broken rock rather than smooth, rounded pebbles or flat plates. In most parts of the country satisfactory washed sharp sand and gravel of different sizes are available from building-supply sources because they are used in mixing mortar and concrete. The owners of most commercial gravel pits know the pH of their sand and gravel.

Loam, on the other hand, varies widely from place to place. If you have ever had a vegetable garden or a perennial border, you probably noticed that the soil differed from section to section. And certainly, if you have purchased topsoil, you will know that no two loads are quite the same.

The most desirable loam is a friable, fine-grained dirt that does not lump and cake when dry, yet tends to hold together when moist. The best way to produce such a loam of uniform quality is to pile sod, dug 4 to 5 inches deep from a good pasture, and let it rot for a year. Except in very sandy or clayey regions, the top 4 to 5 inches of earth make a perfectly satisfactory loam when screened of all weeds, roots, and stones through a ½-inch-mesh screen. This, of course, is not true of soil in recently disturbed and graded building sites, where very often bulldozers bring the subsoil to the surface and compact it with their heavy treads. Barnyard soil is also unsuitable, since it has been pounded too fine and compacted by the hoofs of cattle. Swamp-muck tends to be an unsatisfactory loam because of its fine grain. But even rather poor clayey subsoil can be made acceptable for plant growth in a final mixture if a high proportion of sand and humus is added.

Humus in the form of pure leaf mold is, once again, the ideal, both because of its texture and because its gradual breakdown supplies in the soil-mix a slowly available and long-lasting nutrition in the moderate amounts appreciated by rock garden plants. The usual compost pile is too rich and may contain an abundance of weed seeds.

Sedge peat, frequently referred to as Michigan peat, is a satisfactory substitute for leaf mold but to it should be added some superphosphate, bone meal, and dried manure. Acid sphagnum peat may be used as a soil conditioner, although it is practically devoid of nourishment and tends to acidify the soil mixture. Therefore, to sphagnum peat should be added generous amounts of superphosphate, bone meal, ground limestone, and dried manure. If the final soil mixture is to be used for acid-loving plants, understandably the limestone is not included.

When, because either the loam or the humus is not itself a source of fertility, you add fertilizers, remember that rock garden soils are preferably not really rich. Precise measurements cannot be given because of variations in natural fertility, but not more than a generous double handful of any of the fertilizers should be used for each 3 cubic feet of soil-mix.

Most rock garden plants grow in soils that are neutral in reaction, between a pH of 6 and 7.5. It is probably advisable to have your soil tested if you plan to grow a variety of plants, some needing special soils. To bring a neutral soil down to a pH of 5 or lower for growing acid-loving plants, the addition of sphagnum peat and powdered sulphur will give good results, unless your water is extremely hard and your surrounding soil limy. Under these circumstances it is difficult to maintain acidity except in small isolated and raised beds watered only with rainwater. On the other hand it is far easier to make an acid soil alkaline by adding ground limestone or substituting limestone chips for some of the drainage material. These, also used for roof-dressing or for sprinkling on dairy barn floors, may be purchased in bags. Oyster shell, used by poultry farmers, is also an excellent source of lime.

It is important to mix the components of the soil thoroughly, and no job is more backbreaking than doing this by turning and folding with a shovel. I have found a large canvas or stout burlap sheet a great help. Pile the main ingredients on one end of it, then sprinkle with whatever additives (such as fertilizers) seem necessary. Grasp the corners of the sheet at the end on which the soil is piled and pull the sheet over the mound, rolling the material toward the other end. By doing this back and forth three or four times the ingredients will be thoroughly blended. An added advantage to this method is that there is no waste of any of the precious conglomeration; you can pick up the sheet containing the last bit and empty this where you want it. You may need a partner for this rolling job if your sheet is large and you have as much as a wheelbarrow load of each of the components in your pile.

If you have a mechanical rotary cultivator this is a handy tool for mixing large quantities of soil. It can be run through your pile of ingredients to churn them together very satisfactorily. Such a machine may also be used to improve the soil on the garden itself and make it suitable for rock plants. If the topsoil of your site is of good quality it may be used as the loam content of the mixture to which you need only add the gravel, humus, and fertilizer. A good topsoil need not be a foot deep, of course, since it is only ⅓ of the final mixture, but you should be able to count on a good foot of the proper soil mixture when you are finished, provided the undersoil is not impervious and hard-packed. It is most important, though, that you be particularly careful to remove all weed roots from the area before you churn in the other ingredients, or they will rise to haunt you later when your garden is built and planted.

Once the topsoil is cleaned, spread over the site a 2- to 3-inch layer of gravel (more if your soil is heavy with clay) and churn it in thoroughly. Then mix in a 3- to 4-inch layer of humus that has been sprinkled with fertilizer at the rate of about 1 double handful to each 9 square feet of area. If the top spit of your soil is naturally gravelly or sandy, or is of a poor quality because of grading, loam will have to be brought in to make the final soil right for your plants. You may find when preparing a naturally gravelly soil that little or no gravel need be incorporated, but if your dirt is a hard-packed subsoil brought to the surface or exposed by grading, gravel must be added to provide proper drainage.

If your final soil mixture raises the general level of the garden area too much, it may be necessary to excavate and discard existing subsoil in order to achieve the desired contours and still provide the minimum foot of proper soil mixture. Too often only a thin layer of good soil is added to existing inadequate soil, and the plant roots soon penetrate down to this impoverished subsoil. Better to provide a generous, deep root-run before construction than to try to improve the soil later when planting. Moreover, if you are building a site that needs the addition of rocks, it is far easier to bury them to a proper depth in a soft mixed soil than in the packed earth.

With experience, an observant gardener gets to know a good deal about the quality of his soil by sight and touch and the type of natural vegetation on the property, but there is no mystique about it, as some rock gardeners suggest. There are some connoisseurs who have in their garden sheds, bins and pails of all kinds of special ingredients, such as ground flowerpots, broken slate, burned clay, powdered pumice. Bits of this and that, with special loams and the duff from beneath a particular species of evergreen tree, or ground bark, are blended to precise measurements in the hope of success with difficult plants like *Jankaea heldreichii, Dicentra peregrina pusilla,* or *Androsace helvetica.* Sometimes they succeed and sometimes they fail. It takes more than a special soil mixture, however; it takes proper exposure, proper watering, and frequently a dash of salutory neglect.

Planting

Some special rock garden sites are constructed to meet the needs of plants already on hand, and others are built in anticipation of acquiring them; or an area may be planned purely for landscape effect. In fact, there appear to be two extreme types of rock gardeners: at one pole is the specialist collector whose concern is more with the individual plant specimens than with the general appearance of the garden; at the other is the landscape composer, who works for effects of structure, sweeps of color, and contrast and balance of mass, line, and texture. The majority vacillate somewhere in between. Every rock gardener, nevertheless, must come to terms with the problems of getting his plants into the right spot and maintaining them there.

Let us suppose you have just completed a new garden area: the rocks are set, the final subtle grading has been done, and the carefully mixed soil is covered with a topdressing of gravel. It is good practice to let a new garden settle for a few days, preferably with at least one good soaking, in advance of planting. If you have the patience, it is even better to wait several weeks, to give weed seeds a chance to germinate so that they can be destroyed wholesale. Few gardeners have that kind of patience. A good time to build is late summer and a good time to plant is very early spring; but gardens get built when the inspiration moves and time allows, and plants get set out when they are available. Fall planting has some advantages: cool weather, short days, autumn rains, and less lustily growing foliage make it easier for most plants to establish their roots without excessive demands for water. Fall planting, however, should be done at least one month before hard freezing, to prevent heaving and the consequent tearing of new roots.

With your new site before you and the plants on hand (you will be amazed how many you will need), before you start putting them in it pays to think about the overall effect as the plants mature, about season of bloom, about possible clashes of color, about the posture and aggressiveness of particular specimens. Errors are not irremediable, but established plants become harder and harder to move. It is probably well to underplant rather than overplant. In most natural alpine situations there frequently are considerable stretches of unplanted space; moreover, rarely are the plants you set out mature specimens, and they will need room to expand. Except in the alpine lawn, where you want a solid mass of plants jostling and mingling together, most alpines want space to develop their characteristic growth habit. In general, because no alpine plant is very tall, it is not necessary to worry overmuch about planting mat-formers in the front and grading up to the tallest plants in the back of the bed. In fact, some variation in height throughout the bed adds to the natural effect. It is prudent, nonetheless, to check the growth habit and mature size of the plants before putting them in so that you will not place a rampant spreader near small and delicate tuffets. It is always safer to put your real treasures in a segregated section away from the stronger growers and those producing numerous progeny from self-sowing. It may take a little time to discover which are which, for a plant that barely survives in one spot may become a weed in another, but it is always possible to dig out an encroaching plant and put it somewhere else so that it may thrive without injury to its neighbors. When you have a fair idea of the overall scheme, begin by placing and then planting the stronger growers, the accent plants like dwarf trees and shrubs.

Time spent in careful planting is never wasted, for on this will depend the future success of the individual plant and of the total effect of the garden. Make each hole wide and deep enough to receive all the roots without cramping or doubling them. If the soil is dry, and it is easier to work dry soil closely around the roots to exclude air pockets, use a watering can to soak each plant around the roots before completely filling the hole. For cushion plants, especially those with a heavy taproot, be sure to put a collar of at least an inch of stone chips around the crown and under the cushion. Even if you have spread a topping of gravel over the whole area before planting (as described on p. 23), this tends to get dug into the soil as you make the holes and therefore should be replenished for individual plants that insist on a dry crown. It is not usually necessary, though, to re-topdress the whole garden with stone chips if you have been generous in your original application; soil scattered on the gravel surface by planting operations will be washed down between the stones during the first few waterings. Firm—and it cannot be too firm—planting is an excellent rule for rock garden plants. Tramping them in with the full weight of the body, by treading around each plant as close as possible to the crown, is not excessive.

In early spring or in the autumn, when days are short and cool and rain normally frequent, plants newly set will need little extra watering and shading. But in bright sunny weather, and especially if it is hot or dry, or both, frequent watering is imperative until the plants have sent new roots reaching out into the soil. This ordinarily takes about two weeks. Temporary shading is also helpful if the weather is particularly bright and hot. A strawberry basket with one end supported by a small stone will serve the purpose, or a leafy branch stuck butt-end into the ground on the south side of a newly placed plant will give it shade during its first few days of convalescence.

Generally speaking, rock garden plants are inured to cold and to frequent freezing and thawing, both in spring and fall. Because many of them, however, are accustomed to a protective cover of snow during periods of prolonged cold, the first winter after planting it is good insurance to cover the rock garden. This cover should be put on after the ground is frozen and lifted as soon as new growth begins in the spring. If you are in a section where hard freezes of long duration are often without snow, a protective cover of pine branches, cranberry vines, or a light layer of salt hay may be advisable even in an established garden. Avoid using materials that pack to form a smothering mat.

General Upkeep

Once well established, rock gardens need less attention than almost any other type of garden. Although rock garden plants will not live forever, most persist year after year with a minimum of care. Weeding, watering, and an annual topdressing are the only regular chores.

Weeding in the rock garden is basically a hand operation with the aid of a two-pronged hand-fork for taprooters like Dandelions, and a clawlike hand-scrabbler for scratching out tiny weed seedlings in open spaces. During the first season in a newly planted rock garden the best system is to scratch up the soil periodically to destroy all seedlings. These will almost surely be sprouting weeds. Later, as your rock garden plants go to seed, you will want to be less wholesale in the abolition of seedlings since many of these will be those of desirable plants. A few rock garden plants are annual or biennial and some, such as Alpine Poppies, are short-lived; these must be allowed to self-sow, if they are to become a permanent feature. Therefore the individual uprooting of weeds by hand-pulling is the safest method in a mature rock garden. You will soon learn to identify the weeds in your particular part of the world; in fact, when you first start gardening it is easier to learn to identify your local weed plants than to try to remember the appearance of everything you have intentionally put in the garden. If in doubt, you can always let a plant about which you are uncertain grow up and even flower before yanking it out; just be sure you do not let it go to seed.

A few weed roots will inevitably remain in the most carefully prepared garden site and some weeds will sow into the beds. You may even plant something that will become a weed. But I have found that almost every weed plant, and also the most persistently sprouting tree stump and pernicious perennial, will eventually succumb if you pull off all top growth several times during the growing season. To be successful, this operation requires faithful attention and may take two or three years.

If you are conscientious about weeding for the first few years, never allowing weeds to seed within the bed, there will be practically no weeding to be done in a rock garden maintained with a good stone-chip mulch. Of far greater importance, and a chore to be done at least once (better twice) during the growing season, is the edging of the rock garden where it abuts the lawn. With an edger or sharp spade, cut down 6 to 8 inches around the entire periphery of the garden and remove all grass roots and grass tuffets from within the bed. Grass roots creeping in from the lawn soon find a lodging among the plants and rocks and are then almost impossible to extract. More rock gardens have to be reconstructed for failure to keep out creeping grass than from being overrun by seeded-in weeds.

To help prevent the seeding-in of weeds it is a sound plan to maintain a mowed area around the garden proper. When cutting grass with the type of mower that spews the cuttings off to one side, be sure to run your machine so the clippings and weed seeds are directed back onto the grass and not sprayed over the garden. In a wooded site it is a good plan to mow off the tops of unwanted plants with a sickle or scythe before they have an opportunity to go to seed. If your area is really small, jerking off the tops by hand, which sometimes uproots them, is satisfactory since it tends to weaken their growth. The problem of brush control is taken up on page 60.

It may become necessary to weed out some of the rock garden plants themselves. Many self-sow abundantly, and in time the stronger-growers would take over the garden if not controlled. Some self-sowing is valuable, though, and a few years' experience will teach you which should be left to mature and which should be dealt with rather ruthlessly. Unless you are eager to have your plants self-sow, spent flowers should be trimmed. In the rock garden this is not a frequent chore. Once or twice a season is generally enough. At this time plants that have grown out of bounds or become thin and straggly should be clipped back to renew their shape or prevent their overrunning a less vigorous neighbor. Only a few plants, such as *Daphne cneorum*, are harmed by such clipping. For most plants and especially for early-blooming shrubby sorts, many of which set next year's flowerbuds during the summer, trimming should be done immediately after flowering. Those that persist in blooming much of the summer can be cut back in the fall.

In the late fall there should be a general cleanup. This is especially true if there are deciduous trees in the area whose leaves fall upon or are blown into the garden. Alpines, particularly those essentially evergreen, do not like the damp smother of leaves over the winter. It is also far easier to do this job in the late fall, when the dormant plants can endure being walked on and even carefully raked with a broom-rake. It may be necessary to do a supplementary pickup in the spring, but this will not be a major operation; it must be done, though, very early—before new tender growth commences.

Either after the fall or early spring cleanup an annual topdressing does wonders. Mix equal parts of leaf mold, and coarse sharp sand or ⅜-inch gravel. To each bushel of this mixture add a double handful of dry manure and another of bone meal. Sprinkle this conglomeration over the whole garden in a thorough but light topdressing. If it falls on the cushions and mats of the plants it will soon be washed in by rains and will not smother them.

If the rock garden soil has been properly prepared, very little watering is required in an established garden except in prolonged periods of drought. Err, if at all, on the side of dryness, especially during hot, humid weather. The wet foliage of cushion and bun plants literally steams in sunny, muggy weather; under such conditions the plants mildew and rot. It is safest to water on cool, windy days. Choose such a day, when possible, and water long and deep; then do not water again until absolutely necessary. Better to let plants droop in the hot midday of a muggy spell than to encourage disease of the foliage and root crown. A fairly good rule of thumb is to water only if the plants show signs of wilting in the early morning. Where you have installed an underground watering system such as described on pages 24–26 and 54–56, overhead watering will be seldom, if ever, called for, and because the foliage of the plants is not wet there is much less opportunity for mildew to get a foothold.

Blights and Bugs

If during hot, humid weather a thundershower is followed by strong sun, mildew may occur despite precautions, especially when nights are also muggy. A dusting with sulphur, Captan, or Fermate will help. But some woolly-leaved and tight cushion plants are not aided even by such treatment, and will only escape if properly planted on a north-facing scree or moraine and in a situation with freely circulating air.

Though there are very few insects that attack alpines, close watch should be kept for slugs and cutworms. In some moist gardens slugs are a constant menace, unless kept under control by frequent watering of the whole area with a solution containing metaldehyde. In other gardens they seem to appear cyclically and only periodically require control. Chlordane powder sprinkled around plants attacked by cutworms, by the root borers of columbines and iris, or by occasional invasions of ants will usually eradicate these pests.

4

Propagation

VERY FEW ROCK GARDENS are ever completed. It is only fair to warn you that once you begin the adventure of rock gardening you will be constantly planning revisions and extensions, trying new and more difficult plants, and experimenting to discover the growing methods best suited to your particular conditions, complete pre-scriptions for which no library of horticultural books can possibly supply.

As you embark on these enterprises, you will discover that there are few commercial nurseries in this country that can supply you with the kind and quantity of plants you want. Therefore you will resort to various methods of adding to your collection. With the expenditure of very little time and money, but with a great deal of enjoyment, you can produce your own plants. You will find that rock gardeners are a generous group, always ready to share with fellow gardeners propagations of even their most prized plants. Most rock gardens are liberally endowed with plants acquired by gift or exchange. You will want to have on hand a few sought-after surplus plants for this type of trading, and many more perhaps to furnish those additions and revisions you are likely to be making. Begin, therefore, to build your stock by division, by layers, by cut-tings, by seed, and by collecting from the wild.

The Work Area

Before you begin, it is a great convenience to establish a small propagating area in some inconspicuous corner of the property. One or two cold frames and a couple of nursery beds will be most useful, and it is safe to predict that soon you will be displaying the plants here as proudly as you do your garden. When rock garden enthusiasts get together the propagating area is the Mecca toward which they turn.

A sand frame is almost basic equipment if you plan to do much propagating. This is like a convalescent ward. Into it go divisions, layers, collected plants, and rooted cuttings whose ability to survive has been weakened by the recent operations performed upon them. Even debilitated plants from the garden may revive if placed in this situation. The sides of a sand frame should be no lower than 12 inches. In the bottom spread at least 2 inches of coarse drainage material; over this put a good 6 inches of pure sand or a mixture of 6 parts of sand to 1 of loam and humus, mixed half and half. This frame should be kept well watered and shaded, with a plastic-cloth shading material that cuts out 50 percent of the light or with a lath shading that lets in no more than 50 percent light. When really weakened plants are in the frame, a glass or plastic cover with the shade over it may be used to maintain an atmosphere of high, even humidity. In this case watch out for excessive heating or the formation of mildew, which may call for some ventilation. A few days of careful attention to their needs will frequently bring to full recovery precious plants that might otherwise perish in their invalid condition.

A workbench of convenient height set up under a tree—or, better still, in a shed where you can work on rainy days—will make your activities in the propagating area easier and pleasanter. A supply of pots of differing sizes, labels, plastic bags, mixed soil, and sand, along with small tools at hand, will add to your efficiency. All operations of propagation can be done in the kitchen, garage, or basement, and you may find yourself retiring to these places for some of the work in cold or wet weather; but, as your operations expand, you may outgrow the household areas.

Divisions and Layers

Division is certainly the easiest and quickest method of increasing the supply of a particular plant. There are a few plants with thong-like roots or a single spindlelike crown that do not divide success-fully, and a few others that resent disturbance at the roots; but a very large proportion of rock garden plants may be split up, each division soon forming a new root system and new foliage growth. The two best times for making divisions of most plants is early in spring, when growth commences, or soon after flowering. Yet it is possible to divide plants at almost any time during the growing season if the divisions are treated rather like cuttings and inserted in a sandy soil in a closed and shaded frame until they make new root growth. In many instances, especially if a plant is divided heavily into many sections with only a few roots on each, excess foliage should be cut back and the plants nursed in the closed and shaded frame.

It is generally most satisfactory to lift the whole plant you plan to divide with as much root as possible intact. Shake off the soil or wash it off so that the pattern of the root system is easy to study. Select a section of the foliage crown which you think would make a good new independent plant and trace it down to see whether, when detached, it will have some roots of its own. You will discover that many plants are made up of numerous rosettes or clusters of leaves, each with its own stem and roots. Where they are only tenuously connected together, the rosettes with roots attached may be teased free of the clump. Sometimes it is necessary to cut each rooted section free of the main plant cluster with a sharp knife or a pair of scissors. If, as you work, you find some bits come away without roots, do not discard them; treat them as cuttings.

Vigorous mat-formers that root along the stem may be divided easily by taking rooted pieces from the outer edges of the mat without disturbing the plant at all. These divisions are in a sense layers, and even plants that do not normally root down along the stem may be encouraged to do so by bringing a stem into contact with the soil without removing it from the parent plant. The stem should be covered with an inch or two of sand and pinned down with a stiff bent wire or held down with a stone. When roots have formed, a layer may be cut from the parent plant. As insurance, leave the rooted layer undisturbed for a while after it has been cut free; it can then be dug and transplanted. Some erect and mound-growing plants with stiff stems can be encouraged to form stem-roots by partially burying them in sand. Most herbaceous plants and many woody shrubs will form roots along the stem if layered by one of these methods. As roots usually form most readily at joints or nodes where there are dormant buds, it is advisable, when possible, to make sure that this part of the stem is buried. Many plants, particularly those with woody stems, root more easily if the bark is scraped on one or two sides of the stem where it contacts the soil.

If each division or layer has a good supply of roots, it may be set directly in the ground of the garden or nursery. Newly planted divisions and layers should be well watered and kept shaded for a few days with a small portable shader or a leafy branch stuck into the ground nearby. If, however, the roots seem meager for the amount of top growth, put them in the sand frame for a while before setting them out.

Cuttings

Cuttings, like divisions, will produce a supply of progeny identical with the parent. Both methods are therefore important for propagating hybrids and desirable forms of species not likely to come true from seed, and creating offspring from a stock that sets very little seed or none. From a single plant many more cuttings than divisions can usually be made. Some plants not susceptible to division may be increased by cuttings, but it must be remembered that cuttings are not so sure nor so speedy.

The basic principle is to remove from a plant a stem without roots but with sufficient substance so that it may be encouraged to send out roots, and to place it in an environment conducive to its remaining alive and in a medium that permits and invites the production of roots until it becomes an independent growing plant. Despite the anthropomorphic and nonscientific verbs such as encourage, permit, and invite, the above sentence is a pseudoscientific way of describing what we mean by striking roots on cuttings: in a bed of sand or other material kept moist, you insert pieces of plant and get them to root.

Here is what you do. From the plant you want to reproduce, cut off a stem or shoot with a sharp knife, razor blade, or scissors. The length will depend on the type of plant and the rapidity with which it grows; for most plants this will be about 2 to 3 inches of this year's growth, taken when the shoot is not very soft and tender but while it is still full of vigor. "Half-ripened wood" is what they call it in shrubs and trees. In some cushion plants, like drabas, saxifrages, and androsaces, a shoot is a very short-stemmed rosette requiring fussier but no different handling.

Trim the leaves off each stem for about ⅓ of its length up from the basal cut. In some instances this may be done by gently pulling the leaves downward. In others, this kind of action breaks up the stem itself; therefore you must patiently snip off each leaf with a razor blade or sharp fine-pointed scissors. Only in a few cases can these lower leaves be left on the shoot. Some propagators are known to boast about making 300 cuttings per hour; but most of us are content with three or four or ten.

These stripped cuttings are ready for insertion. There is a definite advantage in dipping or rolling the bare stem of the cutting in a rooting hormone powder. Even if these powders do not have magic principles to put roots on table legs or hair on a bald head, most include a fungicide in their makeup which may help prevent the cutting from rotting before it sends out roots.

The rooting medium used by the old-time masters was a pure, sharp sand—sometimes, to be sure, collected from a particular river shoal by the light of a special phase of the moon. The important thing is to have a substance that will support the cutting and hold moisture and air around the stem until it sends out roots. Pure sharp sand, vermiculite, coarse peat, perlite, ground slate, crumbled brick, fine coal ashes, or various mixtures of these will serve the purpose. Consider how many plants are rooted in the kitchen window from "slips" stood in a glass of water. Not that many alpines are as willing as a begonia or pelargonium, but the basic principle is the same.

Atmospheric moisture around the leaves helps prevent wilting before new roots are formed. This requirement suggests that the rooting medium be contained in something that can be covered to control the beneficial moisture. A frame with a sash will accommodate a commercial lot of cuttings; a single pot inserted in a plastic bag will handle an amazing number; and with a bit of ingenuity other containers can be devised. The modern purveyor of goods who temptingly displays his wares in transparent sanitary packages supplies you with plastic shoe boxes, butter dishes, egg-nestlers, and goody-preservers of many shapes and sizes. All of these make as useful cutting containers as the old bell glass and battery jar: a moist atmosphere within a light-admitting container above a rooting medium that is moist but open enough to admit plenty of air.

The main problem is fungus and mildew. If you start with a sterilized container and a sterilized medium, sterile surgical instruments, scrubbed hands, and a masked mouth you may avoid this—or again you may not. On the other hand, nine times out of ten you may never meet this difficulty. But if on inspection, and certainly you will inspect your cuttings often, you detect the least sign of fungus, sprinkle with powdered Captan, Fermate, or sulphur. Those who are provident will dust the surface of the cutting bed at the time of insertion without harm to anything but the ubiquitous airborne spores of fungus.

Cuttings should not be jabbed into the rooting medium, but set into holes made with a pencil or blunt stick, deep enough to contain most of the portion of the stem that has been stripped of leaves, and far enough apart so that the leafy part of the cuttings do not overlap. The rooting medium is then pressed close and firm about each cutting, and when all are in place they should be watered with a fine spray. Locate your cutting container where it will receive as much indirect light as possible; direct sunlight would heat it up too much. The medium should never be allowed to dry out or be too saturated. You may observe wilting for the first day or two, but the cuttings will soon recover as they take in moisture. Though on some cuttings new growth may begin before roots are initiated, in most cases root and top growth are fairly simultaneous. Some herbaceous material, prepared during the warm part of the growing season, may root in as little as a week; with woodier stems the waiting period may extend to six months or more. Cuttings can be carefully dug up for inspection and reinserted without harm. It likewise does no harm to leave cuttings in the medium for some time after roots have begun to form, but not for too long since there is no nourishment in the rooting medium.

Because the tender new roots emanating from the sides and base of the cutting are easily torn off, careful lifting of the rooted material is imperative. If your container is a small one and most of the cuttings show rooting, it may be easiest to turn the whole lot out onto a piece of newspaper and separate the cuttings from the pile. Rooted cuttings are rarely ready to be set out in the garden; they need hardening off. This may be done gradually by opening the container while they are still in the rooting medium, or the rooted cuttings may be put in a frame, either in pots or directly into a suitable mixed soil. Strong and easy cuttings such as arabis, phlox, aubrietia, and helianthemum may be set in the nursery bed and shaded. Cuttings of very small rosette-plants like saxifrages, androsaces, and drabas may be left in the rooting container till they make small clumps. Here it is best to start the cuttings originally in a large flowerpot or bulb pan with a good growing soil beneath the surface layer of the rooting medium.

In addition to stem-cuttings, pieces of root may be treated like cuttings. This method is useful for such things as geraniums and anemones, which have brittle, heavy roots. You probably have noted new top growth from roots left in the ground after digging up a plant. These are like root-cuttings.

A long thong-root may be cut into segments of about 2 inches and inserted in a container of good but sandy soil with the upper end of the piece of root (and this must be the upper end just as the root was attached to the plant) at the soil surface. Over this spread about 1 inch of pure sand and keep it watered until new top growth has been made. New roots will begin to form in the soil. Though this method of propagation is less generally used than others, it has many advantages; among them is the adaptability to a significant range of plants, not only those with tap and thong-roots but also for fine-rooted material such as Birdsfoot Violets and campanulas. A good general rule is, the finer the root the longer the cutting.

Seed

Propagation by seed must, of course, be the method where no stock material is available for divisions, layering, and cuttings. By this method, also, a large number of plants for mass planting can be produced with very little expenditure of effort, time, and money.

There is, in addition, considerable gratification in having a fine stand of husky plants of some treasured rock garden species which you have watched develop from the tiny, inert seeds.

Seed may be planted in almost any type of container with drainage holes in the bottom which will hold at least a 3-inch depth of soil: wooden flats, clay pots, plastic pots, punctured coffee cans. The small, pliant, plastic garden-pack, 6 x 4 inches, with large drainage holes in the bottom has many advantages. It is rotproof, light to handle, easily stored and cleaned, and does not become brittle and crack.

In the bottom of whatever container you use put about ½ inch of drainage material, such as gravel or pieces of broken flowerpot. This is not absolutely necessary unless the containers are to be left outdoors where they may be flooded by heavy rains. Fill the container with soil of a standard mixture: equal parts of good loam, humus, and sharp sand or grit. Firm and level the surface with a block of wood. There should be about ½ inch of space between the surface of the soil and the rim of the container. Soak the soil thoroughly, preferably by standing the container in a shallow tub of water deep enough to come up the sides but not over the top. When the surface is moist, sow the seeds thinly upon it. Thin sowing is probably more often advocated than practiced but it is urged, because ten husky seedlings are preferable to a hundred pinched and crowded ones. Since many very small rock garden plants are best left in the seeding container until they have reached good size, thin sowing is important.

After the seeds have been thinly scattered on the soil surface, cover them with a light layer of small stone chips or grit; turkey-grit and chicken-grit, sold by poultry suppliers, are excellent in composition and size. There are many advantages to this covering. It will not compact when watered from above, nor will it permit the seeds to wash into the corners if the container is not absolutely level. It supports the delicate seedlings and helps prevent damping-off and the formation of moss. As the small plants develop it provides the perfect surface for the foliage to rest upon, especially hairy or woolly leaves. Though lime-loving plants will do well with limestone grit, granite turkey- or chicken-grit is quite satisfactory for all types of plants.

Not all seeds germinate in the same length of time, nor do they necessarily respond to the same conditions, but it is not essential to subject each container of seed to individual and special treatment after sowing. Since the seeds of many rock garden plants appear to benefit from a period of low temperature, and all germinate best when the atmosphere is not too warm, it is convenient to sow seeds in the late fall, winter, or very early spring. The containers may then be placed on a bed of coal ashes or gravel in a covered frame, or set in a barn or shed until the weather begins to warm up a bit. Though the seeds will not be harmed by exposure to weather, and might benefit from a covering of snow, heavy rains will wash even a grit surface, and other casualties are too likely in the open. If the containers are under cover check occasionally to be sure the soil is moist.

To simulate a cool period to break the dormancy in seeds, you may use the refrigerator. Mix the seed with a small portion of sand or peat in a plastic bag. Moisten with a few drops of water and leave in the refrigerator—not the freezer compartment—for at least six weeks before sowing.

Though many seeds will germinate in total darkness and, in fact, many appear to do so better if light is excluded, a few need light for germination and all need good light when they begin to sprout. Direct sunlight, however, is apt to scorch and dry irreparably the tender new growth, or parch the seeds at that critical moment when they are just beginning to germinate. Some means of shading is consequently necessary. Portable light wooden frames covered with a material such as plastic shading-cloth or lightweight unbleached muslin that excludes 50 percent of the light are handy to place over a cold frame. Or, mounted on legs at the four corners, these can be used over containers set on the ground and later over young material transplanted to the nursery.

It is also important that the containers in which seeds are sown should never be thoroughly dry. With a grit surface, providing the receptacles are resting on a quick-draining material, overwatering is not likely to occur. Thorough watering with a fine spray is the daily routine as soon as the weather warms up enough to stimulate seeds to sprout. Some seeds, especially those from our own West, germinate as soon as the soil begins to thaw in the spring and do not appear to be damaged by the subsequent brief periods of freezing that might occur at night in early spring.

An advantage is to have two sections in your seed area, one with heavier shade, where you leave the containers and water more frequently until germination, the other with more light and a slightly different watering routine, where you transfer the containers when the plants are beginning to develop their true leaves. Since seeds of some rock garden plants are long delayed in their germination, no container of ungerminated seed should be discarded for at least two years. Those seeds needing special treatment are discussed in the Descriptive Catalogue of Plants under the appropriate species.

If the seeds have been sown thinly, the plants may remain in the seedpan until they tend to become crowded, by which time they will have a considerable root system. To facilitate transplanting, turn out the whole batch, permitting the soil to dry out to a considerable degree in advance of this operation so that individual plants can be more easily separated from the mass. These husky seedlings may be potted singly and plunged in a shaded frame or lined out in a shaded nursery bed. If, on the other hand, you find that your thin-sowing was not really thin enough and that the plants, even when quite small, are really crowded, they should be transplanted early and spaced more widely for development in a flat or other receptacle.

Various alternatives for any of the steps in the process of growing plants from seeds are easy to devise for fitting your equipment, your location, and your time schedule. Some growers find that sowing seeds in compartments or rows in large containers is less demanding of attention and that they get superior results. Narrow strips of composition roofing shingle inserted into the soil in a large wooden or metal flat will divide it into compartments of any size wanted. Because of the greater mass of soil, watering does not have to be done as frequently. Also conducive to less frequent watering is a removable lid with wooden sides and a plastic top that is made to fit snugly on top of the flat once the seeds are sown. After the germination, ventilation is provided by raising the lid on small blocks or substituting a lid covered with shading material.

Very similar is the method of sowing seeds in compartments or rows directly in a cold frame filled with a properly prepared seeding soil of at least 6 inches depth over a 2-inch layer of drainage material. Such a frame should be provided with a sash supplemented by a shade cover during the early stages of the process. The shading is used alone when the weather warms up and most of the seeds have germinated. Thin-sowing and a grit surface are just as important in large flats and frames as they are in small containers.

No matter what method you employ, it is only sensible to take precautions against marauders. Mice and birds seem to come long distances to feast on your finest seeds. Ants are particularly fond of carrying off some types of seeds. Slugs, snails, and cutworms can lay waste a whole row of tender young plants in one night. And cats delight to dig and dogs to bed down in loose moist soil. What precautions you take will naturally depend on your feelings about animals and what deterrents your hardware man can suggest.

Collecting

As your garden matures you will wish to gather seeds from your own garden to share with friends and to sow yourself, or you may wish to collect seeds in the wild. Most seeds are ready to collect when the capsule begins to lose its green color. Because some ripen quickly and scatter, it is provident to cut the whole stem bearing the almost ripened capsule and put it head down in a paper bag to be stored in a dry place. Some seeds will be released on drying, others will require your breaking open the capsule and sifting out the seed. Cleaned seeds should be stored in a dry, cool place until sowing, preferably in a closed container, since some seeds lose viability if permitted to desiccate for long.

Seed in pulpy fruit is inhibited from germination by the pulpy covering. To remove the pulp before sowing, steep the fruit in water for a few days until the pulp has fermented and loosened. Scrub in a sieve under running water to remove most of the pulp and the rest will flake off after you have dried the seeds by spreading them on paper.

Because plants of the rarer alpines are almost impossible to obtain from nurseries, growing from seed is what most serious rock gardeners resort to. But it is likewise difficult to buy the less common seeds from commercial sources; consequently, rock gardeners exchange plants and seeds. The plant societies listed on page 455 all have organized exchanges through which members may procure seeds, with the annual offering frequently running to more than 1000 species.

There is yet another way besides division, cuttings, layers, and seeds or trading with friends by which you can augment your assemblage of plants. This is by collecting plants from the wild. Without entering into the controversial field of conservation, it is safe to say that in many places and under many circumstances it is perfectly proper and even desirable to bring into the garden plants collected in the wild.

If the plants are gathered nearby and with all the roots intact in a good ball of soil, they may of course be set directly in the garden, in a site as similar as possible to their original home, and treated like any other transplant; but if the plants have been out of the ground for a considerable time or have damaged root systems, they should be given a chance to recover in a sand frame such as the one described on page 97.

Collected plants can be kept out of the ground for as long as two weeks without serious damage if they are totally enclosed in a sealed plastic bag. To prevent rot, shake, but do not wash, most of the soil from the roots and then immediately enclose each in a separate plastic bag, leaves and all, without additional moisture of any kind. When the bag is sealed with an elastic band or a short length of paper-covered wire, the plant no longer loses moisture and remains alive for a considerable time. The bag should be kept from strong sunlight, but the foliage may lose color if it is stored in total darkness for extended periods. It should also be kept as cool as possible short of actual freezing.

All flowering heads must be removed, and if the plant has a great deal of top growth this must be cut back severely before insertion in the bag, and particularly before planting in the recovery bed. If the foliage is reduced and the roots are treated like those of cuttings, most plants will recover quickly in the convalescent-frame—unless excessive moisture and heat have led to their rotting in the plastic bag.

A plastic label enclosed with the plant should carry basic information about the site in which it was found and the identity of the plant when known. It is very easy to forget, when collecting any number of species, all the details that may later be important to the successful growing of the plant in the garden. A notebook with some kind of key system corresponding to a number on the label enclosed with each plant will permit more adequate information than can be written on the label alone.

PART II

*Descriptive Catalogue
of Plants*

Descriptive Catalogue
of Plants

THE FOLLOWING catalogue of plants does not pretend to be exhaustive. Included in it are most of the genera of plants found suitable for the different sites described in Part I of the book. Under each genus is included those species that the author considers best. Not all readers will agree with the selections; certain species have been included that some readers will think ugly, impossible of cultivation, or for other reasons undesirable; certain species have been omitted that some readers will claim the best and easiest of the genus. But the selection has been made mostly on the basis of firsthand experience with the plants in the garden or in the wild. In a few cases there have been included species not known at first hand but sufficiently similar to those that were to warrant inclusion on good written authority.

The Catalogue is arranged alphabetically by genera and usually alphabetically by species within each genus. In genera where there are many diversities among the species, groupings have been resorted to for convenience of bringing together those similar in appearance or those requiring similar treatment in the garden. Under some genera—as, for instance, lilies—no particular species are described, because the whole genus is so specialized that the reader would be better served by referring to one of the books listed in the Descriptive

Bibliography which deals specifically with the kind of plant in question.

The Catalogue attempts to give a brief description of the species and essential information about where and how to grow them. The descriptions are not intended to be used as botanical keys for identification purposes. Details of size, growth habit, flower color, and season of bloom are included to help the reader decide whether he would like to try the plant. Cultural information is given for the genus as a whole when it fits all species, or for separate species where essential. Included are references to the type of site where the plant is found in nature, to any special aspects of site or soil found important in the garden, and to methods of propagation. The cultural and propagation directions are frequently mere references to type sites and standard procedures described in detail in Part I.

Flowering plants, shrubs, dwarf trees, and bulbs are included alphabetically in the general Catalogue, but a separate section at the end is devoted to the ferns. This last section is in two parts, grouping together in each part those genera and species requiring similar sites in the garden.

The scientific names of plants are not always permanent. For sound taxonomic reasons botanists have over the years made many changes in nomenclature and it is not always easy to keep abreast of all revisions. Because some plants may be known by more than one name I have listed alphabetically generic synonyms with a cross reference and have included in the descriptions alternative specific names. I have relied principally on Bailey's *Hortus Second,* but have attempted to verify each name by reference to other works as well: Fernald's edition of *Gray's Manual of Botany, The Royal Horticultural Society Dictionary of Gardening,* Peck's *Manual of the Higher Plants of Oregon,* Rehder's *Manual of Cultivated Trees and Shrubs,* and Griffith's *Collins Guide to Alpines.* I have used the same sources for common names and horticultural names.

The styling of the common names has been brought into line with modern American practice. Generic common names are made plural and begin with a small letter. Specific common names begin with a capital. The styling of the horticultural names conforms to the International Rules of Botanical Nomenclature. Botanical varieties are indicated by a third (and occasionally a fourth) Latin name in agreement with the specific name. Plant varieties and forms of garden origin may be Latinized or given fanciful or elaborate names, which are indicated by putting the name in single quotation marks. Those of hybrid derivation have the specific name preceded by ✕.

Flowering Perennials, Bulbs, Trees, and Shrubs

ACAENA (Rosaceae)

These are rather undistinguished carpeters, not as dense or rapidly spreading as thymes, but good for ground cover in the alpine lawn and for use over dwarf bulbs as a foil for the blossoms and a cover for the bare ground after the bulb foliage is spent. These are prostrate shrubs with generally gray-green, small roselike leaves. Acaenas are not reliably hardy unless a snow cover protects them from temperatures near zero. The only species generally offered is *A. buchananii,* which lacks charm of foliage and is usually shy of its insignificant greenish blossoms. Divisions are easy to make. When grown from seed, all acaenas are rather slow to establish. The best *Acaena,* if you can get it, is *A. microphylla inermis,* because of its showy, red, spiny seedheads. Other species of much the same general effect, and mostly less hardy, come also from South America, Australia, and New Zealand. The whole genus is disappointing, because it either fails utterly to produce its carpet of neat foliage and burry seedheads or else ramps like Quack Grass.

ACANTHOLIMON (Plumbaginaceae)

Only the species *A. glumaceum* is ordinarily available, and even that demands rather special treatment. All the spiny thrifts belong to the hot limy ledges of Asia Minor, a fact that suggests the proper site in the limy scree. The long needlelike foliage makes a handsome, dark, rather lax hummock about 4 to 6 inches high; it turns a lovely bronze in late fall. The dense one-sided racemes hold their pink papery blossoms well throughout the summer. *A. echinus* has gray leaves and white flowers, *A. venustum* green leaves and larger rose-pink flowers. Fertile seed is rarely, if ever, set in cultivation. Layering seems the best means of increase; yet even when the roots have formed the plants are slow to establish. It seems best to put down layers in early spring and not to move them at least until the following spring. Late summer-cuttings strike, but must be held over in greenhouse or frame for the winter. Cuttings are likely to damp-off without striking root. The essential stem is very slender and lacks food for rooting.

ACANTHOPHYLLUM (Caryophyllaceae)

This name may turn up in catalogues but, alas, it must be suspect. What is usually offered as *A. spinosum* is really *Dianthus noeanus* (see under *Dianthus*). There are true acanthophyllums in the Middle East with small rose-colored flowers on short stems above pincushion foliage.

ACHILLEA (Compositae)

Tight clusters of short-rayed daisies in yellow and white mark the smaller yarrows. The foliage varies from a thick white pelt in *A. tomentosa* to rounder, toothed, hoary leaves in *A. clavennae*. The blossoms last for long periods in summer, but even in the bright yellow of 6-inch-high *A. tomentosa* they never seem quite dense enough or bright and large enough to assert character. These small yarrows are easy to grow in warm, sunny spots, with at least a dash of lime, where their foliage and blossoms contribute unassertively to the general texture of the garden. They are simple to increase by division and can be scattered around the warmer locations to furnish pleasing contrast and break up the splashes of more brilliant neighbors, an important if inglorious role. There are many species and garden hybrids. Read nursery catalogue descriptions of this genus carefully or try out the offerings in a nursery bed before placing them in the garden. For *A. ageratifolia* see *Anthemis aizoon.*

ACONITUM (Ranunculaceae)

We generally think of the monkshoods as border plants, and many forms are admirably suited to such a site, producing in late summer stalwart, stiff plants with terminal racemes of deep blue helmeted flowers. The wild types, from which these garden forms have been developed, are justly fitted to a woodland garden, where in foliage and flower they bring richness of color in late summer. There are also dwarfs of the Asiatic mountains and long-stemmed, leaning species of Appalachian Mountain woods adaptable to many sites. All grow readily from seed, or may be increased by division of large, clumpy plants. They develop most vigorously in rich, open soils with some shade. Dwarf alpines of Asia want rich scree conditions.

A. ferox from the Himalayas, like others from the same area, vary markedly in stature. These pale blue-flowered species may be 6 inches tall, or as many feet. Try them in a lean scree to keep them dwarf, but do not parch them in the sun. *A. fischeri,* a tall Asiatic species with rich blue flowers, is best grown among tall shrubs in the woods garden. The western American—*A. columbianum*—is very similar. *A. hookeri* is a name that covers a wide range of Himalayan dwarf forms—all desirable—to be grown in fairly rich scree out of the full blaze of the sun. *A. lycoctonum,* a widespread Old World plant, varies in height up to 3 feet, depending on the richness and altitude of its home. It brings to the genus a difference in the yellow color of its helmets. *A. napellus* is the species that supplies a gamut of garden forms, all excellent for their rigid, self-supporting carriage and abundant flowers. *A. uncinatum* is a semiclimbing species from Appalachian country which delights in a cool, shady position among shrubs to rest upon. There it produces pale striped helmets.

ACTAEA (Ranunculaceae)

The baneberries are vigorous herbaceous woodland plants growing about 2 feet tall in rich neutral soil. Large compound leaves are borne on the stout stems; in late spring, in terminal spike-like clusters, are produced the feathery white flowers, followed in summer and fall by showy berries. When established, the plants will frequently self-sow. The seed, with the pulpy coating removed, may be sown in fall, or older plants divided in early spring as they develop more than one underground growing point.

A. arguta is the West Coast species with spherical red berries. *A. pachypoda* is the White Baneberry, or Doll's-eyes, so called for the white fruit with persistent black pistil, carried on stout pinkish-red pedicels. *A. rubra* produces its shiny, holly-red berries in dense clusters, each berry carried on a slender pedicel. Red-berried varieties of the White Baneberry and white-berried varieties of the Red Baneberry are sometimes found, distinguished by the thin or thick pedicel of the fruit. *A. spicata* is the European species, with purplish-black fruit.

ACTINEA, sometimes listed as *Actinella* (Compositae)

These little silver-leaved yellow daisies come chiefly from the drier shortgrass plains of the American West. Their early blossoms and dense habit set them off from the general daisy tribe. Perfect drainage in summer seems a prerequisite, and even with the best of conditions they tend to be short-lived. Fresh seed germinates readily. Three perennial species are available: *A. fastigiata,* 4 inches; *A. herbacea,* 8 inches; and *A. simplex,* 10 inches. Except for height all are very similar.

ADENOPHORA (Campanulaceae)

Most adenophoras are too tall and have disproportionately small blossoms in the spike to fit well in the rock garden and compete with the closely allied campanulas. Two Japanese species do have charm and fitting proportion: *A. nikoensis,* with a lustrous dark rosette of leaves from which rise foot-tall spikes of lovely dark blue or burgundy bells; and *A. tashiroi,* even more of a dwarf and with blossoms a pure icy white or sometimes pale blue. In *tashiroi* the blossoms are jaunty, tubby bells with exserted style for clapper. Adenophora does well in differing sites, with sun or light shade, and comes readily from seed. A periodic sowing of home-saved seed seems advisable, since the plants are not long-lived. Summer flowering makes them valuable for the rock garden.

ADONIS (Ranunculaceae)

Very early in spring, *Adonis* produce on short stems large golden suns like glistening buttercups. As the flowers fade the stems elongate above the increasing spire of feathery green foliage. These will flourish in almost any soil, in full sun or light shade, but they are slow to propagate. Only fresh seed will give good germination, and plants from seed are slow to flower. Careful division in the spring is possible. *A. amurensis* is the earliest species. The double form, which is fertile, carries a greenish cast to the flowers. *A. brevistyla,* from the Himalayas, wants a rich leafy soil, where it produces blue-backed, white, cupped flowers. *A. vernalis* has large golden flowers of good substance and is a fine species best planted in solid drifts to furnish early color in the sunny garden.

AETHIONEMA (Cruciferae)

There are no more charming and accommodating rock garden plants than Persian candytufts if they happen to like your garden. What they demand is full sun and a deep, limy, light soil. There these dwarf shrubs, ranging in height from 3 to 10 inches and decked with the loveliest of tiny blue-green leaves, will burst into pink

Aethionema
(½ life size)

showers of refined crucifer blooms—ample, long-lasting, and of most harmonious hue. The pink haze of their blossoming is welcome after the first flush of early spring bloom is over. When happy, they will self-sow into the most unlikely places—some appropriately into the tightest, hottest chinks, and yet again into a tangle of dense, leafy competition in moist semishade. In the latter spot, they do not flower profusely and the stems get long and soft, but for a few years they will persist and cast their blue-green magic.

There are five or six species ordinarily listed in catalogues and seed lists; but by now, species though they may have been in their Levantine homes, they have so intermarried that *A. grandiflorum, A. pulchellum, A. shistosum,* and others, are quite indistinguishable. *A. warleyense,* a sterile hybrid propagated by cuttings, is distinct in its very gnarled, weeping habit and brighter pink bloom. A plant I have grown from seed listed as *A. theodorum* is distinctive; more erect, taller, later to flower, and a slightly harsher, though still charming pink; the foliage is looser and greener. What generally passes for *A. iberideum* is indistinguishable from *Shivereckia bornmuelleri;* and *A. coridifolium* of the nurseries appears to be an *Iberis. A. creticum* and the closely related *A. saxatile* are both easily grown and are quite different in foliage and habit from the narrow-leaved, stiff, bushy stone-cresses. These have rather widely spaced, roundish, somewhat succulent gray-green foliage on long stems that tend to flop over the rocks. They are best grown so as to make a background for the rather minute but pleasingly typical pink crosses; the blossoms are disappointingly small, but early.

Mature aethionemas do not appear to settle down happily after being moved. Even young cuttings tremble on the brink after transplanting and may never become as really lusty as do self-sown foundlings, but good forms like *A. warleyense* should be propagated by cuttings. Seedlings may be moved before the root becomes long and woody. Shearing off the blossoming stems right after the blooming keeps the Lilliputian bushes tight and thick, though it means no self-sown seedlings, which is the only way to have aethionemas in the number and careless array that enhances their beauty. Severe freezing without snow cover will kill-back the late new growth and delay the blossoming for a week or so but will rarely kill vigorous young plants. Ancient specimens with gnarled branches and thick trunks lose their vigor and may be carried off by a severe winter. All are easy to strike from summer-cuttings. A good strain, so propagated, when planted in quantity does wonders for the mass effect in the rock garden or alpine lawn.

AJUGA (Labiatae)

The commonest species, *A. reptans,* has many varieties and they are distinguished either by flower color or leaf color. All are easy-to-grow, invasive plants useful as bulb covers in the alpine lawn. A dry site slows the invasion and encourages flowering. Since this species roots as it runs, propagation is simple by division at any season. *A. genevensis* var. ***brockbankii*** is a more refined plant, fit for the select company of raised bed or rock garden proper. It does not run and root, and the blossoms are larger, of a good clear blue. It wants sun and good alpine soil; propagate by summer-cuttings. *A. pyramidalis* is a compact, many-stemmed mound with good spikes of blue blossoms. It does not run, nor does *A. metallica crispa,* which has burnished crumpled leaves.

ALCHEMILLA (Rosaceae)

If the Lady's-mantle, *A. alpina*—which may be taken as the type for the whole genus—were not so greedy of increase by stolon and seed, its silvery-green palmate leaves would make it an ideal foliage foil, especially since it gathers in its pleats sparkling diamonds of dew from the atmosphere. On the mountains in the wild it is the associate of many delicate plants. It will flourish in any soil and exposure, but keeps neatest in very lean sites. Not to be encouraged among favorite plants in the restriction of the usual rock garden, Lady's-mantle needs a whole alp for setting.

ALLIUM (Liliaceae)

Every seed list has a vast array of the adaptable flowering onions. The season of bloom is from spring to fall, with a color range from purest white through pink and lavender to clear blue (plus a few yellows). They range over the world, and not all the myriad North American species have been brought into the garden. Some are too tall for most rock gardens and some are better relegated to the herb and vegetable garden. Since a few have an insatiable propensity to seed themselves, it is well to invite into the favored locations in the rock garden proper only the more special sorts. All grow well in thoroughly drained, sunny sites and are admirably suited to the mixed planting of the alpine lawn. Seeds of some species are slow to germinate, and others sprout like grass. Clumps of desirable species may be divided either when dormant or when just beginning spring growth.

A. acuminatum produces flowering heads of deep rose-purple on 1-foot stems well above the grassy foliage, a worthwhile American westerner. *A. beesianum* has short flattened leaves and fine flowering scapes about 10 inches tall, from which hang the nodding clusters of deep plum-purple flowers in summer. *A. cernuum* is an American of wide distribution which is good in the alpine lawn, where the clear pink blossoms nod in summer on stems up to 2 feet. *A. cyaneum* makes a fat clump of thin grassy foliage above which for a long period in late summer are nodding heads of clear blue, on 6- to 10-inch scapes. This, with the very similar *A. sikkimensis,* are among the best. *A. flavum* is yellow-flowered and easy to grow. The flowering heads, on 1-foot stems, are subtended by rather long leaflike bracts. It should be grown where it may self-sow, since it freely does. *A. moly* has large clear-yellow flowers and rather broad foliage. This is a showy and adaptable onion, willing to grow even in shade. *A. narcissiflorum* is one of the handsomest, with rather large clear-pink blossoms on stems 6 to 8 inches high. This species does not increase rapidly by bulb offsets as do many alliums, and the seeds are slow to germinate. *A. ostrowskianum* produces large heads of deep rose flowers on short stems amid flattish glaucous foliage. *A. senescens glaucum* is a fall bloomer with pleasant light lavender-pink blossoms. It is a delight all season because of the twisted flattish leaves that make a swirling gray-green cowlick. *A. zebdanense* is an early-flowering 10-inch species with pure-white, miniature lily-like blossoms in a loose head. It will stand considerable shade.

ALYSSUM (Cruciferae)

These plants were once considered to be a cure for the bite of a mad dog; hence the common name "madworts." For brilliance and mass of bloom the species *A. saxatile* is well named Basket-of-gold, with its sharp yellow blossoms. The finer pale moonlight-gold of var. *citrinum* is by all means to be preferred, though it is not reliably true from seed. But cuttings are of easy culture and soon produce full baskets. These large-leaved clumps of soft gray-green prefer a rocky, dry resting place for their elongated stems and do best if the flowering stems are clipped off before they go to seed.

Less brilliant of blossom but charming in leaf and twig and a late bloomer is shrubby *A. argenteum,* which demands a severe shearing after blooming to hold its otherwise straggling growth to a gray mound of tiny, hard, silvery leaves. It attains a height of about 18 inches. For low mats of trailing woody stems studded with small silver-gray leaves and soft-to-shocking-yellow heads of bloom, there are a number of species rather similar: *A. alpestre, A. armenum, A. idaeum, A. montanum, A. serpyllifolium,* and *A. wulfenianum.* All these and *A. argenteum* come easily from seed and may self-sow excessively unless trimmed after flowering.

A. spinosum (also called *Ptilotrichum spinosum*) is quite different, a really dwarf, gnarled-looking ancient, with some twigs mere sharp spines and others ending in small heads of white or pink crucifers. This is a treasure, but difficult to obtain, since the seed germinates poorly and the dry twigs are unsuitable for cuttings. When acquired, it should be grown in an appropriate sunny spot, and moved only when young.

Anacyclus depressus
(⅞ life size)

ANACYCLUS (Compositae)

The procumbent Atlas daisies are charming as foliage plants, forming wheel-like patterns of finely cut grayish-leaved stems. At the tips are the daisies, white when open, red in bud and when closed in the early morning. **A. atlanticus, A. depressus,** and **A. maroccanus** are very similar. They do best in well-drained stony soil, and are indifferent about lime. Fresh seed will germinate readily. Summer-cuttings are satisfactory.

ANCHUSA (Boraginaceae)

This genus is best known for border plants, but there are two species fit to carry the clear-blue blossoms into parts of the rock garden. **A. caespitosa,** if you can secure the true plant, is a cushion-grower of great beauty from the Mediterranean world. If you can procure it, it will probably succeed in deep rocky soil in full sun. It can be grown from seed and from root-cuttings but it resents disturbance of the succulent roots and abhors wetness when dormant. *A. angustissima* is frequently mistaken for it, but is a good plant in its own right, producing all through the summer a succession of foot-high stems abundantly furnished with true blue flowers. As it too wants good drainage in full sun, it brings summer color to the larger rocky ledge or alpine pasture. This will flower the first year from seed and may be increased by early division.

   A. myosotidiflora (also called *Brunnera macrophylla*), on the other hand, is for the woodland garden, where in early spring and for a considerable season, it sends up showers of clear blue forget-me-not-like blossoms. Though it prefers part shade, it will stand some sun. The leaves, which develop later than the earliest blossoms, become as large as small burdock leaves. Seed, root-cuttings, or division will provide increase.

ANDROMEDA (Ericaceae)
   For acid, peaty soil with adequate sun to encourage flowering and make for dense growth, these dwarf heath shrubs are very fine. The small blue-green leaves are elegantly arranged on the thin woody twigs. The leaves, leathery on the upper surface and glaucous beneath, make a perfect setting for the tubby, waxen white and pink bells, which nod in terminal umbels in early spring. The American species, *A. glaucophylla* and *A. polifolia,* are very similar, reaching about a foot in height. The Japanese forms of *A. polifolia* are the real charmers; both var. *minima* and var. *compacta* deserve the best site for display of their exquisite frosty lanterns on the dense twiggy bushes. In acid humus soil, never allowed to become bone-dry, they will form sizable clumps by short underground stolons. To propagate, a sizable clump can be lifted and divided, or stolons severed and rooted. Top-cuttings root in sandy peat. The very fine seed will germinate in chopped sphagnum.

ANDROSACE (Primulaceae)

To the inveterate rock gardener the androsaces are the joy and the despair of his heart. For one year of success with *A. carnea, A. chamaejasme,* and *A. villosa* there are many years when the promising clumps will grow sodden and moldy in the dog days of summer or will slump to mush at the end of a wet, snowless winter. When the androsaces do flourish, and there are some easily grown fine ones,

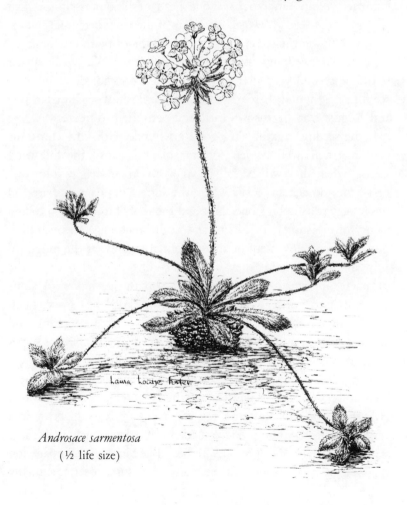

Androsace sarmentosa
  (½ life size)

their exquisite proportions, clarity of color, and intricate pattern of leaf proclaim them as members of the true elite of the alpine clan.

What is more thrilling than the burst of numerous pearly buds, opening on 2- to 3-inch stems above the closely huddled rosettes of silvery silk of *A. villosa?* Year by year new offshoots form on runners so short as to be concealed within the expanding cushion. These may be detached in late summer to form the nucleus of a new, compact colony, and to have one head of bloom itself the next spring. From seed *A. villosa,* like most of the truly perennial androsaces, will flower the second spring after the first tiny rosette has been set out. The seedlings of all this genus will very likely not appear until the second year after sowing, though occasionally conditions seem just right and there may be a sudden flush of seedlings in July and August from seed sown early and permitted to freeze.

If the seeding mixture is a good gritty one with lime chips, the seedlings may well be left for transplanting until the following spring, when they will be full of vigor. As their shaggy form suggests, they do demand a site where the surface drainage is sharp and the foliage rests upon stone chips and the roots can run deep to find plenty of moisture. For bloom and health of foliage an open location with free movement of air is essential to prevent the muggs of July and August. But they will not endure the full blaze of the summer sun, which can shrivel and crisp the cushions. A slope facing east or north, in scree, moraine, or raised bed is excellent.

A. chamaejasme, although less silky, is just as winning and demands identical treatment. *A. carnea* in its various forms is somewhat less fussy, since the foliage lacks all downiness. It forms expanding clumps of narrow pointed foliage, above which goldeneyed flowers of pink or white are carried on stems of 1 to 3 inches. *A. sarmentosa* and its forms are all lovely and easy to grow in a variety of sites. They produce a forest of 4- to 6-inch flowering-stems with heads of bright pink verbena-like blossoms. Propagation is simple by establishment of the many, new, furry rosettes annually thrown out at the end of long strawberry-like runners. Clip the runner after the roots have begun to form in the late summer and move the rooted rosettes in the spring. *A. sarmentosa* will do in almost any site and the rosettes from the same plant will vary amazingly from a dry site in full sun to a rather moist one in shade, those in the dry site being more condensed in all features.

A. sempervivoides is slightly more demanding than *A. sarmentosa,* though similar in general effect. The runners are somewhat shorter and a deep red, the rosette is tight and smooth, the blossom head more brightly colored and on a shorter stem. *A. lanuginosa* also has verbena-like heads of blossom, softer and more lavender than in the sarmentosas. These come in late summer on the long trailing shoots of silvery foliage. The trailing habit and soft leaves require a site where they may sprawl over warm dry rocks with a deep root-run beneath, as in the raised bed or planted wall.

There are a number of annual species of *Androsace* with small pure-white blossoms in a spidery head on wiry 6- to 10-inch scapes. These rise from a flat pad of narrow toothed leaves. Here belong *A. lactiflora* and *A. septentrionalis.* Once established they sow themselves charmingly in rather dry sunny sites. Of similar effect, but fully perennial and easy to grow, is *A. lactea.*

The foregoing species are challenging but not insuperably difficult. There is, however, a whole group of androsaces that challenges even the experts. Some gardeners with a flair for special soil mixtures and an eye for special sites have succeeded with these high-alpine species and are amply rewarded by the perfection of a minute tussock studded with brilliant blossoms. All these difficult high-alpine species require a sharply drained soil mixture made up of at least half sharp sand or fine crushed gravel, or crushed flowerpot or slate. Yet they must not suffer drought. Hence the soil mixed with the drainage material should be one-half peat or pure leaf mold. These fussy androsaces are perhaps best grown in pots in frames or alpine-house for the winter. If tried in the garden they will call for

careful placement, preferably on a north slope, with plenty of overhead light and good air circulation.

For the connoisseur they are worth the trouble, and to succeed is
to glow with pride. Included in this group "for experts only" are:
A. alpina, a mat of hard rosettes with single flowers of soft pink
close on the dome; it wants an acid soil, well drained, and ample
light and air without hot baking sun; and *A. helvetica,* which forms
small hard mounds of minuscule gray-green rosettes, on which sit
stemless white flowers; it should be planted in tight crevices between limestone rocks, avoiding southern and western exposures.
Others of the same general sort are occasionally offered as plants—
or, more often, seed; these are all high-alpine, minutely tight, tufted,
and single-flowered: *A. charpentieri, A. ciliata, A. cylindrica,
A. hirtella, A. imbricàta, A. matildae, A. pyrenaica,* and hybrids
among them.

ANEMONE   (Ranunculaceae)

Windflowers are found in all corners of the world, from lofty
alpine peaks to warm Mediterranean pastures, in fullest sun or in
dense, shady woods, as diminutive plants a few inches high or as
stalwart herbs a few feet tall. Even though one whole group of
anemones has been shifted by botanists to the genus *Pulsatilla*
(which see for descriptions), there are windflowers remaining under
the classification of *Anemone* suited to every portion of the open
rock garden and to the woodland glade. So varied are they in habit
of growth and cultural requirements that particular information
is given for each species or group of closely related species. They
have one characteristic in common, however: all anemone seeds
should be sown as soon as possible after harvesting.

A. apennina and *A. blanda* belong to the group of Mediterranean tuberous-rooted anemones, all of which bloom in early
spring along with crocus and daffodils. In this group is also the
A. hortensis-fulgens complex, whose members, along with florist

developments from this complex, are not reliably hardy, nor do they fit well among less sophisticated wild species. *A. apennina* and *A. blanda* are both to be grown in swatches for best effect, and may be situated among ground covers in the rock garden or alpine lawn, or beneath deciduous trees, preferably in well-drained soil, rather rich in humus. Purchased tubers are apt to be so dried out that they do not grow at all or else take two to three years to catch hold. When finally established they will self-sow, the seedlings flowering usually the second year. *A. apennina,* the taller of the two related species, generally has blue blossoms with the tripartite petticoat of leaves less divided. It also prefers a somewhat shadier location than *A. blanda,* the species commonly offered by bulb dealers in shades of blue, white, and pink. Both species have daisy-like blossoms on stems from 4 to 10 inches high and both grow best with a ground cover and will thrive in a grassy bulb lawn.

A. baldensis, from 6 to 8 inches tall, varies considerably in the size of the blue-backed white blossoms. In the best forms the cup-like glistening flowers are 2 inches across, with a ruff of the divided involucre close beneath. As the plants mature, the flower stems elongate and carry the seedheads in small, hard, cottony globes. Fresh seed germinates readily, and good forms may be propagated by careful division. This species from the European Alps and its American counterpart *A. drummondii* of the western mountains are best grown in a moraine condition with considerable moisture at the flowering season.

A. canadensis has but one flaw: it spreads so rapidly and aggressively that it will invade and overcome even stalwart companions. If you can place it in a ramparted corner in good loamy soil, either in full sun or partial shade—where it can rule supreme—it will become a gleaming sea of white in early summer, as the 2-inch blossoms open above the buttercup-like foliage on 2-foot stems. The thin brown roots, ramifying endlessly just beneath the surface, may be divided at any time, even while in flower.

A. caroliniana and its close relative *A. decapetela* are spring bloomers in open prairies and moist calcareous sandy areas of the southeastern United States. From a tuberous root rise stems of 1 foot, bearing at the top solitary blossoms 1½ inches across, in various shades of white, pink, and violet. It will thrive best in the alpine lawn or the richer parts of the rock garden. This is to be increased by fresh seed, which is borne in a cottony head.

A. cylindrica, the Candle Anemone, is a tall, awkward plant carrying greenish-white blossoms quite small for the 2-foot stems. Even more disproportionate is *A. virginiana.* Both are to be admitted only to openings in the wild-type woods garden.

A. deltoidea is a handsome woodland carpeter from the evergreen forests of the American Far West. It is the finest of the American wood anemones and quite the equal of the European. The 2-inch-wide white blossoms, occasionally tinged with blue or pink, are on 6- to 8-inch stems, well above the glossy, dark green, 3-part leaves. The running roots may be established in leafy soil in the woods garden.

A. hupehensis, the Japanese Anemone (sometimes known as *A. japonica*) in all its forms makes a welcome contribution to the woodland garden. In late summer and fall generous blossoms are carried on strong stems above substantial lobed foliage. The many horticultural varieties range from pure white to carmine in color of flower and from 18 inches to 3 feet in height. Because they are not thoroughly hardy they should, in northern climates, be given a sheltered site in the woodland in humus-rich soil, and for insurance mulched throughout the winter with leaves or pine needles. Mature plants may be divided in the spring and provide generous material for increase by root-cuttings. Seedlings are slow to reach flowering stage.

A. magellanica is to be found in gardens in both a dwarf form of about 6 inches and another measuring up to 18 inches, each with ample creamy-yellow flowers. These two forms and others with even reddish blossoms are probably garden hybrids remote from their South American ancestor. All are of easy culture in rich soil in sun or light shade.

A. narcissiflora of moist meadows in the European and Asian mountains produces clusters of 1-inch flowers on 18-inch plants. The blossoms are most generally white, tinged with pink, but more deeply colored forms are to be found in the Caucasus, with even a good yellow, classified by some botanists as *A. chrysantha.* The North American relative, *A. zephyra,* is creamy white. As with all anemones, only fresh seed will germinate.

A. nemorosa, the European Wood Anemone, in its various forms is one of the finest of all plants for carpeting in the woodland garden. The plant varies considerably in the wild, and named varieties have been selected for size and color of blossom. The brittle brown roots, which may be divided in early spring or in the fall, ramble just beneath the surface and thrive best in humus-rich soil. The foliage disappears soon after the flowers do. The principal horticultural varieties of *A. nemerosa* are: *alba flore-pleno,* double white; *allenii,* lavender-blue; 'Blue Bonnet,' deep blue; *robinsoniana,* blue; 'Vestal,' double white with pompon center. Seed is not commonly produced in cultivation, but increase is fairly rapid in the spreading roots. For best effect clumps should be left undisturbed to form sizable mats and can be encouraged to do so by generous topdressing of leaf mold and bone meal soon after spring flowering.

A. quinquefolia, the American Wood Anemone, does not quite compare, it must be said, with the European, but it does have a delicate charm as a woodland plant. It prefers a rich acid soil that does not parch in summer. The wiry, white, spreading roots form mats of leaves and scattered fine-textured flowering-stems with 3 involucral leaves beneath blossoms that range from ½ to 2 inches across. The sepal color is white, flushed with pink, occasionally with a deep pink on the reverse. Rather similar to this common northeastern species are *A. lancifolia,* taller and larger throughout, *A. oregana,* which runs more to blue in blossom color, and two other small western species, *A. adamsiana* and *A. lyallii.*

A. ranunculoides, the Yellow Wood Anemone, is very like a small-flowered wood anemone in bright yellow. It thrives in sites suitable to other wood anemones and is a fine companion to associate with them. Both the species and its double-flowered variety, *pleniflora,* are easily increased by division of the running root-mat.

A. rupicola is a handsome Himalayan species, behind whose good name too often worthless species hide. The true plant bears large white flowers with pink reverse, generally on a 1-foot stem. The basal and stem-leaves are silky and much cut without appearing feathery. This wants well-drained, rich soil in partial shade.

A. sylvestris, the Snowdrop Anemone, will grow in almost any site, but grows best in open shade with woods soil. It soon makes clumps carrying fragrant white flowers, 2 inches across, born singly or in pairs on 12- to 18-inch stems. Plants divide and reestablish easily, especially in early spring.

There are many other anemones of lesser value in the garden frequently offered in seed lists. Rock gardeners may wish to experiment with these because occasionally good forms of most species or desirable hybrids do occur. Among these are: North American *A. globosa* and *A. lithophila,* both found in moist, rocky mountain soils, with color forms that may run to good reds in *globosa* and good yellows in *lithophila; A. multifida* in many geographic forms, some poor indeed; *A. obtusiloba patula,* from the Himalayas, which carries many handsome blue flowers on stems radiating rather horizontally; *A. parviflora,* with white flowers far larger than the name suggests on dwarf compact plants of the Alaskan mountains.

ANEMONELLA (Ranunculaceae)

This is a genus of only 1 species, the Rue Anemone, *A. thalictroides,* which is separated by botanists from the true anemones on characteristics of the style and the seed. For garden purposes this is a cheerful, many-flowered, early spring windflower growing from a tuberous root on wooded hillsides of eastern North America. The rue-like foliage subtends a branching inflorescence of small white or pink flowers, which continue to open for a considerable season. A double white form is long lasting and a double pink is utterly charming as it continues to send out persistent pink pompons well into July. The fingerlike tubers may be separated after flowering for fairly rapid increase and should be planted in woodsy, well-drained soil in rather dense colonies for best effect.

ANEMONOPSIS   (Ranunculaceae)

The only species in this genus, *A. macrophylla* from Japan, re-sembles the Japanese anemones and like them makes beautiful, husky fall-blooming accents in the woodland garden. In this plant the foliage is more finely cut and the many flowers, in shades of light purple, nod at the summit of 3-foot stems. Because of the nodding habit, plants are most charming when placed on a rise above a woodland path, in soil rich with leaf mold. Older plants with multiple crowns may be divided in the spring. Fresh seed will ger-minate readily, but the plants are slow to mature.

ANTENNARIA   (Compositae)

The pussytoes, or Indian tobaccos, are desirable mostly for foliage carpets, which in many species are almost white with a mat of silken down. In dry, rocky soils, in full sun, the carpets remain dense and make excellent cover for dwarf bulbs. The clusters of undistin-guished small tubular flowers with bristly pappae do not add any-thing to the garden, except perhaps in species like *A. dioica* and *A. rosea,* in which the involucral bracts are pinkish and on stems short enough not to flop and tangle as they do in many species. There are many similar species, especially in the American West, where they make up a conspicuous and pleasant portion of the general ground cover in exposed and well-drained sites. There are perhaps as many as 50 recognized species in North America alone, but only a specialist would wish to distinguish among them or a collector to grow them all. The tribe is easily propagated by division or fresh seed.

Quite different and as entrancing as a bonsai is *A. suffrutescens,* which forms a twiggy, twisted dwarf shrub set with small evergreen spatulate foliage. The leaves are thick and rigid, a shiny green above and silver beneath. This grows on hot rocky slopes in the mountains of southern Oregon. It may be propagated readily from cuttings, but is not always hardy in the Northeast.

ANTHEMIS (Compositae)

For summer bloom the smaller camomiles are useful, with numerous modest daisies above tufts of variously cut and scalloped grayish foliage. They want full sun in the scree or other well-drained rocky soil. The clumps are easily divided in early spring or increased by cuttings or seeds. *A. aizoon* has numerous small white flowers on short stems above the grayish, toothed leaves. *A. biebersteiniana* has yellow daisies above 6-inch mounds of glistening, silvery, cut leaves. *A. cinerea* has fairly large white flowers above the pubescent bipinnate leaves. *A. montana* has silky leaves gashed into linear segments, and white flowers. *A. nobilis* has feathery green foliage, desirable as a ground cover in the alpine lawn, and is white-flowered. *A. nobilis* 'Treneague' is a nonflowering form of this camomile which makes a close turf of pungent foliage, rapidly spreading by stolons. It is excellent for the alpine lawn and as a bulb cover or, indeed, as a substitute for grass, since it needs no mowing. The foliage of most camomiles is deliciously aromatic.

ANTHERICUM (Liliaceae)

Though these summer-blooming members of the Lily Family are a bit tall for the small rock garden, they are such a feature of the alpine meadows of Europe that they deserve a place in the garden. In the alpine lawn, for instance, the large clumps of sedgelike foliage are entirely at home and are enhanced in summer by numerous 2-foot stems that bear racemes of small white lilies. They also look well in openings in the woods garden. The fibrous-rooted clumps may be divided in spring or new plants can be grown from seed, which generally takes two years to sprout. *A. liliago,* St. Bernard's Lily, and the slightly shorter *A. ramosum* are both good. For *A. liliastrum* see *Paradisea.*

ANTHYLLIS (Leguminosae)

For growing among hot, sunny rocks, especially of limestone, are these summer-blooming vetches, most readily grown from seed, or by division of the mat-formers. *A. hermanniae* is a foot-high twiggy shrub with gray leaves and abundant small yellow pea flowers. *A. montana* forms a close gray carpet of leaves with cloverlike heads of pink or red. *A. vulneraria* has clusters of pea blossoms ranging from yellow to crimson on green mats.

ANTIRRHINUM (Scrophulariaceae)

The only snapdragon to be brought into the rock garden is *A. asarina.* This is a fine if slightly tender trailer to be grown on the face of a planted wall or raised bed, or in crevices of the rock garden to spill down over rocks. There it will spread its pubescent ovate leaves, from among which all summer will appear pouched flowers of cream-yellow, frequently penciled with pink. It propagates from seed.

AQUILEGIA (Ranunculaceae)

The host of columbines, although the glory of the mountains, do not achieve such eminence in the rock garden. They frequently grow fat and wheezy, short-lived and pale or they intermarry with the undistinguished to gain longevity and awkwardness. The special beauties of the high places are sometimes offered in seed lists. When

they come true from seed—not often, unless collected in the wild—
it is generally the reward of patience, because most alpine columbines
take two years for germination, with at least one prolonged cold
period. If you do succeed in raising a brood of the more coveted
species, then comes the challenge of providing what all seem to
demand: plenty of sunshine and drainage to invoke flowering and
prevent crown-rot and adequate moisture to strengthen stem and
leaf. They appear indifferent to whether the soil is acid or limy.
They do not readily lend themselves to propagation by cuttings or
division. Cuttings have been made in early summer from a basal leaf
stripped from the crown with a bit of the taproot adhering. It is also
possible to divide a vigorous plant at the very beginning of new
growth in spring. Lift the whole plant and with a sharp knife sever
the main carrot lengthwise (with attached side-roots) into as many
divisions as you have the courage to dare. Treat as cuttings in the
shaded sand frame.

For garden purposes, the columbines may be divided into the tall
species of meadow and woodland or the dwarf species of the cliff
and scree. For the large alpine lawn and openings in the woods
garden are the following species; given a stony, not too rich soil, they
will be longer of life and neater of form. *A. caerulea,* the Colorado
state flower, carries its large blue blossoms well above the mass of
basal foliage. Much seed offered as this species is of garden-hybrid
origin. *A. canadensis,* with its red and gold flowers, is most successful in rocky soil. It is most pleasing in dense clumps or sweeps, in
either full sun or light shade. Permit it to self-sow, because the plants
are short-lived and in some sections are attached by a root borer.
A. chrysantha is a tall yellow westerner for openings in the woods,
best grown among shrubs, where its gawkiness is less conspicuous.
A. formosa is a variable species of the Northwest, rather like a large-
flowered *A. canadensis* and for similar sites. *A. glandulosa* is the
handsomest of a number of Siberian species with large, nodding blue
and white flowers.

Aquilegia flabellata var. *nana alba*
(⅞ life size)

For the rock garden ledges, screes, or rocky pasture are some highly desirable smaller dwarf species to be kept dry at the crown but permitted to reach down deep for moisture and nourishment. *A. akitensis* is a fine Japanese species of about 6 inches with ample blossoms, purple-blue in the sepals and spurs, creamy white in the central petals. *A. alpina* in the true species is a foot-high plant with large, solid-blue blossoms, rather long-spurred. *A. ecalcarata* is an oriental columbine of unique color and shape. Spurless blossoms of a purplish brown are carried on 8- to 10-inch stems. *A. flabellata* is a Japanese species with light green glaucous foliage and firm-textured blue and white blossoms. In var. *nana alba* the blossoms on the 6- to 8-inch stems are a lovely pure icy white. *A. jonesii,* from a few limy rockslides of the American West, makes tight little tussocks of finely cut, silvery foliage. It is a shy flowerer, but when the blossoms appear, erect and solitary just above the 3-inch fan of foliage, they are a rich deep blue with a short curved spur. A feeding with bone meal and dry manure appears to stimulate blooming. In nature the plants frequently go dormant during the dry summer. *A. pyrenaica* in its true dwarf form is one of the most beautiful columbines. The intricately divided foliage-mound is a deep green and makes an excellent background for the deep blue, short-spurred blossoms on 6-inch stems. *A. saximontana,* another gem from the high Rocky Mountains, has short-spurred blossoms of clear-blue sepals and white petals on 6-inch stems just above the glaucous foliage. *A. scopulorum* varies from site to site in the Rockies. It may be as condensed as *A. saximontana* or the flower stems may rise to 10 inches. The long-spurred, upfacing blossoms are pale blue, frequently shaded with white or green.

ARABIS (Cruciferae)

If the rock cress crucifers were not so readily grown, they would doubtless be as cherished by the expert rock gardener as they are by the beginner. The better *Arabis* species are handsome in foliage and spendthrift of blossom in early spring. All come readily from seed and are easily increased by division or cuttings. Though many will endure some shade and thrive in almost any soil, a lean rock garden mixture in full sun keeps the plants compact and floriferous. *A. albida,* the species most common in gardens, forms mats of gray spatulate leaves with coarse teeth at the broad end. The numerous flowers in loose racemes on 6- to 10-inch stems are generally pure white. There are, however, varieties with pink flowers, variegated leaves, and, perhaps best of all because the flowers last longer, the double form, var. *flore-pleno.*

A. androsacea makes dense cushions of silky rosettes with white flowers on short stems, more desirable for foliage than blossom, and best in the scree or moraine to keep the furry cushion tight. *A. aubrietioides* is tight-growing, the foliage in the mat being either gray or green, short and blunt. The 9-inch flower spikes are pink.

A. blepharophylla is one of the finest of the American species, producing large, deep pink, sweetly scented flowers on foot-high stalks above a flat cushion of lucent leaves, serrate and ciliate on the margins. It is for well-drained rocky sites and is not always reliably winter-hardy without snow cover.

A. carduchorum has neat rosetted foliage with white flowers and suggests a magnified draba. *A. kellereri* makes tight, low mounds of small ashy-gray foliage. The white flowers on short wiry stems are sometimes quite sparse. This is an excellent plant—for scree, moraine, and rocky pasture.

A. procurrens has shiny pointed leaves on rapidly advancing long stolons. The white flowers are sparingly produced in rather open racemes. This species is useful under shrubs or for a ground cover in the alpine lawn. *A. sturii* is like a trim, compact edition of the last, and with larger, more abundant white flowers. There are many less valuable or quite similar species. Some of the American western-ers, mostly with rose and pink flowers, may prove to be good rock garden plants when they become available.

ARCTERICA (Ericaceae)

This genus has but 1 species, **A. nana,** sometimes assigned to the genus *Pieris.* It is a minute, mat-forming, evergreen shrub with oval, sharp-tipped, small leaves arranged in 3's around the 3- to 4-inch woody stems. The white bell flowers, usually in 3's nod at the top of the stems, becoming erect as the seedpod ripens. It is very slow in growing from seed but quite readily propagated by cuttings made of the shoots, or more quickly of the underground stolons, which form around the base of the clump. Use it for a peaty, moist spot in either an acid moraine or an acid raised bed, or in a special pocket along a path in the woods garden among cassiopes and other special, restrained, peat-loving plants of the heath.

ARCTOSTAPHYLOS (Ericaceae)

Plants of this genus are known as bearberries, kinnikinnicks, and manzanitas, the first two for procumbent shrubs and the third for erect species. **A. uva-ursi,** Bearberry, forms broad mats of excellent evergreen foliage which conform, in cascades, to the shape of rocks and slopes. Clusters of waxy pink bells stud the mats in spring and are followed by long-lasting bright red berries. The coriaceous foliage turns dark maroon in the late fall. Pot-grown plants from cuttings are the surest method of establishing this species. Seeds are slow and uneven in germination, and older, established plants are practically impossible to move. Bearberry has a curious distribution in the wild. It is found happily progressing in the pure acid sand of beach dunes and in acid rocky soils of lofty mountains in America, Europe, and Asia. Though usually in acid soil, it is occasionally found among limestone and has been successfully grown in rocky limestone soils. It does not thrive in rich clayey soils.

   A. nevadensis is a rather similar species of Oregon and California. The stems are more arching and rarely root down, giving the effect of a low shrub rather than a carpeter. This should be handled as *A. uva-ursi* is. There are other low-growing manzanitas of the Far

West of untested hardiness but worth trying. Still other species are more erect and shrubby, hardy in rhododendron soil in the Northwest and other areas of gentle climate.

ARCTOUS (Ericaceae)

These are deciduous dwarf shrubs, rather similar to *Arctostaphylos* but never trailing, and best planted in peaty acid soil with a cool exposure, since they come from high mountains in the north. *A. alpinus* has leaves that turn bright red in autumn and it bears juicy berries of purplish black, whereas *A. ruber* differs principally in having red berries. Both may be grown from cuttings or seed, but the seed is slow to germinate.

ARENARIA (Caryophyllaceae)

The sandworts are legion. Most make grassy tufts either lax or stiff, upright or creeping, with small white flowers in abundance, and most are also easy to grow in any reasonable soil. The seed germinates readily and many divide with ease. For convenience they may be grouped into those with erect, grassy foliage, those growing in tuffets with short, needle-foliage, and those of rather individual habit.

The grassy-leaved ones are suited to many sites in full sun, but especially in the alpine lawn. Most of the American westerners belong to this group. Some are low and mounded, such as *A. compacta, A. congesta, A. fendleri, A. hookeri,* and *A. kingii.* Others, such as *A. preslii* and *A. tmolea,* are as much as a foot high when in flower.

The tuffet varieties go well in ledge and scree and rocky pasture. These include *A. caroliniana, A. grandiflora, A. laricifolia,* and *A. ledebouriana.*

A. verna caespitosa is rather more mosslike than grasslike. It will spread into a very flat film of bright green turf (yellow-green in var. *aurea*) spotted with minute white flowers.

One of the handsomest of all the sandworts and an all-around excellent rock plant is *A. montana.* It forms good carpets of trailing stems set with lanceolate leaves and in late spring is a solid sheet of glistening white flowers set off by a yellow eye. This wants a sunny aspect, preferably with a large rock over which to drape. It does not root down as it sprawls, nor does it divide willingly, and the stems do not root well as cuttings. Seed is the surest method of propagation.

Unique among the genus is *A. purpurascens,* with fairly large, starry, rose-lilac flowers above the 4-inch-high tufts of ovate-lanceolate leaves. This does best in well-drained, acid soil with some shade at least at midday.

Different too is *A. tetraquetra,* which when grown in full sun in well-drained soil forms a hard mound about 1 inch high. The small, oval, leathery leaves, edged with yellow, are packed closely along each stem. The solitary, white, 4-petaled flowers are rather small, but the plant is charming for its foliage alone. Increase this by division or cuttings of the short leafy stems.

ARETHUSA   (Orchidaceae)

Among the small group of dwarf, terrestrial orchids of eastern North America is the very rare and beautiful *A. bulbosa.* Rising from a bulbous root are a single linear leaf of 6 inches and a flowering stem of 10 inches bearing a hooded rose-purple flower with a long, fringed white lip spotted with purple and yellow. This elfin orchid grows among sedges and dwarf shrubs on hummocks in acid bogs and swamps. It will grow in the drier parts of the garden bog, in the moist pine barren, or among low plants in the peat bed. This is increased by bulb offsets or, rarely, self-sown seedlings. No one has yet learned how consistently to produce seedlings of the American terrestrial orchids.

ARISAEMA   (Araceae)

This genus offers a few species of Jack-in-the-pulpits, odd of blossom and brilliant of fruit. All are easy to grow in rich moist soil of the woodland garden. Propagate them by seed. *A. dracon-tium* is commonly called Dragonroot, owing to the fact that the spadix protrudes from the greenish spathe like a tail. In late summer the spathe withers to reveal the fat spike of brilliant orange-red berries that are produced on the swollen lower portion of the spadix. The whole plant rises from a tuber and may reach 4 feet, the single leaf being divided into many long leaflets. The tubers should be planted from 4 to 6 inches below the surface. This has a wide distribution in eastern North America and, although more common southward, is perfectly hardy. *A. triphyllum* is the common eastern Jack-in-the-pulpit, whose pair of leaves may reach 3 feet and are divided into 3 large leaflets. Beneath and between these um-brellas rises the hooded spathe longitudinally striped green and purple—or white and green in var. *stewardsonii.* Within is the clubby spadix. The whole plant may wither in late summer, leaving only the conspicuous cluster of large, scarlet, berrylike fruits. There are a number of Asiatic species, some with tail-like spadix append-ages and one or two with great flaring hoods to the spathe. All are striking, especially *A. candidissimum* with its large pure-white spathe. Himalayan species are not reliably hardy far north.

ARMERIA (Plumbaginaceae)

The rock garden thrifts form tufts and carpets of grassy foliage above which are carried in late spring and summer a long succession of small papery flowers in tight heads, ranging in color from pure white to various shades of pink. *A. caespitosa* (also called *A. juniperifolia*) forms a dense bun composed of rosettes of stiff, very short, awl-shaped leaves. The heads of flowers sit just above the foliage on stout scapes. The mat is composed of elongating and branching rosettes rising from a single taproot, which does not allow propagation by division. Rosettes stripped off the taproot in spring may be rooted in sand. Fertile seed is short-lived. Seed sown thinly as soon as ripe in summer will provide seedlings that should be undisturbed until the following spring. Because this species has hybridized freely with the commoner **A. maritima** in gardens, the true species, known by its very short, stout flower scape and short awl-shaped leaves (triangular in cross section), should be increased by cuttings. This charming, evergreen, everblooming plant should have full sun in the scree, the rocky pasture, or in a rocky crevice where surface drainage is quick. If the clump becomes hollow in the center with age, topdress with a very gritty mixture of stone chips.

Armeria caespitosa
(life size)

A. maritima has many varieties and forms, some frequently given unjustified specific standing. The species itself ranges the Northern Hemisphere in Europe and America, from the seacoast to alpine heights, and has developed forms distinguished by length of leaves in the grassy mound or by the length of the flower scape and color of the flower head. The flower scapes may be from 6 inches to a foot high. All rise from a bright green carpet of linear, erect foliage up to 6 inches tall. This species and its varieties are easy to grow in any sunny site. Increase by division or fresh seed.

There are taller species very suitable to the alpine lawn, some with fine, grassy foliage, some with broader, flattened leaves. In this general group are: *A. canescens,* to 18 inches; *A. filicaulis,* to 20 inches; the common garden thrift, *A. latifolia,* with 2-foot flower stems above rather broad lanceolate leaves; and *A. plantaginea,* to 2 feet.

ARNEBIA. See *Macrotomia.*

ARNICA (Compositae)

These large yellow-flowered composites look their best in scattered colonies among other plants, as they are seen in the grassy mountain meadows and in the semishade of open woods on mountain slopes of Europe and western America. Since they all have rather stout, deep root systems, they do not transplant easily, and are best moved when young. Propagate them by seed, divisions of young plants, or root-cuttings. Grow them in the mixed planting of the alpine lawn or in rocky, duff-filled soil in openings in the woods garden. Solitary plants in the rock garden look awkward and frumpish. The western Americans with rather tall flower stems above the clustered basal leaves include such species as: *A. amplexicaulis,* to 2 feet; *A. chamissonis,* to 2 feet; *A. cordifolia* to 15 inches; *A. nevadensis,* to 1 foot; *A. pedunculata,* to 2 feet. The European *A. montana* is generally under a foot tall in cultivation, with flowers larger than in the American plants. Alaskan *A. lessingii* and *A. unalaschensis* are neat dwarf plants. All species require abundant moisture and acid soil.

ARTEMISIA   (Compositae)

The silvery wormwoods of the European mountains and the American West are foliage plants of great beauty though inconspicuous of flower. When grown in full sun and lean soil, they maintain a pleasing tight growth habit, improved by a light midsummer shearing to discourage distracting flowers and encourage a dense new growth. Many will need a hard clipping in early spring before new growth, because the old leaves and, in some species, the stems are killed back in winter. Increase is possible by division or by cuttings of summer-wood. These are admirable as a foliage contrast in the alpine lawn and as an accent in the rock garden. Most are pleasingly aromatic in the sun.

A. arbuscula is a 1-foot shrub from the American West, with wedge-shaped, toothed, silvery leaves. *A. bigelovii* is a similar southwestern sagebrush with very small silvery leaves. *A. filifolia,* with feathery, white, tomentose foliage, may by shearing be kept lower than the 3 feet it reaches in Nebraska and Nevada. *A. glacialis* is a rock garden treasure from the Alps, to be grown in scree or rocky crevice. It has much-divided, silvery foliage on 4-inch stems, with yellow flowers of some charm. *A. minuta* is aptly named, being a minute, frosty-leaved little shrubby species of about 4 inches from Alberta, Canada.

The silky, silvery mound of the artemisia sold by nurserymen as 'Silver Mound' may be *A. schmidtiana nana,* originally from Japan. By whatever name, it is a valuable foliage plant of easiest culture. There are other special, dwarf, silvery mounded artemisias in various parts of the world, excellent and worth possessing but essentially so similar that they are rarely available. But no species that meets the descriptions above will be out of place in the sunny scree or rocky pasture.

ARUM   (Araceae)

The only arum hardy enough for inclusion in wooded northern

gardens is *A. maculatum,* the Lords-and-ladies of English and European woodlands. More interesting than beautiful, it is somewhat like a miniature Jack-in-the-pulpit, with arrow-shaped leaves, green spadix in a green spathe sometimes spotted with purple. Like the Jack, it produces red fruit as the leaves yellow and disappear. It will increase by self-sowing to make a nice clump in moist, woodsy soils.

ASARUM   (Aristolochiaceae)

The wild gingers are excellent carpeting foliage plants for the woods garden in rich soil. The blossoms are amusing little tubby jugs, in brown or maroon-red, concealed beneath the foliage and so close to the ground as to be frequently buried by fallen leaves at the time they blossom in the early spring. The husky running roots may be separated at almost any season and planted directly out if not permitted to suffer from the lack of moisture.

A. canadense bears heart-shaped leaves from 2 to 7 inches across on silky petioles up to a foot high. The flowers are a reddish purple. *A. caudatum* from the Far West has somewhat smaller leaves and brownish flowers most curiously devised, with the lobes prolonged into tails about 2 inches long. *A. europaeum,* with small shining leaves, will soon make a dense evergreen ground cover in good soil. *A. hartwegii* is like its western neighbor *A. caudatum,* except that the leaves are most beautifully marked with a conspicuous silvery-white patch in the center. *A. shuttleworthii* of the southern Appalachians is likewise handsomely marked with mottlings and specklings of silver on deep green glossy, leathery leaves that turn deep reddish brown in the fall and persist throughout the winter southward. All but *A. canadense* are reasonably evergreen in foliage.

ASCLEPIAS   (Asclepiadaceae)

Most milkweeds are too coarse to find a place even in the large rock garden, but there are one or two with such real character that where space permits they deserve to be grown. Give them a poorish dry soil and they do not become gross in stature or leaf but put their vigor into the flowers. These should be increased by seed and root-cuttings.

A. quadrifolia is a refined milkweed of dry, rocky woods which produces along the 2-foot stem scattered whorls of 4 leaves and at the summit pure-white, typical milkweed blossoms. The erect pods are gracefully slender. *A. tuberosa,* aptly named Butterfly-weed, is a striking midsummer bloomer, bringing to the alpine lawn or openings in the woods garden, brilliant splashes of orange and gold on stems 1 to 3 feet high. The erect, slender pods are architecturally handsome, changing to mahogany-red before splitting to display the bulging cargo of long silky-haired seeds. *A. verticillata* var. *pumila* of the western plains is like a 10-inch leafy horsetail, with the linear leaves densely arranged in whorls. The greenish-white flowers are followed by thin, erect, spindle-shaped pods.

ASPERULA (Rubiaceae)

This genus is known to most gardeners only as a ground cover in shady places, but there are woodruffs from the sunny cliffs of the Mediterranean which make dense, stoloniferous mats studded with small pink trumpets. They may be propagated most readily by spring division or by the sparsely set seed.

A. cynanchica bears light pink tubular flowers at the tips of the sprawling, thin, green stems, which are set with whorls of small leaves. This is a variable European, ranging from a tight mat in alpine forms to taller, more straggly types on the chalk hills. It wants a well-drained limy soil and not too much sunshine.

A. gussonii makes flat mats of intertwining, short stems thickly set with tiny pairs of dark green lustrous leaves, concealed in early summer by the myriad pink tubular flowers. It should be grown in full sun in a deep, well-drained soil. This is a plant for scree or rocky pasture, to be guarded against the muggy damps of summer or excessive wet in winter. Very similar, varying mostly in size and intensity of color in the blossom but all requiring a well-drained surface for the foliage to rest upon, are *A. lilaciflora caespitosa* and *A. pontica*. *A. hirta* forms more open clumps, about 4 inches high, with linear leaves arranged in whorls. The blossoms are pink. *A. nitida* is quite similar. Both want the well-drained sites suggested for the mat-formers.

A. odorata, Sweet Woodruff, whose white flowers are used in May wine, wants a somewhat dry shaded spot. It is one of the few plants that will thrive at the base of maple trees. Even when not decked with its sweet-scented flowers, the fragrant green leaves, arranged in whorls of 8, make a pleasing carpet.

A. suberosa is as beautiful as a carpet of shaggy-leaved androsaces and as difficult to please. It, and other similar Grecian species, make clumps of 3- to 4-inch stems, bearing tiny leaves, the whole plant furry with thick gray wool. The flowers are brilliant pink trumpets. These are definitely plants for the scree or moraine, and even there may not easily survive the rigors of a snowless winter or the muggs of a humid summer. It is a supreme alpine-house plant.

ASTER (Compositae)

Among the hundreds of aster species, it is difficult for the rock gardener to make choices. None are perhaps indispensable; but, because in the wild they are a conspicuous and charming component of the mountain flora at all seasons, they merit more attention than they usually receive. To be sure, they hardly warrant inclusion in the company of minute tuffets in the moraine or the select treasures of the scree. They are plants for the large rock garden, the alpine lawn, the rocky pasture, and the woods garden. Most are easy of culture and are readily increased by division and from seed, preferably fresh seed, as with most of the composites.

A. alpinus is the type of many handsome, truly alpine species that carry large flowers singly on foot-high stems in early summer in shades of violet with a golden eye. All these come from the high meadows, where they grow among short grasses and other herbage, in full sun but not parched for moisture at the root. The alpine lawn or lower reaches of the large rock garden offer congenial sites. The increasing clump may be divided after flowering and seems the longer-lived treated thus at frequent intervals. They may also be grown from seed. To this showy alpine meadow group belong *A. alpigenus* and *A. sibiricus* of America's western mountains. *A. farreri, A. forrestii, A. himalaicus, A. likiangensis,* and *A. purdomii* are all Asiatic representatives of this group, the last two small enough to warrant being planted in the moraine.

In the mountains of the American West are cluster-headed dwarf asters of considerable charm worthy of inclusion in the mixed planting of the alpine lawn. Among those of rather small stature and good proportions are *A. andinus, A. apricus, A. fremontii, A. meritus,* and *A. scopulorum.* There are many others still to be collected and distributed.

Available, but not as often seen in gardens as it deserves, is the eastern American *A. linariifolius,* the bushy little Savory-leaved Aster, also known as the Stiff or Bristle Aster. The numerous lavender, occasionally white blossoms are long-lasting in September at the top of a cluster of stiff stems about 1 foot long.

The newly developed and indubitably beautiful dwarf hybrid asters carry such a hybrid and garden-border look about them that, despite their lavish and lovely blossoms in early fall, they appear out of place among the wildflowers of rock garden and alpine lawn.

ASTILBE (Saxifragaceae)

The astilbes, almost exclusively of oriental origin, are handsome plants with compound toothed foliage of graceful pattern with large panicles of small flowers in white and shades of pink and red. All want a good, rich soil that does not become entirely dry. They will stand considerable sun if their roots have access to ample moisture; otherwise they are to be grown in shade. There are stalwarts for streamside and bog, and miniatures for the pathside beds of the woods garden and the peat bed of rare plants. These are to be increased chiefly by division. Seed will give fairly mixed progeny. *A. chinensis* is a somewhat variable species with rather long narrow foliage and thin branching panicles. This blooms in August, generally in a soft shade of pink, *A. chinensis* var. *pumila* is altogether different, with flowers gathered into slender stiff spikes about 10 inches tall. These raspberry-colored flowers appear in September above the flat pancake of much-divided foliage. This variety, in the kind of moist, cool site that it favors, can become a nuisance by self-sowing. *A. crispa,* which may be merely another variety of the above or, more likely, of hybrid origin, is most beautiful in foliage, with feathery, curly leaves, reddish-tinted. Short, compact spires of good clear colors appear in June.

A. davidii, a 6-foot Chinese plant, is rarely seen in the pure species. It has contributed much to modern hybrids that remain under 3 feet tall but produce abundant, densely flowered panicles in a wide range of colors, from pure white through pinks and salmons to deepest reds. Though somewhat stiff in habit they add midsummer brilliance to streamside, woodland and bog.

A. glaberrima var. *saxatilis* is the real miniature of the tribe, producing in early summer, on 3-inch stems, small spikes of pale pink flowers above a flat carpet of foliage, cut and toothed like very small Japanese Maple leaves. This one is for a carefully selected spot in woodsy soil in shade, or beside a small pool or in a small bog.

A. simplicifolia, with gracefully arching foliage and open arching panicles of very pale pink in early summer, is never more than a foot tall.

ASTRAGALUS (Leguminosae)

Because these excellent members of the Pea Family are almost impossible to transplant and do not lend themselves to propagation by any method other than seed, they rarely appear in the nurseryman's list. And it is for this reason that they are so rarely seen in rock gardens, though they are abundant and beautiful in hot, dry, rocky soils in many parts of the world. There are species in almost any color imaginable, even if some have these colors in rather dingy hues. In addition to the heads and spikes of pea blossoms, many have handsome tuffets of furry, silvery, compound leaves and decorative seedpods. Whenever seeds of any of the smaller dwarf species are available, scratch them and sow singly in small pots, to be transplanted without root disturbance before the plants grow to any extent or sow the seeds exactly where they are to grow. The scree and rocky pasture offer the most likely places for success.

In addition to the herbaceous species, there are dense, spiny shrub forms, mostly from the Middle Eastern and Asian mountains. All the dwarf species are worth trying whenever seeds become available. A few among hundreds of *Astragalus* that you might watch for are seeds of the purple- to blue-flowered *aculeatus, alpiniformis, goniatus, inflexus, monspessulanus, newberryi, onobrychis, purshii* (especially in var. *glareosus*), *sericoleucus, shortianus, tauricus, tridactylicus, utahensis,* and of the yellow-flowered *ceramicus, gilviflorus,* and *tyghensis.*

ASTRANTIA (Umbelliferae)

One finds the unspectacular but pleasing masterworts along the margins of woods and in hay meadows as one goes upward in the alpine sections of Europe. The show is in the pink, white, or purple bracts of the umbellate blossom heads of small greenish-white flowers on bare stems above the palmately lobed basal leaves. These should be propagated by seed and grown along streambanks or in leafy soil of the woods garden in light shade. *A. biebersteinii,* from the Caucasus, has pink calyx bracts surrounding the white flowers on 10- to 12-inch plants. *A. gracilis* is smaller, with whitish bracts, and *A. major* grows up to 3 feet, with purple umbel bracts beneath the white or pinkish flowers.

ATRAGENE. See *Clematis.*

AUBRIETA, frequently spelled *Aubrietia* or *Aubretia* (Cruciferae)

From the stony, limy pavements and rockslides and ledges of the Mediterranean come these neat mat-forming perennials with bright and abundant cruciferous flowers. The different species represent but minor variations on the theme *A. deltoidea,* which in its various-named garden forms has long dominated stone walls, rockeries, and cottage gardens of England. Success in America appears to depend on growing the plant where it can tumble over rocks, preferably lime-stone and preferably not in the full eye of the summer sun. It is easy to grow from seed, to divide, to layer, and to strike from cuttings. There are doubles and singles; there are lavenders, blues, pinks, and reds, and under each color a host of named forms, some with variegated leaves; all are good if grown as a wall or crevice plant. To keep the clumps floriferous and healthy, clip them back fairly severely right after blooming.

AZALEA. See *Rhododendron.*

BALSAMORHIZA (Compositae)

There are a number of species of these dwarf sunflowers throughout the dry sections of the American West. On open hillsides they spread their large, frequently deeply cut leaves, more or less covered with coarse hairs or matted pubescence. The large, well-proportioned flowers are either bright yellow or cream-colored, on stems from 8 inches to 2 feet tall. All are early-flowering. The roots are gigantic and take poorly to transplanting. Like other deep-rooted westerners, they should be grown from seed, set out when very young, and given full sun and perfect drainage. The rocky pasture is a good site. Species to be especially sought are: *B. hirsuta, B. hookeri, B. incana,* and *B. sagittata.*

BAPTISIA (Leguminosae)

There is a place for these in larger plantings where open areas in the woods want color and low shrubby masses. Though the clumps are herbaceous, the upstanding mound of foliage of *B. australis* in blue or white quickly attains a height of 3 to 4 feet, with flower spikes of lupine-like bloom above cool-green compound leafage. *B. bracteata* is a yellow species, less showy but useful to mix with the blue and white. All want deep, rather open sandy soil and at least half sun to induce bloom. Not commonly offered in nursery catalogues, they may be easily grown from seed.

BECKWITHIA. See *Ranunculus.*

BELLIS (Compositae)

The small English Turfing Daisy, *Bellis perennis,* a weed in the lawns of Europe and our Northwest, may be used in the Northeast as a welcome constituent in the less dry, shadier sections of the alpine lawn. Not as perennial as the name suggests, the plant does self-sow sparingly. *B. rotundifolia* behaves about the same and does have a variety, *caerulescens,* of pale lilac-blue.

BELLIUM (Compositae)

This is like a condensed *Bellis.* The small-leaved tuffet of *B. bellidioides* will slowly increase if given light soil in an open site, though it is not reliably hardy northward. It carries diminutive white daisies on 4-inch stems. Increase this by seed or division.

BERBERIS (Berberidaceae)

The evergreen dwarf barberries are charming as foliage accents in the larger rock garden. *B. candidula* and *B. verruculosa* have holly-like leaves of shining green with silvery reverse. The yellow flowers are in small clusters sweetly lilac-scented. In severe winters branches may be frozen back, but the plants recover and become denser for the pruning. From the far tip of South America come dwarf evergreen barberries with narrow leaves, spiny only at the tip, with yellow or orange flowers that are solitary or in pairs. These species are less hardy than the last two, but worthwhile, given the protection of a good cover of pine boughs to bring them through the winter. Dwarf forms will be found listed under **B. buxifolia, B. darwinii,** and **B. stenophylla.** All seem adaptable in any reasonable soil and may be propagated by top- or root-cuttings.

BERGENIA (Saxifragaceae)

These large-leaved saxifrages are frequently listed as *Megasea* or *Saxifraga*. Because of their large, shining, evergreen leaves and rather heavy spikes of pink bloom, the bergenias are not suited to the company of dwarf alpines, but they are having a definite revival of popularity because of their adaptability in a fairly rich soil in either sun or shade, especially for their handsome foliage. They will increase into sizable clumps with heavy rootstocks, easily propagated by division. The species are all rather similar. **B. cordifolia** has somewhat nodding flowers above large polished leaves. **B. crassifolia** has taller, dense panicles of deeper-colored flowers well above the leaves. These two are the hardiest and are the parents of recent hybrids.

BESSEYA. See *Synthyris.*

BETULA (Betulaceae)

With small leaves, rough and scalloped, the dwarf birch **B. nana** of the Far North will make a twiggy mound up to 24 inches. It should be cut back occasionally to keep it neat in the garden where fierce snow-burdened winds do not provide the natural pruning. This is for acid, moist soils. Cuttings do not root easily, but layers are possible.

BOLAX (Umbelliferae)

Though the rare plant **B. glebaria** comes from the Falkland Islands, it seems perfectly hardy. Too hot a site will scorch the dark shining leaves cut in the fashion of those of a mossy saxifrage. It makes a fine tight mound less than 3 inches high. The yellow flowers, just above the leaves, are of no account. The clump may be divided easily.

BOYKINIA (Saxifragaceae)

Saxifrage relatives from the western mountains of North America, *B. elata* and *B. major* are 2-foot plants for moist woodland sites, whereas *B. jamesii* is a handsome dwarf. The last wants a well-drained soil laced generously with leaf mold, preferably acid, and in half-shade. If happy, it will make a thick clump of wavy, kidney-shaped leaves with short spires of purplish-red, rather tubby flowers on 4-inch stems. Increase these by seed or division.

BRODIAEA (Liliaceae)

Most of these bulbous plants of the Far West are perhaps too lanky in stem to appeal to gardeners, nor are they often offered in the trade. The foliage is scanty and thin, frequently gone at flowering time. But even the taller ones are satisfactory in the alpine lawn or rocky pasture, tucked in among plants whose foliage will act as a foil. The color is usually blue or white, though there are a few yellows. The best for the small rock garden is *B. grandiflora* with quite large blue trumpets on 6- to 8-inch stems. Give all brodiaeas sun and well-drained sites. Though not reliably hardy in severe climates, desirable species are: *B. bridgesii,* 9 inches, pale lilac; *B. capitata,* 2 feet, blue; *B. douglasii,* 1 to 2 feet, blue; *B. hendersonii,* 9 inches, yellow; *B. ixioides,* 1 foot, salmon; *B. laxa,* 2 feet, purple; and *B. ida-maia,* 2 feet, scarlet.

BRUCKENTHALIA (Ericaceae)

The Spike Heath, *B. spiculifolia,* is one of the most beautiful and easiest to grow of the heathers. Indeed, it is a rival of the fussy and difficult *Phyllodoce empetriformis* and is far superior to *Empetrum nigrum,* both of which it resembles in foliage. The blossoms, which literally sheet the ever-increasing low carpet of needled stems, are at the tips of the shoots well above the foliage. The color is uniformly a charming pink. It is absolutely hardy and adaptable in any acid soil. Full sun is best, since shade reduces the June and July bloom. The stems root down as the carpet spreads, especially if you work into the base some sandy, peaty soil. Rooted divisions can be taken off in spring and treated like rooted cuttings. Water them frequently until well established; then the Spike Health will ignore drought. It may also be increased by cuttings. Color forms, as found among the other heaths, have not been offered in the trade, if they exist.

BRUNNERA. See *Anchusa.*

BULBOCODIUM (Liliaceae)

This very early flowering bulb, **B. vernum,** is rather like a cross between a crocus and a colchicum in the flower shape, but there is something distinctive about this plant, which is not as commonly grown as its beauty warrants. The color is a glowing raspberry-pink, a bright and luminous spot in the very earliest days of spring. It will flourish in the alpine lawn in sun or light shade. In some soils the bulbs are short-lived; in others they persist and multiply slowly. They seem to do best in moist but well drained areas.

BUXUS (Buxaceae)

The dwarf forms of **B. microphylla** and **B. sempervirens** have excellent evergreen foliage in the hardier forms. They tend to be somewhat formal in shape, but can be used for accent or in a large rock garden to form dark evergreen patches. They stand shearing, but this is not necessary. The Korean Box, **B. microphylla koreana,** is the hardiest, and itself has many forms. Some remain dark green in winter and others tend to brown in the leaf. They also vary in height. **B. microphylla compacta** stays dwarf and a good green. All boxwoods are adaptable as to soil and site, even doing well in fairly heavy shade. Cuttings of half-ripened wood root easily.

CALANDRINIA (Portulacaceae)

C. umbellata is a 6-inch portulaca cousin with fleshy, linear leaves and bright, satiny, magenta flowers. It grows best in a hot, sunny site. The individual flowers are evanescent, but a new crop each day is produced over a long season in summer. They are easily propagated from seed sown where they are to stand. *C. caespitosa,* a fairly recent introduction from Patagonia, has a clump of very short succulent leaves and white flowers on short, wiry stems.

CALCEOLARIA (Scrophulariaceae)

None of the perennial calceolarias of remote places in South America have proved easy to grow in the Northeast, and for that reason alone they are much sought after. The ones sometimes offered as seed are *C. biflora, C. darwinii, C. polyrrhiza,* and *C. tenella.* All have small pouched flowers, basically yellow, with various stripings and specklings, on fine stems that rise from among a tuft of close-growing leaves. They want cool, moist summers and cold, dry winters. If these are carefully located in peaty moraine soil, success may briefly reward the devoted gardener. The alpine-house, however, provides the most likely conditions under which the bewitching pouches are finally and consistently produced.

CALLA (Araceae)

C. palustris, the Wild Calla, is a showy plant for the wettest parts of the bog garden, growing in nature in shallow pools of black, still water in northeastern American bogs and swamps. It is, indeed, like a miniature Calla Lily, with a pure-white spathe enfolding a yellow spadix. For a good show of flowers it wants some sun, and must be constantly moist. The pulpy red berries enclose seeds that may be sprouted in sphagnum soup, but division of the heavy rootstock after the flowering period is the surest and easiest method of increase.

CALLIANTHEMUM. See *Ranunculus.*

CALLIRHOE (Malvaceae)

The spreading poppy mallows can fill the sunny reaches of the big rock garden or a rocky bank with brilliant color from late June till frost. Rambling among a planting of blue and white *Campanula carpatica,* their glossy, glowing crimson cups strike a charming note. The branching stems, clothed with long-stalked, deeply cleft leaves among which the wine-cups sit, splay out along the ground from a deep and sizable, carrot-like root. Increase is best by seed and the plants put in their permanent positions while young. They will grow in heavier soils than is generally supposed, and their reputed short life may be due to starvation more than anything else. *Callirhoe involucrata* is the commonest species, only slightly different from *C. digitata, C. papaver,* and *C. triangulata.*

CALLUNA (Ericaceae)

Heather, *C. vulgaris,* the only species in this genus, is available in many sizes and many shapes, with pink, white, or purple flowers that are single or double. Hence, in acid soil and at least 50 percent sun, it is a charming plant for many different sites. There are literally hundreds of named varieties and forms described in lists of special growers and in books devoted to heaths and heathers. There are miniature horticultural forms such as '**Dainty Bess,**' '**Mrs. R. H. Gray,**' and '**Sister Anne,**' and also tuffet varieties of the species, such as *foxii nana, minima,* and *pygmaea.* All the smaller varieties are suitable for growing among the select plants in the peaty rock garden; the taller varieties are best in a heath, either alone or mixed with other ericaceous shrubs.

During muggy summer weather the dense cushion types may be attacked by a fungus that, if not arrested, will cause browning of top growth. An immediate liberal dusting with flowers of sulphur will halt the infection. In exposed sites callunas may burn during the winter if not covered with snow. Pine boughs placed on them in the fall will generally provide sufficient protection, but even if they are badly burned they will soon break new growth after a spring shearing. Spring shearing is a good practice for all the taller-growing callunas to keep them neat. This does not diminish the flowering if it is done early, since they bloom on new wood in late summer.

All heaths and heathers are best transplanted in very early spring and given plenty of water until established. Once they are growing well, they will endure long periods of drought. A topdressing of a sand and peat mixture worked into the crown encourages renewal of vigor by root development along the base of the stems. This also provides rooted layers that may be severed from the plant and then grown-on in pot or frame for future planting-out. It is best not to transplant established plants. Cuttings of new growth, taken in late summer or winter, root readily in an acid medium not permitted to dry out. Plants may also be grown from the fine, dustlike seed. Seed collected from the forms and varieties will give an interesting collection of variants.

CALOCHORTUS (Liliaceae)

These handsome western American bulbous plants do not thrive in the Northeast. From purchased bulbs, planted in late summer or fall and protected by a mulch during the winter, there may be a single season of bloom; or, as frequently happens, nothing at all shows up in the spring. Most failures are probably due to insufficient drying of the bulbs in summer. As pot plants in the alpine house they can be given a thorough dormant drying and sufficient winter protection. They are so beautiful, however, that whenever available they should be tried in very well drained but never rich soil. The rocky pasture and scree offer possible sites. The smallest and hardiest are *C. amabilis, C. eurycarpus, C. gunnisonii, C. maweanus, C. nitidus, C. purdyi,* and *C. uniflorus.*

CALOPOGON (Orchidaceae)

These are native American orchids of sphagnum bogs and wet, acid meadows. *C. pulchellus,* in early July, carries conspicuous blossoms of deep rose in a loose raceme of up to 10 flowers on a stalk of about 1 foot, which springs from between 2 long narrow leaves. The lip, which flares curiously at the top of the blossom, is fringed with golden hair. White and pale pink forms are occasionally found. The roots are rambling and rather brittle, but may be cautiously teased from the sphagnum-moss bed and transplanted to an acid bog site in sun or light shade.

CALTHA (Ranunculaceae)

The Marsh Marigold of the Northeast, *C. palustris,* is a congenial plant for the very wet swamp site and stream margins. The tangle of white fibrous roots will anchor the plants in even fairly swift water, where the ample shining leaves are a perfect background in early spring for the large clusters of glossy buttercup-yellow blossoms. This species is also found in Europe, from which varieties with double flowers and giant flowers have been brought into the garden. It is also found in the Far East, where white and even purple blossoms have been reported.

Other species for planting in similar sites, very moist at least in the spring, are *C. biflora* and *C. leptosepala* of western America, both white-flowered. In *C. biflora* the flower segments are rather better proportioned and fuller than in the other. Large plants of marigold may be divided, especially in late summer when the plants have died down. Seeds sown as soon as ripe germinate readily, old seeds reluctantly. The seedlings are rather slow to reach flowering age.

CALYPSO (Orchidaceae)

The single member of this genus, the beautiful little orchid *C. bulbosa,* grows from a tiny pseudo-bulb found buried in the acid duff of cool, moist, coniferous forests in the Northwest and rarely in the Northeast. One large basal leaf clasps the flower scape of 6 to 9 inches. The solitary blossom of purple, pink, and yellow has a rather large rolled lip, lined and mottled with maroon. Collected plants are sometimes offered, but so dried out that they rarely flower for more than one year. Plants carefully collected and protected from mice may be successful in a duff of rotted wood and pine needles in dense shade. Do not water this in summer.

CAMASSIA (Liliaceae)

The camass lilies are a prominent late-spring feature of the moist meadows of the Far West. Tall for the rock garden proper, they are good for planting in clumps in the alpine lawn or in moist, loamy spots in light shade in the woods garden. The generally blue flowers are produced in full spikes at the end of 1- to 3-foot stems with long straplike basal leaves. Bulbs should be planted 3 to 4 inches apart and about 4 inches deep. *C. cusickii* has pale blue flowers on 3-foot stalks; *C. esculenta,* an eastern species, has light blue spikes on 2-foot stems; *C. howellii* is only 10 to 18 inches tall, with blue-violet flowers; *C. leichtlinii* is creamy white; *C. quamash* is dark violet.

CAMPANULA (Campanulaceae)

From all the corners of the Northern Hemisphere come charming bellflowers to grace the rock garden. From the beginning to the end of the flowering season, you can have campanulas great and small. So numerous are the species, in fact, that a whole authoritative volume by H. Clifford Crook, in which about 300 species are recognized, has been devoted to their description and culture.

Most campanulas are in the lavender to blue color range, and white forms are found in many of the species. They are ordinarily of easy culture, for they make their homes in nature in the less lofty reaches of the mountains—some, to be sure, demanding rocky conditions and others consorting with meadow plants. Seed is minute but abundant, and will usually germinate with ease. In fact some kinds, like *C. carpatica* and the Harebell, *C. rotundifolia,* may become a slight nuisance because of their proclivity to self-sow in the garden. Particular color forms and hybrids should be increased by division very early in the spring, by root-cuttings or by stem-cuttings taken with a bit of rootstock at the base of the shoot. Because of their long season of bloom and the beauty of their flowers, campanulas are the real backbone of the rock garden. Only a sampling of the various kinds, mostly those of easy culture and neat habit, can be here listed.

Campanula garganica
(½ life size)

Flat, Trailing or Creeping Species

These are mostly useful on the face of the planted wall or raised bed and in the fissures of the rock garden, where their foliage can splay out over stones. Or the more fussy ones can run about in the chip surface of the moraine.

Like elfin Harebells on short, wiry stems, the light blue or pure-white flowers of *Campanula cochlearifolia* dance 2 to 3 inches above the carpet of ever-increasing tiny rosettes of typical campanula foliage. There are many named horticultural varieties of the species and synonyms for the species itself, but whether called *C. bellardii, C. pumila,* or *C. pusilla,* it is always charming when permitted to run about a rocky surface in any site not too parched. It has a way of disappearing from precisely where it was last year and appearing a good foot or two away, by the magic of an underground running rootstock. Because of its low stature and delicacy of carriage, it wants to be near a path or in a raised bed where its miniature proportions can be closely enjoyed. Division is easy at almost any time of year. Seed is abundant and easy, though it does not seed itself as generously as some of the campanulas.

There is a puzzling array of names based on what are frequently either minor or local variations on the general theme, *C. garganica.* The theme is altogether charming, a splaying of numerous neatly proportioned and well-spaced stems, along which sit a prodigality of more or less starlike blossoms. The color is in shades of blue and violet, frequently with a white center eye-ring, or occasionally a pure *alba* form. The leaves of the basal tuffet are round and crenate, with a pronounced cleft at the petiole end. The foliage varies in size, color, and amount of hairiness from species to species, but there is a recognizable family resemblance.

The most delicate of the *garganica* tribe is probably the one called *C. fenestrellata* and the huskiest is *C. cephallenica,* with flowers proportionately larger on the more erect mounds of bloom. All species in this group are admirably suited to location on the face of a wall or among rock ledges, where the flowering-stems lie flat over the rocks in a brilliant display. With good soil at the roots they stand considerable sun, but flower well and increase most rapidly in partial shade. Increase in spring is easy by division of the clump, if the segments are given a chance to develop a husky new root system in the shaded sand bed before being put in permanent location. Seed is abundant and will germinate easily when the soil becomes really warm. The seed is so fine that it is best to mix it with dry sand for sowing to avoid overcrowding, though even this does not appear to discourage the seedlings' remarkable willingness to live. A tight wad of tangled seedlings may be shaken apart and set in flat or frame for the most eager and rapid rejuvenation.

C. portenschlagiana, because of its neat habit, ease of culture, and especially its abundance of flower, is unquestionably one of the outstanding plants for rock garden or wall. It was once called *C. muralis* ("of the wall"), and may still be found so named in lists. With a tight tuft of shiny green leaves like miniature ivy and up-facing bells of light violet with reflexed lobes crowded in a many-flowered panicle at the top of 4- to 6-inch leafy stems, this campanula never fails to enchant. The tuft always stays compact as it increases slowly year by year, adding new rosettes on rather woody stems. These may be removed from the edges of the clump and rooted at almost any time of year, but especially in the spring. Though not fussy about soil, *C. portenschlagiana* does its best in soil that does not become bone-dry, and it flourishes in light shade. It is a splendid plant for the top of the raised bed or in an ample pocket in the face of the wall. It self-sows sparingly, but does not appear to hybridize and has not been known to show up in white, though this is something to be prayed for in any batch of seedlings.

C. poscharskyana is in effect a magnified *C. garganica*. The foliage is similar but larger and the longer stems, splayed out from the crown, have more ample starry flowers. Since it is so vigorous and easy that it may smother tiny neighbors, it is best grown on the face of the wall, or fittingly at the foot, where the long sprays of pale lavender stars flatten against the rocks. It is not an abundant seeder, but is easy to increase by division. In very rich soil it is almost too vigorous, but, if given a lean diet among constricting rocks, its beauty is long-lasting and permanent.

All through the Mediterranean mountains there are numerous minute rock-dwelling campanulas—most, unfortunately, mono-carpic. Of these **C. *sartori*** maintains itself by self-sowing in the narrowest fissures of the wall or ledge. The first-year seedlings form a minuscule rosette of ivy-shaped, slightly downy leaves. The following year elongating and prostrate stems form around the crown, and by July are decked along their ground-hugging length to the very tip with upfacing, neatly proportioned, glistening-white bells. After flowering and setting seed, the plant passes away to its reward, leaving room for the host of self-sown progeny to carry on.

Erect-growing Dwarf Campanulas

The difference between this group of bellflowers and the last is frequently a matter of degree and general effect. The blossom stems of many of the first group are in reality erect, but because of their tendency to make mats of foliage they create an emphasis different from that of those whose carriage is more upright from crown to bell. ***Campanula carpatica,*** the Carpathian Bluebell, is the type for this group. It is a real standby, producing over an extremely long period, from midsummer to frost, a magnificent and unfailing supply of large blossoms. In color the range is from dark lavender through china-blues and blue-grays to the most icy white. The size of the blossom varies up to as much as 3 inches across, and in shape from a deep bell to an almost flat salver. Variation is also marked in the flowering-stems above the long-stemmed leaves in a clump at the base; they may range from 6 to 18 inches. All combinations of these variables are to be found in a batch of seedlings, the best of which can be increased by division and cuttings in the spring. A good dwarf form with solitary upfacing bells above foliage rough with hairs is known as *C. turbinata* and tends to come fairly true from seed. The one mark against *C. carpatica* is its insatiable urge to self-sow. Because of its long season of bloom, with new buds opening on old stems and new stems thrusting up from the crown, the earliest flowers shed their seed before the last are budded. Unless you hand-pick the seedpods before they ripen, self-sowing is a real problem. For this reason it is the best part of wisdom to keep *C. carpatica* away from rare and prized alpines that cannot survive the smothering blanket of a neighbor's foliage. Except for this restriction on its placement, you may safely insert it in almost any kind of site, since it will flourish in full sun or part shade in rich, moist soil or in dry, rocky places where the root run is deep. In the latter location it blooms more profusely on shorter stems and the self-sown seedlings are less likely to survive.

Whoever has seen a sweep of the bearded *C. barbata* glistening in the sun among the grasses of an alpine pasture must surely have coveted them. Nor need this yearning go unsatisfied, for *C. barbata* is easily raised from seed and will give at least one season's display of bloom. Though apparently perennial in the wild, it is frequently short-lived in the garden. Give it a deep, fairly rocky soil, in a site not too baked. These prescriptions are quite the opposite of those given in English books, where a lean, rapidly draining soil is advocated for long life. Perhaps it is after all not a true perennial in nature and shares with many fine campanulas the taint of the monocarpic. At all events, seedlings must be set in whatever location you finally decide on while they are still small because of their great carrot-like roots. Once established, they should be allowed to go to seed to carry on their tribe.

C. collina is in effect a refined and darker-flowered *C. sarmatica*. It differs also in that it increases yearly the size of its clump of narrow, rough foliage and number of foot-high stems. It is an early bloomer, and quickly past, but of such charm that we remember it with regret when the rush of later bellflowers have burst into bloom. *C. collina* of the high hills in the Caucasus does not endure droughty sites, but given good, deep soil will flourish and flower in full sun.

C. glomerata is typical of the cluster-head bellflowers and is really too tall and heavy for most sites in the rock garden, having coarse leaves and flowering-stems that reach 2 feet; but the dwarf form variety *acaulis* makes a fine floriferous plant of only a few inches. Although it increases fairly rapidly in good soil, if grown in full sun in a pocket among rocks where it is not too richly nourished it may stay reasonably well put. The whole tight mound of rough, long-pointed leaves will be smothered in tight heads of upfacing flowers for an extended period in summer. If grown from seed only a proportion of the plants will be really dense and short-stemmed; but, since it is easy to propagate by taking off, in spring, one or more of the advancing stolons, the best forms may be multiplied and the rest relegated to some out-of-the-way corner or to the border garden. Color variations from deep blue-purple to pure white add spice to your selection of superior forms.

C. planiflora is a curious plant. In its best form it makes a rosette of firm, very dark green rounded leaves, shallowly waved around the edge, from which rise 1 or more stiff stems, 6 to 9 inches high and sparsely decked with narrow pointed leaves. In the axils of these stem-leaves are displayed, flat against the stem, large, very shallow platters of firm-textured flowers in white and soft lavender. The curious thing about the plant is that it either dies out after a year or two (unless the new offsets are removed and reestablished) or else it assumes (frequently) in the second year or so a bewildering spurt of growth, so that the flowering-stem reaches 3 feet and the plant looks exactly like *C. persicifolia* of the border garden. It is probable that *C. planiflora* is a Mendelian recessive form of this Peach-leaved Bluebell, not always consistently produced from seed. In any batch of seedlings grown from *C. planiflora*, you can spot very early the ones that will be dwarf and those that will be more like *C. persicifolia*. The young plants of the pygmy form have very dark green, somewhat rounded leaves of quite a leathery texture, whereas the tall ones have longer, narrow, peachlike leaves. Perhaps persistent roguing may establish a strain that will come true from seed.

C. raddeana has something of the effect of a richer, fuller *C. rotundifolia* with much larger blossoms and bigger leaves. From the rapidly increasing carpet of cordate, toothed leaves, which are glossy and prominently veined, spring numerous stems up to a foot long and frequently forked into branchlets and then rebranched. From these hang large deep lavender bells in July. The full flush of blossom is so bountiful that the stems are often laid prostrate with the weight. A lean soil, containing lime chips, and plenty of sun give greater stiffness to the stems. A closely allied species, very similar in foliage and blossom, *C. kemulariae*, is even more prone to flopping its blossoming heads to the ground; so a position at the top of a wall or above a large rock displays the tumble of great bells to the best advantage in both these species. They are very easy to divide.

Every country of the Northern Hemisphere has some form of the airy and graceful *C. rotundifolia,* the Harebell, or Bluebell-of-Scotland. The process of genetic variation and segregation has given rise to a multitude of different races of the species, some so distinctive as to merit separate names. The individuality of most of these subspecies, becomes canceled out when they are grown in the garden and permitted to mingle their characters in a miscegenetic progeny. Select forms, such as dwarf or large-flowered individuals, can be multiplied easily by vegetative means. Some have nodding bells on long, wind-yielding stems; others, like the variety from the Olympic Mountains of the American Northwest, have their flowers on short stems close to the tuft of rounded, dentate leaves. Still others are stiffer and hold the bells more erect. The variations are endless, yet all forms are of the easiest culture in sun or light shade, demanding but the barest crack in the rock for a foothold. It is never more bewitching than when swaying its blue or, rarely, white bells out from the fissured face of a massive ledge, but it can become a weed by self-sowing.

C. sarmatica is a husky plant, with large grayish leaves and rugged stems of 1 foot, from which hang in a one-sided raceme ample bells of soft gray-blue. Though the foliage is too massive to associate with more delicate alpines, *C. sarmatica* has an attractiveness that is enhanced when given a setting where the campanile of pale bells may chime against a background of bold rock of dark color. Easy to satisfy in any exposure and deep soil, it is not easy to propagate except from seed, which it does not always set freely. It blooms in the latter part of the summer and for a long period, the new buds opening as the old ones fade.

C. tommasiniana is a trim little plant, in many respects quite individual. From a forking taproot, which makes division impracticable, there rise a multitude of wiry stems 4 to 6 inches high, forming a rounded bush, clothed in stiff, narrow, serrate leaves. In late summer the bush becomes laden with long narrow bells of pale blue, individually undistinguished but because of their dense mass really effective. Seedlings should be transplanted when young, and for vegetative propagation full stem-cuttings with a bit of the rootstock attached are possible early in the season. A more generous, open blossom on the same sort of bush marks the hybrid × *standsfieldii*, which originated in the native haunts of *C. tommasiniana* in Istria. In the same part of the world is a separate species rather similar to *C. tommasiniana*, *C. waldsteiniana,* with upfacing lavender bells that make it a more desirable plant, but unfortunately it is less frequently available. All these closely similar plants enjoy an open site with good drainage—not parched, however. The requirements suggest a humus-rich gravelly soil out of the blaze of the sun. Under these conditions the plants enlarge year by year without at any time running or sprawling.

There are a number of excellent closely related species, all from the Caucasus or Asia Minor and very similar to each other in appearance, cultural requirements, and earliness of bloom: the *tridentata* group. *C. aucheri*, *C. bellidifolia*, *C. saxifraga*, and *C. tridentata* are the most distinctive and available, though other names will be found for some species closely resembling them. All make a compact tuft of rosettes of firm-textured, rather small leaves with shallow indentations. The flowers are carried erect on short stems and are large in proportion to the plant. The texture of the petals is sturdy and long-lasting, giving a depth to the color, which tends toward the violet end of the blue range. There is a conspicuous white zone at the base of the cup. All want plenty of light to encourage bloom, yet must not be parched; good soil for the long, heavy thong-root to run in, with a deep layer of stone chips around the crown, seems to offer the best solution. Propagation is not easy except from seed because of the carrot-like root structure. Leaf-cuttings in spring, having a bit of the root crown carried along with the base of the leaf, can be made for especially desirable forms of the various species. The plants appear longer-lived than many campanulas.

There are handsome taller bellflowers, too numerous to list, that are suitable both for the woods garden and the large alpine lawn. Those interested in these species would do well to consult a general garden encyclopaedia or a book specializing in this huge genus.

Campanulas for the Connoisseur

Though there has already been listed a sufficiently wide selection of bellflowers to furnish different sites in the garden, enthusiasts and experimenters will sooner or later wish to try some of the more challenging species to be found in the genus.

Campanula allionii is a temperamental prima donna. Its large bellflowers are opulent-looking as they sit rather stolidly among the narrow, rough leaves of the foliage tuft. It longs for the pure air, the gravelly root-run, and the ample underground moisture of the high-alpine moraines. In the humid heat of lowland gardens *C. allionii* languishes to the point of death. It is easy to grow from seed, and in youth, given as homelike a condition as possible, will put up with less than the ideal. After flowering in the second year, however, it is likely to succumb. Light shade and an almost vertical position may persuade this beauty to linger beyond a hopeful adolescence. Eventually a race of immigrants may evolve with a greater tolerance for adverse conditions, though it is unlikely that this will ever be an easy plant to grow.

C. alpina seems less willing to bloom than most. It is easily propagated from seed and soon makes a trim rosette of hard, dark green, narrow leaves. If given the sunny well-drained site it demands for flowering, it is likely to shrivel away. If grown in richer soil or shade it will persist as a lush rosette but fail to send up its 10-inch pyramid of rather large stiff bells. When finally persuaded to flower it is apt to die of exhaustion. Seed is the only means of increase.

C. arvatica has a tight tuft of small shining leaves rather like the basal leaves of *C. rotundifolia.* The tuft increases slowly in well-drained limy soil in full sun and sends up abundant, short-stemmed, rather starry blossoms of violet to light purple in June and July. Though native to northern Spain this miniature species seems hardy if given good drainage. It may be increased by cuttings or division in the spring, or by seed.

C. betulaefolia is a beautiful species rather recently introduced from the rocky places in the mountains of Armenia. The birch-shaped leaves are carried on fairly long petioles, forming a clump from which splay out stems that branch and produce clusters of 2 or 3 good-sized bells opening over a long period in summer. The color of the open blossoms is white with a flush of pink, this quite conspicuous in the bud and deeper in some plants than in others. Because the stems tend to bend down with the weight of the flower clusters, it is advantageous to grow the plants high on a ledge or wall. It does best in a position out of the full sun and in fairly deep rich soil. Root-cuttings offer a method of increasing particularly good color forms, but seed is the easiest method.

C. cenisia challenges the keenest gardener but must disappoint the unprejudiced eye. In the garden, if you can bring the plant to flowering stage, flowers are small, scanty, short-lived, and of a pale cast. Rather tiny rosettes form along the wandering root-thread, from which rise the 1- to 2-inch, hairlike flowering-stems. In native haunts it meanders in a shaly detritus with constant moisture seeping beneath the well-drained surface.

C. lasiocarpa presents a lavish display of erect blue bells on short stems above an ample and neat tuffet of toothed leaves. For best growth the plant demands good, well-drained soil in a spot shielded from the hottest sun. The blossoms are produced over a long period in summer. Division of the clump in spring as growth begins or leaf-rosettes with a length of older stem treated as cuttings are means of vegetative propagation especially for superior forms. There is some variation in size and color of bloom among seedlings, though all are good.

C. pilosa shares with other Western Hemisphere campanulas an uncertainty of disposition, at least in the literature. Yes, and in the garden, too. The stalwart heavy-textured leaves of this species suggest a disposition at least as assertive as *C. carpatica*'s. But the single rosette may sit and sit, year after year, without offset or bloom. Perennial it is, however, unlike such a bizarre species as *C. formanekiana*, which bursts into bloom and expires. Once it decides to flower, *C. pilosa* will slowly, year by year, magnify its clump of flowering rosettes, from which rise, on short, stiff stems, really ample blossoms of a clear color. Each blossom is edged with short, bristly hairs, hence the specific name. In Japan, which is the center of its native distribution, many forms have been selected. Like most of the fussier bellflowers, it demands, for optimum vigor and longevity, a fairly rich neutral soil with plenty of drainage, enough sun to encourage bloom, and an absence of any blistering, baked aspect.

C. piperi restricts itself in nature to the mountain screes and tight fissures of the Olympic Mountains of the State of Washington, where it finds special conditions seemingly difficult to reproduce under cultivation: a hard, rocky root-run with considerable moisture about the roots during the growing season and a rather steadily cold and dry condition during the winter. The alpine-house is excellent for its winter requirements of dry cold, but *C. piperi* needs moving water about the roots as the season advances, a demand hard to meet in this artificial location. This requirement called for during active growth and the plant's great resentment of stagnant moisture would suggest the under-watered moraine as a satisfactory location—and it is in spring. The plant breaks into new rosettes along the thin procumbent stems, and buds form. Then in July, just as they should break into a shower of wide-open stars of clear deep lavender, come a few days of torrid, muggy weather and the whole plant—bud, leaf, and aboveground stem—turns to a limp, sodden ghost. Eastern growers may do well to search for the surest clue to success with this attractive campanula, as well as with other challenging Westerners.

C. raineri is a name more honored in the breach than the observance. From time to time it turns up in catalogues of plants and lists of seeds; but, alas, it always seems to develop as a form of *C. carpatica*. The true plant is, to be sure, on the order of an etherealized *C. carpatica* with large, satiny, upfacing bells on very short stems, above a creeping mat of hairy gray-green leaves. In the limestone mountains of its limited distribution near Bergamo, Italy, it laces the narrow cracks in sunny sites. The plant may be increased by careful early-season division and then treated as a cutting before being placed in a limestone crevice or in a limestone scree. Seed called *C. raineri* is likely to provide some trim hybrids with probably some genes from the true plant.

By selection and vegetative propagation a race of worthwhile garden bellflowers has evolved. Hybrids among the dwarf species have been made from time to time and are occasionally offered in the trade. Vegetative propagation by cuttings or division are, of course, the only means of getting plants true to the original hybrid type. The requirements for growing these hybrids can be devised through consideration of the parents. A good many tend to have a lighter and frequently yellowish foliage. Hybrids with *C. carpatica* tend to be dominated by that species. A few easy and desirable ones are *C.* × *stansfieldii, C.* × *wockii,* and *C.* 'Mrs. G. F. Wilson.'

CAREX (Cyperaceae)

The large plantain-leaved sedge *C. fraseri,* of the southern Appalachian Mountains, is the best of the genus, producing large evergreen leaves and in early spring a flowering spike of white and gold fringe. Grown in clumps among other woodland plants in rich soil, it is excellent all year. Large plants may be divided. Other sedges, though widely scattered in alpine situations around the world and a pleasing constituent of most alpine turf in nature, are to be banned from the rock garden as too aggresive.

CASSIOPE (Ericaceae)

All the dwarf heathlike cassiopes would be perfect shrubs for the acid rock garden if only they were easy to grow. They demand ample moisture and an exposure away from the sun but not too closely overhung. A north slope is perhaps best. The soil should be peaty, with enough grit or sand to give body and drainage. All species are enchanting and to be sought after.

C. fastigiata and *C. salaginoides,* both from the Himalayas, are advisedly grown in the alpine-house, unless a good snow cover can be assured in winter. Mosslike *C. hypnoides,* lovely as it is, is rather slow-growing and rather temperamental. The easiest, if given acid soil and shade, is *C. lycopodioides,* from Siberia and Alaska. This, as the name suggests, looks like a tight mound of ground pine with the diminutive white lantern-like blossoms on thin reddish stems shooting out from the small leaves along the whipcord stems.

C. mertensiana, C. stelleriana, and *C. tetragona* are more erect and grow to 1 foot. All are similar in appearance and from the general region of the northwestern mountains of the United States, including Alaska. To see these plants in the wild forming mounds and sheets of healthy green growth, hung with the glistening white bells, makes one think that they must be as simple to grow as heaths and heathers. And they probably would be if we had in our gardens thin, cool air, underground moisture, a constant refreshing breeze, and only a brief bright-season free of the blanket of snow. All we can do is to approach these ingredients and rely on the universal adaptability of plants and their urgency to grow. Cuttings taken in late summer and early autumn will root in an acid cutting bed. Carefully made layered divisions should be treated like cuttings.

CASTILLEJA (Scrophulariaceae)

The brilliant Indian paintbrushes of the western hills and mountains of the United States are well known to every visitor to the great National Parks of the region. The reds and oranges and yellows literally paint the rockslides and flowery hillsides with splashes of far-carrying color. But futile it is to dig and transplant them to the garden. Authorities in such matters accuse the castillejas of being parasitic on the roots of other plants. Some species have been brought to flower when grown from seed, and an adventurous gardener may someday find the secret of how these gorgeous flowers can be brought into cultivation. Botanists have classified many species but have not suggested one that can assuredly be grown in the garden, including the chief eastern species, *C. coccinea.* When seed of any species is available, sow it on a rocky slope, particularly among other existing plants.

CAULOPHYLLUM (Berberidaceae)

C. thalictroides, Blue Cohosh, is an excellent plant for the woods garden. The uncurling rue-like leaves glow with reddish purple, and the clusters of yellowish-green flowers come early on top of the forking branches of the 1- to 2-foot plant. It is the long-lasting, blue, berrylike fruits, however, that are its chief glory. A group of Blue Cohosh planted in rich, woodsy soil in fairly dense shade display their beauty for a long season. Root-cuttings are the quickest means of increase, though seed planted in the fall and permitted to freeze will give some germination the first spring and another crop of seedlings the following year.

CEANOTHUS (Rhamnaceae)

This is a large genus of North American shrubs mostly too large and too tender for use in the rock garden. However, two species, *C. prostratus* and *C. pumilus* (both known as Mahala Mat), make prostrate shrubby carpets densely clothed with coarsely-toothed evergreen leaves. They deck the ends of the branches with rounded clusters of small blue flowers like miniature lilac blossoms. These creeping ceanothus should be transplanted when young, grown from cuttings, and well watered when first set out, preferably on a slope with well-drained soil in full sun or part shade. A north slope is best. *C. americanus* is a useful low deciduous shrub of neat habit with small but showy white blossom spikes. This eastern American, known as New Jersey Tea, thoroughly hardy in well-drained soil in sun or light shade, is most likely to succeed in acid soil.

CELMISIA (Compositae)

These white-flowered daisies from Australia and New Zealand occur more frequently in rock garden literature than in rock gardens. Some of the high-mountain species with silvery foliage and short-stemmed blossoms are good rock garden plants, hard to aquire and as hard to keep. Only fresh seed germinates and this is difficult to come by. Like most plants from Down Under they want an acid, moist but well-drained soil in partial shade. *C. bellidioides* is an easy and reliable species, forming a shining mat that can be divided for increase.

CENTAUREA (Compositae)

This genus is principally for the border and annual bed. Occasionally offered are some of the dwarf silver-leaved species, mostly with shaggy bachelor's button flowers on short stems. These hail from both sides of the Mediterranean, mainly from hot sunny sites in the mountains. Given a similar situation, plants raised from seed, which is sometimes available, are worth growing for their silvery foliage and summer bloom. Desirable species include *C. depressa, C. leucophylla,* and *C. simplicicaulis.*

CENTAURIUM (Gentianaceae)

These dwarf pink relatives of the gentians are sometimes listed under *Erythraea.* Though not reliably perennial, once a group of the charming small plants are established from seed in a moist sandy soil, they will persist by self-sowing and carry the bright pink blooms on 3-inch stems for a long period in summer. Most frequently available are seeds of *C. chloodes, C. diffusum,* and *C. pulchellum.*

CERASTIUM (Caryophyllaceae)

Many beginning rock gardeners are tempted by the fine gray foliage and sheets of white bloom of *C. tomentosum,* the Snow-in-summer, but they regret eventually its introduction into the garden. It is so invasive and persistent, once established, that it is almost impossible to eradicate. *C. alpinum lanatum* is, however, a restrained and suitable little chickweed with intensely woolly leaves and short-stemmed white flowers. It resents muggy weather and all excessive dampness on its foliage, but neither will it flourish in a baked site. It does best as a crevice plant in good soil on a north or east slope and in the moraine. Rooted layers may be severed from the plant and established in spring or fall. Equally desirable for their restrained habits are two alpine species, *C. latifolium* and *C. uniflorum.*

CERATOSTIGMA (Plumbaginaceae)

C. plumbaginoides (also known as *Plumbago larpentae*) is desirable both for the clear azure-blue of its flowers and for its late blooming period in September and October when its leaves are tinged with red. It creeps slowly at the root, sending up diffuse stems of about 1 foot. The clumps are easy to divide, preferably in the spring as growth commences. It will grow in any well-drained good soil in an open site, and will likewise endure considerable shade.

CHAENACTIS (Compositae)

Of the many species in the western American mountains and dry plains the majority are annual. Perhaps the most desirable of the perennial species is *C. alpina*, a scree plant at high elevations, with large clear-pink heads composed of small ray flowers on 4-inch stems among ferny gray leaves. Also good though less refined is *C. douglassii.* Increase these by seed or division.

CHAMAECYPARIS (Cupressaceae)

Among the various species of the false cypress are to be found some of the best dwarf evergreen trees for the rock garden. Names in the catalogues tend to become interchanged and mixed. You might buy two quite different plants under the same name or the same plant under two different names. Some of the best are: (1) *C. lawsoniana*—var. *ellwoodii compacta,* a narrow column of blue-green, var. *forsteckensis,* a very tight, dark green mound, var. *nestoides,* a low, spreading shrub; (2) *C. obtusa*—var. *gracilis nana,* an erect but irregular bush, var. *minima glauca,* a rounded mound of dark green; and (3) *C. pisifera*—var. *plumosa minima,* a flat, fine-leaved, low mound, var. *squarrosa pygmaea,* a blue-green, feathery mound, var. *squarrosa pygmaea aurea,* a mound with golden tips to the foliage. Since so many others are available, it is best to pick out the plant yourself at a reliable nursery. They are easy to grow in any not too limy, good soil. Propagation is by cuttings of half-ripened wood in fall, or occasionally by layering.

CHAMAEDAPHNE (Ericaceae)

C. calyculata var. *nana* in nature is a dense dwarf shrub that makes great thickets in acid, sunny bogs. The leaves are small and leathery, evergreen but more brown than green. Near the tips of the arching shoots are hung small white lantern-like blossoms very early in the spring. It is a good shrub for acid soil in the heath garden or dwarf-rhododendron thicket and does not require bog conditions in the garden. Cuttings provide the best method of increase. Seed germinates well but plants are slow-growing.

CHAMAELIRIUM (Liliaceae)

C. luteum, the Devil's-bit, is an uncommon native plant of the American Northeast with shining green lily-like leaves at the base of a foot-high stem that carries a dense spike of white flowers in a wand. This forest plant should be grown in good leaf-moldy soil. Seed is the only satisfactory means of increase.

CHELONE (Scrophulariaceae)

The American turtleheads with penstemon-like flowers are plants of swamps and moist woods. *C. glabra* has showy white flowers in a spike at the top of the 2- to 3-foot leafy stems. In *C. lyonii* the flowers are a clear pink. Planted in good soil in light shade, these plants do not demand a swamp. Propagate them by seed or division.

CHIASTOPHYLLUM. See *Cotyledon.*

CHIMAPHILA (Pyrolaceae)

The two species of the eastern American pipsissewa, *C. maculata* and *C. umbellata,* have been somewhat ignored as excellent subjects for the shady garden. From evergreen tufts of holly-like leaves (marked with a varied pattern of white in *C. maculata* and solid green in *C. umbellata*) rise stiff 5- to 6-inch stems, from which hang good-sized waxy white flowers. The westerner of the genus, *C. menziesii*, with either solid green or spotted foliage, has reddish stems and generally pink flowers. They occur in scattered colonies, usually in acid, sandy sites, where beneath oaks or conifers a good duff has accumulated. They increase slowly by underground stolons that are very lightly anchored by only a few fine roots. Collected plants are not easy to establish unless treated like cuttings in the sand frame or in pots to stimulate new root action. Careful division is a possible method of increase. These operations are to be done only in early spring.

CHIOGENES. See *Gaultheria.*

CHIONODOXA (Liliaceae)

These early-flowering bulbs with short racemes of large upfacing flowers of purest blue look best planted in drifts in the alpine lawn or along paths in the woodland garden. Plant the bulbs about 3 inches deep and very close together. *C. luciliae*, the principal species, is offered by bulb growers in a variety of forms.

CHRYSANTHEMUM (Compositae)

The common white Field Daisy has a high-mountain dwarf counterpart in *C. alpinum*. The leaves are finely cut and silver-frosted, a perfect foil for the short-stemmed and neatly proportioned glistening-white daisies with golden disks. Like many of the dwellers in the lofty places, *C. alpinum* languishes in hot, muggy weather, especially as it grows older. Young yearling plants, which self-sow sparingly around the older clumps, seem to endure the adverse conditions and will flower the following year before the heat of midsummer. Young and old have a tendency for a second burst of bloom in late summer. A rich scree in full sun and with good air circulation offers the best chance for a long life and abundant flowering. Seed sown as soon as ripe will give good germination and supply plants large enough to flower the following summer.

CHRYSOGONUM (Compositae)

C. virginianum is an accommodating and cheerful native of the eastern United States. In either light shade or sun, it produces a constant display of bright yellow daisies, starry in effect because the rays are broad and widely separated. They bloom at the tips of stiff branches that splay out just above the low clump of dark green, somewhat coarse leaves. When the cluster increases, it can be propagated easily by dividing the clump into as many pieces as have rooted down. It will grow in almost any soil or site that is not very dry or very moist.

CHRYSOPSIS (Compositae)

These late-flowering golden asters are not as generally grown as their merits deserve. The common species from the eastern United States, *C. falcata, C. mariana,* and *C. villosa* are coastal, in acid, sandy soil, but do perfectly well transferred to the rock garden in ordinary soil. *C. falcata* is perhaps the handsomest, with dark basal leaves copiously matted with long gray hairs. The flower stem is about 1 foot tall and stout and stiff, with a flat cluster of golden daisies in late August and September. *C. mariana* is like a husky form of *C. villosa,* with larger blossoms on the tips of the 1- to 2-foot stems. It has a long season of bloom from midsummer to early fall. *C. villosa* is the least attractive, with thinner leaves and smaller blossoms. A fine western form of *C. villosa* is var. **prostrata,** which sprawls in a low mound and flowers from June to September. All are easy to raise from fresh seed, or may be divided early in the season.

CIMICIFUGA (Ranunculaceae)

The large bugbanes are stalwart accent-plants for the woods garden. In rich soil, **C. americana** produces large compound leaves and racemes of white blossoms in summer on 5-foot plants. *C. racemosa* is the same but larger in all its parts, reaching a height of 8 feet, and blooming somewhat earlier. **C. simplex** reaches only 3 feet and produces its handsome white wands of flowers in late autumn. Propagate these by seed or by division in the early spring.

CLADOTHAMNUS (Ericaceae)

A deciduous ericaceous shrub to plant among rhododendrons and azaleas is *C. pyrolaeflorus* of the far American Northwest. The solitary pink flowers, in June, are about 1 inch across, on twiggy tips of the 3- to 5-foot shrub. Propagate this by seed or summer cuttings.

CLAYTONIA (Portulacaceae)

The spring-beauties of the eastern woods of the United States are best grown in large groups, where the delicate pink-striped white blossoms are delightful in early spring. The two eastern species are very similar. *C. caroliniana* has shorter, broader leaves and blooms a week or two earlier than *C. virginica*, which is distinguished by very long narrow leaves; these are fleshy in both species. After the flowering the foliage yellows and withers; so it is wise to plant claytonias with such companions as hepaticas, Maidenhair Fern, and others that delight to grow in the rich duff of deciduous woods.

Some western American claytonias, like alpine *C. nivalis* and *C. megarrhiza*, do not have the hard underground corm or tuber of the eastern species, though the general effect is rather similar. These westerners are more difficult to grow in the East, calling for good scree conditions with a northern exposure not overhung by trees. *C. megarrhiza* is unique in that it appears to be larger and more vigorous the higher it grows in its rocky haunts in the western ranges. Other westerners are very like the eastern species. Where happy, claytonias will self-sow. Some western species of *Claytonia* are described under *Montia*.

CLEMATIS (Ranunculaceae)

There is no room for the great vines of most clematis in the rock garden, though some clambering over stumps, bushes, or trees in the wild woods garden are very effective. For open sites, especially among large rocks, are some bushy clematis. *C. alpina* (frequently listed under *Atragene*) may climb in time to 6 feet, but is generally a bushy shrub with nodding violet-blue flowers 1½ inches long. Very similar is *C. pseudoalpina* of the western United States, though with larger, more open blossoms. More like a western pulsatilla in foliage and in fluffy seedhead is *C. douglasii,* called Old-maid's Bonnet, with nodding purple flowers. Not easily transplanted, but successful from slowly germinating seed, all of these will do better if not in direct sun, and planted among low shrubs over which to climb.

CLINTONIA (Liliaceae)

The cool, moist woods of North America, both East and West, are the home of the clintonias. They will increase by underground stolons and have broad shiny basal leaves that declare their membership in the lily tribe. Often great patches of these leaves, handsome as ground cover, are to be found without flowers. The flowers are handsome and the berrylike fruit is brilliant. All may be increased by division in early spring, or be grown from seed. They need a moist, acid soil in rather dense shade. If fed some dry manure and bone meal mixed with leaf mold, they are more likely to flower.

C. borealis has an umbel of yellow flowers followed by bright blue berries on 1- to 1½-foot stems. *C. umbellata* is similar but has white flowers and black berries. *C. uniflora,* from the deep woods of the Northwest, is shorter in stem, with larger pure-white flowers, 1 or 2 to the stem, and Prussian-blue berries. *C. andrewsiana,* from among the Redwoods of northern California, is the giant of the genus, with larger leaves, somewhat taller stems of pink, nodding lily-like flowers, and blue berries also. It is not reliably hardy northward.

CODONOPSIS (Campanulaceae)

These campanula relatives have intricately patterned and varicolored hanging bells. All come from the mountains of Central Asia, some growing in brushy sites where the flower stems elongate and twine for support. They grow from a fairly stout white carrot-like root, difficult to transplant when large. Unless covered with snow, most are sensitive to extreme cold. They are best grown on a raised bed of good soil out of the full glare of the sun or among low shrubs to support the long, otherwise procumbent stems. Seed is abundant and easily grown. Most have a strong skunky smell. *C. clematidea* has flowers of pale blue with maroon and orange markings on erect 12-inch stems. *C. meleagris* has stems up to 2 feet which flop or clamber according to the support; the terminal flowers are yellowish lanterns with purple spots and veins. About 40 species have been named, but many are similar or very rare.

COGSWELLIA. See *Lomatium.*

COLCHICUM (Liliaceae)

The autumn crocuses are ideal for planting in the alpine lawn or among low ground covers in the woods garden. In both sites the blossoms will have a foil of foliage they otherwise lack at blossoming time, having produced them in spring along with the conspicuous seed capsules of the previous year; these yellow and die as summer advances. There are many species of fall bloomers, large ones to 5 inches across and smaller ones of crocus-size. Most bulb catalogues list these. There are a few less well known spring-blooming species. All want good soil and are to be planted shallowly. The bulb clumps are best divided and replanted when the foliage withers in summer. Colchicums come in lavender and white.

COLLOMIA (Polemoniaceae)

This genus, related to *Polemonium,* contains mostly annual species. In the talus slopes and rockslides of the Cascade and Rocky Mountains of the American West are *C. debilis* and two sub-species—all perennial—which produce heads of small tubular flowers of white, pink, or blue on clustered, flopping stems that vary in length according to the site. These should be grown from seed or by division, among the rocks of the scree or rocky pasture, or on the face of the planted wall or raised bed.

CONANDRON (Gesneriaceae)

A rare and enchanting relative of the African Violet and ramondas is **C. ramondioides.** Crinkly light green leaves erupt in early spring from a tight resting-bud densely covered with brown fur in winter. In summer comes a succession of short-stemmed lavender flowers with orange eyes, quite like those of the African Violet. A pure-white form is known. This is a difficult plant from the rocky hills of Japan. It must be grown in a sheltered pocket among rocks in full shade, preferably near the foot of a slope or wall where moisture is assured and where snow may pile over the crown in winter. Late frost may nip the first leaves. It is advisable to grow it from seed, though careful division of large plants is possible. Seed should be sown very thinly in a fairly peaty mixture and never permitted to dry out (best watered by plunging), and the seedlings left until they reach a good size before transplanting.

COPROSMA (Rubiaceae)

There are many species of this shrubby genus from New Zealand, many large, none showy in flower, but valued for their handsome berries. The only one suitable to the rock garden is **C. petriei,** which makes a creeping mat of stems clothed in small hairy leaves with minute white solitary flowers at the tips of the branches. The half-inch, bloomy, blue fruit is handsome. This should be grown in peaty, acid soil, as in the heath bed, and is best in the alpine-house northward. Propagate it by cuttings.

COPTIS (Ranunculaceae)

The goldthreads, so named for the brilliant golden, running, underground stolons, are excellent dainty ground covers for shady moist sites. The small white flowers, like miniature buttercups, stand on short wiry stems above the dark shiny-green scalloped leaves. The spreading mats are easily divided for increase and need ample water until well established in rich, woodsy soil. *C. aspleni-folia,* from the Cascades of northwestern America, has lacy, finely cut foliage; *C. laciniata* and *C. occidentalis,* also western American, are more robust, with larger leaves on stems of about 4 inches and somewhat larger lacy flowers; *C. trifolia* is the eastern forest-dweller of neat and sturdy habit.

COREMA (Empetraceae)

C. conradii, the Broom-crowberry, is a heather-like shrub useful for its evergreen needled foliage and its neat, compact habit. The early-season blooms, in dense terminal heads, are inconspicuous, either pistillate or staminate and without petals and sepals. The plant is found—but never commonly—in either rocky or sandy acid sites near the East Coast of the United States. It will grow where heaths and heathers flourish but is not as easily propagated from cuttings; nor is it so showy in flower. It is rather like *Empe-trum* in appearance, without the berrylike fruit. Layering is the most successful method of increase.

CORNUS (Cornaceae)

C. canadensis, Bunchberry, is a diminutive relative of the Flower-ing Dogwood and, like it, a native American. On mats of whorled leaves, which turn fine colors in autumn, sit dogwood blossoms of 4 pure-white bracts beneath the cluster of tiny yellow flowers. In its northern haunts, in deep, moist, acid woods or in more sunny situations as it moves into Canada, the blossom cluster elongates above its 4- to 6-inch stem to produce in late summer a bunch of brilliant, gleaming red berries. In its southern reaches it neither blooms so well nor fruits so efficiently. Give it acid soil, never dry, with as much light as is consistent with moisture. There, if it can be established at all, it will spread by underground stolons into a magnificent carpet. Divisions of established plants are possible—but difficult. Seed sown in fall will provide young plants that will grow through the following summer for setting in permanent sites the following fall or spring, when they will settle down far more easily than older divisions or collected plants.

CORONILLA (Leguminosae)

The crown-vetches provide a long season of summer bloom with pea blossoms in crownlike heads, mostly in shades of yellow. They want well-drained limy soil in full sun. Seed is the easiest method of increase; seedlings should be set out when young where they are to grow, since the roots become deep and carrot-like. *C. cappadocica* is a procumbent, glaucous plant with summer-long golden blossoms on stems up to 12 inches long; its var. *balansae* is particularly trim and dwarf. *C. minima* is rather prostrate, with small blue-gray leaflets and pale flower heads. *C. vaginalis* is a stronger, better *C. minima* with more and brighter flower heads. Beware of *C. varia,* pretty as it is with its rambling 2-foot stems and pinkish-white flower clusters: except on the most remote and driest sites, it will overrun everything in sight and will resist eradication just as a bad habit does.

CORTUSA (Primulaceae)

C. matthiolii is an enchanting primrose relative for shaded soil rich with leaf mold, where the plants fatten in time to neat clumps of downy geranium-like leaves. In June, on about 6-inch stems above the clusters of foliage, dances a shower of hanging bells, somewhat jagged at the tips; the color is a clean rosy purple, sometimes enhanced by a winsome white. This plant is no more difficult to grow from seed than *Primula acaulis,* and the clumps may be divided as they increase, or the heavy late-summer roots may be treated as root-cuttings. The whole plant dies down to an underground resting-bud in late summer.

CORYDALIS (Papaveraceae)

There are many species of *Corydalis,* suitable for many different sites. Most have fine-cut foliage of soft blue-green and spikes of blossoms somewhat suggesting narrowed bleeding-hearts. Blossom color varies from white through yellow to pink and blue. There are literally hundreds of excellent species, especially in Asia, though many have not been brought successfully into cultivation; whenever seed of any corydalis is available, it will be no mistake to experiment. All species are to be propagated by seed, which is frequently slow to germinate unless fresh. All grow best in light shade.

C. cashmeriana is a most cherished species from the Himalayas, of finest fernlike foliage and brilliant blue blossoms; it is for a rich scree in a cool site, and probably is successfully grown only in the alpine-house. *C. bulbosa* (also known as *C. halleri* or *C. solida*) grows from a tuber. In early spring, in either full sun or part shade, come full spikes of rosy-purple flowers above a cluster of blunt, much-divided foliage. The tubers increase rapidly and may be separated after the foliage dies down in summer. *C. lutea* is almost everblooming in rocky sites in either shade or part sun. The bright yellow flowers arch above the ferny green foliage and ripen and scatter their seeds throughout the summer. Though this species is invasive by self-sowing, young plants are lightly anchored and easily can be twitched out; or these may be transplanted, although even young plants do not establish easily. The species is best propagated by sowing the seed where the plants are to grow, but patience is necessary since seed usually takes two years to germinate.

C. nobilis is indeed a noble plant, rising from a husky tuber that should be inserted about 2 inches deep in good humus-rich soil in shade. The substantial cut foliage of vivid green provides a handsome base for the 10- to 12-inch stalks, which carry a dense spike of 10 to 20 large yellow-tipped white blossoms spotted with purple-brown. *C. sempervirens* is a delicate annual or biennial native that, when established in the garden by seed, will maintain itself by self-sowing. It will grow in very poor, thin soil and in full sun, but develops huskier plants with more copious tubular flowers of pink-tipped yellow in richer soil and in part shade. *C. wilsonii* is a dwarf plant with blue-green leafage and bright yellow flowers for a sheltered spot in a rich scree mixture.

COTONEASTER (Rosaceae)

The dwarf and creeping cotoneasters, with small rose-like flowers and bright berries and generally evergreen leaves, are excellent shrubs for the rock garden. They flower and fruit better in full sun, though they will succeed in quite dense shade, and seem quite indifferent to soil. None are easy to transplant except from pots or other containers or when rather young; early spring planting is most successful. All come rather easily from cuttings of young ripened shoot-wood, and usually layer themselves. The seed is slow to sprout, sometimes lingering in the seedbed two years before germinating.

C. adpressa is a prostrate species, which in time will make sizable low mounds. It loses its leaves in winter but not before assuming lovely autumn colors to accompany the bright red berries. *C. congesta* is sometimes listed as *C. microphylla* var. *glacialis,* to which species it is quite similar. It is evergreen and compact, occasionally dying-back at the shoots when not covered with snow during a severe winter. *C. dammeri* (sometimes listed as *C. humifusa*) runs flat along the ground, rooting as it runs. In exposed sites the thick, round evergreen leaves may brown in winter. The fruit is abundant, large, and a shining red. Rooted layers may be severed and potted for increase.

C. horizontalis, evergreen in favored locations, has a distinctive fishbone arrangement of branchlets along the main stems, which naturally espalier themselves against a wall or rock. Var. *perpusilla* is to be sought for the rock garden proper because of its less vigorous and neater growth. *C. microphylla,* with small lustrous leaves, will make an erect spreading shrub up to 3 feet. Growth above the snow is frequently damaged, though the plant is root-hardy. Var. *cochleata,* which is almost prostrate and is tighter, has the same shiny leaves and excellent scarlet berries. Even smaller and twiggier and very slow-growing is var. *thymifolia.* Forms of dwarf cotoneaster, perhaps of hybrid origin, are offered by nurserymen under the names 'Cooperi' and 'Little Gem.'

COTULA (Compositae)

C. squalida is an invasive carpeter that makes a solid turf of flat, dark green, fernlike foliage, turning bronzy in autumn and brown in winter. The flowers are infinitesimal and inconspicuous. If placed between stones in a paving, or as a ground cover among shrubs, beneath which bulbs may be planted, this plant is a useful thing. Division is simple and spread is rapid, and it will hence make a solid turf in the alpine lawn. Since it comes from New Zealand, the tops may kill back in a severe winter, but the roots persist and soon renew the foliage, especially in shady areas.

COTYLEDON (Crassulaceae)

These are succulent plants distributed by some botanists among other genera. Most are not hardy. The two hardy ones listed below are sometimes classified under *Umbilicus* or *Chiastophyllum.* *C. chrysantha* is like a soft, downy sempervivum with 4-inch stems carrying light yellow flowers above the globular clusters of foliage. Increase this as you would sempervivum—by division—and grow in sites where hens-and-chicks thrive. *C. oppositifolia* (also called *C. simplicifolia*) is quite different. The basal foliage is smooth and succulent, rather like the leaves of a large sedum. The golden flowers are in dangling chains on 4- to 6-inch stems. This species requires good drainage and shade and is best grown in a shady wall. It is not ironclad in hardiness, but charming and different, and easily grown from seed, cuttings, or division. *C. spinosa* is described under *Sedum.*

CRASSULA (Crassulaceae)

C. sediformis (also called *C. milfordiae*), the only hardy species, makes a neat, compact carpet of small, rather succulent rosettes, which take on rich bronze color in autumn. Just above the mat in summer sit the numerous small white flowers on short red stems. Though native to Basutoland, this plant survives under snow cover or with light protection. Grow it in partial shade in good, well-drained soil. It makes a pretty alpine-house plant and can be multiplied by division of the clump.

CROCUS (Iridaceae)

Though the fat hybrid Dutch crocuses in all their splendor are those most commonly seen in beds and borders and grass patches, it is the hundreds of species crocus, from *C. aerius* to *C. zonatus,* that offer the rock gardener bulbous plants to use lavishly in all the sunny sections of the garden. There are species to open the flowering season in spring and to close it in autumn. Any good catalogue of bulbs will offer a wide choice of species. Plant the bulbs in generous patches in good, well-drained soil, 2 to 3 inches deep. The alpine lawn offers the best site for tucking them beneath ground covers, creeping junipers, and among the taller perennials. In the rock garden proper they never interfere with even delicate bun-plants and may be safely and lavishly scattered. Grown under turf they are more likely to escape the depredations of chipmunks, which are excessively fond of the corms. To acquire an ample supply of some of the rarer species, grow them from seed. If the seed is sown in a special frame or in large pots or flats, the bulbs may be left to enlarge for two growing seasons and set out to begin flowering the third.

CRUCIANELLA (Rubiaceae)

C. stylosa (frequently put in the genus *Phuopsis*) rapidly—too rapidly for restricted areas—makes a solid mat like a prostrate bedstraw with showy, summer-blooming, deep rose flowers in globose heads. Easy to increase by seed or division, it will grow in sun or shade. Its one and most positive drawback is the strong skunky smell.

CRYPTOMERIA (Taxodiaceae)

The tall, handsome Japanese evergreen, *C. japonica,* has a few dwarf forms admirably suited to the rock garden. They make a dense, prickly mound of dark green short needles. Where winter temperatures go below zero the tree may brown badly or be killed if grown in full sun. A blanket of snow or some other form of protection and a position shaded from winter sun and wind will bring it safely through. It will grow in any soil and can be propagated from soft-wood cuttings.

CUTHBERTIA. See *Tradescantia.*

CYANANTHUS (Campanulaceae)

These Asiatic relatives of the campanulas bear large upfacing blooms of clear blue at the ends of trailing stems. The alternate leaves are very trim and small. It is difficult to find for them the right site and soil where they will have sun enough to produce their late-summer blooms and yet coolness enough to keep them happily growing. Since they die-back to a winter resting-root, they are hardy when once established but frequently grow so poorly that they lose vigor and perish. An acid soil composed of coarse sand and humus in light shade is the most likely prescription for success. Though many species have recently been introduced, those most commonly offered and probably most likely to succeed are: *C. integer,* which makes a close-growing mat of rather fine uncut leaves and clear-blue salver-shaped blossoms with conspicuous white hairs in the throat; *C. lobatus,* with larger leaves, divided into lobes, and large lavender-blue flowers, especially ample in var. *insignis;* and *C. microphyllus,* distinguished by very small leaves and purple-blue flowers. The seed is fine but not difficult to handle after the manner of the finer campanulas. Summer-cuttings root readily.

CYCLAMEN (Primulaceae)

If we could grow in the garden all the Mediterranean species of these charming, dwarf, cormous plants, we would have an almost year-round display of the pink and white butterfly-like blossoms. Except in favored sites or in the alpine-house—where all species are superb—only two are reliably hardy north of New Jersey. *C. europaeum* makes an almost evergreen cluster of beautiful leaves close to the ground. These are somewhat round and lightly marbled, the upper surface a deep green and the undersurface purple, with holly-like points set irregularly around the edge. Rising just above the foliage, from July or August right up to frost, is a succession of bright crimson and utterly charming blossoms. After the flowering period, the fat seed capsules are slowly brought to earth by a spiral coiling of the flower stems. Plant the corm so that the top (the flat, slightly hollowed side) is 2 to 3 inches below the surface of the soil. *C. neapolitanum* is rather similar, though here the leaves are longer and more ivy-shaped, with more conspicuous splashing and marbling. Leaves and flowers appear together in September and October. The flowers are pink with a central zone of red or, in var. *album,* with purest white blossoms. Plant this shallowly, but protect against chipmunks. *C. coum,* a late fall and early winter bloomer, is fairly hardy around New York City and south. This and other species may be tried where winter temperatures do not go below 10°F.

The only assured way to propagate cyclamen is from seed; these will produce a few flowers the second year after germination, almost as fast as from the purchased dried corms, which are slow to establish. The corms are long-lived, increasing year by year in girth and flower production. Once they have reached good size rodents seem to ignore them, but one- or two-year-old corms will attract mice and chipmunks and be devoured greedily. Seed, which will not ripen until the summer after the blooming period, should be sown on top of good leaf-mold-rich soil and covered with fine gravel. If the seed is sown thinly the plants should be left growing for two years, protected against mice and heavy freezing the first year. The second year they may be set out in groups in a shady or semishady well-drained but leaf-mold-rich soil. Limestone grit mixed with the soil is of distinct benefit and appears to stimulate flowering. An annual feeding of dried manure and bone meal mixed with leaf mold is a fine tonic. Established plants will begin to self-sow and the tiny seedlings may be lifted and grown-on for later establishment.

CYMBALARIA. See *Linaria.*

CYMOPTERUS (Umbelliferae)

Not often seen in gardens, these western American umbellifers are among the showiest of the family. The basal leaves are much divided and pleasantly dusty-looking. On very short stems, the dense umbels are variously colored. Because, as with most of the Carrot Family, the roots are stout and long, these should be grown from seed and planted in deep, well-drained soil in full sun, such as in the alpine lawn or rocky pasture. Good species to search for are *C. acaulis, C. alpinus, C. bipinnatus,* and *C. utahensis.* There are many many more worth growing to bring summer bloom. Watch for these in seed lists.

CYNOGLOSSUM (Boraginaceae)

Because of its forget-me-not-like blossoms and striking large hairy leaves, *C. grande,* a native of the forests of the American Pacific Coast, deserves a place in the woodland garden. Propagate this by seed.

CYPRIPEDIUM (Orchidaceae)

The hardy lady's-slipper orchids demand rather special conditions, but repay the extra care necessary because of their long-lasting and exotically beautiful blossoms. Where they will grow in the wild, they are likely to be abundant, but to provide identical conditions in the garden is not at all easy. There are no secret formulas for success. If, however, you attempt to reproduce natural conditions, the chances of succeeding are greater and may even exceed your expectations. One of the essential conditions may be a soil bacteria, which you might already have in your soil or might by chance import with the plant and establish as a root companion for the orchid. The need for this has been suggested but not proved. All species have been successfully grown in gardens, a particular garden apparently suiting one species better than others. It is well to start conservatively with a single plant or two before venturing on great beds of lady's-slippers. Correct planting is essential. The growing point of the crown wants to be just below the surface, upon which a leaf or pine-needle mulch should be maintained.

C. acaule, which lifts its solitary large pink slipper on a 10- to 12-inch scape above the 2 large ribbed basal leaves, is hardest to please. In the wild it grows in acid woods of oak or pine, in soil generally rather sandy and well drained. It is occasionally found on hummocks in swampy ground. No secrets have yet been divulged which absolutely assure that it can be kept growing for more than a year or two, though it definitely is long-lived in nature.

C. calceolus var. *pubescens,* the Yellow Lady's-slipper, is in all ways an easier plant to please. It will even grow in ordinary rich garden soil if given some shade, but it thrives best in a neutral or even limy leaf-mold-rich mixture. Year by year the clump of 12- to 18-inch leafy stems increases in size; the stems carry single or sometimes twin blooms with a waxen pouch of gold and long, twisting, brown petal segments. When the foliage has died down in the fall, or in very early spring before growth commences, the clump can be lifted and each crown, with its attached fleshy roots, gently teased from the general mat and replanted immediately.

C. reginae, the queen of the American lady's-slippers, seeks as its home brushy swamps and bogs in areas where the underlying limestone sweetens the acid of the decomposing vegetation. There, on hummocks or about the fringes of the swamp, the stalwart stems, amply furnished with broad ribbed leaves, will carry great pink pouches, backed with crystalline white petals and sepals, up to 3 feet above the wet muck. Success in the garden depends on copious moisture about the roots in rich black soil generally peaty in structure but not acid. The crown does not want to be under water, though it does endure temporary flooding in spring. It starts into growth in May and blooms in July, well after the others.

There are other species of *Cypripedium* both in Asia and America worthy of trial under conditions similar to those given above. Though lady's-slippers frequently set great fat seedpods in cultivation as in the wild, full of thousands of very fine seeds, rarely do we find self-sown seedlings and never can we get them to germinate in any seeding mixture.

CYTISUS (Leguminosae)

The brooms provide dwarf shrubs, both species and hybrids, which flourish in light soils and sunny sites, where they deck themselves in pea blossoms, mostly in shades of yellow and cream. The genus is close to *Genista,* and many of the best dwarf species are frequently listed under that heading. *C. decumbens* makes an arched mound of long stems somewhat pubescent. Along the stems are clusters of small gray-green leaves, and in early summer bright yellow pea blossoms. *C.* × *kewensis* is a hybrid of *C. ardoinii,* which is not very hardy, and is an erect white broom. The hybrid is hardy and very beautiful; it is prostrate, producing in May large clear cream-colored blossoms. It is best planted above a good-sized rock over which the branches can fan out to display the garlands of bloom. All *Cytisus* resent transplanting when mature. Species may be grown from seed and set in position when young. Hybrids must be grown from cuttings, which should be taken early, when the green wood is just beginning to harden. Layers are also possible. Newly formed roots on both layers and cuttings are easily broken.

DABOECIA (Ericaceae)

The Irish Heath, **D. cantabrica,** is a low heathlike shrub with large hanging bells. The foliage instead of being needlelike is small and round, silvered beneath. It is reasonably hardy if covered with snow or given the protection of pine branches. The long season of flower begins in June and continues till frost. Colors range from white through pink to purple. It should be given sun or light shade in acid, peaty soil, handled like other heathers and heaths, and increased by seed or cuttings.

DALIBARDA (Rosaceae)

D. repens is a native of the northeastern United States, where it makes mats of violet-shaped evergreen leaves in rich acid woods. The white, single, rose-like flowers are scattered over the carpet from June to September. The foliage colors attractively in the fall. It is an excellent ground cover among shrubs in the acid peat bed— never invasive but slowly increasing. The clumps can be carefully divided and must be kept well watered until established.

DAPHNE (Thymelaeaceae)

Prescriptions for success with the lovely sweet-scented daphne shrubs vary from grower to grower. Some urge that they do well only when growing among limestone rocks, others say most daphnes are lime-haters and all do well without it. There is fairly general agreement that they want generous amounts of leaf mold mixed in the soil. Most will flourish in full sun, though many grow well in partial shade. Like other temperamental plants, they are best described as doing well in some gardens and failing utterly in others, for no apparent reason. Recent experiments show that the roots of most species are sensitive to cold. A mulch over the roots is important unless plants are growing among rocks where frost does not penetrate deeply.

D. alpina comes from the limestone regions of the southern Alps, where it makes sparse twiggy bushes up to 18 inches high. Clusters of small, starry, fragrant white flowers tip the twigs early in the year before the gray-green leaves have developed. The fruit is a showy red berry, from which new plants may be grown as well as from new-wood cuttings.

D. blagayana sends out prostrate branches from the crown with a foliage cluster of shiny oval leaves at the tips. Among the leaves in early spring appear clusters of large creamy-white flowers, sweetly fragrant. The flower buds are formed in the autumn and may be frozen by zero weather unless protected by snow or pine branches. The long bare woody stems benefit by being buried in stony soil. This induces rooting and also provides a ready means of increase. Rooted layers should be potted up until well established.

D. cneorum, the Garland Flower, is as temperamental as it is charming. In one garden it will spread into great yard-wide mounds smothered in May and June with deliciously scented pink blossoms; in another garden it will languish and depart in conditions that seem identical. Let not the owner of the former become too complacent, though, because next year his stalwart, healthy plants may begin to perish branch by branch. A soil of loam, leaf mold, and lime-stone chips does seem to assure the greatest health. In full sun it stays more compact than in shade and seems less inclined to sickness, once established. Perhaps most important, this daphne deeply resents cutting back, though it does not seem to mind a very conservative removal of material for cuttings. Exposed plants may suffer burning of the foliage in winter, but will generally send out new leaves in late spring; these apparently winter-killed branches should never be cut back until late summer, when it can be ascertained that the wood is really dead. Once established, the Garland Flower should never be dug up and moved. Pot-grown plants are far surer than ones dug from the nursery row. An annual generous dressing of leaf mold and stone chips gently worked around the crown and an inch or two up the bare lower branches will induce new roots and increased vigor. The rooted shoots may be removed and potted in the spring and the blossom heads pinched off. Cuttings of half-ripened wood, without a flower bud at the tip, root readily in a peat-sand mixture.

D. collina is more tender to winter cold than the others listed here. Given a favored site, or in gardens south of New England, it becomes a neat evergreen bush up to 18 inches, with large heads of deep rose, sweet-scented flowers in early summer. Its soil needs are the same as for other sun-loving daphnes. Half-ripened cuttings strike roots easily.

D. genkwa is too tall for the rock garden proper, but at the edge of woods-plantings or as a background for a heather bed the garland of lilac blossoms along the stems makes a sight of delicate beauty in early spring before the leaves emerge. It is not reliably hardy north of New York City, but is worth trying in a sheltered position where the early-breaking buds are protected from winter sun and icy blasts. The thin twigs make poor cutting-wood. Root-cuttings are a possible method of increase.

D. mezereum, though it will grow to 3 feet, brings color so early to the garden that where it can be used in proper scale it should be generously planted. The white-flowered form, which produces yellow berries, is easier to use in color combinations than the rather faded magenta of the species, which has bright red berries. Both forms are very fragrant. As soon as the berries begin to show their red color and sometimes even before, Rose-breasted Grosbeaks come to feast on the pulp and scatter the seeds for distant self-sowing. It has thus naturalized in open woods in some areas. The plant may be increased by summer-cuttings of new wood, or by seed sown as soon as the berries are thoroughly ripe in July or August. This daphne, even more than most, resents root disturbance and should be established young and preferably from pot-grown material. It is also subject to attack by red spider if grown in the sun, or even in shade during a droughty summer.

D. retusa is rather like *D. collina* but seems to be slightly hardier and much slower growing. Small plants with their hard, shiny leaves and ample clusters of purple buds and starry, pink, open flowers, will grace the rock garden for years before they grow out of proportion. Summer-cuttings will root and should be held over and potted in frames or the alpine-house for planting the second spring.

D. 'Somerset,' a hybrid between *D. cneorum* and *D. caucasica,* is also rather large for the rock garden, but is a splendid small shrub up to 3½ feet, with clusters of large, sweet-scented, pale pink blossoms. It thrives more readily in differing sites than do the other daphnes. Propagate this from summer-cuttings.

DARLINGTONIA (Sarraceniaceae)

If you have a bog, plants of this bizarre insectivore, *D. californica,* will make a striking picture as they send up tubular pitcher-leaves with conspicuous white-spotted hoods and 2 forked appendages. The solitary flowers are yellow and brownish red. Increase them by division or seed. They will need some protection in the North and constant moisture all season.

DEINANTHE (Saxifragaceae)

These uncommonly seen Chinese relatives of the hydrangeas are remarkably effective plants in a shady spot in acid soil. From a husky root rises a 1- to 2-foot sheaf of stout deciduous stems that carry 4 large-toothed leaves at the summit. In terminal panicles above them are formed fat round buds that are as handsome as the open blossoms. The flowers are pure white in *D. bifida* and pale violet in *D. caerulea.* The fine seed should be sown thinly and the plants permitted to reach good size before transplanting. They will flower in late summer the third year from seed or may be increased by root-cuttings.

DELPHINIUM (Ranunculaceae)

Among the vast number of dwarf delphiniums suitable for growing in the rock garden, very few have been brought into cultivation. They range the mountain regions around the world in the Northern Hemisphere and deserve the attention they have missed in the shadow of the spectacular border breeds. The lofty mountains of China and India shelter species that have been described in tantalizing terms, and a few have been briefly introduced to cultivation. The mountains of North America, principally in the Far West, offer a wide range of species, many dwarf, early-flowering, and summer-resting in the form of underground tubers. Some of these are short-lived in cultivation, if not in nature, yet many of them, once established, appear to carry on by self-sowing. The Asiatic species call for better soil, more moisture, and, curiously, more sunlight than do the Americans, which want in general a well-drained soil, fairly moist in spring but drying out in summer, and at least half-shade. So little reliable experience with the array of species has been gained in American rock gardens that the best suggestion is to experiment on your own. Whenever seeds are offered of species that are of proper stature, grow a few (they are mostly easy from seed), and try them in various sites. Species of *Delphinium* to be sought out are: from Asia, ***brunonianum, cashmerianum, likiangense, przewalskii, pylzowii, zalil;*** from America, ***andersonii, bicolor, carolinianum, decorum, depauperatum, distichum, geyeri, glareosum, menziesii, nelsonii, nudicaule, nuttallianum, scaposum, tricorne,*** and ***uliginosum.***

DENTARIA (Cruciferae)

It is odd that these spring-blooming crucifers have not been as widely used as their charms would suggest. There are many species in Europe and Asia, none of them commonly offered in the trade. And the same may be said for the American species. The two northeastern natives, **D. diphylla** and **D. laciniata,** are easily grown in the shady garden in rich woodsy soil, where they produce in spring arabis-like clusters of pink-tinged white flowers. They will increase slowly to sizable clumps and are easily divided at any season by breaking up and replanting, just below the surface, the husky but brittle, toothed white rootstocks. They may also be grown from seed. The American West offers other species, some with rose-purple flowers. Desirable species, besides the two mentioned above, are **D.** *digitata,* **D.** *glandulosa,* **D.** *quinquefolia,* and **D.** *tenella.*

Dianthus alpinus
(life size)

DIANTHUS (Caryophyllaceae)

Vast indeed is the number of species of *Dianthus,* and as vast is the general confusion about the names of many of the lesser-known. Among those easily identified and readily available are "pinks" of almost every color and stature, and so extended a blooming season that the rock garden can be daily decked with dianthus from early spring till late summer. Most are lovers of full sun, well-drained soil, and lime, though a few shun the last ingredient—nor do any appear absolutely to demand it. All come easily from seed, though garden-cultivated seed is apt to produce a mongrel lot because the various species interbreed, thanks to every bee that passes. Species may be grown from seed collected in the wild; species or good forms of hybrids may be readily produced from cuttings, some, to be sure, more easily than others.

D. alpinus is in many ways the apotheosis of rock garden dianthus. In June, on short stems and from a close mat of grass-green, broad, short foliage, come large, rounded, flat blossoms of glowing rose-pink, flecked in the center with a ring of crimson. Blossom color may be pure white or a ravishing salmon-pink that in full sun fades to a pearly hue. When grown in well-drained limy soil, not in the hottest sun but with plenty of light, the flowers are so densely provided as to conceal the foliage underneath. Forms with good color and habit should be reproduced by summer cuttings or division of the clump directly after blooming. From garden seed there is likely to be variation in color, foliage, length of stem, and size of blossom because, though *D. alpinus* is a precious aristocrat of the high limestone alps, it will breed in the garden quite indiscriminately. Many of its offspring, however, carry the patrician mark and are quite admissible to the most stuffy conclave of dianthus. An annual topdressing worked down into the foliage clump will prevent dying-out in the center of the cushion, a calamity otherwise rather common.

D. caesius is the famous Cheddar Pink. It is not always easy to come by in the pure state in this country and is sometimes listed as **C. gratianopolitanus.** When true, it forms a dense mound of bluegray grass above which, in June and July, on 6- to 7-inch stems come multitudes of sweet-scented, fringed blossoms of rose-pink. It wants full sun, flourishes in a limy, well-drained mixture, and is admirably adapted to ledges in the rock-garden or to sheeting a planted wall. **D. callizonus** carries flowers rather like those of *D. alpinus* but of a more delicate pink, with a central ring of flecked crimson and white. The foliage is thin and glaucous, the flower stems longer and less rigid than in *D. alpinus*. Though it comes from hot limestone ledges of southeastern Europe, it appreciates light shade here to compensate for the dreadful humidity of summer. It seems utterly hardy to winter cold, but does languish in hot, muggy weather.

D. deltoides, the Maiden Pink, is obligingly easy in almost any spot. Though the type-species is a rather poor magenta, there are many varieties with pleasing colors, from pure white to a real crimson, some flecked and striped. It has smaller flowers than most but is very floriferous. Because the plant spreads rapidly and self-sows generously, it should be kept away from the precious wads and buns. It is a strong competitor and will grow in the midst of *Phlox subulata* and thymes. It is a fine plant for pavements, walls, and the alpine lawn.

D. glacialis is generally a disappointment. The tight foliage clumps of bright, blunt, grassy leaves are very neat, and the blossoms sit above them on short stems; however, the color, a slightly muddy pink, and size of the blossoms do not measure up. Nor is the plant long-lived or easy to handle. Young plants, raised from wild seed, will usually flower the second year if given a moist scree site, but many fail to survive much longer. *D. knappii* is a short-lived plant, calling for frequent replacement by cuttings or seed, which in this species comes true. The trouble is worth while only for the color—a rather pale yellow that is unusual in a dianthus. The flowers are carried in a head on stems of about 1 foot without much basal foliage; it is a rather awkward plant. Give it sun and drainage. *D. microlepis* is as trim in clump of foliage as *D. glacialis,* but the blossoms are a far better pink and in better proportion. It is also more permanent and warrants a prominent position in good, limy soil with a mulch of chippings. It may grow for a few years before it displays its charming blossoms.

D. neglectus is a true alpine beauty to be classed with *D. alpinus* and *D. callizonus.* It is distinguished by the brilliance of its pink blossoms with a dusky-blue eye and a distinctive buff on the back of the petals. These are carried on stems 2 to 6 inches above the grassy-green foliage tuft. It flourishes in well-drained but not parched soil—preferably without lime, though it seems to tolerate some lime in the soil. *D. noeanus* (usually offered as *Acanthophyllum spinosum*) is a tight spiny bun that arouses great expectations. The first time you have it you expect that here is one of the lovely plants that will spatter the pincushion tufts with bright coins of bloom; instead, in late summer, long, lank stems are topped with white blossoms so laced and ragged as to be almost invisible. That they are sweet-scented and with excellent foliage habit suggests that some enterprising plantsman might try hybridizing them with a short-stemmed bright colored dianthus. These are worth growing, however, for foliage effect alone and will thrive in any well-drained sunny site. Increase them by seed or cuttings. *D. squarrosus* is another with fringy, white fragrant flowers; but here the blossoms appear early in the season above mats of soft green grassy foliage.

There are many other species suitable for the sunny rock garden, ledge, wall, and alpine lawn which are described more or less accurately in seed and plant catalogues. Most are of easy culture and useful for generous summer color in the garden. The species of distinctive quality and best suited to association with alpine plants are listed above. Many of these have also entered into hybrids, too numerous to list here but quite worthy of trial; when you find some that please you, perpetuate them by division or cuttings.

DIAPENSIA (Diapensiaceae)

D. lapponica is an alpine of wide but rare dispersal. It inhabits the loftiest granite peaks of the Far North, where in the peaty accumulations among the rocks it forms hard evergreen cushions composed of tight rosettes of shining, crispy leaves. These turn a lovely russet and rose before the long winter rest beneath the snow. With the quick awakening in the late spring thaws, on 1- to 2-inch stiff stems, open glistening-white 5-petaled flowers rather like magnified androsace blossoms. This belongs to a noble family which includes such beauties as shortias, schizocodons, and pyxidantheras. To grow and flower *D. lapponica* in the garden is a real challenge. It is difficult to reproduce its home conditions of peaty, gritty, acid soil, perfect drainage with cool water running at the roots, and frequent fogs and cool nights. To promote flowering, sun—or at least considerable light—also is necessary. The best prescription is an open north-facing slope with peaty, gritty soil, ample moisture in spring, and a snow cover in winter. It is extremely slow-growing, and hence difficult to produce from seed. Large clumps from the mountain habitat are impossible to move successfully because there is only a very deep main taproot with delicate feeding-roots easily torn away and almost impossible to regrow. Young, small tufts collected with as much soil as possible about the roots have the best chance of establishment. Single rosettes torn from the taproot have been induced to root—slowly, to be sure—and so feebly as to defy successful establishment. Without doubt this is a most beautiful and temperamental alpine.

DICENTRA (Papaveraceae)

The dwarf bleeding-hearts are lovely and delicate plants for growing in light woodsy soil among rocks in the shady garden. Seed is slow to germinate, but increase is easy by division of the fleshy roots and tubers after the flowering period. It is best to grow along with them some of the smaller ferns such as *Woodsia obtusa* and Oak Fern, to fill the space left when the leaves of some species shrivel away in late spring or early summer.

D. canadensis of the northeastern woodlands of America is called Squirrel-corn from the collection of round bright yellow tubers just beneath the surface. From these comes tender fernlike foliage in early spring, 6 to 10 inches high, within which are the brittle flowering-stems decked at the tip with a raceme of short, earlike, white, spurred flowers, usually tinged pink at the throat. **D. cucullaria,** also from the Northeast and called Dutchman's-breeches from the shape of the flower, has almost identical foliage but differs in the white underground tubers and fat and prominent spurs of the blossoms, which are white with a golden throat. A form from the Northwest is very similar, though the "breeches" are more densely hung on the tip of the stem.

D. eximia is a medium-sized bleeding-heart with glaucous foliage and pink blossoms. It blooms for a long season in spring and summer, spreads fairly rapidly, and is easily divided and moved at any time. It thrives in light woodland soil and shade. Slightly shorter but quite similar is **D. formosa** from the Northwest, and even finer is **D. oregana,** with blue-gray foliage and white pink-tipped flowers in dense nodding panicles. There are pure-white and deep red forms of these taller species. Their foliage persists until late summer.

D. uniflora is the smallest. On 3-inch stems, from rather broad-cut foliage, comes a single flower of white or pink with very short spurs but with the long outer petals strongly recurved to form 2 horns that give the flower the appearance of a steer's head. This is a species of rocky, shady places in the mountains of California, Washington, and Oregon, local in distribution. From the same area is **D. pauciflora,** also white or very pale pink, with up to 3 flowers on a somewhat taller stem. It has fatter spurs than *D. uniflora,* rather like abbreviated "breeches," and with the outer petals less strongly recurved. **D. peregrina pusilla,** from Japan, is a challenge to every expert rock gardener, even the Japanese. It is all-silver finely cut silk with spikes of ethereal pink blossoms on the order of *D. uniflora's.* An acid moraine on a north slope offers the most likely site for success.

DIGITALIS (Scrophulariaceae)

There are a few perennial foxgloves suitable for growing in light, humus-rich soil in open woods. They come easily from seed, which needs light to germinate and will self-sow where fallen leaves do not lie thick. Species to choose among, for a range of color from a good pink to orange, yellow, and white, are: **D. ambigua,** yellow marked with brown; **D. dubia,** purple; **D. lutea,** yellow or white; **D. obscura,** yellow marked with red; and **D. orientalis,** cream marked with red.

DIPHYLLEIA (Berberidaceae)

The Umbrella-leaf, **D. cymosa,** of moist soils in the mountains of Virginia and Tennessee, is well named for the great, deeply 2-lobed leaf that may be up to 2 feet across. The flowering-stem rises just above it, carrying 2 smaller leaves and a cyme of white blossoms followed by showy blue berries; an uncommon plant worth giving a prominent position in a moist spot in the woods garden. Increase this by seed, or by root-cuttings—a quicker method.

DISPORUM (Liliaceae)

The fairy bells are woodland plants of about 2 feet, rather like twisted-stalks in growth habit, but here the drooping bells of creamy white or greenish yellow are in a cluster near the tips of the spreading, leafy branches. The flowers are followed by showy red or orange berries, effective when planted in a woodland setting among ferns and other appropriate companions. They are easy to transplant, can be grown from seed, or divided early in the spring. Two eastern American species are **D. lanuginosa** and **D. maculatum.** Far-western species are **D. hookeri, D. oreganum, D. smithii,** and **D. trachycarpum.** All are rather similar, and all desirable.

DODECATHEON (Primulaceae)

The shooting-stars are a strictly North American genus of wide distribution and considerable variation in height and color. All are similar in general effect, having a rosette of many fleshy leaves from which rise naked flower scapes carrying at the summit an open umbel of cyclamen-like blossoms with reflexed petals and a narrow cone of protruding anthers. The base of the flower is frequently ringed with a color different from that of the petals. All are simple of culture in rich soil that has plenty of moisture in the spring. They will endure drying out in summer when the foliage withers and disappears. They are easy to grow from seed, which should be sown thinly, thus permitting the seedlings to remain in the seed pan for at least a year until they have reached size enough to handle easily. The spidery, fleshy roots break away from the crown readily and will make a new plant. It takes about three years from seed for dodecatheons to bloom. Root-cuttings generally flower the second year. For best effect grow them in clumps.

More than 25 species have been named, many rather similar. Some distinctive ones are: *D. alpinum,* a low, mountain species with rather narrow foliage. The red-purple flowers, on 9- to 12-inch scapes, have basal ring-bands of white and yellow, through which protrude the deep purple stamens. Other species of the same effect, distinguished by size of leaf and length of scape, are *D. hendersonii, D. jeffreyi,* and *D. tetrandrum.*

D. conjugens has fairly large leaves and large flowers on 6- to 10-inch scapes. Flower color is quite variable, from pure white to brilliant magenta-red. It is widely distributed in the intermontane country of the Far West, where it blooms very early when the ground is moist and dries out and disappears in summer. *D. dentatum* is a woods plant of the shaded sites in the northwestern mountains, where it carries white flowers with a purple basal zone, 8 to 10 inches above broad, rather thin-textured, toothed leaves. *D. meadia* is the more eastern species, a taller plant with flower scapes up to 24 inches. In moist meadows the husky plants, with large rosettes of firm leaves, bloom for a long period in early summer and stay green far longer than the westerners. Flower color ranges from white to a red-purple. The whole classification of these lovely *Primula* relatives is undergoing a complete revision and simplification, but by whatever name the many types may be called, all are magnificent.

DOUGLASIA (Primulaceae)

Brilliance of blossom, neatness of growth, and challenging obstinacy all make the American douglasias alpines of distinction. The one European species is no less beautiful and in most gardens is more amenable to cultivation. The American species are rather like the difficult high-alpine androsaces, both in their charm and in their temperament. The north-facing scree offers the best chance of success. Seed, when available, will germinate abundantly, although generally not until the second year and while the soil is still quite cool. Large cushions may be divided in early spring, but cuttings of ripened shoots root easily enough to make digging the plant for division too risky.

D. dentata, with rather loose rosettes of glaucous foliage, serrate at the edges, has something of the effect of a harder-leaved *Androsace lanuginosa.* The flowers are a violet-pink in 2- to 6-flowered umbels. The color of this scree or moraine plant is not as gleaming as in other species. *D. laevigata* is more compact, with hard, shiny, pointed leaves. The long-tubed, primula-like blossoms vary from deep carmine in the species to clear rose-pink in the Columbia Gorge form. They are carried on short stems in a few-flowered, open umbel, very like an alpine androsace. Plants begin to flower the second year from seed. It is definitely a plant for acid scree or moraine. *D. montana* has slightly smaller blossoms, generally 1 to a stem but so numerous as to make a dome of bloom above a tight tuffet of narrow short leaves, almost needlelike in effect. The flowers vary in the pink range of color, and a white form has been reported. This species will stand considerable sun and may even dry out completely in summer, although it wants plenty of moisture in spring. Grow it in the scree and rocky pasture. *D. nivalis* is a tiny, rather woolly mound with clear-pink flowers. It is a rare species in the northern Coast Ranges at high elevations and difficult to tame. *D. vitaliana,* of the European Alps, is similar and yet quite different. Here the blossoms are bright buttercup-yellow and quite stemless, sitting solitarily but thickly, close down on the bun of small linear leaves, gray with fine hairs. This plant thrives in full sun in well-drained soil. It divides with great ease.

DRABA (Cruciferae)

Except for a few rather difficult species, this vast race, found mainly in the mountains of the Northern Hemisphere, is less grown than its merits deserve. Most are tight, clumpy little plants with an abundance of short-stemmed crucifer-flowers of white or yellow. Though there is a basic similarity among many, some are distinctive of foliage and blossom. They carry the alpine trademark in their compactness of growth, hairiness of foliage, clarity of blossom color, and cultural needs. The majority succeed best in a light gritty soil with some leaf mold, in full light but not in the all-day glare of the sun. Grow them in the scree, the moraine, the rocky pasture. They are deep-rooted and, once established, the perennial species increase the size of the tuft from year to year. As the old leaves on the stem die, new rosettes are formed at the tip. A topdressing of gritty soil encourages new tight growth and stem-rooting, which in turn provides material for divisions. Seed germinates with the greatest ease and is generally true to species, since there seems to be very little natural hybridization.

There are literally hundreds of good perennial species and there are a few that are not worth growing, mostly those of loose habit and ungainly flower stems with disproportionately small flowers. Though there are similarities among certain species, as a whole they do not fall clearly into separable groups, and all are difficult of identification even by trained taxonomists. The alphabetical list given here is based on the author's personal experience with plants grown under these names. Confusion is common in nursery lists and seed lists, however; these seem a few of the most desirable species.

D. aizoides is the type for a whole range of species with mostly yellow or orange flowers in terminal racemes on short stems above mounds composed of many rosettes. The tiny rosette-leaves are longer than broad and edged with bristly hairs. *D. aizoon* is very similar, with rosettes a bit larger and the leaves slightly longer. *D. andina* is quite different in effect, with very small, rigid leaves, quite dusty gray, that have stellate hairs. The leaf-rosettes huddle into a hard, dense cushion when grown in full sun in a well-drained soil. *D. athoa* of the aizoides type has rather longer leaves, in larger rosettes, and tends to make more ball-like, domed cushions with good-sized yellow flowers.

D. arabisans is like a diminutive smooth-leaved arabis with rather small white flowers and twisted seedpods. It is not an outstanding plant but the only truly perennial draba of eastern North America. *D. bertolonii* is another of the aizoides type, with especially long bristles on the leaves.

D. bruniifolia carries orange flowers on short stems above the cushion of small green rosettes. The tiny blunt leaves, about as broad as long, are covered with soft hairs. *D. bryoides imbricata* forms an almost mosslike cushion of rosettes formed of minute, infolded leaves. The flowers are yellow, the flower stems fine and wiry. *D. dedeana,* one of the loveliest, carries a compact head of pure-white flowers on 1- to 2-inch stems above the compact cushion of small hairy-leaved rosettes. *D. densifolia* has condensed rosettes heavily decked with short gray hairs—a pleasing background for the head of good, yellow flowers.

D. fladnizensis is like a magnified *D. arabisans* with broad, dentate, gray foliage forming an open mat and with good-sized white flowers on 3- to 4-inch stems. *D. incerta* has large clear-yellow flowers above a cushion of gray foliage, like a looser and larger *D. andina. D. lutescens* repeats the aizoides pattern but here the rosettes appear almost spidery because of the long, very slender leaves, with especially long shining bristles.

D. mollissima is an excellent plant for pot-culture in the alpine-

Draba dedeana
(life size)

house, where it will form a rounded dome of packed miniature
rosettes, gray with fine wool. The yellow flowers are on short wiry
stems just above the foliage. It is possible to grow *D. mollissima* out-
of-doors, but it must be placed in a vertical crevice where no moisture can lodge among the furry foliage. **D. oligosperma** is very
similar to *D. andina,* but not quite as compact and with somewhat
longer flower stems. **D. paysonii,** in the same group as the last two
species, is very dense, very gray, and very handsome. **D. polytricha**
is on the order of *D. mollissima,* with more open and larger rosettes
and longer woolly hair, and is far easier to grow in scree conditions,
where it produces its clear-yellow flowers just above the rosettes in
earliest spring.

    D. rigida is quite similar to *D. bryoides,* but the effect is more
grasslike because the leaves are smooth and green. **D. siberica**
(sometimes listed as **D. repens**) is quite unlike the others. Light
green leaves are arranged along trailing stems that root down into
a mat. In very early spring, good-sized heads of yellow flowers are

carried on wiry stems up to 6 inches tall. This plant is easy to grow in almost any site except deep shade, and is readily propagated by division, preferably right after flowering.

DRACOCEPHALUM (Labiatae)

The dragonheads bring summer flowers of rich blue and purple to the garden. Though many species are suitable only to the border, there are neat clumping plants that carry 2-lipped blossoms in whorls and spikes on fairly short wiry stems. Propagate these by seed, or by division in early spring. They are to be grown in rich soil in a position not too hot and sunny. Some of the best are from the Caucasus and eastward. Good species are *D. alpinum, D. botryoides, D. bullatum, D. hemsleyanum, D. ruprechtii,* and *D. ruyschianum.*

DROSERA (Droseraceae)

The insectiverous sundews are never very showy in blossom but fascinating in leaf. The basal leaves, of many shapes, are thickly set with sticky glandular hairs that glisten in the sun. They want a sunny spot with constant moisture, and are ideal for the small bog. *D. filiformis* has long, linear, erect leaves with purple hairs. The bright purple flowers open one at a time up the uncurling spike at the top of the scape to reach a height of about 18 inches. This species wants a sandy, boggy, acid soil. *D. intermedia, D. longifolia,* and *D. rotundifolia* all have a whorl of basal leaves that lie flat out from the crown. The glistening hairs are brilliant red, the flowers white. These species are most commonly found growing in sphagnum bogs. Propagation is by seed sown in a sphagnum soup.

DRYAS (Rosaceae)

These prostrate shrubby evergreens are truly rock-and-sun-lovers, where they sprawl in dense mats of scalloped evergreen leaves like small oak leaves. The blossoms are large single "roses" of white or pale yellow followed by swirling, fluffy seedheads. Though in the

Dryas octopetala
(½ life size)

wild they are generally found on limestone rocks, this is not a requirement in cultivation. A normal rock garden soil in a position of sun and air makes them happy once established. Potted plants are most easily handled. Rooted layers may be taken off in spring and treated like cuttings, or cuttings of mature wood root readily. Seed is possible but slow to germinate and slow to grow.

D. drummondii is very handsome in foliage, since the leaves have an undertone of pink and are woolly on the back and sometimes covered with gray bloom on the upper side. The blossoms are creamy yellow and nodding, but do not open fully. *D. octopetala* has larger, pure-white blossoms held erect on 2- to 4-inch stems that elongate above the shiny green leaves as they go to seed. There are varieties with gray, woolly, and very small leaves, one of which is named *D. tenella.* The hybrid between *D. drummondii* and *D. octopetala* is called *D. ✕ suendermannii* and is yellow in bud, opening to white nodding flowers.

DUCHESNEA. See *Fragaria.*

EDRAIANTHUS (Campanulaceae)
This genus, which is closely related to campanulas, has upfacing bell flowers, frequently in a cluster at the tips of the procumbent leafy branches that lie out from the crown like wheel spokes. All come readily from seed and most of the wheel-bells are easily grown in ordinary rock garden conditions. The flower clusters of lavender, blue-purple, or white appear in early summer. The typical wheelbells are quite similar and may be variants of a single species, *E. graminifolius.* Those like it are *E. dalmaticus, E. caudatus,* and *E. tenuifolius.*

E. pumilio is very different. Here is a tight mound of grassy, grayish foliage, quite covered in June by solitary, almost stemless, upfacing, deep blue-purple bells. A scree site is essential, and though it wants plenty of sun it tends to brown and rot in prolonged muggy weather in summer. An open north-facing slope is probably best.

Winter does not disturb it since the foliage quite vanishes. *E. serpyllifolius,* with larger and greener leaves, somewhat longer stems that tend to splay out, and larger, rich-violet flowers, wants a similar site.

ELMERA. See *Heuchera.*

EMPETRUM (Empetraceae)

The Crowberry, *E. nigrum,* is a heather-like shrub of dwarf habit. The flowers are inconspicuous and are followed by black berries. This should be grown among other acid-soil plants on an open north slope or in the heath. It transplants poorly except when very young and may be grown from seed or soft-wood cuttings, but both methods are rather slow.

ENDYMION. See *Scilla.*

EPIGAEA (Ericaceae)

The Trailing Arbutus, *E. repens,* is not so difficult to grow as is frequently hinted. Most failures have sprung from trying to move large plants from the wild, or from insufficient attention to soil and moisture requirements, the latter especially after the transplanting. As its name suggests, this is a trailing woody shrub with evergreen leaves and clusters of deliciously fragrant pink and white bells early in the season. The flowers are followed by white pulpy fruits, peppered with minute black seeds, much beloved by ants. The best prescriptions are to start with really small plants, potted if purchased, and seedlings if gathered in the wild. Plant in acid soil, a sandy, peaty mixture, preferably on a north or east-facing slope but not in deep shade. It is most important to cover the plants with pine needles or oak leaves and water frequently until the plants are established. Once established the plants will endure almost anything. *E. repens* may be propagated from seed sown as soon as ripe— usually in July—and will bloom in about three years; it also may be propagated from cuttings of half-ripened wood of shoots that show no signs of flower buds. *E. asiatica* is quite similar, with larger, heavier-textured, pointed leaves and longer, more tubular, pink flowers. It should be propagated in the same manner as *E. repens* and protected with a covering of pine needles in winter since it is less hardy and the foliage burns easily.

EPILOBIUM (Onagraceae)

For the most part species of willow-herbs are rather leafy for the amount of flower. The tall Fireweed, *E. angustifolium,* spectacular when the pink flowers bloom in large masses in summer, may be established in open woods by seed where the fallen leaves and duff do not lie thick. There are a few dwarf western American species worth trying in moist gravelly sites along streams. Most showy is *E. latifolium,* which forms a low mat of broad foliage with leafy flower stems about a foot high bearing large red-purple blossoms similar in shape to those of the evening-primroses. Others are *E. luteum* and *E. obcordatum.* Most beautiful and desirable of all is *E. rigidum* from the rocky screes in the Siskiyou Mountains of northwestern America, where it forms close mounds of light green foliage above which are borne, on short stems, dense racemes of bright clear-pink flowers about an inch across.

EPIMEDIUM (Berberidaceae)

These are delightful plants for the shady garden. All are lovely in foliage and charming of flower. Most species make a low close-growing cluster of divided foliage, especially beautiful as it uncurls in the spring. Above the foliage clump of 6 to 9 inches rise the wiry flower stems, frequently opening blooms before the new foliage has expanded. The flower stems do not much exceed the foliage in some species and in others they display fine branching bouquets of delicate spurred blossoms well above the leaves. Flower color runs from purest white through creams and yellows to deep red. All grow in leafy, woodsy soil. Division of the clump soon after the flowering period is the best method of increase. *E. alpinum* has pale foliage tinged with light red when first unfolding. The blos-

soms are like small, dark red, spurless columbines. **E. grandiflorum,** from Japan, comes in many forms and colors and has been
the parent of a number of garden hybrids. The flowers in this
group are large and bright, frequently bicolored; **E. macranthum**
is a synonym. **E. pinnatum,** from the Caucasus, supplies the yellow
color to the genus and the hybrids.

ERANTHIS (Ranunculaceae)

The early-flowering Winter Aconite, **E. hyemalis,** with its short-
stemmed, green-ruffed, buttercup-like blossoms, should be mass-
planted in rich, fairly moist soil in sun or light shade. The tuberous
roots should be buried only about 2 inches deep. Self-sowing will
provide increase or the tubers may be divided.

ERICA (Ericaceae)

A collection of different forms among the various species of
heaths will give a fairly long season of bloom, and when out of
bloom the dwarf evergreen shrubs are neat and fresh. They enjoy an
acid, sandy peat soil in full or half sun. *E. carnea* is the only heath
that will flourish in soil containing lime. Though these shrubs may
be used as accents in the acid rock garden, they look their best, perhaps, in association with other acid-loving sun-lovers in a heathlike
setting. They may also be used in company with rhododendrons
and to underplant azaleas. The foliage may burn in a cold, snowless winter, but if cut back, new stems quickly fill out the plant. An
annual dressing of sandy peat worked down into the crown and
among the prostrate stems induces rooting. This not only keeps
the plants vigorous and more hardy but provides material for layered
divisions. Old plants are difficult to move. Small potted plants or
rooted cuttings, which are made from shoot-tips in summer and in
winter made indoors, are easier to establish (spring is most favorable) and soon make sizable plants.

E. carnea is very early to flower. The buds form in the fall and
may even open during a mild spell in winter or just as the snow

disappears. Varieties in pink and red are numerous. 'Springwood White' is a fast-spreading prostrate variety, among which dwarf lilies and appropriate daffodils can be planted. *E. ciliaris* bears large bells of rosy red in a long raceme at the tip of the branches. It blooms for a long period in late summer and fall. Since this is not quite as hardy as *E. carnea,* a snow cover or winter protection of evergreen branches will bring it through and be well worth the trouble. *E. cinerea* is a summer bloomer with distinctive, fine, gray-green foliage. It needs the same treatment as *E. ciliaris,* but prefers a hotter, drier site in general. *E. tetralix* is even grayer in foliage, especially in var. *mollis,* with rather large hanging bells in terminal clusters. It enjoys more moisture than the other species. Flowers are produced for a long season in summer. *E. vagans* is dense with both needlelike leaves and flowers among the leaves near the tips of the branches. The whole plant makes a thick shrub about a foot high, as hardy as *E. carnea.* There are numerous hybrids among the ericas, each as hardy as the parents, generally with red to pink flowers, or occasionally white.

ERIGERON (Compositae)

In general the erigerons are like small asters with narrower and more numerous ray flowers surrounding the yellow disk. There are literally hundreds of species in the mountains, especially in western America. Most of them have nice proportion, with trim basal foliage, usually rather grayish. Ray flowers may be white, pink, purple, or blue, and in at least one species a brilliant gold. Though most come readily from seed and self-sow when established, some seem short of life in the garden and may be in the wild. All want excellent drainage and full sun. The perfect site is a gravelly slope where, grown in sizable groups, they bring a long season of color to the garden in summer.

Some that have proved satisfactory in the East, though there are many more excellent ones awaiting trial, are listed here. *E.*

aureus is a golden dwarf of high mountains and one of the few that insist on acid soil. It is not for a hot, dry site; a north slope suits it best. **E. compositus** has small white or blue flowers above a lovely silver filigree of foliage. **E. leiomerus** has very short stems and good violet flowers above a close mat of glabrous gray leaves. **E. simplex** is a variable species with large solitary blossoms that unfold from fat, reticulated buds. **E. ursinus** is a very floriferous dwarf with densely tufted, narrow, gray foliage and lavender-pink flowers. Every State manual of botany will list numerous other species very worth growing in typical sites in the garden.

ERINACEA (Leguminosae)

E. pungens is a strange shrub of Spanish limestones, rarely seen in this country but perfectly hardy in spite of its origin. It is composed of a stiff tangle of gray-green thorns that in summer erupt with lavender-blue pea flowers and a few green leaves. The whole plant is never more than 6 inches high by a foot across. Cuttings of the stiff green branches will root slowly in late summer. It is best grown among limestone rocks in either sun or shade.

ERINUS (Scrophulariaceae)

E. alpinus makes a dense low mound of overlapping, sharply toothed leaves of bright green. The typical 5-part flowers, in a dense raceme on 3- to 4-inch stems, are a rosy color. The white variety comes true from seed and good pink forms are occasionally seen. Good color-forms may be increased by cuttings. This is a fine plant for the crevices in walls where the winter moisture does not lodge in the foliage and rot the plant. Even if some plants die during severe winters, self-sown seedlings are abundant. It is best grown in a well-drained soil in partial shade.

ERIOGONUM (Polygonaceae)

This genus makes splashes of color during the summer in the mountains and meadows of the American West. The most desirable dwarfs are sub-shrubby, with basal leaves frequently felted with hair. The small flowers of cream, pink, or yellow are in dense heads on naked stems. Each cluster of flowers is held in a sort of papery cup, often of a color different from that of the blossoms. All are difficult to transplant, since they grow from a deep taproot. Seed is abundant but sometimes not highly fertile and offers the only means of propagation. Either sow where the plants are to grow in well-drained sunny sites, or transplant to permanent quarters when small. Some of the best are: *E. douglasii, E. flavum, E. multiceps, E. ovalifolium, E. polyphyllum, E. pyrolaefolium,* and *E. umbellatum.*

ERIOPHYLLUM (Compositae)
This is a group of far-western American yellow "daisies" known as Oregon sunshine for the abundance of the golden-rayed blooms on foot-high stems above the gray carpet of cut leaves. They ask for good drainage and a sunny site. Seeds grow easily, or the mature plants may be divided in spring. Species all rather similar are *E. caespitosum, E. lanatum,* and *E. multiflorum.*

ERITRICHIUM (Boraginaceae)
Two or three species of these high-alpine beauties are found in the Rockies and Coastal Ranges of western America as well as on other alpine peaks of the world. All are characterized by tight buns of small leaves utterly swaddled in woolly hair. Brilliant blue forget-me-not-like flowers spangle the little cushion in the wild. Few are the gardeners who have succeeded in growing these plants, and fewer those who have succeeded in making them flower. They can be grown, and have been grown, but not easily or for long; yet every dedicated rock gardener eventually rises to the challenge. Collected plants are difficult to transport from their lofty homes and harder to reestablish. The best chance of success is to grow them from seed.

Seed of American *E. argenteum* and *E. elongatum* (probably only geographical varieties of the European *E. nanum*) are sometimes available. They germinate easily, grow slowly, and perish quickly if they become sodden and hot. Success is most likely if the seeds are sown thinly in a large pot with a stone-chip mulch. Thin the seedlings to stand about an inch apart. Water the pot only by plunging. Plenty of light and air but no baking sun are requisite, and, above all, protection from the heavy beating of thunderstorm rain. Soil should be a gritty leaf mold, though in nature they may be found growing in a stony, red-gumbo clay. With luck they will flower the third year from seed on tuffets about 2 inches across. Spare seedlings may be potted singly or set in the scree on the north side of a rock when the single rosette has begun to make new rosettes.

E. strictum is quite different and far easier. It has smooth, grayish, linear leaves and an upstanding stiff flower stem about 6 inches high, which branches and carries lovely pale forget-me-not-like flowers. The flower color tends to become washed out in a limy soil; an acid scree mixture on a north slope is the best position.

ERODIUM (Geraniaceae)

Though there are many desirable heronsbills for the rock garden, most are not hardy in northern gardens. The best are from the Mediterranean region, where in sunny sites all summer long they produce above the ferny foliage small geranium-type flowers, often delightfully striped. They tend toward various shades of pink and rose. Once acquired by growing from seed, plants of the less hardy species may be lifted and wintered in frame or alpine-house. They are worth the effort because of their beauty and long season of bloom. In general they are easy to divide in spring as growth starts. Most likely to prove hardy and desirable in rocky, limy soil are *E. macradenum, E. manescavii, E. petraeum,* and *E. supracanum.*

ERYNGIUM (Umbelliferae)

The spiny steel-blue leaves of the genus are strikingly beautiful. Most species are suited, however, only to the border. *E. alpinum* does keep below 2 feet and has a neatness to invite it into the alpine lawn or sunny rock garden, where it wants a deep fertile soil. It is to be grown from seed or cuttings. American species worth searching for are *E. alismaefolium* and *E. articulatum,* which grow in moist open sites in the Far West.

ERYSIMUM (Cruciferae)

The dwarf wallflowers produce their orange and gold crucifers for a long period during the summer. They are easy to raise from seed and should be grown in poor, gritty soil in full sun to increase their chance of permanence. There are many species in the mountains of the American West and in Europe. Some species have low-altitude, impermanent forms and more permanent alpine forms. As with most members of this family, they come quickly from seed, frequently blooming the first summer. *E. kotschyanum* is a low mat from the high mountains of Asia Minor, with good-sized orange-yellow flowers; *E. pyrenaicum* bears large golden flowers just above a tuft of grassy foliage. *E. wheeleri* is a variable species from the American Rockies, especially to be hunted out in the dense, dwarf, large-flowered form from high places in Colorado.

ERYTHRAEA. See *Centaurium.*

ERYTHRONIUM (Liliaceae)

For the shady garden no group of bulbs is more rewarding than the trout lilies. There are Europeans of considerable charm and eastern Americans neat in foliage and blossom. But it is the species of the mountain valleys of the American Far West that are most beautiful and enchanting. They are generally easy to establish in a good woodsy soil full of leaf mold. The bulbs should be planted 6 inches deep and left to increase year by year. Their tendency to bury themselves more deeply and hence diminish flowering may be curtailed by placing a rock or two beneath each bulb at the time of planting. The first year's display will be disappointing, but from then on there will be an increase in the number of flowers per bulb and increase in the bulbs by offsets and self-sowing. It is a slow process to increase your supply by seed. Seeds should be sown as soon as ripe, and even then they may take two years to germinate and another three to flower. The wait is worth it, because no garden ever has too many erythroniums.

E. americanum, the eastern American, yellow-flowered and with mottled leaves, increases so rapidly by offsets that the stand becomes too dense to flower. The remedy is to dig up the bulbs and replant them on a stony base. A generous dressing of wood ashes and bone meal will also stimulate flowering. *E. albidum* and its close relative *E. mesochoreum* are lovely, nodding, white trout lilies, sometimes tinged with a smoky blue-gray on the outside. The leaves are mostly unmottled. *E. dens-canis* is the European representative, with broad, mottled foliage and short-stemmed blossoms in a range of colors. They increase by offsets. It is the western Americans, however, that provide the greatest assortment of most spectacular blooms. Some have unmarked green leaves, and in others the leaves are magnificently mottled. All except untamable *E. montanum,* the Avalanche Lily, are easy to establish in shade and good, rich, stony forest soil. These are to be sought whenever dealers offer them: *E. citrinum, E. giganteum, E. grandiflorum, E. hendersonii, E. howellii,* and *E. revolutum.* There are others, plus hybrids, and not a poor one among them.

EUONYMUS (Celastraceae)

Dwarf forms of *E. radicans,* especially var. *minimus,* are valuable carpeters for sun or shade, doing well in limy soil. They make ideal bulb cover, and since they root as they run, can be increased readily by layers or cuttings. They will also climb upward, though not to great heights, by clinging to rock or bark.

EUPHORBIA (Euphorbiaceae)

It is the bracts beneath the small blossoms which give color to the euphorbias. The rapidly spreading *E. cyparissias* should be kept out of the rock garden, enticing as it is in feathery foliage. Once in and rampaging, it is almost impossible to eradicate short of major reconstruction of the garden and so it should be left to cemeteries and roadsides. No such complaint can be issued against *E. poly-chroma,* which makes an erect, branching, herbaceous bush a foot tall, with bright yellow bracts beneath the small heads of bloom. It may be increased by cuttings or division. *E. myrsinites* is prostrate, with large blue-gray leaves densely arranged. This is to be grown in a warm sunny spot, trailing over rocks.

FESTUCA (Gramineae)

Though grasses and sedges play a large and important role in the natural rock gardens of the high mountains, it is generally prudent to exclude them even from the alpine lawn and rocky pasture. An exception may be made for the Sheep's Fescue, *F. ovina glauca,* which produces restrained clumps of short, blue-gray, fine grass. Increase by division and grow in lean rocky soil to keep it neat.

FRAGARIA (Rosaceae)

The wild strawberries make a rapid and dense ground cover, rooting as they produce stolons. Though they provide a pleasant spattering of white flowers followed by red fruits, they should be used only as an underplanting for husky companions in the wild-type garden. There have been developed some erect, nonrunning forms that also tend to be everbearing on erect clumpy bushes of 8 to 10 inches, suited therefore to planting in more select company. All are easy to propagate by division in the spring and will thrive in almost any soil. For flower and fruit they want some richness in the soil and considerable sun. There are species from every part of the world—all very similar, and one, *F. indica* (also called *Duchesnea indica*), with yellow flowers and brilliant, tasteless berries.

FRANKENIA (Frankeniaceae)

F. thymifolia is a prostrate shrublet with heather-like leaves, among which sit very pretty pink blossoms in July and August. It is not hardy outdoors in the North but makes an excellent plant for the alpine-house or planter. Cuttings taken at any season are easy to root, or a branch may be encouraged to root by placing a small stone on it.

FRITILLARIA (Liliaceae)

The genus has its enthusiasts, who see in the nodding flowers a strange beauty and in the difficulty of their culture a real challenge. The Guinea-hen Flower, *F. meleagris,* with its checkered blossom, and the Crown Imperial, *F. imperialis,* with a cluster of yellow, orange, or red bells at the summit of 3- to 4-foot stalks, want rich soil, moist in spring but well drained and dryish in summer, and some shade in this country. The same is true of dusky *F. camschatcensis.* These three are tall and should be planted in openings in the woodland garden. Other species from the Mediterranean regions and from western America—including *F. pudica,* a dwarf yellow, and *F. recurva,* with brilliant scarlet and orange flowers on 1-foot stems—all want sun and a site that is quite dry in summer. For these the alpine lawn or rocky pasture are best.

FUNKIA. See *Hosta.*

GALANTHUS (Amaryllidaceae)

All of the snowdrop species and forms are desirable. Though only the early spring *G. nivalis* is commonly grown, there are others for spring and some for fall blooming. These are all available from most good bulb houses. Snowdrops should be planted in mass for best effect and preferably in rather good soil in partial shade. They do well when planted among deciduous shrubs such as azaleas. Bulbs should be buried about 4 inches deep. If happy they will self-sow and multiply by offset.

GALAX (Diapensiaceae)

G. aphylla is a gorgeous foliage plant for acid soil in shade or half-shade. From the running roots come long-stalked shiny evergreen leaves, round and sharply toothed. These turn lovely shades of red and bronze in the fall. In early summer rise the tall wands (up to 2½ feet) of small white flowers, effective in mass. This is a perfect plant to mix with and use under ericaceous shrubs. Established plants may be divided in spring or fall. Seed is easy to germinate but the seedlings are slow to reach mature size.

GAULTHERIA (Ericaceae)

These evergreen shrubs and carpets have charming, hanging waxy bells followed by bright berrylike fruits. They all demand acid, rather moist soil, and shade to keep them from drying. Large plants are difficult to establish; so it is best to acquire rooted runners, or small divisions, or soft-wood cuttings, treated with care in a propagating medium till a new vigorous root system is formed. Seed germinates slowly and the plants are dilatory in reaching flowering dimensions.

G. adenothrix is a dwarf, upright shrub from Japan, with quite large pink and white bells, followed by bright red berries. *G. cuneata,* from western China, has unbranched stems splayed out from the woody crown. The branches reach about a foot in length and are set thickly with narrow pointed leaves. The berries are pure white. This, like other oriental gaultherias, may be cut back by severe cold without snow cover; but if plants are growing in a congenial site they will break new growth in the spring. The roots seem quite hardy.

The Creeping Snowberry, *G. hispidula* (sometimes listed as *Chiogenes hispidula*), spreads into sizable carpets on very moist, cool duff, rotted wood, or sphagnum moss. The fine rambling stems are beaded with very small, rounded evergreen leaves, among which are hidden the tiny white bell flowers and the pure-white wintergreen-flavored berries. Rooted divisions, after nursing in the acid sand frame or pot, can be established as a ground cover among dwarf shrubs in the shady heath or acid bog.

G. humifusa makes dense mats of light green rounded leaves. This western American is difficult to establish, but once adjusted in acid, moist, peaty soil, with an annual dressing of decayed evergreen needles, it will make an excellent ground cover with a scattering of small white bells and bright red fruit. *G. miqueliana* is the easiest and hardiest of the oriental species. It makes a neat twiggy shrub about a foot tall. The leaves are thick, glossy, and abundant, coloring to pink and red in the fall. The fruit is white, sometimes pink-tinged.

G. ovatifolia is rather like a denser, flatter *G. procumbens*. It is easier to grow than its fellow westerner, *G. humifusa,* and carries the same pink and white bells followed by scarlet fruit, eaten by mice and birds. *G. nummularioides* is like a magnified Creeping Snowberry. The leaves along the procumbent viny branches are round and ciliate. Under the leaves, scattered along the stem are solitary, pink-white bells followed by blue-black berries.

G. procumbens, the common Checkerberry, or Wintergreen, of acid soils in eastern North America, will succeed in drier sites than do any of the other gaultherias. Carefully dug sods will transplant, but need generous amounts of water until reestablished. Sections of running root with one of the erect, small, treelike stems can be treated as a cutting in the propagating frame. This is a good method of propagation for selected strains that produce an abundance of the pinkish-white blossoms and scarlet fruit. This quality of the plant is somewhat affected, however, by soil and light; in ideal soil and sun there are more flowers and fruit.

There is a whole group of gaultherias, some up to 3 feet tall, with dark blue, indigo, or azure-blue fruit. They are not considered hardy north of Philadelphia. *G. veitchiana* is of this type.

GAYLUSSACIA (Ericaceae)

There are two dwarf huckleberries of the eastern states admirably suited to join the collection of small shrubs and ground covers in the acid heath bed. They may be propagated by division of the creeping roots or by soft-wood cuttings. **G. brachycera** is a rare, evergreen, creeping shrub with small shining "box"-like leaves. Once established it will run fairly rapidly, with a disconcerting habit of sending up new plants at considerable distance from the original rather than in a trim, dense mat. The foliage colors handsomely in the fall. Flowering (and consequently the blue berries) is scanty. **G. dumosa** is a deciduous species about 1½ feet tall, which in the wild grows in acid bogs in a close tangle. It will, however, flourish in the drier, acid heath, where it produces hanging bells of pink and white, followed by edible black berries.

GENISTA (Leguminosae)

This genus is closely related to *Cytisus,* and like it produces a lavish display of pea blossoms on twiggy dwarf shrubs. All like full sun in well-drained soil. Cuttings of new wood root fairly easily. Seeds germinate well and provide a method of rapid increase. Old plants of *Genista* do not transplant easily.

G. dalmatica makes a tight rounded dome about 6 inches high with small leaves and numerous thin spines. In June and July the plant is covered with dense spikes of butter-yellow blossoms. This will grow in half-shade as well as sun. **G. delphinensis** is a miniature of *G. sagittalis,* with the same leafy, winged stems and heads of golden flowers. The plant never grows much taller than 3 inches. It does not thrive in limy soils. **G. horrida** earns its name from the stiff green spines that tip the silvery stems. On this rigid little tree of 6 inches or so are hung heads of bright gold in summer. **G. prostrata** (sometimes listed as **G. pilosa procumbens** or as a *Cytisus*) is an absolutely flat carpet of branches decked with hairy leaves and scattered yellow blossoms. **G. sagittalis** makes a large mat of tangled, green, winged stems that carry terminal blossoms of bright yellow in early summer, rising to about a foot. Allow for a good 2-foot spread.

GENTIANA (Gentianaceae)

No genus supplies the rock gardener with more gorgeous blue flowers. The range of species and hybrids provides plants adapted to a multiplicity of sites and to differing blooming seasons. They vary in stature and have flowers of numerous shapes and of colors other than gentian-blue. To describe and prescribe for even the better garden-worthy species would require a good-sized volume. Such a book has been produced by the late David Wilkie, for years connected with the Royal Botanic Garden, Edinburgh, and long acknowledged expert on gentians.

Gentians all want humus-rich soil, not boggy but definitely never dry. Though in most climates they flower best in full sun, in the eastern United States most require some protection from the midday sun. They thrive best on a north slope in a bed made spongy and moist by the incorporation of leaf mold and peat, and made fertile by including well-rotted manure or such organic fertilizers as cottonseed meal. The fine seed is best germinated on a ½-inch layer of chopped sphagnum moss above a proper soil mixture in pot or flat. If thinly sown they may stay in this seed mixture until large enough to set out in permanent sites; otherwise they should be transplanted when quite small and grown-on in separate pots or in such a way that the roots are not disturbed on final transplanting to the bed. All gentians resent root disturbance and require firm planting. Though many have deep taproots and cannot be propagated by division, some can be increased by careful lifting in the early spring; the crowns, with roots attached, are teased apart, and the divisions immediately replanted and well watered. Some will furnish cutting material of short, nonflowering shoots from the crown early in the growing season.

G. acaulis, which along with *G. verna* is called Spring Gentian, may be used as the name to encompass a group of similar species that grace the alpine turf of Europe. All have shiny, broad, evergreen leaves in an ample tuft, above which in late spring rise large

Gentiana acaulis
(⅔ life size)

gorgeous blue trumpets on scapes from 2 to 6 inches. In some gardens plants do not flower well, and no explanation has been discovered, though many theories have been propounded. Certain it is that they want rich, moist soil and as much sun as they can endure without drying; they respond to frequent division. In this group, and with minor and geographical differences, are **G. alpina, G. angustifolia, G. clusii,** and **G. dinarica.** These and the next group will endure lime in the soil but do not demand it.

G. angulosa with **G. bavarica** and **G. verna** form another group of spring-flowering gentians of most intense clear blue. Here, instead of forming trumpets, the flowers open flat in a starry effect. The foliage clump is evergreen, like diminished *G. acaulis* leaves. They grow in small grassy hollows in the mountains where there is copious underground moisture. All spring-blooming gentians as seedlings are most impatient of transplanting and should be sown very thinly for direct planting when of adequate size. However, once they have formed sizable clumps with many crowns, they may be divided right after flowering. Lift the clump and tease apart the crowns with roots attached. Such divisions are best grown-on in a frame or shaded nursery bed of rich soil until new offsets are formed. Division and replanting in fresh fertile soil does seem to renew vigor and may actually stimulate blossoming, especially if bone meal is worked into the earth at root depth.

G. andrewsii is the Closed or Bottle Gentian of eastern American woodlands and moist meadows. Though there are dwarf forms of this species and other American species with bottle-shaped blossoms, this is the plant commonly used in woodland gardens, where it makes an erect sheaf of stout stems up to 2 feet. In August and on into September the flowers of blue or blue-purple with white tips, or rarely of pure white, are carried in a cluster at the tips of the stems and in the upper leaf axils. Seed is the best means of increase, though careful spring division of the crown with its heavy thong-roots is possible for propagation of especially desirable forms. Moist acid soil suits it best, though it will tolerate any woodsy soil and even some lime.

G. asclepiadea, the Willow Gentian, makes a sheaf of graceful wands up to 2 feet tall, with large azure-blue flowers in the axils of the willow-like leaves all along the stem in late summer. This should be grown massed in shaded, moist, rich soil. A few white-flowered plants, which come fairly true from seed, give an added charm when mixed with the blue. Seed is the best method of reproduction. When they are established, there will be considerable self-sowing.

G. decumbens is the name for a group of oriental gentians too dowdy to compete with the select, except in odd corners of the shady garden, where their rather heavy foliage and somewhat pinched blue blossoms in the upper axils do give a show of color in the summer. They are not to be compared with the gorgeous spring gentians or the late fall ones with large blossoms and grassy foliage. Too often, alas, seed listed as that of the finer species turns out to be one of the *decumbens* group in masquerade.

G. farreri may be taken as the type or, better, the apotheosis of the group of fall gentians which have no competitors for neatness of habit, brilliance and abundance of flower, and ease of increase. Here may be gathered, in spite of differences of flower shape and color, all those that send out a multitude of procumbent stems in a great wheel about the crown, feathered with narrow leaves and graced at the tip by large single upfacing blossoms in shades of clearest blue with various markings of white and luminous green. Under this heading are **G. hexaphylla, G. lawrencei, G. ornata, G. sino-ornata,** and **G. veitchiorum.** It is this group that has produced the gorgeous hybrids, as magnificent as and frequently easier than the parents. Without exception they want deep, cool, moist, acid soil, with ample leaf mold or peat. Fresh seed will germinate very readily. From then on follow the general directions for growing all gentians. Seed of the hybrids will not produce identical plants, but all are worth growing. In fact, no one ever has too many. They may also be increased by early division of the crowns, by spring-cuttings, and by root-cuttings.

Though **G. gracilipes** has affinities with the *decumbens* group, this gentian carries its family resemblance with distinction. The blossoms at the ends of the decumbent branches, which arch up at their outer reaches, are a clear rich blue, more open and graceful than in its relatives. This species will endure considerable sun if not parched. Moreover, it does not insist on acid soil.

G. porphyrio, the Pine-barren Gentian, is undoubtedly the most gorgeous of all the perennial American species. From a deep taproot rise to a height of 2 feet, in late summer, fine, wiry stems set with linear leaves. In September the bright blue flowers, spotted with brown, are 2-inch goblets, solitary at the tips. This is to be grown from fresh seed and planted among other plants in the pine-barren garden. Increase is possible by root-cuttings.

G. saxosa is worth growing for its unique qualities. Coming from New Zealand, it is not quite hardy in New England except when protected. The plant forms a small rosette of dark procumbent stems, at the tips of which come clusters of starry white blossoms in summer. Seed is very easy, and cuttings in spring are also possible. It should be grown in acid soil in good light.

There are two different forms and many variations of the beautiful late-blooming Japanese species, **G. scabra.** The upright form produces compact leafy-stemmed bushes about 12 to 15 inches high. The decumbent form flattens the stems along the ground. Both produce clusters of deep blue flowers at the tips of the stems and in the upper leaf axils. It grows best in moist rich soil with at least half shade. The blossoms do not appear until October and will carry on into November, but even so late it quickly ripens abundant seed, which is the best means of propagation.

G. septemfida is the type of a number of valuable and easy summer-blooming gentians: **G. freyniana** and **G. lagodechiana** belong here. In good soil, not necessarily acid, in either sun or shade, the husky, lax bushes carry clusters of good-sized bright blue bell-shaped flowers at the tips of foot-long stems. Some forms are more compact, with fewer but larger blossoms. Color variations are in the blue to blue-purple range. These are easy to grow from seed, and good forms may be reproduced by cuttings.

G. crinita, the eastern American Fringed Gentian, is a biennial species, rather demanding in its requirements. In the wild it grows in old, moist pastures and mowed meadows and in roadside ditches. It is not a woodland species, except where woods have been heavily thinned and the soil disturbed. It is, however, immaterial whether the soil is limy, neutral, or acid. The seeds apparently need mineral soil and considerable moisture for germination and the tiny first-year rosettes are intolerant of heavy competition. It may be grown from fresh seed, as you would any other gentian, and transplanted into moist but not boggy soil at the end of summer, when the small plants are no bigger than a 25-cent piece. The following summer the plants increase in size, and in August and September send up 1 or more flowering-stems (frequently branched), on the tips of which bloom the clear-blue fringed flowers, sometimes as late as October. Seed is ripe in November and should be sown immediately either in pots and flats or in the specially prepared site where they are to grow. If happily placed, Fringed Gentians will self-sow, though it is advisable to plant them two years in succession in order to produce bloom every year. Some seedheads will harbor worms that destroy the seeds.

There are many other gentian species, some only annual. Most are worth trying from seed and will respond to careful handling, grown in rich moisture-retentive soil with some shade from the hot sun. It must be admitted that most American gentians, other than those listed above, are not very showy; yet some forms of the western **G. calycosa** are fine for moist, open sites.

GERANIUM (Geraniaceae)

The rock garden and woods garden geraniums are numerous and varied, mostly blooming for rather long periods in early summer. The blossoms are salver-formed, frequently with striations darker than the ground color. Most are comparatively easy to cultivate in ordinary soil mixture. Seeds germinate readily, if somewhat tardily, in some species. They may also be increased by divisions of the crown in spring. Root-cuttings provide a further means of propagation.

G. argenteum makes a dwarf branching plant with silvery cut leaves and large flesh-pink blossoms with lines of darker pink. It should be grown in limy, gritty soil in full sun, where the plant will keep its dwarf 4-inch stature and will bloom from June to August.

Grow this from seed. Stems pulled from the crown may be rooted
as cuttings. **G. *cinereum*** is like a paler *G. argenteum* with gray
foliage. It wants similar treatment.

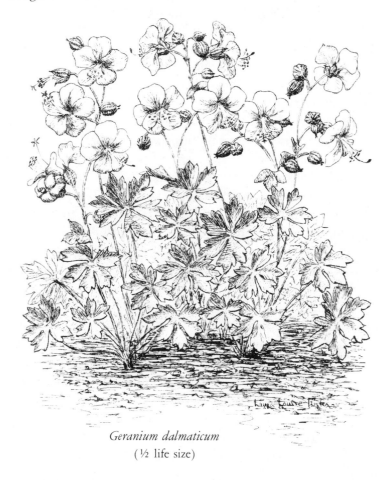

Geranium dalmaticum
(½ life size)

G. *dalmaticum* is a geranium of rather recent introduction. It is
an altogether easy and delightful plant, with dark, shining, indented
leaves. In June it becomes a mass of clear bright pink blossoms on
6-inch stems, with individual flowers about 2 inches across. It will

grow in sun or light shade in any reasonably open soil. Propagation is very easy by division of the clumps either in early spring or after flowering—so easy that to resort to slower and more difficult methods is not necessary, though seed is easy, if not abundantly set.

G. farreri (also called *G. napuligerum*) is neat and tuffeted with flat flowers of pale lavender-pink having conspicuous black anthers. It is best grown in rich scree. Seed germinates readily, or the plant may be divided carefully. Slugs and cutworms are especially fond of both foliage and blossoms.

G. endressii, with flowers of a particularly lovely shade of pink, is one of the large group of geraniums that grow 1 to 2 feet tall, all floriferous through late spring and on into the summer with blossoms of white, pink, through blue-purple. These are a bit tall and somewhat floppy to be grown among small alpines, but are excellent for the alpine lawn, for light shade in woodsy places, and for the large rock garden. Increase by seed, division, and root-cuttings. In this group are: *G. fremontii,* rose-purple; *G. grandiflorum,* lilac to rich blue-purple with purple veins; *G. ibericum,* blue-purple; *G. maculatum,* pale rose; *G. psilostemon* (also called *G. armenum*), rich purple with a black center; and *G. renardii,* large purple-veined white flowers and gray foliage.

G. macrorrhizum is a quick-spreading plant with strongly scented, robust leaves and smallish flowers of deep pink. It makes a thick mat about a foot high in sun or shade and is excellent for steep, rocky banks. Propagation is simple by division or root-cuttings.

G. pylzowianum is another fast-spreading plant, but of quite different character: small and neat in leaf, with sparse but lovely flat blossoms of clear pink on thin wiry stems. A starvation diet in full sun keeps it less rampant and perhaps more floriferous. Divisions are easily established.

G. sanguineum is a variable, easy species with a long season of bloom. The type is rather large and sprawly for the small rock

garden; it has bright magenta flowers, or white in husky var. *album.*
G. s. var. *lancastriense* is much finer, and flatter in habit, with soft
pink blossoms brightly etched. Named forms of *G. sanguineum* are
available, with dwarf habit and good flowers. All flourish in ordinary rock garden soil in sun or semishade and are of easiest propagation by seed, or for the varieties and forms, by division and root-
cuttings.

G. subcaulescens has luminous carmine blossoms with a distinctive dark, almost black center. These are carried on stems about 6
inches high above a slowly increasing tuft of small scalloped leaves.
Though sometimes classified as a variety of *G. cinereum,* it is quite
distinct. Reputed to be rather too rampant in the English garden,
here it stays neat in ordinary rock garden soil. Seed is never abundant and increase by root-cuttings is slow, but possible.

G. wallichianum, especially in '**Buxton's Variety,**' is a gorgeous
thing with large blue white-eyed blossoms on a prostrate plant. It
wants good soil in a sheltered site. As it comes from the lower
reaches of the Himalayas, it is not hardy in the North unless well
protected by snow. Seed is the easiest method of propagation.

GEUM (Rosaceae)

Avens are a race of summer-flowering plants with rather large
pinnate basal leaves and erect stems bearing solitary or clustered,
bright, single, rose-like blossoms. They do not bloom so abundantly
as to make a great show, but the brilliance of the individual flowers
makes a vivid spot of color. Seed or divisions are both ready means
of increase.

G. borisii bears orange-scarlet flowers on 6- to 12-inch stems
above ample clumps of divided, bright green foliage. Good soil in
sun or half-shade will fill its needs. *G. montanum* is an accommodating alpine species with large golden blossoms on short stems
above a good mat of pinnate leaves. The long feathery styles
attached to the ripening seed add a summer dividend. It is easy of
culture in sun or light shade, in limy or acid soil. *G. peckii,* endemic

to the White Mountains of New Hampshire, has blossoms rather like those of *G. montanum* on slightly taller stems and the leaves are quite large, with great rounded terminal leaflets. Good, acid, moist soil and a position out of the brightest sun suit it best. *G. pyrenaicum* is less neat than *G. montanum,* and without its indefinable quality; it requires the same treatment.

G. reptans is the gem of the genus, with great golden blossoms close above the rambling mats of almost ferny foliage. It comes from the highest places in the rocks of the Alps and is scant of flower and very difficult to keep in northeastern America, where the heat of summer is too torrid and too moist. Try it in a rich stony scree on an open north slope. *G. × rhaeticum* is a natural hybrid between *G. montanum* and *G. reptans,* with the latter's elegance and the former's disposition. It is occasionally offered as seed and should be eagerly sought. It will grow with the freedom of *G. montanum* and may be increased as readily. *G. rivale* is the avens of wet meadows, not at all showy, but a pleasing plant with nodding flowers of curious terracotta and ivory-silk shades. Give it moisture in sun or semishade. *G. rossii* of arctic North America is in habit like a mixture of *G. montanum* and *G. peckii,* with the best features of both. It wants rich, well-drained soil out of the glare of the sun. The foliage is almost as ferny as that of *G. reptans* and colors a rich reddish purple in fall.

GLAUCIDIUM (Ranunculaceae)

G. palmatum is like a huge anemone with big dark green palmate leaves. It wants a deep peaty soil in shade, where the large flowers of blue or white gleam on stems a foot high or more. Seed is the only simple method of increase, but seeds may not germinate until the second year. Root-cuttings are possible.

GLOBULARIA (Globulariaceae)

The globularias make trim tight mats of dark green foliage, above which in early summer are borne on short stems a pompon head of small, fluffy, blue flowers. They will grow in any soil, but for abundance of flower and compactness of growth, give them a limy scree soil in full sun with a rock to spread on. Seed is not always fertile. Cuttings strike easily and division is simple. **G. cordifolia** is the commonest species in gardens, soon forming mats of woody stems, among which bulbs may be grown for good effect. **G. incanescens** adds to its beauty by having silvery evergreen foliage and clear-blue flowers. **G. nana** is minute in leaf, short in flowering-stem, and slow of increase. It deserves a special spot among treasures of the limy scree. **G. trichosantha** makes a tuft of basal foliage and sends up 6- to 10-inch stems topped with steel-blue heads.

GOODYERA (Orchidaceae)

These are the rattlesnake plantain orchids with beautifully mottled foliage, white on light green. The rather tall spikes of dense, small white orchids are sometimes spirally arranged. Established plants may be carefully divided in early spring. All species grow in woodsy acid soil in shade. Native to North America, there are 4 or 5 species, all rather similar. They are often grown in terrariums for their foliage.

GYPSOPHILA (Caryophyllaceae)

This genus has an airy charm to the blossoms, well adapted to the rock garden in the dwarf species. Most are of easy culture in deep soil and a sunny location. They develop long thonglike roots and are best transplanted when young. They are easy to grow from cuttings and seed when available. **G. aretioides** makes a compact hard cushion of gray-green foliage sprinkled in June with almost stemless pale pink flowers. Coming from the lofty peaks of Iran, it wants perfect drainage and protection from winter wet. Plant in a crevice or in a vertical wall where moisture will not settle in the clump. Spring-cuttings, with a heel of older wood, root slowly. **G. cerastioides** has larger blossoms than most of the genus—lovely round white flowers veined with purple. These are on 3-inch stems above the dense mat of downy spoon-shaped foliage. The cushion may be divided for increase, or rooted by cuttings. It is on the border of hardiness in New England, suffering in a severe winter without snow cover. An open north slope with acid soil suits it best. *G. repens* is a quick and ample spreader, producing a beautiful, airy effect when decked with showers of small white flowers, or the showier pink of var. *rosea.* Seed is abundant and germinates easily. It will grow in almost any site but looks best when tumbling over a rock. Belonging to this clan are *G. dubia, G. franzii nana,* and *G. fratensis. G. tenuifolia* makes pads of small shiny leaves, from which rise wiry stems with heads of rather small pink flowers. This is an easy plant of delicate charm, to be increased by seed.

HABENARIA (Orchidaceae)

There are many orchids in woods and swamps of North America with spike-like flower heads, from small, greenish-flowered wood orchids to great fringed orchids in white, purple, or orange. Nurseries dealing in collected material sometimes offer the showier species, but none are easy to establish or generally persist more than a year or two when moved into the garden. Careful handling to prevent damage to the brittle fleshy roots and planting in fairly heavy but peaty, moist soil in half-shade, plus the magic of a "green thumb," may persuade these gorgeous plants to grace your woods garden or bog garden edge in the summer months after the flush of spring bloom.

HABERLEA (Gesneriaceae)

This genus proclaims its alliance with the African Violets and *Ramonda* by its rosettes of hairy, rugous foliage and by the clusters of blossoms that are lavender on the backs of the 5 petals, with white faces flecked in the throat by gold. These are carried on stout 3- to 4-inch stems that radiate from the leaf clump. These Middle European gesneriads want a leafy soil with a northern exposure; never permit them to dry out completely. They are most effectively grown in crevices of a north-facing wall or among rocks on a north slope. Leaf-cuttings pulled away from the crown with as much stem as possible will root in a peat and perlite mixture in a closed frame. The dust-fine and abundant seed germinates on a peat-sand surface, never allowed to dry out. They are best sown thinly and permitted to remain in the sowing medium until fair-sized for growing-on. *H. ferdinandi-coburgii* is the Bulgarian type, and *H. rhodopensis* has slightly smaller, if darker, blossoms—pure white in var. *alba* and var. *virginalis.*

HAPLOPAPPUS (Compositae)

This is a large American genus of yellow composites with some high-mountain forms of mat growth habit and large solitary golden daisies, rather on the order of arnicas but easier to grow and more permanent. Forming a close mat of fairly rough foliage with inch-wide blossoms on 2- to 6-inch stems is *H. acaulis,* and somewhat similar, with slightly taller stems and toothed leaves is *H. uniflorus.* These and others to be sought in the high elevations of our western mountains ask for sun and sharp drainage, as in a scree or rocky pasture. Established plants may supply root-cuttings or divisions as well as seed.

HEBE (Scrophulariaceae)

These shrubby veronicas from Australia and New Zealand, frequently listed under the genus *Veronica,* are mostly too tender to grow in the garden north of New York City. Where protected by snow in winter some, however, prove surprisingly hardy. The hardiest are dwarf shrubs with leathery evergreen leaves, frequently with a glaucous cast. All are easy to grow from seed and increase rapidly from cuttings taken in late summer. They appear quite indifferent to soil and will grow in sun or semishade. *H. decumbens* is the most reliably hardy, making wide mats with white flowers in terminal racemes. It has scant bloom but is an excellent foliage plant. *H. lycopodioides* makes a clumpy bush about 6 inches high. The foliage is almost needlelike, of light gray-green mossy effect. It should be protected in winter to prevent browning and die-back. Others of the broadleaf species may prove in time hardier than supposed. None of the curious whipcord species, with hard, scale-like leaves, is really hardy, but *H. hectori* is worth trying and should prove useful south of New York.

HEDERA (Araliaceae)

The English Ivy, *H. helix,* in its rapidly climbing form can hardly find a place in the garden except possibly as a ground cover in large woods gardens or as a cover for a dead tree. There have been developed, however, dwarf, compact forms, some with curiously shaped and twisted foliage. These are offered by florists and nurserymen under a collection of rather confused common names, and they are to be purchased advisedly only on inspection. Good forms are easily propagated by cuttings. Ivies like rich soil and prefer light shade, particularly to prevent burning of the ever-green foliage in winter.

HEDYSARUM (Leguminosae)

This genus is very like *Astragalus* and *Oxytropis,* with pinnate leaves and spikes of pea blossoms. The flowers of hedysarums are of bright colors from white through yellow to red and purple; the pods have restrictions between the seeds. These plants are best grown from seed and transplanted when young into deep, well-drained soil in full sun. The summer display of blossom is always welcome, though seldom seen in gardens. There are many species in Europe, Asia, and America awaiting the adventurous rock gardener, who cannot go wrong by trying any species. Some may reach 2 or 3 feet but are more spreading than erect.

HELIANTHEMUM (Cistaceae)

The sun- or rock-roses are less used in America than they deserve.

These are twiggy dwarf bushes, no more than a foot high, ablaze with a display of transitory flowers through early summer and with a spattering thereafter. The color range is from purest frosted white through pinks and yellows to the deepest red, both single and double. Once established, and this should be done with young, potted plants, the alpine species carry on for years if grown in full sun and deep soil that is not very rich. They will come readily from seed, blooming the second year. Named varieties—of which there are many—and hybrids are best increased by summer-cuttings, all very easy to root. It is well, particularly with the showy named sorts, to give them an annual late-summer shearing after the main season of bloom; and to·root some cuttings every fourth year or so to replace those that exhaust themselves with flowering or succumb to a hard winter in their old age. The species that come from southern Europe are remarkably hardy and persistent.

H. alpestre makes a close carpet of twiggy growth with shiny small round leaves and small golden flowers in profusion. Other species with gray-green leaves or narrow, straplike green leaves are brilliant with fleeting blooms of yellow or white that renew themselves daily for a long season in early summer. *H. vulgare* (also called *H. nummularium*) supplies a long list of horticulturally developed varieties and forms in singles and doubles, of all shades except blue. Most are hardy, even if tops are occasionally pruned severely by a hard winter. Bushes of this species become so large and sprawly that they must be kept away from less stalwart plants.

HELICHRYSUM (Compositae)

These are a strangely fascinating group of "everlasting" daisy-like flowers, mostly with silvery foliage, that have never caught on in America. The majority come from Down Under and do not thrive; they are just on the border of winter hardiness and are impatient of humid heat in summer. Moreover, seed imported from Australia and New Zealand rarely germinates; the fresh seed, as with so many of the composites, does not hold its viability very long. All should be sought and tried in different sites, preferably in full sun in well-drained acid soil. It is worth trying a north-facing scree with plenty of light. Summer-cuttings of rosettes from the clump, taken with as much stem as possible, will root easily but will have to be potted and held over in the closed frame or alpine-house. *H. bellidioides* is a good species to begin with, as most likely to survive both muggs of summer and blasts of winter.

HELIOSPERMA. See *Silene.*

HELLEBORUS (Ranunculaceae)

Establishing the Christmas Rose (*H. niger*) and Lenten Rose (*H. orientalis*) is not always easy because of their great fleshy thong-roots. But careful planting in deep rich soil in partial shade will generally succeed. Once established the plants will increase in size, producing large buttercup-like blossoms of green, white, madder, and sometimes pink from late fall to spring. Large clumps may be divided in early summer. Seed is slow to germinate, occasionally lying dormant for two years. The seed should be planted about 1 inch deep in a shaded frame and left until sprouted. An annual topdressing of well-rotted manure applied to older plants will increase the number and size of the flowers. Though there are other species, the finest for flower color and size are *H. niger* and *H. orientalis,* and especially the modern hybrids between them.

HELONIAS (Liliaceae)

H. bullata, the Swamp-pink, is a native plant of the coastal bogs from New Jersey to North Carolina. From a tuft of long lily-like leaves come drumstick stems of about 12 to 18 inches topped with a dense spike of clear-pink flowers early in spring. Two or three plants in a small bog garden are effective both in foliage and flower. The clumps are easily divided. Seed germinates very poorly.

HELONIOPSIS (Liliaceae)

These are small lily-like plants from Japan which produce from a stout rhizome a clump of evergreen leaves on the order of a broad-leaved sedge about 3 inches tall. Just above the foliage in a 3- to 10-flowered raceme are nodding, inch-wide pink "lilies" with spreading segments. This is *H. japonica,* which blooms in early spring. Plant it in woodsy rich soil in light shade and increase by seed or division.

HEMIEVA (Saxifragaceae)

This rather rare but prized saxifrage relative grows on moist cliffs in the mountains of the American Far West. The somewhat round basal leaves are divided into segments and are toothed, glossy, and dark green. On 6- to 8-inch stems sizable heads of saxifrage-like flowers are produced in late spring—pure white in *H. ranunculifolia* and lavender in *H. violacea.* These need a moist soil with some duff, and in shade, but may safely dry out in summer when the whole plant dies down and leaves only a cluster of small white tubers shallowly buried in the soil. These may be divided for increase. Self-sowing also occurs in favorable sites.

HEPATICA (Ranunculaceae)

These very early spring flowers should be planted in close masses for optimum effect of both flower and leaf in deciduous shade in the woods garden. They like a site rich in leaf mold yet well drained, especially on a slope, and need to be muffled in fallen leaves. They divide easily or may be grown from very fresh green seed, which will not sprout till the following spring. The best forms should be propagated by division, and carefully dug plants can be transplanted easily from the wild even in full bloom.

H. americana is the smaller of the two dwarf species native to eastern North America, with rounded lobes to the 3-part, frequently mottled leaves. The blossom color tends to be a deeper blue in this species, though it may run to white. The European *H. triloba* (also called **H. nobilis**) is very similar but has larger flowers and more showy stamens. **H. acutiloba,** the other North American, carries its larger sharp-lobed leaves on longer, hairier stems. The flowers on long scapes are likely to be white, pale blue, or pink. Double forms and deep-colored flowers are occasionally found. **H. transsilvanica** of eastern Europe (also known as **H. angulosa**), with typical blossoms, has the 3-part leaves puckered and notched at the tip. There are named forms and hybrids, particularly of the Europeans. All species respond with more copious and larger flowers to feeding with organic fertilizer.

HERNIARIA (Illecebraceae)

These plants make dense mats of minute stemless leaves that bronze in winter. Flowers are insignificant, but the plant makes a good ground cover for dwarf bulbs in the alpine lawn or for walk crevices. **H. glabra** is smooth, whereas **H. hirsuta** has hairy stems and leaves. Increase by seed or division.

HESPEROCHIRON (Hydrophyllaceae)

Two species appear soon after the snow melts in somewhat wet spots in the Cascade and Siskiyou Mountains of the western United States. **H. pumilus** has flat ¾-inch, saucerlike blossoms, white with blue veins, lying out on short stems above the rosette of smooth, rounded, rather thick leaves. In **H. californicus** the blossoms are more bell-shaped and the foliage is gray and pubescent. Both species dry out and die down in summer. Increase them by seed or spring-cuttings. The plants should be grown in clumps in low pockets of the rock garden in neutral to acid soil.

HEUCHERA (Saxifragaceae)

There are many select forms of the species **H. sanguinea,** but most have taken on a character more suitable to perennial borders than rock gardens, though these may be used as woodland plants. There are other species from the mountains and woodlands of North

America more in character, but it must be admitted that few have flowers of sufficient size or brilliance to compensate for the rather large serrate foliage and the tendency to lanky flower stalks. There is one very fine species growing in the rocky talus slopes of the lofty Olympic Mountains of Washington, **H. racemosa** (also called *Elmera racemosa*), which has dense 10- to 12-inch spikes of large, creamy-white, firm-textured blossoms above a low cluster of cordate leaves. This species should be grown on an open north slope or in light shade in a very stony soil; others are suitable in the woods garden, in sun or light shade. All heucheras are easy to grow from seed and by division.

HEUCHERELLA (Saxifragaceae)

This hybrid between *Heuchera* and *Tiarella,* named **H. tiarelloides,** combines the characteristics of the two plants in a clumpy mass of toothed leaves above which are carried panicles of rather small pink blossoms. It is a handsome plant suitable for the humus-rich soil of the woods garden.

HIERACIUM (Compositae)

Though awkward in flower and prone to fierce self-sowing, the hawkweed genus does offer a few good foliage plants. They are easy to grow from seed but not easy to move when large. Give them full sun and good drainage to keep the foliage gray and furry. **H. bombycinum, H. villosum,** and **H. welwichii** are gray-leaved plants with yellow dandelion-like flowers on tall branching stems. The last species is perhaps the grayest of all.

HIPPOCREPIS (Leguminosae)

H. comosa is a mat-former with pinnate foliage and heads of yellow pea blossoms in midsummer. Give it a rock to sprawl on, more especially a limestone rock and in full sun. Grow it from seed and transplant it when young, or increase by removing a rooted stolon.

HORMINUM (Labiatae)

H. pyrenaicum has perhaps too much leafage for the spikes of bluish-purple salvia-like blossoms. It is a true alpine and if grown in poor limestone soil, in sun, offers a patch of color for midsummer. It is easy to grow from seed or division.

HOSTA (Liliaceae)

The plantain-lilies, *Hosta,* sometimes listed as *Funkia,* are chiefly grown as foliage plants. The large basal leaves are of various sizes and shapes, sometimes glaucous, sometimes streaked and mottled. The flowers, which in some species are shapely and well proportioned, may be white or in shades of lavender-purple. Though hard to place in conjunction with other plants, the hostas have their uses in moist soil in sun or drier sites in the shady garden. They are usually propagated by division, though they come easily from seed. New varieties are frequently produced by specialists, from whose lists may be culled species and hybrids to suit many purposes.

HOUSTONIA (Rubiaceae)

The American bluets, or Quaker ladies, are less used in the garden than they deserve. *H. caerulea* makes a small tuffet of tiny leaves, covered in spring with light blue, 4-petaled blooms. Old pastures and poor, rundown fields in New England are sometimes a shimmering carpet of these blossoms in May. It seems indifferent about the acidity of the soil; it wants moisture in spring, but endures considerable drying thereafter. Though the individual plants are not long-lived, they self-sow in the most unlikely places when established. Seed is easy of culture and clumps may be divided, a treatment that seems to renew their vigor. *H. serpyllifolia* makes a spreading mat of fine foliage and carries deeper blue flowers than *H. caerulea.* It wants moist soil and shade and makes an excellent ground cover for trilliums and erythroniums, or such plants as Jack-in-the-pulpits. It prefers acid soil. Division of the mat is easy. There are also upright-growing species 1 to 2 feet tall, with small leaves and summer-blooming loose cymes of purplish flowers—*H. longifolia, H. purpurea,* and *H. tenuifolia*—all for dry, rocky sites in acid woods.

HUDSONIA (Cistaceae)

The beach heathers are natives of the sandy acid soils near the eastern coast of the United States, where they make compact, needle-leaved, green or gray shrubs about 6 inches high, with bright yellow flowers in summer. They root deeply and are difficult to move. Seedlings, either collected or grown from seed, can be established in sandy acid soil that does not become too dry at root level. A sandy or gravelly surface in full sun will protect the plants from the fatal rotting affecting them outside their native haunts. Peat mixed with the soil about 6 inches to a foot beneath the surface will keep them thriving. It is possible to root cuttings in sharp sand and peat. These are plants for the sunny sections of the pine-barren garden. *H. ericoides* has green needlelike leaves on tufty bushes of about 7 inches. *H. tomentosa* is denser and bears scale-like leaves of frosty gray.

HUTCHINSIA (Cruciferae)

H. alpina and the very similar *H. brevicaulis* are charming little tuffet plants with dark green, much-divided foliage and clear-white arabis-like blossoms for a long season in early summer. The clumps, which may reach 8 to 10 inches across, can be divided easily and should be, because old plants tend to die off in patches. Seed is also very easy to germinate. For success the plants want good, fairly moist soil and will stand considerable shade. The more light, the more bloom, so long as they never dry out at the root.

HYDRASTIS (Ranunculaceae)

H. canadensis is an eastern North American woodlander for moist rich soil. Two large leaves on foot-high stems make hand-some umbrellas, just above which are carried a small white flower with a conspicuous brush of stamens. The fruit is a head of crimson berries. Increase this species by seed or division of the roots.

HYDROCOTYLE (Umbelliferae)

A small shiny-leaved carpeter for moist soil in either sun or shade, *H. moschata* carries on creeping stems small, round, scalloped, shining leaves and inconspicuous flowers. It is not a select plant and tends to ramp, but it is useful and is easily propagated by pulling off rooted runners.

HYDROPHYLLUM (Hydrophyllaceae)

The waterleaves are plants for the woodland garden. The small bell-shaped flowers with prominent stamens are gathered in dense clusters. The long-stemmed leaves are much divided into broad segments. The 3 eastern American species are rather tall and leafy for the size of the flower, besides being rather aggressive. The best of the 3 is *H. virginianum.* Better still is the westerner *H. capitatum,* which has dense heads of lavender blossom on stems from 4 to 8 inches high. Increase these by division and plant in good, moist soil in shade.

HYPERICUM (Hypericaceae)

This genus supplies the garden with a sizable number of species worthy of admittance. Who is to make final selection among these plants that are sunbursts with flashing golden boss of numerous glistening stamens? Some are prostrate, some are erect and shrubby, some are magnificent, many insignificant. All are of the easiest culture in almost any soil, in full sun or part shade. They set abundant, easily grown seed, and one wonders not so much that there are so many but that they have not dominated the world. They are mostly summer bloomers and may tend to be neglected just because they are so easy and so late. The finest Mediterranean species are remarkably hardy if given a site where they can "ripen" in full sun and not suffer cruel blasts in winter or heaving by frost. Mature plants develop massive woody roots resentful of disturbance, but seedlings are easy to grow and cuttings of especially fine forms may be rooted. Some of the best species are: *H. balearicum, H. calycinum, H. coris, H. olympicum, H. polyphyllum, H. reptans,* and *H. rhodopeum.*

HYPOXIS (Amaryllidaceae)

Yellow-eyed Grass, *H. hirsuta,* is the North American stargrass of rocky open woods, where it makes tufts of erect grasslike foliage among which are carried the starry yellow flowers for a long period in spring and summer. This should be planted in well-drained but good soil, in either light shade or full sun. A neutral soil is best. Established plants may be divided.

IBERIS (Cruciferae)

The perennial candytufts are compact evergreen shrubs with full heads of white flowers admirably suited for the rock garden in full sun or light shade. The foliage may burn in a severe winter but the plants soon recover if pruned back. In fact, taller species benefit from an annual clipping immediately after flowering. All species are quick to develop from seed and are readily increased by rooted cuttings or layers. *I. saxatilis* is a close-growing, prostrate species to be grown in the scree, preferably limy. *I. sempervirens* (also listed as *I. semperflorens*) has given rise to many named forms—all good, dwarf, upright evergreens. Some with *I. saxatilis* in their breeding are almost prostrate.

ILEX (Aquifoliaceae)

Among the hollies is *I. crenata* var. *helleri,* a fine, dwarf, compact shrub with small oval evergreen leaves. It may be used as an individual accent or in mass plantings to make a flat-topped evergreen ground cover of a foot or less. Given a humus-rich soil, it will grow in sun or half-shade and can be propagated by half-ripened-wood cuttings. There are other dwarf varieties of *I. crenata,* some quite similar to var. *helleri* but none superior. All hollies should be transplanted in the spring, and some require acid soil.

INCARVILLEA (Bignoniaceae)

These plants display in early summer great flaring trumpets of rose-pink on 8- to 10-inch stems above large pinnate leaves. Roots are long and heavy, demanding deep, rich soil in sun. Seed is plentiful though somewhat slow to germinate. In the North the plants want some winter protection but do not want to be smothered. The commonest species, *I. delavayi,* is a bit large, reaching 2 feet in height, but *I. grandiflora* and its varieties are handsome and more compact.

INULA (Compositae)

These are rather large, narrow-petaled, yellow daisies among wide grassy foliage, hairy and rough. They should be grown in good soil in full sun and propagated by division or seed. *I. acaulis* has practically stemless flowers surrounded by the leaf cluster, whereas *I. ensifolia,* with somewhat broader leaves, carries its daisies on foot-high stalks. Both flower for an extended period in early summer.

IRIS (Iridaceae)

This is a vast race of varied growth habit, with dwarf members suited to almost every site in the rock garden, the woods garden, or the bog. Though not a sound botanical separation, the irises may be grouped into bulbous, rhizomatous, and fibrous-rooted kinds. This is a useful classification for general cultural prescriptions.

Bulbous irises thrive best in full sun and limy soil and require a good baking in summer. Their reputed impermanence is largely because they do not get the thorough summer dormancy they need. They are excellent for pot-culture in the alpine-house, where they bloom in February and March. Rhizomatous irises, with heavy surface rhizomes, are of easy culture in any reasonable soil. They are most successfully transplanted soon after flowering, when they may

Iris cristata
(life size)

also be divided. Fibrous-rooted irises are not technically separable from those with rhizomes, but their cultural requirements are quite different and more exacting. These are best transplanted and divided in the early spring when root growth is active. Most want acid soil and moisture or light shade. Some western American species stand summer-drying. All irises are easy to raise from seed. If sown in fall, seed will germinate copiously at least by the second spring, many plants blooming the second year thereafter if transplanted into proper sites.

I. bracteata, fibrous-rooted, is from western America and is 18 inches high, the flowers cream with purple veins. *I. chrysographes,* fibrous-rooted and from western China, is about 12 inches tall, with blossoms of deep blue stenciled with gold. *I. chrysophylla* is a dwarf fibrous-rooted western American with large flat blossoms of white to yellow, finely brown-veined. *I. cristata* has thin mat-forming rhizomes but prefers woodsy soil in half-shade, where in late spring it bears multitudes of light blue gold-crested flowers on 6- to 9-inch stems. There is a pure-white variety, *alba,* and others of differing shades of blue. It is best divided after the flowering season.

I. danfordiae is a charming bulbous iris of clear lemon-yellow flowers on 3-inch stems. In alpine lawn or rocky pasture this blooms along with the crocuses. *I. flavissima* resembles a dwarf golden Siberian iris 3 to 6 inches tall. It blooms in early summer and though fibrous-rooted should be grown in well-drained soil and full sun, as in the rocky pasture.

I. forrestii is an Asiatic fibrous-rooted iris and should be treated as such. It looks like a short Siberian iris, 12 to 18 inches high, with yellow flowers in early summer. *I. gormanii,* a western American, is fibrous-rooted, with straw-yellow blooms on 12-inch stems. *I. gracilipes,* from Japan, is to be treated like a fibrous-rooted iris. It carries its flat, delicately lilac-pink or, rarely, white blossoms most charmingly on thin arching stems above frail narrow foliage. The whole mat is about 9 inches high. It wants shade and rich, leafy, acid soil. *I. innominata* is a fibrous-rooted western American, graceful and delicate, only 6 to 10 inches tall. The flowers of blue, white, or coppery shades are all penciled with brown. *I. lacustris,* form the Great Lakes region, is like a light blue, somewhat smaller *I. cristata* and should be treated as such.

I. mellita, rhizomatous, is like a dusky-red *I. pumila* with red-margined foliage. *I. pumila,* also rhizomatous, somewhat resembles a very delicate dwarf bearded iris. The species is dark red-purple and flowers in early spring, almost stemless among the stiff foliage. It has color variations in the wild and there are now hundreds of named forms and hybrids in many colors (some of these rather coarse) and ranging in height from 6 inches to 2 feet. All are of easy culture in any ordinary rock garden soil. *I. reticulata,* bulbous, blooms very early in various shades of blue. It is not easy to maintain. *I. ruthenica,* rhizomatous, forms a mat of narrow foliage and has blue and white, sweet-scented flowers about 6 to 8 inches tall. It blooms in early summer. *I. tectorum* is rhizomatous and has broad thin-textured leaves. The flowers, blue-lilac with darker pencilings, come 2 to 3 on 12- to 18-inch stems in early summer. There is a form with frosty-white blossoms.

I. tenax, another fibrous-rooted iris of western America, resembles a dwarf and delicate Japanese iris. *I. tenuis,* a western American fibrous-rooted iris of very local distribution, is narrow-leaved and about 10 inches tall, with many white flowers, veined with purple and yellow. It needs shade and good drainage. *I. verna* is somewhat similar to *I. cristata,* and like it is eastern American and for moist woodland sites. There the taller, sharper, *evergreen* foliage mass of *I. verna* is alive with brilliant blue orange-crested flowers in May.

ISOPYRUM (Ranunculaceae)

The European *I. thalictroides* is not unlike the American Rue Anemone and delights in the same open woodsy sites. It is easy to grow from seed and by division. Two western American species are rather similar: **I. stipitatum,** only 2 to 3 inches tall, and **I. hallii,** taller and somewhat coarser. All are to be grown in colonies in the woods garden.

JANKAEA (Gesneriaceae)

J. heldreichii, from the shady rocks of Greece, is a difficult plant, closely allied to ramondas but even more demanding in its requirements. From the rosette of hairy leaves spring stems of 2 to 3 inches, each bearing a crystalline lavender blossom like a diminished gloxinia. Try it in a crevice on a north slope with good leafy soil mixed with sand at the roots. It is better as an alpine-house plant set between two chunks of sandstone in a deep pot of leaf mold and sharp sand, kept quite dry in winter and copiously watered—by frequent immersion of the pot—when the growth commences in spring. The fine seed is to be handled as for ramondas, or leaves with a stem may be rooted in summer. This genus is sometimes included in *Ramonda.*

JASIONE (Campanulaceae)

This is a group of low-alpine meadow plants, related to campanulas, but with small fluffy heads of pale blue, like refined scabiosas. Grown easily from seed, or by division, they want good, loamy soil in a site that does not become too dry. All rather similar are *J. jankae, J. montana,* and *J. perennis,* all reaching about 12 inches. Only about 4 inches high are *J. humilis* and *J. supina.*

JEFFERSONIA (Berberidaceae)

There is something about the carriage and design of these woodland plants that wins more admiration than the size of the blossoms would suggest. They are sometimes compared to lanky hepaticas or shrunken anemones, but they have a distinctive quality all their own. The genus is sometimes listed under *Plagiorhegma.* The American species, *J. diphylla,* bears a pair of irregularly kidney-shaped leaves on 10-inch stems. Above these are carried in May, on a separate stem of 2 to 3 inches, 1-inch-wide, pure-white flowers, followed in August by strange cornucopia-shaped, leathery seed capsules. These open to reveal the large seeds in the boatlike cavity. Seeds are soon scattered, and after two years young plants will form a handsome group. Where grown close together they make a fine display. The roots may be divided either after the foliage dies down in the fall or in very early spring. Even fresh seed is likely to take two years to germinate. *J. dubia,* from Japan, is similar but even finer in its somewhat denser growth habit and in its heart-shaped, irregularly margined leaves (glaucous beneath) and larger, soft blue flowers. A clump of this plant in a woodland setting in rich leafy soil is a real delight.

JUNIPERUS (Cupressaceae)

These evergreen trees in their dwarf erect forms or in their spreading carpets are ideal for giving stability and design to the garden. Among most of the species, varieties well adapted to the sunny reaches of the small or large rock garden have been discovered and propagated. Increase by cuttings of new wood with some two-year wood at the base. Fall cuttings kept in a closed frame and given bottom heat are the surest. Layering of the procumbent forms is usually easy. There are a vast number of new forms being introduced yearly. All want open sites with considerable sun. They do not move easily when large, and even when small must not be permitted to dry at the roots during transplanting and immediately after. Once established they can stand dry conditions. Below are listed some of the best forms.

J. chinensis japonica is a bushy procumbent form of this highly variable species, up to 3 feet. *J. c. procumbens* (sometimes listed as just *J. procumbens*) is flat, stiff, and slow-growing and one of the best. The Japanese cultivated form, *J. c. shimpaku,* is very tight and neat.

J. communis is the low prostrate juniper of New England and the mountains. Suitable for the rock garden are: var. *compressa,* a dense, narrow column of light green, slowly reaching 3 feet; var. *depressa,* low and spreading, turning reddish in winter; var. *saxatilis,* low and flat, a mountain form. *J. conferta* is the Shore Juniper from Japan, a twisty, flat, bunchy species, distinctive and slightly less hardy than most.

J. horizontalis is, in all its forms, flat and quick-spreading, usually following the contours of the ground or rocks. *J. sabina* in var. *tamariscifolia* is another good trailer. *J. squamata* has 2 varieties well suited to the rock garden: var. *meyeri,* a dense, upright shrub, with beautiful silvery-blue foliage, to be kept low by bold pruning; and var. *prostrata,* one of the very best, which forms hard, tight billows about 4 inches high, rolling to fit any contour, even tumbling like a green waterfall over a ledge.

KALMIA (Ericaceae)

The Mountain Laurel, **K.** *latifolia,* is too large a shrub except as a background in the heath or acid rock garden or in the woods garden. The Bog Laurel, **K.** *polifolia,* carries blossoms like diminished blooms of the Mountain Laurel on low shrubs with small, evergreen leaves. It will grow in acid, peaty soil, best in semishade. The var. *microphylla,* from the high mountains, makes an almost flat mat of wider but shorter leaves. Division of established plants may be made and treated like cuttings. Cuttings of new wood will root. Both the plants—*K. polifolia* and its variety—are ideal for the heath garden.

KALMIOPSIS (Ericaceae)

K. *leachiana,* native to a few regions in the mountains of Oregon, is a beautiful dwarf evergreen shrub that bears over a long period bright clear-pink blossoms rather like a cross between those of laurel and of azalea. Var. *le piniec* is denser and more floriferous, best grown in well-drained acid soil with plenty of humus and in semishade. Where snow cover is not assured, some protection of ever-green boughs is advisable. Increase these plants by cuttings and careful division.

KELSEYA (Rosaceae)

K. uniflora is a rare American native of limestone ledges and screes in Montana, Idaho, and Wyoming, where it makes hard-domed cushions spattered with small white flowers. It is rarely successful in cultivation but is always a challenge to the expert. Seed, when available, is not difficult to germinate. It is resentful of humid conditions and should be grown so that the deep root may penetrate open, limy soil, and the cushion sit on pure rock: in a crevice or beneath a deep layer of limestone chips or on a piece of limestone with a hole drilled through it to accommodate the root in the soil beneath. Cuttings of the woody stems generally rot before rooting.

KNAUTIA. See *Scabiosa.*

LATHYRUS (Leguminosae)

The perennial peas are mostly too spreading and climbing for inclusion in the garden, but there are some bushy types that produce large showy flowers for a long season. *L. bijugatus,* from rocky mountain areas of the American West, is a bush about a foot tall with purple flowers. Related to it and from the same region, but varying in color from white to rose are *L. cusickii, L. nevadensis, L. rigidus,* and *L. torreyi.* From Europe comes the early-flowering bush, *L. vernus* (also called *Orobus vernus*). All are advisably grown from seed and established in the alpine lawn or rocky pasture while still young.

LAVANDULA (Labiatae)

Only *L. officinalis nana* is hardy and suitable to the rock garden. It makes a compact gray-leaved shrub with spikes of long-lasting lavender-blue flowers. A white-flowered form is a smaller dwarf and tighter in growth habit. Grow them in ordinary soil in full sun. The cuttings strike readily.

LAVAUXIA. See *Oenothera.*

LEDUM (Ericaceae)

The Labrador tea shrubs are all to be given acid, peaty soil, where the twiggy evergreen bushes bear interesting foliage and small clusters of white flowers at the tips of the shoots. They may be grown from seed or soft-wood cuttings. *L. groenlandicum* has thick leathery leaves felted beneath with rusty, woolly hair. It should be grown in sun to keep it dense and flowery. *L. columbianum* has a lighter texture, with leaves silvered beneath. It will grow about 2 feet high. Blossom buds can be damaged by a severe winter. Both are good shrubs for a large heath garden.

LEIOPHYLLUM (Ericaceae)

L. buxifolium is an excellent dwarf shrub for sunny, acid sites. The small evergreen leaves are shiny, and each twig of the 8- to 10-inch bush is tipped with a cluster of pink buds opening to white stars. Var. *prostratum* is a miniature form from the southern Appalachians. Increase these by seed or cuttings of half-ripened wood. Layers are perhaps easiest and quickest of all. They are well suited to the pine-barren type of site or in the heath garden.

LEONTOPODIUM (Compositae)

This is the famous, or infamous, Edelweiss with woolly, starfish blossoms above gray, hoary leaves. It is an easy plant to grow from seed or division, and should be planted in any fair soil in sun. *L. alpinum* is the species that adorns the traveler's hat and grows in alpine pastures in Europe. Var. *crassense* is a good dense form with heavily felted flowers. *L. sibiricum* is similar but taller, up to 12 inches, and with broader flowers. Many other species, from a range of sites in Europe and Asia, are similar, and all want considerable moisture to prevent flagging and wilting but must have sun to keep them compact and healthy.

LEPIDIUM (Cruciferae)

This genus gives to the dinner table the annual garden cress, but has in the Rocky Mountains a perennial species, *L. nanum*. This, in its native limestone screes, makes a hard-domed mound of small divided leaves sprinkled with almost stemless heads of small arabis-like blossoms. It demands full sun in a well-drained scree or crevice. It is easy to grow from seed, or from spring cuttings.

LEPTODACTYLON (Polemoniaceae)

In dry rocky sites in the Cascade and Rocky Mountains these relatives of the gilia and phlox form stiff little shrubby plants close-set with needle-leaves. The campanulate flowers of pink and white are carried in heads at the tips of the shoots and in the axils of the upper leaves. *L. pungens*, the commonest species, has grayish pungent foliage. These plants are to be propagated from seed or cuttings and grown in the scree or rocky pasture.

LEPTOTAENIA (Umbelliferae)

L. purpurea is known only from the drier sections of the Columbia River region, where in spring the flat, broad umbels of bright purple rise to 14 inches above ferny, fine foliage. Grow it in rocky, acid soil on a north slope and from seed when available or by division of established plants. The seed is deliciously pungent.

LESQUERELLA (Cruciferae)

This genus is rather like yellow-flowered arabis with hairy gray foliage. The seedpods are bladderlike. These plants are to be grown from seed and planted in light gravelly soil in full sun. From the American West comes *L. alpina,* a small bun of narrow leaves with short-stemmed blossoms. *L. condensata* is similar but an even smaller dwarf, and other species but play variations on the theme.

LEUCOCRINUM (Liliaceae)

L. montanum is the delightful Sand Lily of the drier western American mountains. Pure white, sweet-scented, almost stemless, narrow-petaled, crocus-like blooms cluster in a tuffet of grassy foliage. It is to be grown in sandy or gravelly well-drained soil. The fleshy roots may be divided and replanted when dormant in late summer.

LEUCOJUM (Amaryllidaceae)

The snowflakes are huskier and later-blooming than the snow-drops, yet rather similar in effect, with hanging white bells tipped with green. *L. aestivum, L. autumnale,* and *L. vernum,* as the names suggest, provide a long season of bloom. Plant the bulbs 3 to 4 inches deep in well-drained but good soil. They will endure considerable shade.

LEUCOTHOE (Ericaceae)

The Japanese *L. keiskei* is in stature and hardiness the best of the genus for the rock garden. In semishade and acid soil it becomes a trim evergreen shrub with stems that arch up about 8 to 10 inches. The foliage is glossy, turning red in fall. Large, waxy, white bells are pendent at the tip of the stems. Increase this plant by cuttings or division. It is for growing with heathers and other dwarf erica-ceous material in the heath bed. *L. davisiae* and *L. grayana* are a bit taller, with smaller flowers, and not quite so hardy.

LEWISIA (Portulacaceae)

This strictly American genus has contributed much beauty to the rock gardens of the world. In the mountains and valleys of the West are many species, all worth the effort to make them flourish in eastern gardens. They have succulent, brittle leaves, and heavy, fleshy roots that call for a number of rather special conditions in the garden. All grow readily from fresh seed, frequently all the seeds germinating within a day or two of each other after having waited as much as a year in the planting medium. They germinate best at a cool temperature, even just above freezing, as though anxious to make as much growth as possible before summer drought and winter rest. Some species are evergreen; others have leaves for only part of the year.

L. brachycalyx, like most of the deciduous species, wants a place in the sun. Early in the spring spatulate 3-inch-long leaves rise in a rosette; then from the crown come 2-inch stems carrying solitary pure-white flowers, 2 inches across. This is to be grown in quickly draining but fertile soil, half sharp sand or fine gravel and half mixed loam and leaf mold. As with all lewisias, a collar of dry stone chips on the surface keeps fatal root-rot from the crown. Spring moisture and summer dryness are the rule in its native haunts.

L. columbiana has evergreen, narrow straplike leaves in a neat rosette. Numerous 8- to 10-inch stems carry sprays of small flowers with dark pink stripes on white to light pink petals. The whole plant has a graceful effect and should be grown with a northern or eastern exposure, never sunbaked, in well-drained, nourishing soil. It seems indifferent about lime.

L. cotyledon is the most varied and most widely grown of the evergreen lewisias. With all its variants of leaf and flower, it is sometimes listed as these separate species: *L. eastwoodiana, L. finchii, L. heckneri, L. howellii,* and *L. longifolia.* They grow in the mountains of southwestern Oregon and northwestern California from about 1,000 to 8,000 feet. From husky rosettes of evergreen tongue-shaped leaves (frequently wavy or jagged on the edges) rise many stems of 8 to 10 inches, each carrying a panicle of clear-pink to orange-pink blossoms, the petals striped with darker color, the individual flowers as much as an inch across. Plants with pure-white crystalline blossoms have also been found, but rarely, and a pure-yellow form has been reported. In the East they need to be grown under as cool conditions as possible, preferably on a north-facing slope or in the crevice of a shady wall. A gritty soil containing at least half neutral or acid leaf mold, with special drainage at the crown, suits their requirements. Old plants may develop many crowns, which may be separated and rooted in the spring.

L. *leana* has evergreen rosettes of quill-like foliage with panicles of many, small, bright magenta flowers on 9-inch scapes. It has been found—but very rarely—with white and delicate pink blossoms. A gritty soil among rocks, acid in reaction, in sun or light shade, will usually make it happy. Where this species grows in company with *L. cotyledon*, in the Siskiyou Mountains, natural hybrids between them have occurred; these look very like *L. columbiana*.

L. *nevadensis* is an early-blooming deciduous species that carries many solitary white flowers on short scapes among 2-inch cylindric leaves rising from a fleshy tuber-like root. It will endure considerable moisture in spring, but wants a dry site in summer. Rather similar are *L. pygmaea* and *L. triphylla*.

L. *oppositifolia*, with 3-inch linear leaves that dry up and disappear in summer, carries 2 to 4 white water-lily-like blossoms on 8-inch stems. It wants a site that will be moist in spring but dry in summer. **L. *rediviva*,** the Bitter-root, is widespread in the mountains and the dry intermontane reaches of the West. In late summer tufts of green needle-spikes erupt from a wizened cluster of fleshy red roots and persist throughout the winter until the warmer days of June. As they begin to wither, from the crown comes a succession of almost stemless, great pink or white many-petaled chalices, unfolding from the fleshy reddish wrappings of the bud. This wrapping persists as a papery envelope for the seeds. *L. rediviva* wants very good drainage in a rocky soil that will dry and bake in the summer. When dormant, it may be transplanted and divided. Most effective in good-sized clumps, it poses the problem of what to do with the spot from which the clumps disappear during the dormant period of late summer, since the plants resent any smothering competition.

L. *tweedyi* is without question the most beautiful of the lewisias and would rank near the top of any list of the best alpines of the world. From a heavy carrot-root come numerous rosettes of broad, fleshy leaves, among which in May rise numerous 4- to 6-inch stems,

Lewisia tweedyi
(⅞ life size)

each bearing 2 or 3 large flowers of pale apricot-pink, shimmering with pearly opalescence. A single established plant may carry more than 50 blooms, which open over a long period. This plant has a narrow range in the wild, being found only in the rockslides of the Wenatchee Mountains of central Washington.

A common experience in the garden is the utter collapse and death of the plant after flowering. This demise is due to a crown-rot in the great fleshy root. To avoid this, grow the plant in a vertical position in a wall or crevice facing east or north. Let the feeding-roots, which grow from the lower part of the heavy taproot, run back into fairly rich neutral or acid soil. Let at least an inch of the crown of the great root protrude from between the rocks. Side-rosettes will form, each with a husky, fleshy tuber; these may be removed with a sharp knife and rooted in sand to increase the supply. Some growers advise removing all side-rosettes in the spring before the flowering period to permit circulation of air, but this is not essential. It is a wise precaution to dust with fungicide the wound where a rosette has been removed.

To get a set of seed in the East it is necessary to hand-pollinate the flowers. Seed germinates very early in spring and by fall will produce plants large enough to insert in a crack. They will flower when about three years old. If grown in a pot in the alpine-house, the crown must be set well above a pair of rocks sunk in the pot, between which the feeding-roots may run down into well-drained rich soil. Avoid overhead watering.

LIATRIS (Compositae)

Most of the American gayfeathers are too tall for the rock garden. A few species, such as *L. punctata* and *L. squarrosa,* carry their spikes of purple buttons on stems under 2 feet. They will bring late color to the alpine lawn, if the tuberous roots are planted in light sandy soil in full sun. Increase these by seed or division of the root in spring.

LILIUM (Liliaceae)

Vast, indeed, is the tribe of the lilies, many excellent ones for the woods garden and a few for the open rock garden. Special books of lily culture are the best source of information on description and prescription.

LIMONIUM (Plumbaginaceae)

These dainty statices, or sea-lavenders (sometimes listed as *Statice*), are rarely seen in American rock gardens. Their effect is not brilliant but is most graceful, and they bloom in summer and fall. The dwarf sorts make small tuffets of foliage, in some a lovely blue-gray, above which rise on wiry stems heads of small "everlasting" flowers with papery bracts. The color of most is in rather pale smoky shades. Though the best come from the Mediterranean coastal region, they are hardy and flourish in well-drained soil in full sun. Propagate them by seed or division. *L. bellidifolium* has pale lilac flowers on 6- to 8-inch stems. *L. incanum nanum* carries red flowers on 8- to 10-inch stems. *L. minutum* has reddish-purple flowers on 6- to 9-inch stems.

LINARIA (Scrophulariaceae)

Many of the linarias from the Mediterranean are not hardy but may be treated as annuals that self-sow. *L. alpina,* however, is a good perennial, if short-lived. It too scatters its seeds where they will produce all summer long a trailing circle of fine stems clothed with small blue-green leaves and numerous little "snapdragons" of brilliant purple and orange. Var. *rosea* has pink flowers. Though it will grow in all sorts of locations and soils, it is more permanent in well-drained, sunny sites.

LINDELOFIA (Boraginaceae)

L. longiflora offers a long season of bright blue flowers, rather like deep blue anchusas, uncurling from pink buds on a foot-high leafy stalk. The basal leaves are large and rough. This is easy to grow from seed, in good soil in sun or light shade. Coming as it does from the Himalayas, it is not always hardy in the North without snow cover.

LINNAEA (Caprifoliaceae)

L. borealis var. *americana* is the almond-scented Twinflower of our northern woods, where it rambles in flat festoons over old stumps and logs. The fine woody stems, which root as they run, are set with pairs of small round evergreen leaves with a russet cast. From the leaf axils, on 2-inch stems, are borne in May and June a pair of lovely pink bells. It is best increased by division of rooted sections established in moist, humus-rich acid soil in shade. It will run rapidly, once established, and is well adapted to ramping beneath the shrubs in the heath garden.

LINUM (Linaceae)

The perennial flax offers summer bloom in blue, white, yellow, or pale pink. Most are delicate of stem and leaf and fleeting of flower, but charming mixed with heavier plants in well-drained soil in sunny sites, such as the alpine lawn. They should be grown from seed and set out when young because they resent transplanting. Usually most will self-sow. *L. alpinum* makes an arching sheaf of wiry 10-inch stems with small grayish leaves and ample heads of chicory-blue flowers. *L. austriacum* is similar to *L. alpinum*, but more erect, with somewhat larger, greener leaves. *L. flavum* bears a head of yellow flowers throughout the summer on rather stiff leafy stems about a foot high. Old plants may succumb in a severe winter. *L. salsoloides nanum* makes a tight low tangle of fine stems with needlelike leaves. For a long period in summer this is covered with good-sized flat blossoms of smoky white, shaded almost blue in the throat. A sunny well-drained spot with deep soil among rocks is essential for health and longevity. This may be propagated by late summer-cuttings of stems with some thickness. *L. tenuifolium* is variable in habit and stature, from 2 inches to a foot, lax to somewhat shrubby, always with narrow, needlelike foliage. The flowers are a pale pink washed with light blue. There are American flaxes, not generally in cultivation, worth searching for: *L. lewisii,* very like *L. alpinum; L. kingii* and *L. sedoides,* dwarf, yellow-flowered species of the high western mountains.

LIRIOPE (Liliaceae)

The lily-turfs of Japan have recently received much attention as turfing and rock garden plants. The grasslike foliage is evergreen, in carpets that can be grown in either sun or shade, so dense that these make excellent plants to stop erosion. In late summer, spikes of blue or white blossoms are thick among the foliage spears. The plants are easy to propagate by division. *L. muscari* in many varieties is a husky species up to 18 inches with thin or heavy cluster-spikes of lavender, blue, or white blossoms. There are also dwarf forms 6 to 7 inches tall. *L. spicata* is narrow in foliage and very rapid in spread, with short spikes of white flowers. *L. graminifolia* is even smaller, with spikes of purple-blue flowers among prostrate strap-shaped evergreen foliage.

LITHOPHRAGMA (Saxifragaceae)

The fringecups are delicate-stemmed wildflowers of the American West, sometimes listed as *Tellima.* From a tuberous root comes a rosette of round leaves in early spring, and then stems of 6 inches to a foot bearing white or pink flowers with deeply slashed petals. These are best grown in rich but well-drained soil with some shade and are propagated by seed or division of the tuberous roots. *L. affinis* may reach 16 inches and is a woodland species. *L. parviflora* has deeply cleft petals. *L. tenella* is a dwarf of 6 inches.

LITHOSPERMUM (Boraginaceae)

From the western United States and the Mediterranean basin come these handsome and difficult plants. The bright orange-yellow of *L. canescens* is as brilliant in its way as the gorgeous true-blue of *L. diffusum.* Authorities differ about how to grow these plants successfully, but there is some general agreement that the principal source of difficulty is in the character of the heavy, brittle root system that needs deep, penetrable soil, rich in nourishment. In the eastern United States some shade from the hot midday sun is a prerequisite.

L. *canescens* is a western prairie plant with long hairy leaves and a fiddlehead of bright yellow flowers. It blooms early and should have a rich, limy, well-drained soil. Propagate it by seed. **L.** *diffusum* is a dwarf evergreen subshrub with dark, hairy green leaves and beautiful "heavenly-blue" salver-form blossoms for a long season. It wants a deep, peaty soil without a trace of lime and on a north slope, but seems impermanent and not safely hardy. It is so beautiful that it is worth rooting cuttings annually. In late July take 2-inch tip-shoots, treat with rooting-compound, and insert in a peat and sand mixture. Rooted plants should be carefully lifted and carefully potted in rich, peaty, leaf-mold soil mixed with ¼ part sharp sand and held in the frame or alpine-house for the winter. Set early in the garden, they will bloom that summer and supply a new batch of cuttings and occasionally, with good snow cover, will persist throughout the winter. To be treated like *L. canescens* are other American species: **L.** *angustifolium,* **L.** *californicum,* and **L.** *carolinense.* To grow like *L. diffusum,* but with the addition of limestone chips, are: **L.** *graminifolium,* **L.** *intermedium,* and **L.** *oleifolium.* Treatment for the last is the same as for *Daphne cneorum.*

LLOYDIA (Liliaceae)

A minute alpine lily of lofty screelike places in the high mountains of Europe and America, **L.** *serotina* produces among grassy foliage small white flowers, tinged with pink, and purple-veined, which are carried singly on 3- to 6-inch stems. Though not showy, a group of the bulbs planted in the scree among other diminutive plants has a certain alpine charm.

LOBELIA (Lobeliaceae)

The American lobelias are suited to moist spots in the wild garden, especially along streams. Once established they will seed themselves. If they do not like the site they will perish after a single blooming, though they are quite perennial. *L. cardinalis,* the Cardinal Flower, up to 4 feet tall, is a gorgeous splash of brilliant scarlet when in flower at the end of the summer. It will grow anchored among rocks in running water, but will also thrive in moist acid soil. It may be propagated by seed, or by pinning one of the stems flat to the ground, where it will send out roots at each leaf node. This is the best method of reproducing the rare white and pink varieties. *L. kalmii* is a swamp-dweller in limestone areas. It is difficult to transplant because of the very slight, thin white roots. The small light blue blossoms on foot-high stems are effective in mass. It is best established by seeding in moist soil where the plants are to stand. *L. siphilitica,* and especially in its pure-white form (the flowers are usually blue), are fine companions for the Cardinal Flower, though they do not insist on quite such a moist site, and they do prefer neutral or limy soil. The plants are long-lived if periodically divided.

LOISELEURIA (Ericaceae)

Those who have seen a large carpet of the prostrate evergreen shrub *L. procumbens* sprinkled with tiny pink azaleas—in the White Mountains of New England or in the European Alps—must have longed to possess such a carpet in the garden. But, alas, it is not an easy plant to grow and nearly impossible to induce to flower in captivity. Collected plants rarely settle down, because their roots are long and woody, with few feeding-rootlets. Cuttings of young shoots can be rooted in sand and peat; and seed, though it will germinate, is extremely slow. Once you have a cutting established in a pot, the selection of a place for it in the garden poses the next problem. It wants acid, gritty soil on a north slope, where it will keep as cool as possible but will have light and air to encourage flowering. Try it in the heath garden with cassiopes and other difficult plants.

LOMATIUM (Umbelliferae)

These dwarf members of the Parsley Family are found in the mountains of western North America, where early in the season, among the fine, green parsley-foliage appear dense umbel heads of small pincushiony flowers. They should be grown from seed, since the roots are rather heavy and carrot-like. *L. ambiguum* has bright yellow flowers on 1-foot stems. *L. gormanii* and *L. piperi* have short-stemmed "salt and pepper" blossoms of white with prominent stamens. *L. macrocarpum* has finely dissected carrot-like leaves and large umbels of white lacy flowers on arching stems. There are many other lovely species that contribute prominently to the wild alpine gardens of the western mountains. There are 37 species in Oregon alone. All want a sunny exposure in rocky well-drained but deep soil.

LUETKEA (Rosaceae)

L. pectinata is a fine-leaved little creeper of the American Northwest, where in high-mountain peaty screes it forms mats suggesting a mossy saxifrage. The carpet is decorated in summer with 2- to 3-inch spikes of pale yellow spirea-like flowers. In the East it wants a cool moist site, a north slope by preference; try it in the heath garden. It will grow from seed and strikes easily from summer-cuttings of the woody stems.

LUINA (Compositae)

The common name for this uncommon composite is Silverback. In rocky screes and crevices of the coastal and Cascade Mountains of the United States, *L. hypoleuca* forms close clumps of veiny leaves, frosted above and downy beneath with dense wool. In flower the plants may rise to a foot, producing spidery, pale yellow button-blossoms in a close head during the early summer, rather like Edelweiss without the felted bracts. It should be propagated by seed or division and grown in scree or rocky pasture.

LUPINUS (Leguminosae)

Besides the wild Blue Lupine of sterile sandy pastures and open woods of the Northeast, there are many dwarfs of the hills and mountains of western America, some too tall for the rock garden, but others dazzlingly beautiful, with the short stalk of "heavenly-blue" flowers rising from a filigree of silver foliage. Unfortunately, to date these small species are very little seen in cultivation. All require excellent drainage and plenty of sunshine, and deeply resent transplanting. They may even be short-lived in nature, depending on self-sowing for perpetuation. They are easy to grow from seed, sometimes flowering the first year. Because of the difficulty of transplanting them (except when young and vigorous) it may be the wisest plan to sow seed directly in a proper site of the garden: a rocky, porous soil in full sun with at least 2 inches of stone chips about the crown and under the foliage. The dwarf perennial species have silky compound leaves and dense heads of pea blossoms, mostly lavender and blue, with white centers. Species of *Lupinus* to look for are: ***arcticus, breweri, caespitosus, confertus, cusickii, lepidus, lyallii, minimus,*** and ***saxosus.***

LYCHNIS (Caryophyllaceae)

The campions, or catchflies, are not easily distinguished from silenes, except that the foliage is generally sticky and the blossom color is less clear. They are easily raised from the abundant seed and grown in fairly rich soil. *L. alpina* makes tufts of narrow foliage with short-stemmed heads of bloom in June. The color is rose-purple or white. It thrives in good soil in a sunny or semishady spot. *L.* × *haggeana* has large blossoms of brilliant red, orange-scarlet, or pink on leafy stems about 10 inches high. This favors rich, moist soil, for June and July flowering, and is a hybrid that breeds true but variable from seed. *L. lagascae* is to be found under *Petrocoptis*.

LYSICHITUM (Araceae)

The Yellow Skunk-cabbage, of western America, *L. americanum,* lights up the woodsy bogs with its large yellow spathes in early spring before the massive leaves unfold. This is a big plant with big, heavy roots, suitable only to large swampy areas but sufficiently beautiful to warrant attempting to grow it from seed or root-cuttings. Even more beautiful and with no taint of the skunk to blemish its beauty is pure-white-spathed *L. camtschatcense.*

LYSIMACHIA (Primulaceae)

L. japonica is a neat creeping plant of moist soil, where small gold coins sit among the cool green leaves during the height of summer. It is like a dwarf and restrained *L. nummularia,* the Moneywort of wet meadows and ditches, which is pretty but prudently left out of the garden because of its ramping ways.

MACROTOMIA (Boraginaceae)

M. echioides (sometimes listed under *Arnebia*) is an unusual-looking plant whose borage-like blossoms are light yellow with purple spots that fade out to leave the flowers pure yellow. These flowers are numerous, in racemes about a foot high, above rosettes of long rough leaves. It grows in very light sandy or gravelly soil in sun. Seed germinates readily, and increase is simple by removal of side-rosettes in spring and treating them as cuttings.

MAHONIA (Berberidaceae)

These evergreen shrubs, the grape-hollies, closely allied to barberries, have excellent spiny foliage and clusters of yellow flowers in spring followed by small blue fruit in grape-like bunches. To prevent winter-burning of the evergreen foliage, a position protected from high wind and winter sun should be selected. They are quite indifferent to soil acidity, but grow best in well-drained soil with leaf mold added. Seed germinates after winter freezing, and cuttings of half-ripened wood can be rooted in summer. Taller species are excellent background shrubs for the rock garden, and the smaller ones make good companions for bulbs and other dwarf plants.

M. *aquifolium,* from the American Northwest is the species most generally available. It will endure rather dense shade and does best out of full sun. Various forms are available but the type will in time become a large, handsome shrub up to 4 feet high and as much across. This plant is suitable for the surroundings of the rock garden or in the woods garden. M. *nervosa* is rather similar to M. *aquifolium* but remains lower and more compact, up to about 2 feet. M. *pumila* is even smaller, about 1 foot, with smaller flower clusters and fruit. M. *repens* is a ground-covering plant that produces stolons and remains under a foot high. Grown in sun and ordinary soil it will in time make a dense mat with thin, spiny foliage, turning wine-red in autumn. It will grow in shade, where it increases more rapidly but not so densely.

MAIANTHEMUM (Liliaceae)

These delicate woodland lilies-of-the-valley are fine carpeters for shady sites in good, leafy soil. Propagation is easy by division. The 3 wild species are quite similar. M. *bifolium* of European and Asian woods reaches a height of 9 inches, whereas the spikes of small, starry, white blossoms on the eastern American, M. *canadense,* only reach about 5 inches. The largest in all respects, including larger flowers, is M. *dilatatum* of the Northwest and Japan.

MALVA (Malvaceae)

To see M. *moschata,* native to Europe, escaped into some moist corner of an abandoned New England meadow or along the roadside ditches of Canada is to recognize its value in the large alpine lawn or in moist openings in the woodland garden. The pink or white mallow blossoms are produced in clusters for a long period in summer on branching plants up to 2 feet tall. This is easy to grow from seed, or from root-cuttings of desirable dwarf large-flowered forms.

MALVASTRUM. See *Sphaeralcea.*

MAZUS (Scrophulariaceae)

This is a genus of flat carpeters with blossoms like those of large lavender-blue and gold linarias spattered on the close mat for a long season in summer. These mats, when happily growing in rich, quite moist soil in semishade, are easily divided for increase. If the winter is bare and frigid, the plants may not survive. The hardiest species is *M. reptans* from the Himalayas.

MECONOPSIS (Papaveraceae)

Though the gorgeous blue poppies of Tibet are not at all easy to grow in the Northeast, every ambitious gardener makes a trial. Enough success rewards careful and patient management to whet the appetite and spur the experiments. Except for the easy Welch Poppy, *M. cambrica,* all the magnificent species want a deep, moist but well-drained soil, rich in leaf mold and peat. The site should be protected from winds, out of the sun, though it must not be dank and gloomy. Many die after flowering, but they come easily from seed. Seedlings should not be moved into permanent sites until fairly large. First transplant the minute seedlings into a flat or deep pot in preparation for setting out the following spring.

M. betonicifolia, with large, silky, sky-blue blossoms at the tip of 3-foot stems, is one of the best and the easiest. If you find the right spot, self-sowing will keep the planting going. *M. cambrica* is an easy plant to grow in shady locations in any reasonable soil. All summer there will be a succession of yellow or orange poppy-blossoms on stems about a foot high. Self-sowing is the surest means of maintaining the species, since it tends to perish after flowering. *M. bella* and *M. quintuplinervia* are lovely dwarf and perennial species but not easy to acquire, because the seeds do not germinate as freely as those for other members of the genus.

MEDEOLA (Liliaceae)

M. virginiana, Cucumber-root, is not brilliant, but has a graceful charm in the woods garden. This native carries on erect stems, without basal foliage, a whirl of leaves that are frequently reddish near the stem. In flowering plants come another short spurt of stem and a second whirl of smaller leaves, just above which dangle fine-petaled, greenish-yellow blossoms; these are followed by purple berries. The fleshy white roots, tasting of cool cucumber, may be divided for increase; seed is also quite possible.

MEEHANIA (Labiatae)

M. cordata is an uncommon carpeting plant from the southern Appalachians. It makes long rooting runners with small, round, rough leaves and clusters of large purple and white snapdragon-like blossoms close on the carpet. This is to be grown in good, woodsy soil and shade and propagated by seed or division.

MEGASEA. See *Bergenia.*

MELANDRIUM. See *Lychnis* and *Silene.*

MENYANTHES (Gentianaceae)

The Buckbean, *M. trifoliata,* is a rather rare but showy American plant of bog and pond edges. From a husky creeping root-stock rise large, 3-part, cloverlike leaves. The flowers, in a raceme of 10 to 20 blossoms on a 10-inch scape, are waxy white and filled with glistening-white hairs. Grow it in a very wet soil—especially an acid one—or in shallow water, and increase by division or seed sown in sphagnum soup.

MERTENSIA (Boraginaceae)

For a lovely shade of clear sky-blue mixed with pink and white, no genus is more prized than the early-flowering mertensias.

America has native species to fit a diversity of sites, with tall leafy sheafs for the shady woods garden and dwarfs for the rock garden proper. Other excellent species hail from the Himalayas. There is not an unattractive species in the whole genus, though some have flowers in the unfurling crosier in finer proportion to the leafage than others. In general the dwarf mountain species require rich, well-drained conditions, moist in spring but drying out considerably when the plants go dormant in the summer. Even the taller kinds lose their foliage and vanish soon after seeding, but they need rich soil in shade. Seed of mertensias germinates readily, but it is not until the third year or afterward that plants show their full beauty. Division of the woody, chunky roots is possible as soon as the plants go dormant.

From the American West come a number of dwarf species, all most desirable and quite similar. The leaves are glaucous, a pale blue-green, from 2 to 4 inches long, and diminishing in size up the flowering-stems, which may be from 5 inches to a foot high. The light blue flowers are in full crosier-form heads at the tips of the stems, opening in succession over a long period in early summer. Any of the following *Mertensia* species should be eagerly sought, planted in rich scree condition, and permitted to self-sow: *alpina,* 8 inches; *bakeri,* 1 foot; *horneri,* 5 inches; *humilis,* 8 inches; *lanceolata,* 1 foot; *longiflora,* 10 inches; *nutans,* 8 inches; *oblongifolia,* 8 inches; and *pulchella,* 8 inches.

From the Himalayas come dwarf species very similar in blossom but different in leaf. Here the leaves are dark green and hairy, mostly basal. These want a rich, acid scree in half-shade. *M. echioides* has deep blue flowers on 1-foot stems; *M. elongata* is very dense and flowery at 8 inches; while *M. primuloides,* which may perish in muggy weather, is an absolute charmer, with deep bright blue flowers on 3- to 4-inch stems.

The taller species have the same sky-blue flowers in uncurling crosiers, pink-tinged in bud, and the same glaucous blue-green foliage as the smaller dwarf American species. Like these, the taller mertensias disappear in summer but not before the stems turn yellow and flop disconsolately, so it is important to surround these woodlanders with other plants, such as ferns, whose foliage will conceal them after their spring bloom is over. Some scatter seed so widely when in a congenial site as to become a bit of a nuisance. The eastern American *M. virginica,* the Virginia Bluebell, is the best known—an adaptable plant in shade or semishade, reaching 2 feet. Westerners of the same general character and requirements are *M. ciliata* and *M. paniculata.*

MICROMERIA (Labiatae)

These are fine-stemmed dwarf shrubs with aromatic foliage and pink labiate flowers, about halfway between those of *Thyme* and *Satureia.* The vast number of rather similar species, ranging in height from 3 to 8 inches, are found in fully sunny sites about the Mediterranean. These should be grown in ordinary rock garden soil among limestone rocks, and may be speedily propagated from seed or summer-cuttings. The one American species, *M. chamissonis,* is a rapid-spreading carpet suited as a bulb cover in the alpine lawn and will endure considerable shade.

MIMULUS (Scrophulariaceae)

The monkeyflowers are New World plants, coming from stream-banks and wet meadows of North and South America. None seem permanently perennial, but when grown in good moist soil with light shade they tend to self-sow. Since the root system is meager, it is well to sow seed where the plants are to stand. They bloom for a long period in summer. Many of the showiest species are tender, but the following will flourish if given a proper setting. *M. cardinalis* is a brilliant short-lived perennial species, about a foot high, with sticky, hairy leaves, and narrow, scarlet and yellow hooded flowers. *M. lewisii* is taller, with broader, deep rose-pink flowers, and is best grown in drier, rich soil in semishade. *M. guttatus* is a variable species, yellow-flowered and easy to grow in wet meadow or on streamsides. Though a western species, it has naturalized along streams in the Northeast. In a lean, moist site the plant may be kept dwarf and somewhat more perennial. *M. moschatus, M. primuloides,* and *M. tillingii* are creeping, yellow-flowered species of wet rocks at high elevations in the western mountains.

MINUARTIA. See *Arenaria.*

MITCHELLA (Rubiaceae)

The Partridgeberry, *M. repens,* is a common plant of rich woodlands that are generally slightly acid. Though common, it is one of the best carpeters for semishaded or shaded sites. The paired oval leaves are evergreen, dark with paler veins. Spattered on the carpet are shining red berries that persist for a full year, even beyond the June flowering of the next year's blossoms. Each 2-eyed berry is the product of a pair of pinkish-white, sweet-scented, waxy trumpets that are united at the base. There is a white-fruited variety of less vigorous constitution. Mats may be divided or cuttings rooted. Seed is slow, but sure. This is an excellent ground cover for dwarf ericaceous shrubs and other acid-soil plants wanting a shady or semishady home.

MITELLA (Saxifragaceae)

The blossoms of the bishop's-caps are not large and showy but most intricately lacy and graceful on close inspection. These are woodland plants to be grown in generous clumps for early flowering. They have a delicate root system that does not fight against neighbors. The general effect is like a *Heuchera* of refined and modest disposition. Seed is the simplest means of increase. In fact, self-sowing is common in rather moist, rich, leafy soil. *M. diphylla* has lacy white blossoms in a slender spike above a pair of stem-leaves. *M. nuda* is smaller, without stem-leaves, and here the blossoms are of reddish-gold threads. Western species comprise two whites, **M. *diversifolia*** and **M. *trifida*,** and greenish-flowered **M. *breweri*, M. *ovalis*,** and **M. *pentandra*.**

MOLTKIA. See *Lithospermum.*

MONARDELLA (Labiatae)

The dwarf, compact horsemints of the far-western United States make dense clumps of hairy, aromatic foliage about 1 foot high and as much across. The blossoms of purple and pink labiate flowers are gathered in close terminal heads. To keep them dwarf and floriferous, give them good drainage and ample sun. The increasing clumps may be divided and must be watched for invasion of less stalwart companions. **M. *macrantha*** of the California mountains reaches a foot in height and has bright orange-red flowers. **M. *odoratissima*** is slightly shorter, with pink and white flowers. **M. *parvifolia*** is dense and woody, with lilac-purple flowers. **M. *villosa*** will reach 1½ feet, with purple, pink, or white flowers. All species are mint-scented.

MONESES (Pyrolaceae)

The elfin shinleaf, **M. *uniflora*,** of dark, cool, acid woods, does not like to be tamed. The solitary nodding flowers are waxy white and deliciously scented, on 2- to 3-inch stems above the mats of round, shining, evergreen leaves. The white roots are sparse and brittle, and may require specific plant or fungus association. It is generally found growing in the needle-duff of pines where it is not too dry—a fact that suggests the only practical method of establishment: young plants, carefully lifted with a good ball of soil, may occasionally be transplanted to a moist site under pines.

MONTIA (Portulacaceae)

These western American spring-beauties are dwellers of wet, mossy, shady places along streams. Though the flowers are as large and beautiful as those of claytonias, the flowering-stalks are much taller and weaker. The basal foliage is succulent and may be eaten as salad. These plants are best propagated by seed and per-mitted to self-sow. Perennial species are **M. cordifolia, M. flagel-laris, M. parvifolia,** and **M. sibirica.**

MORISIA (Cruciferae)

The single species, **M. monantha,** makes a rosette of much-cut leaves, in the center of which are stemless, 4-petaled yellow flowers in early summer. As a Corsican plant, it craves sun and good drainage in the scree but is not reliably hardy north. Seed or root-cuttings provide means of increase.

MUSCARI (Liliaceae)

There are many recognized species of grape-hyacinths. A great number are similar, their color blue, blue-purple, and white. Most bulb houses carry these; they are of the easiest culture in ordinary soil in sun or light shade. Once established they increase by multi-plying the bulbs rather rapidly and by abundant self-sowing. Though they are usually considered too coarse for the small rock garden, they are admirably suited to the alpine lawn, where they will maintain themselves in the midst of the fiercest competition.

MYOSOTIS (Boraginaceae)

The common, azure-blue forget-me-nots are mostly short-lived but set such an abundance of seed that in moist soil in sun or shade they can soon dominate the situation. They are, therefore, to be kept out of the best locations, though their beauty and easy culti-vation encourage the gardener to find a spot where they may have their way. **M. alpestris** and **M. sylvatica** are typical and, though usually blue, there are white and pink forms available—also forms of short stature and neater habit, such as var. **'Ruth Fischer.'** Propagate these by seed or cuttings.

The very different species from New Zealand, with rather stiff rosetted foliage and dwarfed white or yellow flowers, are as tricky in eastern America as the blues are easy. **M. explanata** may be taken as the white-flowered type and **M. *uniflora*** as the yellow-flowered representative. Both have mats of gray-green foliage and short flower stems. A shaded, well-drained but moist site offers the only hope of success.

M. *rupicola* (formerly thought to be a high-alpine form of *M. alpestris*) is horticulturally quite different and most desirable even among the finest rock garden inhabitants. It is an altogether charming plant, forming a dense mound of dark green foliage which in June becomes a mass of clear sky-blue, yellow-eyed flowers in full heads only a few inches above the foliage-mound. Summer humidity frequently blackens the oldest and largest clumps. Young vigorous new plants made of rosettes taken early from the edges of the cluster and rooted in sand, resist mildew and assure perpetuation. A site on the semishaded moraine keeps the plant trim and healthy. Seed will produce flowering plants in two years.

NARCISSUS (Amaryllidaceae)

The larger trumpet daffodils are suited only to the fringes of the large rock garden, or to naturalizing in open areas in the deciduous woods garden and in the large alpine lawn. For the rock garden proper there are a number of dwarf *Narcissus* species that look their best and flourish in rich well-drained soil and sunshine. Specialist growers are beginning to recognize a new interest in these small species, and their catalogues describe many charming varieties with cultural directions.

Bulbs of the most desirable species of *Narcissus* are not, however, always readily available commercially and may be expensive. The easiest way in which to produce a sizable crop of bulbs for group plantings is to grow them from seed. In a frame or other smaller container filled with rich but well-drained soil, plant the seeds with a covering of at least ½ inch of soil. The fine, hairlike foliage will appear in early spring and remain evergreen if given protection during the following winter. The small rice-like bulbs at the base should be left to fatten in the seeding mixture for at least one year before planting-out. When transplanted at an early age they should be treated as any herbaceous plant and not allowed to dry out. In fact, even mature narcissus bulbs should be planted as early in summer as they can be procured. Established clumps may be lifted, divided, and replanted with foliage intact immediately after they finish flowering.

NEOBESSEYA (Cactaceae)

Some of the cacti of the Rocky Mountain area are hardy to well below freezing. Though somewhat exotic-looking when mixed with typical alpines, a sunny pocket of well-drained poor soil among rocks provides a home-like site, where they display large silky blossoms of yellow or red during the summer. They also look at home in the rocky pasture. *N. missouriensis* is a small ball-type cactus with yellow and orange flowers. Give it a soil of almost pure gravel and sand with only a dash of loam and a dash of lime. *N. vivipara* carries carmine flowers on top of the small spiny balls.

NEPETA (Labiatae)

The catmints are of very easy culture and make neat gray-green mounds with spikes of lavender-blue flowers for a fairly long period in summer. Old plants tend to die-back in severe winters, but periodical division of the clumps keeps them vigorous and hardy. Cuttings of half-ripened wood strike easily. Poor soil also tends to keep them stocky and healthy. *N. cyanea,* though small in flower, is low-growing, a 6-inch mound from the Caucasus. *N. grandiflora,* also from the Caucasus, is a 2-foot plant with ample spikes of large blue flowers. *N. mussinii,* is the species most generally grown in America; large-flowered forms are available and most desirable.

NIEREMBERGIA (Solanaceae)

The South American cupflowers are not reliably hardy north of New York City. The blue or white flowers of good size sit neatly on the tops of short shoots above the mat of narrow foliage.

Ordinary, rather rich garden soil, in sun or light shade, will produce flowering plants the first year from early sown seed. Cut back and given some protection they will be permanent. Late summer-cuttings of the heaviest stems will provide increase for good forms. **N. caerulea** is generally treated as an annual, though plants carried over winter in the frame make stocky foot-high bushes with numer-ous 2-inch blossoms of lavender-blue all summer long. **N. rivu-laris** runs and roots, making a sizable clump of thick small-leaved foliage, among which, on short stems, appear upfacing cups of gleaming white with a golden throat. This species seems rather hardier than the lavender one more commonly seen. Divisions carried over in the frame are a good insurance against winter-killing.

OAKESIA. See *Uvularia.*

OENOTHERA (Onagraceae)

The evening-primroses come chiefly from the drylands of the American West, where many dwarf species bear large satiny flowers of white (fading pink with age) or yellow. The individual blossoms, of brief duration, come in daily succession for a considerable period during the summer, the fat buds opening with amazing rapidity in the evening. Because the roots are long and fleshy, they should be grown from seed, transplanted when young, and placed in a gravelly soil to ensure rapid drainage at the crown. Damp, cold soil in winter will rot the roots. Most grow best in a scree or rocky pasture.

O. acaulis is a Chilean plant that carries 4-inch white flowers, which fade to pink. As the plant ages the flowering-stems, at first very short among the gray dandelion-like leaves, elongate and sprawl; it is not long-lived. *O. caespitosa* is variable in leaf but uniform in the short-stemmed white flowers about 3 inches across that turn pink with age. It needs good drainage for the woody roots. *O. missouriensis* has immense yellow flowers on foot-long, sprawling stems, with narrow leaves more or less frosted with silver. It is a long-lived plant, easily raised from seed formed in great winged pods up to 3 inches across. This will grow in any sunny site without special concern about soil. *O. speciosa* is a colonizing plant, sending out underground runners in ordinary good but well-drained garden soil. From the runners rise small rosettes of somewhat lobed leaves and foot-high leafy stems that bear lovely 3-inch blooms, less fleeting than most. The type has white flowers, whereas var. *rosea* is a beautiful clear pink. For increase it must be divided and moved only in the spring. There are many other species of the types described above, mostly similar to one or another.

OMPHALODES (Boraginaceae)

The navelworts have large gentian-blue forget-me-not-like flowers. Two are shade-lovers, increasing fairly rapidly to good-sized mats, easily propagated by division. All may be grown from the curiously shaped seed. *O. cappadocica* has bright azure flowers in graceful sprays on stems about 8 inches high, well clothed with pointed dark green leaves. It wants good soil in shade, where it makes a brilliant display of blossom in June. *O. luciliae* is a sun-lover, to be grown in well-drained limy soil among rocks, where the 6- to 8-inch plants with spoon-shaped gray foliage produce large, clear lavender-blue flowers all summer long. An established clump may be divided, with divisions encouraged to make new roots by insertion in a cutting-frame during late spring. These first two may not prove completely hardy in the north, but *O. verna* is completely winter-hardy. It earns its name of Blue-eyed Mary by the abundance of brilliant blue flowers early in spring. It is easy to grow in woodsy soil in light or deep shade, and easy to increase by simple division of its rooting runners.

ONONIS (Leguminosae)

The restharrows are dwarf pea shrubs for sunny sites in deep well-drained soil. They are best grown from seed and set in place when quite small, since they soon develop long rat-tail roots that resent disturbance. *O. cenisia* forms a small silvery mat of 3-part leaves above which, on fine stems, come solitary pink pea blossoms in summer. It is not reliably hardy unless grown in well-drained soil. *O. rotundifolia* is a dense, twiggy shrub about a foot high with round, serrate leaflets. From the axils of the leaves, throughout the summer, come small clusters of large pea blossoms that combine two shades of clear pink. Though sometimes nipped back by cold in winter, new growth is rapid and full of flower.

ONOSMA (Boraginaceae)

The gold-drops all have rough, hairy leaves and hanging almond-scented flowers in unfurling croziers during the summer. Dwellers mostly of Asia Minor and the Mediterranean region, they are children of the sun, most successfully grown in light stony soil on a sunny ledge. Seed is the simplest method of propagation but cuttings of side-rosettes can be rooted in sand in the summer. *O. albo-roseum* is an especially good species with narrow, gray-green, rough foliage and flowering-stems of 6 to 9 inches carrying a succession of tubular white flowers, flushed pink as they age. *O. echioides* will grow to 18 inches as the numerous flowering-stems, above the long rough leaves, open the unfurling croziers of golden pendants. *O. emodi,* from the Himalayas, has small purple flowers on tall stems above typical *Onosma* foliage. *O. stellulatum* and its var. *tauricum* are the easiest to grow and are quite permanent in differing sites. Above typical foliage, large pendent golden drops over an inch long dangle from 8- to 10-inch flower stems for most of the summer. There are other species—some even with blue flowers—not often available or simple to please but all worth every effort. They are quite easy to raise from seed.

OPUNTIA (Cactaceae)

The prickly-pear cacti, in the hardy western American species and the 1 hardy eastern species, *C. humifusa,* are adapted to hot gravelly or sandy soils, where they decorate their unfriendly lobes and balls with huge silken flowers. The treatment is the same as for *Neobesseya*. Some western species hardy in the Northeast if grown quite dry are: *O. basilaris, O. fragilis, O. imbricata,* and *O. polyacantha.*

ORCHIS (Orchidaceae)

The Showy Orchis of eastern American woodlands, *O. spectabilis,* is generally rather impermanent when moved from its native forest into the garden. Success will depend on matching the deep, well-drained yet moist leafy soil. In the wild it is generally found near the base of a wooded rocky slope occupied mostly by deciduous trees. The soil is neutral in reaction. Here, in late spring or early summer, from between a pair of fleshy, glossy green basal leaves usually found in small clumps, rises the flowering-spike (from 4 to 12 inches) with up to 10 flowers 1-inch long having a rosy-purple hood and white lip.

ORNITHOGALUM (Liliaceae)

Star-of-Bethlehem, *O. umbellatum,* is a very easy-to-grow bulbous plant with starry white flowers rising on short stems from grassy clumps in late spring. It is admirable for the alpine lawn but so adaptable and such a free-seeder that it should be kept out of sections of the rock garden where there are delicate plants, lest it take over. It will send up its sprightly flowers in either sun or shade. Less well known and difficult to obtain is *O. nutans,* with large, rather drooping flowers of a soft jade-green and white. It grows in sun or light shade, the stems occasionally reaching 18 inches.

OROBUS. See *Lathyrus.*

OURISIA (Scrophulariaceae)

These mat-forming low figworts, though they come from South America and New Zealand, are hardy when grown in fairly rich acid soil in part shade. Fresh seed germinates readily but division of the clumps is the quickest means of increase. *O. coccinea,* from

Chile, has tubular red flowers on 6- to 10-inch stems above a mat of heart-shaped foliage. *O. macrocarpa* and *O. macrophylla* are white-flowered New Zealanders that suggest large-blossomed penstemons.

OXALIS (Oxalidaceae)

The flowering shamrocks, or sorrels, are found in many different geographical regions and in a wide range of sites. All carry satiny, bright-faced blossoms—that tend to close on cloudy days—among the trefoil leaves. Some have underground tubers, and others run about underground on fine, fleshy stolons. Both types may be increased by division.

O. acetosella, the Wood Sorrel of Europe, and the eastern United States equivalent, *O. montana,* are summer blooming, with the delicacy of early spring woodlanders. In very acid soil, most frequently in the dense shade of evergreens, the mats of cloverlike foliage are decked for a long period in summer with a succession of short-stemmed, pink-veined white blossoms. The species of the United States West Coast mountains are similar, but larger: *O. oregana* and *O. trilliiflora.*

O. adenophylla sends up in summer, from a bulb, a neat cluster of fan-shaped, rounded leaves of soft gray-green. Among these, cup-shaped blossoms of soft pink, deepening to red at the base, rise on 3-inch stems, singly or in clusters. Try bulbs in a number of sites in well-drained rich soil, searching for the proper proportions of shade and sun to keep the plant from languishing, away from its native Andean heights, yet with enough sun to open the lovely array of blossoms. *O. enneaphylla* is similar to the last, except here the solitary blossoms are paler and the clumps increase more rapidly. It thrives in a good mixture of leaf mold and sand, and ample but not baking sunshine.

O. violacea is another native American woodlander. This grows from a small tuber, producing a head of lavender blossoms in early summer in rocky acid woods, generally beneath oaks and on hill-sides. There are other bulbous species from South and Middle America, some with very brilliant flowers, but less reliably hardy in the north.

OXYRIA (Polygonaceae)

The Mountain-sorrel, *O. digyna,* is a pleasing if minor feature of the alpine flora in the mountain ranges throughout the Northern Hemisphere when the plant wears its spike of bright pink winged fruits during late summer. From a tuft of fleshy kidney-shaped leaves, the flower stalks grow 6 to 12 inches tall, with the insignificant green flowers in a dense raceme at the top. Mountain climbers find the acid-flavored leaves thirst-quenching. This wide-ranging plant may be increased by seed or division and must be grown in moist rocky soil.

OXYTROPIS (Leguminosae)

This genus is very like astragalus, with pinnate leaves and cluster-heads of pea blossoms. Here the petals forming the keel are conspicuously long-pointed. These legumes want deep, well-drained soil in a sunny site. Among the many desirable species, best grown from seed and established young, are: *O. argentata,* a dwarf from Siberia, with silky foliage and pale yellow, dense heads of flowers; *O. montana* of European alpine sites, with yellow and purple flowers on 6-inch stems; *O. sericea* from the American West, with ample racemes of light purple blooms just above the silky foliage tuft; *O. uralensis,* with short spikes of bright purple flowers; *O. villosus,* similar to *O. sericea,* but with creamy blossoms in a short spike.

PACHISTIMA (Celastraceae)

This genus comprises two North American dwarf evergreen shrubs, grown for their foliage alone since the tiny reddish flowers are inconspicuous. They will grow in sun or light shade, making a dense clump of small, shining leaves. Soil requirements are easily met by ordinary garden conditions. *P. canbyi* forms an ever-increasing thicket about 10 inches high, with small parallel-sided leaves having a toothed apex. As it increases by underground stolons, it may be propagated by division, or by cuttings. Old plants do not move well. *P. myrsinites,* of the western mountains, is taller and nonstoloniferous. It makes a trim, small-leaved evergreen shrub of about 3 feet. This is not quite as hardy as *P. canbyi.*

PACHYSANDRA (Buxaceae)

The Japanese *P. terminalis* is well known as an evergreen ground cover for poor, shady sites. Its prevalence should not discourage rock gardeners from using it among shrubs and to carpet areas at the base of trees. Because of its density and stoloniferous habit, however, it must be kept where it cannot overrun more special shade-lovers. Rooted divisions or cuttings should be set about 6 inches apart for solid effect. The white spikes of bloom are not generously produced. Quite different is *P. procumbens* of the Allegheny Mountains. This has a much more wild look, with running stems, partly deciduous leaves, and abundant purplish feathery blossoms on short spikes in early spring. This is most successfully grown in the woods garden in humus-rich soil.

PAEONIA (Ranunculaceae)

Peonies are generally thought of as belonging only in the border or in special beds, where, to be sure, the modern hybrid giants with heads the size of basketballs certainly belong. But the wild single forms from scattered parts of the world are found in nature growing with other plants frequently invited into the rock garden. They look especially appropriate in openings in the woodland garden. They need a good deep soil with room and time to develop. Though they resent disturbance, it is possible to divide them in late summer. Seed is slow, requiring often two years before germination and another three years before flowering. From the Caucasus comes **P. mlokosewitschii,** with 5-inch single yellow flowers on 2-foot plants. From the Orient, **P. tenuifolia** is about 18 inches high, with 4-inch dark crimson flowers. **P. microcarpa,** from the mountains of Spain, is of similar stature, with even larger flowers of bright crimson. The only species from America is **P. brownii,** which bears rather small cup-shaped flowers of deep red and yellow hanging just above the cut foliage. The whole plant is about 12 to 15 inches high and has very little value except for the collector.

PANAX (Araliaceae)

The true Ginseng, **P. quinquefolium,** is a fabled plant, and is now very rare because of commercial collecting to supply the Chinese market. It is still, however, to be found wild in a few places in rich deciduous woods of the eastern United States. On 12- to 18-inch stems it carries a whorl of 5 coarsely toothed 5-inch leaflets and a small round cluster of white blossoms, which are followed by red berries. The Dwarf Ginseng, or Groundnut, **P. trifolium,** is without medicinal value and is therefore more common in wide patches in deciduous woods. The whorls of delicate leaves are on stems of 6 to 8 inches. The flowers, on short scapes, are gathered in small round pincushion heads. Both plants bloom in spring and may be grown by root division or from seed.

PAPAVER (Papaveraceae)

The true Alpine Poppy, **P. alpinum,** in its many forms and varieties and geographical ranges, is the poppy supreme for the rock garden. No other can compare with the compact silvery filigree of its foliage nor the neatly proportioned beauty of its blossoms. Wild types with differences in the hairiness of the foliage and the color of the flower have been given variety rank, but these differences have been modified and mingled in the garden race of *P. alpinum.* From a packet of seed—except when collected in wild stands of separate color—will come white, yellow, red, orange, and pink flowers, some frilled and laced at the edge of the petals. In the wild, *P. alpinum* haunts the screes and rock ledges of lofty mountains of the Old World, where in full sun the silken flowers tremble and dance in the wind; but in our parched and torrid summers they shrivel and die away in such a site. Give them a good, gravelly but rather moist soil, with a surface of stone chips, and they will flourish in sun or half-shade and persist for two or three years till their vigorous offspring take over. The roots are so delicate that they are almost impossible to transplant. In fall or very early spring sow the seeds directly in the garden, just scattering them on the surface, and some plants will bloom the first summer.

P. nudicaule, a larger species with less delicate foliage and a less alpine character, is the New World related species. It will dominate the Old World dwarf if they are grown together in the garden. Because the gardener must depend on self-sowing to maintain the glorious Alpine Poppy year after year, it is best to grow only *the* Alpine Poppy.

P. fauriae from Japan, which may be the same as the poppy listed as *P. myabeanum,* is somewhat midway between *P. alpinum* and *P. nudicaule.* It is a dwarf with large lemon-yellow flowers and hairy foliage, much divided but not so finely as in the true *P. alpinum.* A lovely plant, however.

PARADISEA (Liliaceae)

Like a magnified and glorious anthericum, St. Bruno's Lily, *P. liliastrum,* displays 2-foot wands of large white trumpets from a grassy tuffet. This is a plant of alpine pastures, best grown in the alpine lawn in good, deep soil in sun or part shade. The fleshy rhizomes may be divided in spring or the plants grown—if you are patient—from fresh seed.

PARNASSIA (Saxifragaceae)

This is a race of late-summer and fall flowering plants that grow in nature in wet ditches of the country roadside or in wet and marshy land, sometimes high in the mountains. All the species are but variations on the theme of a basal cluster of gleaming, smooth, heart-shaped leaves and numerous single-flowered scapes from 3 inches to a foot high. The flowers are white saucers veined with green. For garden purposes, it is not important to distinguish among the many species, which vary mostly in the basal foliage and the single small leaf on the flower scape. The eastern American native, **P. glauca,** is typical and differs little from other species recognized in Europe, America, and Asia except for the fringing of the petals in **P. fimbriata** of the western United States. Grown in constantly moist soil, especially with moving water beneath, the clumps will increase till they can be divided. Or new plants may be easily grown from the abundant seed, particularly when sown soon after ripening, for early spring germination.

PARONYCHIA (Caryophyllaceae)

There is nothing dazzling about the flowers of the whitlow-worts, but in many species the papery bracts that surround the minute blossoms have immense appeal. Most species are carpeters of dry, craggy mountains, sprawling over the rocks their fine stems in-tricately patterned with small leaves and their numerous flower clusters with frosty, papery bracts that last all summer. They are excellent light carpeters for the smallest of mountain bulbs. Most root as they run, but not smotheringly, and may be increased by division or from seed.

P. argentea and **P. serpyllifolia** form absolutely prostrate, delicate mats shimmering with frosty bracts. **P. argyrocoma,** from the North Carolina peaks, forms a tufty little cushion with silvery awl-shaped leaves, above which are carried open heads of papery-bracted fuzzy flowers. **P. nivea** makes a twiggy small bush up to 5 inches with large papery bracts among the tiny flowers in the dense head. **P. canadensis,** unlike other species, is an annual plant, native to the rocky woods in the eastern United States. When permitted to self-sow into dense patches wherever the ground is open, it gives a

misty green effect with delicate stems up to 1 foot high, profusely
branched and covered with minute green leaves and greenish flowers.
Because it does not spring to life till early summer it makes a strate-
gic successor to the early-flowering primroses and to dwarf bulbs
that have gone by.

PARRYA (Cruciferae)

The purple-flowered crucifer, *P. menziesii,* outshines many of
the family and yet is seldom seen in gardens. It grows in the high
intermontane areas of the far-western United States, where dry
summers prevail. The plant forms a 6-inch mound of gray spatulate
leaves with pink to purple 4-petaled blossoms in many-flowered
heads. Because the root is long and carrot-like, only young seedlings are easy to move. Plant this in the scree or rocky pasture in
full sun.

PATRINIA (Valerianaceae)

These yellow-flowered valerians add a great splash of gold in
summer to the sunny or half-shady portions of the rock garden. The
flowering-stems reach 12 to 18 inches above handsome, divided,
heart-shaped leaves. *P. triloba* (also called *P. palmata*) from
Japan is the species most commonly grown. *P. intermedia* and
P. sibirica are distinguished by longer, narrower leaves. Propagate
these by seed, or spring division.

PEDICULARIS (Scrophulariaceae)

The wood betonies, or louseworts, have a peculiar fascination
in the varicolored, heavy, ferny leaves and stiff spikes of 2-lipped
blossoms among colored bracts. The colors in some species are
brilliant and in others curiously muted and odd. Alluring as some
of the species are, they pose a problem of culture because of apparent
parasitic dependence. A few may be lured to grow in the garden
in rocky semishade or in the alpine lawn. Since they transplant from

the wild reluctantly, the best chance of success is to grow them from seed. **P. canadensis** is the common eastern American species in yellow or red. The finest westerner for dry woods is red-flowered **P. densiflora.** Western **P. groenlandica** is a handsome, stalwart, red-flowered plant of boggy places. Europe and Asia produce many handsome species just as intractable.

PENSTEMON (Scrophulariaceae)

There are so many beautiful species of this American genus, native principally to the western states, that a special horticultural society is devoted exclusively to their study and cultivation. Even so, there are many rare species still uncultivated and many aspects of their satisfactory culture not entirely mastered. Because they are so varied and grow under such different conditions, no simple prescriptions for success will fit them all. For the rock garden proper, the best are the dwarf shrubby species found growing in lofty rocky places of the West. In general, a well-drained rocky soil—the typical rock garden mixture—suits the penstemons. Though they want abundant light, most do best on a slope facing away from the full blast of the sun. Seed is sometimes slow to germinate and may stay in the ground a year before sprouting. All may be rooted fairly easily from summer cuttings, and this is the best method of increasing good forms. A special handbook published by the Penstemon Society is the best source for descriptions of the literally hundreds of species. Among the many excellent ones a few are here listed by type of growth habit, with a few hints of their quality.

Dwarf mat-forming species of *Penstemon* for scree, rock garden, and rocky pasture are: **acaulis,** 2 inches tall, small leaves, blue flowers; **albertinus,** 6 to 8 inches, small leaves, light blue; **aridus,** 4 to 6 inches, grayish-green leaves, purple-blue; **caespitosus,** mat-forming, small thyme-like leaves, lilac-purple; **crandallii,** mat-forming, narrow leaves, blue and white; **hallii,** 6 to 8 inches, narrow leaves, violet; *montanus,* 8 to 10 inches, grayish leaves, large pink-purple flowers; and *tolmiei,* 6 to 9 inches, small shiny leaves, dense head of pink-purple flowers.

The dwarf, evergreen, shrubby species of *Penstemon* all prefer to sprawl on rocks with roots deep in a crevice or among stones. They may be sheared back after flowering to keep them vigorous. A north slope is the best site for these species: *barrettiae,* to 1 foot, thick leathery leaves, large lilac-purple flowers; *cardwellii,* 10 inches, dark finely toothed leaves, large purple flowers; *davidsonii,* flat mat, small round leaves, scattered large purple flowers; *fruticosus,* variable, toothed leaves, purple flowers; *menziesii,* to 6 inches, small leaves, blue to purple flowers; *newberryi,* to 20 inches, round leathery toothed leaves, red flowers; *pinifolius,* to 1 foot, needle-leaves, narrow scarlet flowers all summer; and *rupicola,* to 4 inches, round glaucous leaves, rose-crimson flowers.

Taller herbaceous species of *Penstemon*—of which there are hundreds of beautiful ones—which are to be grown in good soil in the alpine lawn or in openings in the woods are: *azureus,* to 3 feet, narrow entire glaucous leaves, blue flowers; *cobaea,* to 2 feet, large toothed leaves, large purple flowers; *cyananthus,* to 3 feet, glaucous entire leaves, blue flowers; *erianthera,* to 16 inches, narrow entire leaves, purple flowers; *glaber,* to 2 feet, narrow entire leaves, blue to purple flowers; *nitidus,* to 1 foot, blue-gray leaves, clear-blue flowers; and *procerus,* to 1 foot, shiny narrow leaves, purplish-blue flowers.

PERNETTYA (Ericaceae)

These dwarf evergreen shrubs are not always as hardy as one could wish, since they form handsome bushes with bell flowers and colored berries. Given peaty, acid soil on a north slope, where snow cover may linger as a protection all winter, the species *P. nana* may be successfully grown. It makes an almost prostrate mat suggesting a small-leaved wintergreen. *P. tasmanica* is similar.

Slow from seed, pernettyas are most successfully propagated by summer-cuttings of half-ripened wood.

PETROCALLIS (Cruciferae)

P. pyrenaica is in many ways similar to a cushioned draba, and by some botanists so classified. Here the small cruciferous blossoms are a pale lavender on very short stems, huddled above the tight dome of tiny wedge-shaped leaves with cleft tips. To keep the foliage mound tight and induce blossoming, grow this in scree soil in a sunny site. Lime is of benefit but not essential. Propagate it by seed or shoots pulled from the edge of the clump and treated as cuttings in late summer.

PETROCOPTIS (Caryophyllaceae)

P. pyrenaica is frequently confused with *Petrocallis pyrenaica* because of similarity of name. This one is a silene relative, sometimes listed as a *Lychnis,* making a tidy clump of small leaves and in early summer sending up 6-inch, rather thin stems, each carrying a head of ½-inch pale pink to white blossoms on short pedicels, the petals slightly notched. It is easy to grow from seed but is not long-lived. Self-sowing will occur when it is grown in a good rock garden soil that is never very dry, in half-shade. *P. lagascae* is very similar and to be distinguished by glaucous foliage and long-pediceled flowers.

PETROPHYTUM (Rosaceae)

Sometimes listed as *Spiraea,* these are ground-hugging shrubs with proportionate, "bottlebrush" spikes of white feathery flowers. The foliage forms a dense mat of small blue-gray leaves, increasing till the mat may be a foot across in its mountain home in the far-western mountains of America. The 3 species, very similar in effect, are best grown in scree soil on a slope with a northern exposure. Lime in the soil appears to stimulate flowering. Plants are possible but slow from seed. Shoots, carefully taken from the edges of the mat soon after flowering, can be rooted as cuttings. *P. caespitosum* has short flower spikes and leaves with only 1 nerve. **P. cinerascens** and **P. hendersonii** have slightly longer flower spikes and leaves with 3 nerves, the leaves of *P. cinerascens* being densely gray pubescent.

PHACELIA (Hydrophyllaceae)

There are many annual species of *Phacelia* in western America, and two rather similar perennial species of great charm. The foliage is silky and feathery, especially delightful when spangled with dew. The dark blue spidery flowers are produced in early summer on a dense spike that may rise as high as a foot, though generally shorter when grown in the very meager, stony soil of the sunny scree. Rapid drainage is essential, since the taproot is easily rotted at the crown. Seed provides the only means of increase. **P. lyallii** has foliage not cut into linear segments and only coarsely hairy, with the flower spike about 8 inches tall. **P. sericea** is silver-gray, with fine, silky hairs covering the deeply cut leaves and with a taller flower spike.

PHLOX (Polemoniaceae)

This strictly American genus provides the rock gardens of the world with a vast array of profusely flowering plants. Some species are of easiest possible culture, and others challenge the expert. Though the Moss-pink, **P. subulata,** has become—in some eyes only—a garish commonplace, even it, in forms of restrained growth and refined blossom color, furnishes the best and surest delight for every rock garden. Other cushion species and hybrids are equally desirable, if not so easy. The cushion types, if they root down along the stems as they advance across the soil, are easy to increase by division at any season, most easily in early spring or late summer. Many of the western cushion species rise from a heavy, deep taproot and are not capable of division, nor do they take kindly to transplanting. Seed or cuttings offer the best means of propagation for these. Except for the woodland types, all phloxes

want a lean, rocky soil, generally neutral to alkaline, and a fully
sunny exposure. They will endure in some shade but lose their
tight growth and flower less abundantly. The groupings below are
horticultural rather than taxonomic.

Cushion Types—Western

Here are included a large number of species of needle-leaved
cushions from the dry plains and mountain screes. Most have a
deep, ranging taproot, bloom early in the spring, with blossoms
from purest white to deep rosy pink. They are subject to long
periods of very dry conditions during the summer, when they become quite brown, until fall rains green them up again. Except
when very young they transplant poorly. Early spring-or late summer-cuttings are possible. Seeds, difficult to collect and rarely
available, offer the best means of establishment. All should be
grown in scree conditions to prevent the fatal rotting of the taproot
beneath the cushion. In this group of *Phlox* may be included:
alyssifolia, andicola, caespitosa, diffusa, hoodii, missouliensis
(one of the easiest), ***rigida,*** and others of very local distribution.

P. bifida, the Cleft or Prairie Phlox, has longer, broader leaves

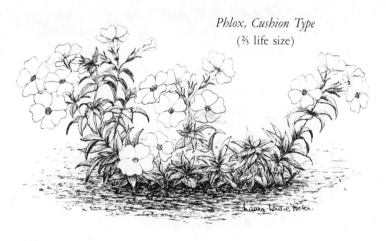

Phlox, Cushion Type
(⅔ life size)

and forms a more erect clump up to 10 inches tall. It varies in color from pure white to a lovely soft blue, enhanced by the snowflake effect of the deeply cleft petals. This is not a difficult plant and will do well in any well-drained garden soil. Though the stems do not normally root down, layering can be practiced by heaping sand into the crown of the plant. Tip-cuttings do not strike easily except under mist because of the very thin, brittle stems. Heavy basal cuttings, taken in late summer, will root at the nodes fairly successfully in sand.

Cushion Types—Eastern

Easy to grow and propagate by division are the two eastern cushion- or mat-forming species, **Phlox nivalis** and **P. subulata.** More southern in origin, P. nivalis is not so vigorous and hardy as P. subulata and it comes into bloom almost two weeks later. As to colors of these phloxes: species, varieties, forms, and hybrids range from pure white through pinks—some lovely, some harsh—to deep red, and a few blues—some very washed out, some good. Flower size and shape also vary considerably. The variety **P. subulata brittonii** is especially desirable for its close growing habit, short-needled foliage, and light pink or white starry flowers.

There are a few very special color-forms of P. nivalis such as **'Avalon White,'** pink **'Camla,'** crimson **'Dixie Brilliant,'** and there are numerous good named forms of P. subulata that will be found listed and described in nursery catalogues. Hybrids between these two species and between these and western species are also commercially available. The named forms developed in England under the designation **'Douglasii hybrids'** probably belong among the hybrids of eastern and western species.

Woodland Species

Suitable for open woodland slopes in medium-acid soil are a number of quite distinctive phloxes. Many, like P. stolonifera, root down along the procumbent stems and hence make sizable clumps. Most have flowers larger than those of the needle-leaved phloxes and produce them in ample heads on comparatively tall stems. *P. stolonifera* forms large mats of rooting stolons set with fairly broad leaves, above which are carried loose heads of bloom on stems of about 6 to 8 inches. The color ranges from a strong rose-pink through light lavender to pale pink: 'Blue Ridge' and 'Pink Ridge' are good varieties. A white form has recently been discovered. Hybrids between this species and *P. subulata* (frequently and wrongly called *P. amoena*), which is properly designated as *P. × procumbens*, have leaves intermediate between the two species and a flowering habit more like *P. stolonifera*'s. These hybrids, especially in good color-forms, are very desirable since they will endure full sun, have a long blooming season, and propagate readily by division and cuttings. Though in the wild *P. stolonifera* grows from Pennsylvania southward in the hills, it is perfectly hardy northward and will succeed even in considerable sun. It thrives best in light shade but seems indifferent to the pH of the soil. Propagation is made very simple and rapid by separating from the parent plant as many of the rooted stolons as are needed. Seeds may produce plants with desirable color variations.

A western relative of *P. stolonifera* is considered by many the most beautiful of all the phloxes, *P. adsurgens.* In a rather limited area of northern California and southern Oregon, westward from the Cascades, this species blooms in late spring. It is the wonderful clarity of color that gives the blossoms their magnificence. The 5 rounded and large petals are in shades of purest pink and peach, paling somewhat lighter in the central eye, each petal penciled with a darker central stripe. There are occasional pure-white-flowered plants. The growth habit is loosely mat-forming, the long procumbent stems amply clothed with dark, shining, elliptical leaves and the flowering-shoots standing a few inches above. If only the plant were as easy to grow as it is beautiful. In the area of its native home and in other states of the Pacific Northwest, it is quite successfully grown in gardens, but efforts so far to tame it in the East have been rather discouraging.

In the wild *P. adsurgens* is found in a range of soils and sites, occasionally in considerable sun on a rather sterile roadbank but in more abundant and handsome colonies in the duffy but rocky acid soils beneath scattered Ponderosa Pine and other conifers. Though it may reach altitudes of 6000 feet in the Siskiyou and Cascade Mountains, where winters are cold, the plants are there protected by deep snows. When planted on a fairly steep north-facing slope in an acid rocky soil containing considerable leaf mold, or in a shaded rocky crevice, plants in the East have lived and flowered for as long as two years. But in spring, unless snow cover has been fairly constant, or the plants have been protected by a good cover of pine needles, much of the growth has been killed back and the stems are bare of their normally evergreen leaves. The fact that potted plants in a closed frame or alpine-house have flourished and bloomed well suggests that *P. adsurgens,* in addition to being fussy about site, is not thoroughly hardy. Eventually adaptable clones may be discovered or some of the splendid qualities of the genus bred by hybridizing into the hardy and adaptable *P. stolonifera* or *P. × procumbens.*

Though the procumbent shoots of *P. adsurgens* root down only sparingly in the wild or in the garden, cuttings taken after the flowering period root speedily and easily. Even as late as October, husky shoot-tips up to 4 inches long will root within two weeks if inserted in a sand and peat mixture. Strip only a few leaves off at the base, since the roots will form in the leaf axils above the rooting medium and reach down and bury themselves. Pot the well-rooted cuttings in an acid soil of sharp sand and leaf mold with a little loam and carry them through the winter in a protected frame or in the alpine-house.

There are a number of taller phloxes suited to the rock garden, especially in semishaded sites. Most will endure considerable sun if given a fairly rich, moisture-retentive soil. Of these, one of the most adaptable and commonly grown is *P. divaricata.* The light lavender-blue blossoms are produced during late May in great abundance on stems about a foot high. At the base are numerous decumbent evergreen stems that root at the leaf nodes and increase the clump, permitting generous division either in early spring or after flowering. Seed is abundantly set, germinates readily, and produces flowering plants the second year. Where it is happy, *P. divaricata* commonly self-sows generously and creates great drifts. A powdery mildew that may appear on the flowering-stems during the summer does not seem to harm the plant. White and, very rarely, pale pink forms have been found. *P. divaricata* has notched petals, whereas in the more western extension the var. *laphami* has entire petals. It too is found in white as well as the lavender-blue color of the type.

P. pilosa and its many geographical variants are about the same stature as *P. divaricata* with the flower color running more to the pink and rosy purples. This species does not have stolons, but older, many-stemmed clumps may be divided after the flowering season, or cuttings may be made from basal shoots. It will grow in many soils and sites, from well-drained open woods to rich meadow-land. For later bloom, there is a group of phloxes with fairly deep green leaves and many-flowered heads of blossom, the *P. ovata* complex, including *P. carolina, P. glaberrima, P. pulchra,* and others quite similar, mostly with pink to purple flowers. Division in early spring is the best means of increase.

In addition to the many recognized species somewhat similar to one another within the groups already mentioned, *P. speciosa* and its variants should be given special mention because of their beauty. These all form narrow-leaved, low, woody-based plants like dwarf shrubs. Flowers in the best forms are large and very colorful in a range of vivid pinks. They are not easy to grow because they like

considerable moisture only in the early spring, then require a long
dry period. They should be tried in the scree, with the addition of
clay about the roots. Mature plants are difficult to establish and it
has proved very reluctant to propagate by the usual methods. Seed,
when available, is perhaps the surest way.

PHUOPSIS. See *Crucianella.*

PHYLLODOCE (Ericaceae)

These are dwarf evergreen shrubs of the greatest charm. The
crowded foliage is needlelike, and the clustered urn-shaped, delicate
flowers swing on thin stems from the summit of the dense leafy
branches. In the cool mountains of America and Japan these beautiful shrubs frequently make extensive sheets, brilliant as a mass of
heather. There, in peaty screelike soil, they begin to flower as the
snow melts after blanketing them for the long winter. They are
rather difficult in the garden and generally very reluctant to bloom.
They thrive best in a sunny bog or pine-barren type of site and
would make perfect alpine-house plants but for the fact that they
resent being grown in pots except when very young. In the open
a light covering of pine needles or pine branches should be put
over them in the winter as protection. Cuttings of new wood may
be rooted or the plants may be grown from seed. Seed should be
thinly sown on a very peaty mixture, kept constantly moist and
shaded. The easiest method is to start seed in a plastic container
with the lid left on until the plants are about an inch high. Then
the minuscule plants are hardened-off gradually by removing the
lid. Never permit them to become dry, though.

P. aleutica has bells of pale yellow. *P. caerulea,* a rare native of
the mountaintops of the American Northeast and arctic regions,
bears light pink to purplish-pink urn-shaped blossoms. In *P. empe-*
triformis, perhaps the commonest and most vigorous in the western mountains of America, the blossoms are bell-shaped and of a
rosy purple. *P. glanduliflora,* somewhat taller and more lax,

bears yellowish blossoms, slightly pinched, whereas **P. nipponica** carries tubby pure-white bells above the rather serrulate needle-foliage.

PHYSARIA (Cruciferae)

These gray-leaved tuffet plants, with yellow crucifer flowers, come from dry sites in the western American mountains. The species are quite similar, varying somewhat in the shape and cutting of the leaves, in the hairiness of the foliage, and the length of the flowering-stems. All want full sun and an open, stony soil, best in the scree or rocky pasture even though in the wild some are found in a rather heavy, stony clay. The inflated seedpod gives them their common name, bladderpods. Though never a brilliant mound of color when flowering in May, the flowers are produced over a long period and the foliage is attractive throughout the season. All are easily grown from seed, or may be increased by division or cuttings. Desirable species are: **P. alpestris,** 4 inches; **P. didymocarpa,** 6 inches; **P. floribunda,** 10 inches; **P. geyeri,** 4 inches; and **P. oregana,** 4 inches.

PHYTEUMA (Campanulaceae)

The horned rampions are more interesting than beautiful, and are to be grown near a path or on a raised bed where you may view close at hand the fascination of their delicately shaded blossoms, like long-necked bottles clustered in a spherical head above leafy bracts. There are a number of rather similar tall species suitable for growing in the alpine lawn or among carpeting plants in the rock garden proper. As summer bloomers they are valued, and will scatter seeds sparingly, frequently into the narrowest crack, into which they somehow fit their white carrot-like root. They do not propagate easily except by seed.

P. orbiculare and **P. scheuchzeri** have light blue flowers on foot-high stems. Slightly different but of the same stature is **P. lobelioides,** its flowers arranged in a loose spike. Of dwarf sta-

Picea

ture, and worthy of the most prominent spot, are **P. hemisphae-ricum** and **P. pauciflorum.** The former has grasslike foliage in a dense, spreading clump, with full heads of clear-blue blossom on 3-inch stems; the latter has a somewhat broader blunted foliage in clumps, above which—on even shorter stems—are heads of dark blue, slightly larger flowers. Both want good neutral soil and a position where they will not be parched in summer.

The real outlander of the genus is **P. comosum,** like a weird cross between a stemless artichoke and a porcupine—odd, bewitching, and improbable. At the top of the white taproot is produced a ruffle of serrate, shiny leaves, for all the world like a glossy, hard Harebell. Then in summer, from the center of this ruff of foliage erupts a devil's claw of long inflated bubbles (or old-fashioned light bulbs), the necks prolonged and darkened as they elongate into lashing, fringe-tipped whips. In the wild this rare plant springs from narrow crevices of hard limestone rock high in the mountains. What it demands in the garden is well-drained, deep, limy soil, especially with rocks for the roots to burrow among, and a dry, rocky support for the crown. Plentiful light is required but not by any means the hottest exposure. From seed—rarely available, but easily germinated—young plants should be set in their permanent positions and guarded against the attack of slugs. After three years you may begin to expect bloom. Root-cuttings are possible in very early spring, if you have the heart to disturb an established plant.

PICEA (Pinaceae)

The spruces in all species, and particularly in the Norway Spruce, **P. abies,** possess dwarf varieties admirably suited to growing as evergreen accents in and around the rock garden. These are most accommodating about soils and exposures, merely demanding a fairly deep soil for the run of their extensive and rapidly expanding roots. Only young plants or pot-grown material move easily, preferably in early spring; and none are easy to propagate. Cuttings of half-ripened wood may be rooted in a sand and peat mixture in a closed cutting-box or under mist. The modern interest in bonsai is fortunately leading nurserymen to propagate the dwarf conifers, and hence to provide a supply for rock gardeners. The list of really dwarf varieties is remarkably long but the nomenclature is frequently muddled. The best way to secure what you want is to see it growing in a reliable nursery.

PIERIS (Ericaceae)

These broad-leaved evergreens for acid soil are generally rather too large for the rock garden proper though admirably suited to the woods garden and for background plantings. There are also dwarf varieties of two species quite small enough and elegant enough to find a place in the acid rock garden, the bog, the pine barren, or the heath. Andromeda, **P. *japonica,*** as a species is rather formal and rigid; when well placed it is a perennial joy, with its early display of waxy white bells arranged in drooping panicles, followed by reddish new foliage shoots—really crimson in some named forms—among the lustrous, narrow, evergreen leaves. The dwarf form **P. *j. pygmaea*** has very narrow, abbreviated leaves on a ground-hugging shrub. It is not as easy as the species, requiring moist, acid soil, in a site that would please a cassiope or phyllodoce, with which it is eminently fit to consort. Like many dwarf forms of otherwise stalwart shrubs, it is rarely known to flower. Both species and variety are comparatively easy to root as cuttings in a peat and sand mixture.

P. *floribunda* from the southern Appalachians is perfectly hardy and easy, once established. Because it does not make a dense, fine root system, it transplants poorly except as a young plant and prefers a well-drained site. As a plant it is less formal in growth habit than the Japanese species; its flowers are similar but held in an upright, more rigid, handlike panicle. This should be propagated by either seed or late summer-cuttings. There is a comparatively new dwarf of dense habit about 1 foot tall, *P. floribunda* '**Millstream Dwarf**,' so far unflowering but neat in habit and easy to propagate by layers or cuttings. *P. nana* is described under *Arcteria*.

PIMELEA (Thymelaeaceae)

This is a race of Australian shrubs noted for abundance of small flowers and handsome berrylike fruits. Only *P. coarctica* is dwarf enough for the rock garden, forming as it does a prostrate, gray-leaved, twiggy bush with small white flowers and translucent white berries. It is not hardy north of Philadelphia, but charming as a pot plant in the alpine-house. It wants an acid, open soil and is easily propagated by cuttings of soft wood.

PINGUICULA (Lentibulariaceae)

The butterworts are exotic insectiverous plants for constantly moist peaty or sandy soils. The various species bear flat, ground-hugging, sticky leaves in pairs, from which rise stems of 3 to 8 inches bearing single, gloxinia-like flowers. The only species generally available are *P. vulgaris,* with purple flowers on 6-inch stems, and *P. alpina,* with flowers of white and gold on shorter stems. The latter grows on limy muds. Other species—some being handsome southern ones not hardy enough for most garden purposes—are but variations on the theme. The sole means of increase is from seed sown on a constantly moist medium (and best in a closed container), except under perfect conditions, when husky plants may make offsets suitable for division.

PINUS (Pinaceae)

There are not as many dwarf pines as there are spruces suitable for growing in the rock garden, but there are a few very handsome ones. *P. aristata* is a dense, slow-growing, erect but irregular tree with short needles. If grown from seed there will be considerable variation, as there will be in other pines so propagated. *P. mugo* varies even more than most, and its high-mountain prostrate forms offer the ideal pine for association with rocks and ledges. Short-needled, compact clones are to be sought out. Others worth considering for the large garden are **P. cembra, P. cembroides,** and dwarf varieties of **P. densiflora, P. strobus,** and **P. sylvestris.** All pines do best in well-drained soils with ample sun, but must be watched for attacks of scale on the needles. Because cuttings are extremely difficult to root, desirable forms should be propagated by grafting.

PLAGIORHEGMA. See *Jeffersonia.*

PLATYCODON (Campanulaceae)
The balloon flowers should find a place in the larger rock garden, not only for the beautiful sheen of the swollen buds and wide blossoms of blue or white, and occasionally pink, but more particularly for the late season of their bloom. They are easy to grow from seed and by early-spring division of the thongy white roots. **P. grandiflorum,** the all-embracing species from Japan, has many forms—varying in stature, season, and color of flower. True dwarfs of only a few inches are occasionally found and should be propagated by division or root-cuttings for growing in a favorite site. All grow readily and are permanent in deep, well-drained soil in sun.

PLUMBAGO. See *Ceratostigma.*

PODOPHYLLUM (Berberidaceae)
The umbrella-leaved Mayapples thrive in a good leafy soil in the woodland garden. They should be given plenty of room, because they develop rapidly into large groves from the underground rhizomes. Through separation of these rhizomes in early spring they are easily propagated, or they may be grown from fresh seed. Both the Himalayan **P. emodi** and the eastern American **P. peltatum** carry handsome lobed leaves like umbrellas about a foot across on stems up to 1½ feet tall. They should be grown on a rise above a

path to show the large, waxy white flowers that nod solitary beneath the leaves. These are followed by handsome fruit up to 2 inches in diameter; when ripe, they are red in *P. emodi* and yellow in *P. peltatum.* In severe climates *P. emodi* should receive some protection.

POGONIA (Orchidaceae)
The Rose Pogonia orchid of bogs and wet meadows of the eastern United States, *P. ophioglossoides,* is not difficult to establish in comparable sites in the garden. It has a simple basal leaf and a solitary flower on a foot-high stem. The soft rose-pink blossom is beautifully proportioned, and has a conspicuous fringed lip.

POLEMONIUM (Polemoniaceae)
A great many species of the Jacob's-ladders have been recognized by botanists and named, but frequently they are so similar as to make identification difficult. For garden purposes you need only distinguish between the tall ones and the dwarf ones, the shade- and moisture-lovers, and the dry-site species—and, perhaps, the mat-formers as different from the solitaries. All have pinnately dissected leaves with numerous leaflets arranged in a ladder pattern. At the tips of the stems in early summer are produced clusters of open-faced bells, frequently nodding, ranging in color from blue (the commonest) to salmon and yellow and white. All come readily from seed or may be divided after flowering.

For growing in good soil and particularly in light shade are most of the taller species, such as: *P. caeruleum,* up to 3 feet, with blue flowers; *P. carneum,* with large salmon-pink flowers on stems to 2 feet; *P. pauciflorum,* with small yellow flowers on 1-foot stems; *P. reptans,* 1 foot, with blue flowers on rapidly increasing dense mats; and *P. van-bruntiae,* 2½ feet, with dark blue flowers.

To be grown in the rock garden in not too parched stony soil are some excellent dwarf species from the mountains of the American West: *P. confertum, P. delicatum, P. haydenii, P. viscosum,* all with blue flowers, and *P. mellitum,* deliciously fragrant and with large flowers of creamy white. These smaller species do particularly well on the face of a wall.

POLYGALA (Polygalaceae)

The milkworts carry their small butterfly-like blossoms in abundance during early summer. The most desirable species are rather shrubby in habit but so dwarf as to make leafy mats, above which dance the somewhat orchid-like blossoms. They may be increased by seed, stem-cuttings, or root-cuttings. *P. calcarea,* as its name suggests, grows best in a rocky limestone soil in full sun, where it will make dense evergreen mats only an inch or so high. Completely covering the foliage in early summer are short-stemmed flowers of a clear sky-blue with a fringed crest of paler color. When well grown, this is an outstanding plant. *P. chamaebuxus* has slightly heavier foliage, and flowers of pale yellow with a deeper yellow tip; in var. *grandiflora,* flowers are lavender and yellow. Both are best planted in a cool location in either neutral or acid soil, but with much light to encourage blossoming. *P. vayredae* has narrower leaves than *P. chamaebuxus,* and here the blossoms are brilliant purple on branches that tend to bend and droop.

The eastern American species *P. paucifolia,* Gaywings, is a trailing plant with roundish leaves clustered at the tips of the shoots. From among the leaves rise on short stems 1 to 4 ample blossoms of a rich rose-purple with conspicuous, fringed white lip. The pure-white form is lovely and rare. The plant succeeds best in fairly deep shade, in a rich duff, neutral to acid. It may be increased by careful division in the spring or by cuttings of the bare running-stems, or by layering. It is, however, not always easy to establish because of a suspected dependence on special root associations in the soil.

POLYGONATUM (Liliaceae)

The Solomon's-seals are woodland plants of easy culture in deep, rich soil. From a heavy, warty rootstock rise slender gracefully arching stems with pairs of glaucous green leaves set along the upper portion. In early summer small, greenish-white, lily-like flowers hang either singly or in groups from the axils of the leaves; these are followed by greenish berries. The heavy rootstocks may be divided in spring or fall. **P. biflorum** is 2 to 3 feet tall, with generally paired hanging flowers. **P. commutatum** is larger in all its parts, with more and larger flowers, and larger and more glabrous leaves on stems that may reach 8 feet. These two are native to eastern North America and are quite similar to the European **P. latifolium** (up to 4 feet) and **P. multiflorum** (somewhat shorter). All species, though not showy in flower, have considerable architectural grace for the woodland garden.

POLYGONUM (Polygonaceae)

There are hundreds of species of knotweeds throughout the world, some of which are, in mass, a colorful part of alpine meadows, but most have such insignificant flowers that they are of indifferent value in the garden; only a few have dense enough and brilliant enough spikes of blossom. **P. affine** forms mats of basal leaves that turn bronzy in winter, just after the autumn display of dense rose-red 6-inch spikes. This is from the Himalayas, as is **P. vaccinifolium,** a quickly spreading trailer with narrow, shiny, evergreen leaves. It carries a profusion of rose-pink spikes in late summer and autumn. Both may readily be increased by division, and P. vaccinifolium by cuttings also. Because both flower better in exposed sunny sites, they may suffer in a severe and snowless winter and therefore appreciate a light covering after the ground has frozen. They are worth the trouble because of their abundant, late-season flowers.

PONTEDERIA (Pontederiaceae)

Our native Pickerelweed, **P. cordata,** is a handsome plant for the edge of a large pool, where in water up to a foot deep it will produce bright blue spikes of bloom among long, pointed, arrowhead-shaped leaves. The quick-spreading rhizomes may be divided at will.

Potentilla nitida
(¾ life size)

POTENTILLA (Rosaceae)

Cinquefoil is a vast, worldwide genus, containing a multiplicity of plants ranging from stalwart shrubs to minute cushions. The 5-petaled rosaceous blossoms are mostly yellow, but there are fine whites and a few pinks and coppers. From so extensive a collection it is difficult to choose, especially since many are rather similar. Full sun and good drainage is the general rule for all species. Among the finest are the ones listed here.

P. alba, with 5-part silky leaves in a low mat, has large white blossoms produced for a long period in summer. **P. alpestris** makes a 6-inch mound of 5-part leaves and large clear-yellow flowers that darken at the center. **P. fruticosa** is the Shrubby Cinquefoil of wide distribution and great variation. Low, spreading, silky-leaved, with large white flowers is var. **mandshurica;** yellow-flowered var. **montana** (or **nana**) is an erect, stiff shrub under a foot high; var.

tenuiloba has linear leaves, arching stems, and yellow flowers. There are other erect varieties that are tall and many named clones that have superior flowers. All varieties bloom for a long period in late summer. The unsightly and persistent seed-capsules should be removed in the fall.

P. nevadensis makes a flat pancake of silky, much-divided leaves and splaying flower stems bearing 3 or 4 yellow blossoms. **P. nitida** is one of the true prizes of the tribe, to be given a limy scree site in full sun, where it will make wide, low mats of silvery 3-part leaves spangled with delicately rosy blossoms. **P. tonguei** blooms late and long, with a profusion of burnt-orange blossoms (shading to a dusky brick-red in the center) on ramifying, prostrate branches. It will make large mats in well-drained but good soil, in a site not too hot and parched; nonetheless, it may suddenly collapse from a rust or fungus attack. Young seedlings generally spring up to replace it.

P. tridentata is in effect a very small stoloniferous dwarf forming a mat 6 to 10 inches high; the woody stems are clothed with 3-part leaves, each leaflet sharply 3-toothed. The small, white, clustered flowers pleasantly grace the carpet in summer, but the plant's true glory is the brilliant blood-red of the leaves in autumn. A native of high rocky places in eastern North America, this is an accommodating plant, consenting to grow in either acid or limy soil, though it colors more handsomely in acid. It is easy to propagate by division or cuttings, and makes an admirable ground cover in the alpine lawn or among heathers in the heath. It is open enough so that bulbs will flourish beneath it.

P. verna forms tight dark green cushions decorated in early spring with copious bright golden coins on very short stems. It will grow in any sunny spot, indifferent to soil, and is easily divided for increase after flowering. There are numerous other species worth growing, but it is only fair to say that most of the western Americans, dwarf and charming as many are when starved in the dry shingles and mountainous rocky places, are disappointing because of the proportion of the rather inconspicuous blossoms to the frequently most attractive compound leafage. Warning should be given about **P. anserina,** the Silverweed. It is better left to lace the rocky shores of all continents with its handsome silvery plume-like foliage than to race ineradicably across your garden.

PRATIA (Campanulaceae)

These small relatives of the lobelias are a genus of New Zealand carpeters of considerable appeal but, alas, not great hardiness. They are nevertheless of sufficient charm to warrant their being introduced into the alpine-house or into rock gardens where temperatures do not go much below 10°F. Somewhat like the Partridgeberry in effect, the mats are studded with short-stemmed lobelia-like flowers with a deeply cut lip which are followed by showy berrylike fruit. Increase these by division or seed and grow in rich woodland-type soil. **P. angulata** has white flowers and reddish-purple fruit and in **P. macrodon** the fragrant flowers are yellow.

PRIMULA (Primulaceae)

The vast and wonderful tribe of primroses furnishes the gardener with such a range of magnificent plants that many have quite under-standably forsaken all other genera and devoted their gardens and energies to primroses alone. Though this may seem an excessive fanaticism, yet to go to the other extreme and exclude them from the garden because of a mistaken, reversed snobbery that says primroses will not grow in eastern American gardens seems just as fanatic. There are easy ones; there are difficult ones. There are species for the moraine and scree, for the meadow, for the streamside and bog, and for the woodsy copses. For so varied a clan few general pre-scriptions can be laid down, except to say that all want considerable humus in the growing medium and plenty of moisture in the season of their active growth and flowering. For convenience, primulas may be divided roughly by the nature of the sites where they are most likely to succeed in the garden.

Alpine and Moraine Primulas: The Auricula Group

Under this heading are included primulas of the Auricula Group
(or Section, as it is known to botanists) which are found in the
mountain areas of Europe: in the Alps, the Pyrenees, the Apennines,
and the Carpathians. The common characteristics are rather thick,
almost succulent leaves, long cordlike roots, and short, rather heavy
flowering-stems. These characteristics are associated with alpine
habitat, where among rocky soils the long roots reach down for
abundant water, where crowns are well drained, and where the leafy
portions are subjected to extremes of temperature and wind along
with high light intensities. All these factors suggest that the true
alpine primulas be grown in the moraine, the raised bed, or the
planted wall.

Many of the species are restricted in nature to limestone sections
and none seem to demand acid conditions. Because lowland temperatures are not alpine, it is advisable to provide high shade during
a part of the day or to plant them on a north-facing slope. All these
make excellent pot plants for growing in the alpine-house. Species
in the Auricula Group are not difficult to grow from seed, but many
seeds will not germinate until the second year, after at least one
prolonged cold period, and take three or four years to reach flowering size. With age they develop multiple rosettes of leaves which
may be detached—frequently with some roots attached—and treated
as cuttings. In addition to the species listed below there are numerous natural hybrids among them and named garden forms developed
by hybridizing and selection.

Primula allionii is very rare and very beautiful, coming from
hard limestone crannies of the Maritime Alps, where it makes rather
long, bare stems below the leaf-rosette. The large pink flowers with
white centers are carried on very short scapes. It grows well in pots,
but in the garden demands a really stony soil with plentiful spring
moisture. **P. auricula,** which gives its name to the group, is one

of the easiest of the lot, wanting a fairly good but well-drained neutral or limy soil on a bank not too sunny. The wild species in its various forms has a clarity of color and a charm sometimes lost in the bizarre and rather odd combinations produced in the Garden Auriculas. Only seed collected in the wild will produce the true, clear-yellow, fragrant species, because when grown in the garden auriculas have a strong tendency to miscegenate. Good forms are easy to reproduce by rooting offsets.

P. apennina is a very small species with reddish hairs on the foliage. It is rare in nature and scarce in gardens, but because of its neat growth and short-stemmed deep pink flowers is most desirable as a pot plant in the alpine-house or in the moraine. **P. clusiana,** an inhabitant of the Austrian Alps, is easy to grow but difficult to make flower. The rosettes of narrow, sharply pointed, shiny leaves rapidly increase to a sizable clump, blooming inconsistently from year to year and not always in spring as they should. Division and replanting sometimes encourage flowering. It will grow in considerable sun, if the well-drained stony soil is plentifully laced with humus. Some bone meal worked gently into the soil and watered

Primula clusiana—Auricula Group
    (¾ life size)

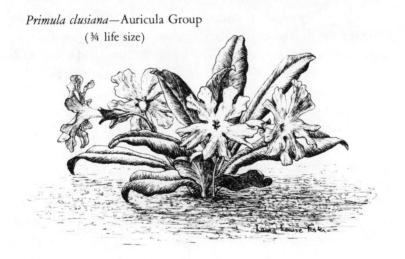

around the roots sometimes stimulates the plant to produce its crimson white-eyed blossoms. It will do poorly if given too much shade.

P. carniolica grows on wooded hills near the Adriatic Sea. It is like a small-leaved *P. auricula* without meal on the foliage. Taking a clue from its native haunts, you should give this small treasured plant considerable shade and a humus-rich soil to encourage the fragrant white-eyed pink flowers to open on 6-inch stems. *P. cottia* is difficult to distinguish from others bearing reddish hairs on the leaves and may be only a small development of *P. villosa,* local to the Cottian Alps. Plant this in a sunny moraine where it will get the light it needs to produce the large rose-pink flowers on glandular scapes but will not suffer from drought. *P. glutinosa* is found in the Austrian Alps growing in moist peaty pockets. The underground-watered moraine or raised bed with an extra measure of peat or leaf mold worked in at planting time may induce this primrose to provide the handsome royal-purple sweet-scented flowers. But, as for most of this group, young seedlings are slow-growing and should be nurtured in a pot of good but well-drained soil until large enough to risk open ground. *P. hirsuta,* unlike the last, is one of the easiest of the alpine primroses, as it is one of the commonest in the Alps. It thrives in rich scree or moraine, where it will slowly make clumps of neat rosettes. The foliage is broad and blunt, with many serrations, especially at the leaf ends. The gland-tipped hairs are numerous on the margins of the leaves and are generally more yellow than red as in related species. The ample early flowers, rose with white centers, are on scapes barely rising above the leaves. This species is frequently listed as **P. rubra.**

P. integrifolia is distinguished by small oblong leaves without serrations on the margins. The flower heads are meager, carrying only a few large rosy-purple flowers on stems about 2 inches long. Give it scree treatment. **P. marginata** will not be mistaken for any other species in the Auricula Group. It is distinctive in producing, with age, branching, woody stems at the ends of which are clumps of sharply serrate white-margined leaves. It may be grown in a rocky crevice, in either sun or shade, where the branches can splay out over rock or gravelly soil. The flowers are freely produced on powdered short scapes springing out of each leaf clump. The flower color is a lovely pale lavender or lilac, with a conspicuous powdery, pale center. But even without a flower the white-edged foliage is very handsome. The plants may be increased most easily from cuttings made by stripping rosettes from the woody stems. Seed, though quite possible, usually takes two years to germinate.

P. minima is as distinctive as *P. marginata* but with a different charm. This is a minute ground-hugging plant with small, wedge-shaped, shiny leaves, sharply serrate at the broad tip. The delicate pink flowers, 1 or 2 to a stem, with each petal deeply cleft, are large for the size of the plant and sit closely on the handsome leaves. This elfin species is most successfully grown on the raised bed among small companions where it may be seen closely for enjoyment. Plants grown from seed will not flower for at least three years, but will eventually form fat clumps. *P. pedemontana* is rather similar to *P. hirsuta,* except that the hairs on the leaves are reddish, giving to the whole leaf a rufous cast. Also, the flowers are carried on scapes well above the leaves. *P. pubescens* is really a general name for various hybrids within the Auricula Group and as *P.* × *pubescens* will produce a host of varying plants, mostly rather close to *P. auricula* itself.

P. spectabilis has large leaves forming a flattish rosette, with the upper surface of the leaf conspicuously pitted. Flowers of a good rose-pink are carried well above the foliage. This is best grown in a stony soil with considerable sun. *P. tyrolensis* has distinctly reddish flowers, 2 or 3 together. It prefers to grow between rocks in a rich scree mixture. *P. villosa* has narrow, very sticky leaves, which are happiest on a stony surface with plenty of stones in the soil mixture. The flower color is not always clear, nor are the flowers large on their 4-inch scapes. *P. viscosa* also has narrow sticky leaves, but here the flower stem is unusually long for this group, up to 6 inches, and the flowers are frequently arranged in a one-sided umbel. *P. wulfeniana* is like a smaller *P. clusiana* with a white edge to the foliage. It will grow as cheerfully as that species, but is likely to produce its large short-stemmed blossoms more readily. Grow it in the stony soil suited to this group.

Primulas for Bog and Waterside

Grouped under this heading are plants whose requirements for moisture are more constant than for other types of primula. Included are some of the pygmies as well as some of the giants of the genus. Aside from their demand for moisture, they do not all want identical conditions, but in general they inhabit soils containing considerable clayey loam. For the most favorable growing conditions one would like to have running water percolating about the roots, especially during the active growing season; some, at this stage of growth, will even endure water flowing over the crowns, but none endure for long a stagnant sinkhole that will heave with the frosts of winter and parch with the droughts of summer.

The garden sites that supply the essential moisture for this type of primrose must of necessity be in low-lying pockets. There the waters of spring thaw supply the life-giving dampness and coolness. The plants bloom and thrive, especially if into the soil has been worked an abundance of organic matter in the form of leaf mold, sedge-peat, and manure. But in our fickle climate, instead of a dry fall and snow-covered winter, we have heavy rains, a succession of freezing nights and thawing days, and the humus-rich soil rises up in a crust of icy crystals, carrying with it the crowns of the primroses. The deep thonglike roots are wrenched and heaved, and by spring the small tuffet of leaves at the top of the cluster of long white roots lies prostrate and limp as a dying squid on the soggy ground. Very young seedlings will probably settle back; old plants are anchored feet-deep by the ramifying holding rootlets; it is the adolescents that suffer—while the soil is still soft, poke them back, hard. By all means set young plants into new soil as early as possible in summer so that they may anchor down before freezing weather. Some of these primroses can endure less than boggy conditions if given a deep humus-rich soil such as that prescribed for the woodland primroses and given constant high shade in a woodland site. In general it may fairly be said that this group is hungry for rich feeding. Another characteristic they have in common is that their seeds require a period of low temperature before germination. Within the group are included the tiny birdseye primroses, the Farinosa clan. There are also the large Candelabra primulas, which carry aloft whorl upon whorl of flowers. In addition there are those of the Sikkimensis Group and some of unique carriage.

The Birdseye Primroses: The Farinosa Group

No one knows the primal grandfather of these fine diminutive primroses. Worldwide in distribution, from Scotland to Iran, from the Gaspé to the Falkland Islands, from the Alps to Japan, in early spring they lift their mealy scapes from the pointed resting-bud of leaves. The clusters of flowers are in general closely held in full heads, with each of the 5 petals prettily notched. The open-faced flowers have a white or golden eye. All members of the Farinosa Group (or Section) look best in close masses, where in early spring the rosy blossoms stand well above the silvery, mealy clumps of foliage.

Members of this Group are easy to raise from the fine, abundant seed but not easy to transplant when young because of the delicate, fine roots. It is wisest to sow the seed very thinly in a flat or large pot of rich, well-drained soil that is never permitted to dry out: ⅓ coarse sand, ⅓ humus, ⅓ loam. Leave the plants to continue growing without disturbance until ready to set out in their permanent site the second spring. If happy they will self-sow and eventually make good-sized clumps that can be lifted for division after flowering and gently teased apart.

Primula algida, from the alpine meadows of the Caucasus and Middle East, is typical of the Farinosa Group but is larger in all its parts than *P. farinosa* itself. It will endure somewhat drier sites than most, but will do its best along a streambank, where it should be permitted to self-sow to make good-sized clumps. *P. auriculata* has the typical tightly packed and pointed resting-bud of foliage which characterizes the farinosas in winter. In this species, however, there is no silver or golden meal. As the spring advances the leaf-rosette expands to reach 10 inches across and the flower stems elongate to 14 inches with disproportionately small pinkish-lavender flowers with a white eye. The one good feature of this species from the Middle East is its long and late season of bloom.

P. chrysopa is a Chinese representative of the farinosas, neat in leaf and with golden-eyed lilac flowers on 10-inch stems. This species prefers a comparatively dry site and is best grown in clumps among dwarf shrubs in good humus-rich soil in the woods garden. *P. clarkei* is one of the smallest and brightest of the group. The clear-pink flowers are carried on stems so short as to bring the blossoms just above the cluster of rounded, stalked leaves. Clumps increase rapidly and may be divided easily. This species demands considerable moisture at all times. Because of its minuteness, beauty, and demands for moisture, it is generally grown as an alpine-house specimen; but if the right conditions can be found, as at the edge of a bog, it is thoroughly hardy. *P. darialica,* from the Caucasus, has little to distinguish it from typical *P. farinosa* except its denser, more squat habit of growth.

P. farinosa gives its name to and sets the style for this large group of primulas. The type-form from the moist meadows of Europe and Britain has a rosette of 5-inch leaves, silvery farinose beneath. The powdery flowering-scapes, up to 10 inches high, carry an open umbel of many half-inch flowers, lilac-purple through pinks to white, with a yellow eye. In most gardens this is neither easy nor long-lived. It seems most successful near running water in a rich moraine in sun.

There are a number of geographical forms of *P. farinosa,* sometimes listed as separate species, which are slightly, though recognizably different. Two may be found in the Gaspé peninsula. Var. *laurentiana* is on the north shore along the St. Lawrence River, where in humus-rich pockets in the rocky cliffs it makes typical rosettes and carries lilac flowers on erect pedicels at the top of scapes that may reach 14 inches. On the south shore, in moist, limy mud among the river cliffs, is var. *mistassinica,* with small incurving silvered leaves and pink blossoms on stems less than 4 inches high. Var. *scandinavica* and var. *scotica* are also very tiny and local; var. *decipiens* from Colorado and Utah and var. *magellanica* have white or pale bluish flowers on rather tall scapes.

P. frondosa is perhaps the best of the Farinosa Group from the garden point of view. It is easy to grow, long-lived, and altogether charming. This Balkan mountain species grows best in a moist gravelly soil in light shade, where the tight mounds of silvery, dentate leaves carry many 5- to 6-inch farinose scapes, each with a full head of numerous rosy-pink blossoms. When it is grown in mass, the early spring display is a highlight of the garden. It sets abundant seed, self-sows into the most unlikely places, and the thick clumps are easily divided for increase. *P. longiflora* differs from *P. frondosa* in the shape and the size of the flower. Each blossom in the many-flowered umbel has a corolla tube that can be 1½ inches long. As easy to grow as *P. frondosa,* it has a distinctive quality in the handsome blossoms, which open slightly later in the spring.

P. modesta and its variety *fauriei* are charmers from Japan. The leaf-rosette is half the size of that in *P. frondosa* and is powdered with golden rather than silvery meal. The yellow-eyed flowers of light lavender-pink or purest white are carried on 3- to 5-inch mealy scapes in a full head. These delicate primroses will grow in moist, gritty soil or in humus-rich woods soil in light shade.

P. rosea is not farinose, though generally included in this group. The leaves unfold very early from a glabrous reddish resting-bud, and soon after the brilliant, glowing rose-pink flowers open in loose heads on 3- to 4-inch stems. These flowering-stems rapidly elongate and may reach 10 inches when in seed. This Himalayan species wants a great deal of moisture in spring and may be grown close to a stream or pond edge. If given light shade and peaty soil, it does succeed without the water close by, but water is better for it. The rapidly enlarging clumps can be divided after the flowering period. In ideal sites there is self-sowing of the fresh seed. Old seed germinates poorly.

The Candelabra Primulas

Primula japonica may be taken as the type of the Candelabra Group (or Section). It is the easiest to manage and has great variation in blossom color, though it is not the handsomest. It will thrive in fairly heavy moist soil in full sun or in a humus-rich soil in light shade. Like other tall large-leaved candelabras, it will benefit from an annual feeding with manure and bone meal when the plants go dormant in the late fall. *P. japonica* will grow to 2 feet and carry as many as 6 whorls of blossoms, opening the first tier just above the expanding leaves in late spring or early summer and elongating the flower stem to carry the wheels of flowers upward, tier on tier, for about three weeks. Flower color ranges from pure white through pinks and red-purples to almost clear red. Good color-forms may be propagated by division in late July or by root-cuttings, methods useful for all species of the Candelabra Group. Seed is easy of culture in this group, sprouting readily after a period of freezing. There is apt to be considerable self-sowing if the plants are suitably located, with blooming the second spring after germination.

P. aurantiaca is a smaller, more delicate Candelabra whose principal merit is the brilliance of the deep orange-red flowers that open from red buds. The smooth flower stalk is also reddish, as is the midrib of the leaves. This species comes from the moist meadows at lofty elevations in Yunnan, and in the garden will endure more dryness than some. It disappears underground in winter and is very tardy in making an appearance in spring. In the top whorl of flowers during July are developed small leaf clusters that may be detached and rooted as independent plants. Though not always vigorous or floriferous itself, it has lent to some modern hybrids its reddish leaf ribs and stalks and its fiery blossom colors.

P. beesiana, with its densely superimposed whorls of large individual flowers, blooms just as *P. japonica* is finishing. The blossom color is a clear rose-carmine with a golden eye. The long white thong-roots may be divided at the crown after flowering or used individually as root-cuttings to produce new plants. *P. bulleyana,* which blooms at about the same time as *P. beesiana,* has clear, deep yellow blossoms tier on tier in a slender pagoda. Combined with the last it has produced rainbow colors in the hybrids known as *P.* ✕ *bullesiana.* These two species and their hybrids combine admirably in massed plantings either in a really wet sunny site or in a deep rich soil in shade. *P. burmanica* is rather like *P. beesiana,* blooming somewhat earlier, with larger individual flowers in densely packed tiers. The color of the blossoms is a reddish purple with a large yellow eye. *P. chungensis* is like a smaller *P. bulleyana,* with somewhat lighter yellow flowers in less husky looking candelabras. The back of the flower and the tube are a deep orange-red.

P. cockburniana is the smallest among the candelabras, rarely achieving more than 2 whorls of flowers on its 10- to 14-inch stalks. The leaves are comparatively small and thin. But the plants make up in color what they lack in size and permanence. With their glowing orange-scarlet flowers, they stop the eye. To hybrids like '**Red Hugh**' they have contributed the purest red of the whole primula tribe. It is difficult to find for it a favorable site: spring moisture well drained, winter dryness, rich soil, and a modicum of open sun. In such a site they are soundly perennial; otherwise they must renew themselves by self-sowing or be replaced by seedlings (easily enough produced from the abundant seed).

P. helodoxa is a handsome pure-yellow-flowered Candelabra that is, however, rather difficult to grow well. It should be planted in deep rich soil in some shade and never permitted to get dry in summer. It is during the winter, though, that it really suffers, especially if subject to alternate freezing and thawing. A good cover of pine branches is advisable. The extra care is worthwhile, since a group of these plants with flowering-stems up to 3 feet is a brilliant sight. **P. pulverulenta** is rather similar to *P. japonica* and is as easy to grow. It is distinguished by a heavy dusting of silvery meal on the flower stalks and calyx lobes. Against this silver-gray the whorls of reddish-purple flowers with a deep purple eye stand out luminously. Lovely pure pinks and salmon-pinks have been selected in the **'Bartley Strain,'** and the species has contributed depth of color and farina to many hybrids.

Tall Primroses with Nodding Flowers in Umbels: Sikkimensis Group

There is another group of long-stalked primulas for moist sites which differs from the candelabras in carrying bell-shaped blossoms in nodding, umbellate heads. The individual flower petioles bend downward at flowering time but become erect when in seed. This group may be propagated in the same ways and wants a situation very similar to that of the candelabras and are good companion plants for these, generally blooming later than the tiered pagodas. **Primula alpicola** hangs out its broadly expanded bells in a loose umbel on top of 16-inch stalks. Within the species are two varieties: var. *luna,* with pale yellow flowers, and var. *violacea,* in shades of purple and violet. Both varieties are enhanced by rings and lines of white farina in the throat of each sweet-scented blossom. *P. alpi-*

cola wants a less boggy site than most of this midsummer group. It does best in good humus-rich soil in light shade.

P. florindae is a very tall late-blooming and sweet-scented primula for definitely wet sites: at the edge of a woodland pool, in a wet bog, or on the verge of a shaded brook. There it will form great clumps of dark green cordate leaves, and, from midsummer on, will carry a succession of stalks up to 4 feet tall. The flowers hang in a large moplike head at the summit. Though the true species bears yellow flowers, lavender and rose shades have been produced by hybridization. Flowering plants may be had the second year from seed; also clumps can be divided or the great thong-roots used as cuttings.

P. secundiflora forms a dense cluster of oblong, serrate leaves about 5 inches long. From this rosette in early summer rise a few slender scapes about a foot tall. The flowers at the summit are arranged in a one-sided umbel and are a dark ruby-purple. This species wants deep humus-rich soil in light shade. **P. sikkimensis,** which gives its name to this group, has rather small, oblong, serrate leaves. The rocket of hanging yellow bells is carried on a 2-foot stalk, produced in early summer. This species is like a refined and earlier *P. florindae* and wants a similar site, but is less hardy. Winter-heaving is frequently fatal and the plants should be protected by pine boughs.

Primroses of Unique Form

There are a few other species suitable for the moister sites of bog and waterside that do not fit into the groups already described. **Primula chionantha** looks like a compressed Candelabra primrose with dense superimposed umbels of large pure-white flowers topping 18-inch mealy stalks. The leaves are large and upstanding, dusted beneath with yellow farina, placing the plant close to the farinosas. Botanists place it in the Nivalis Group (or Section), which is a large division of the *Primula* genus containing some of the most beautiful and the most difficult. This member will succeed in a site that has ample spring and summer moisture but enough drainage to prevent the fatal rotting of the crown in winter. Because young seedlings do not transplant easily, it is advisable to sow thinly and transplant the seedlings when of good size. Methods of raising from seed and growing are similar to those required for *Meconopsis.*

P. denticulata will thrive in either very wet, miry sites or in rich woodsy soils. Fat resting-buds are produced in the fall, and from these very early in the spring erupt numerous stout scapes with globular heads of flowers that begin to open when the scapes are barely above the slowly expanding leaves. Late spring snows do not harm the blossoms, which continue to open as the stalks elongate and the leaves unfurl and give about three weeks of bloom. By early summer the touseled seedheads are aloft on 12- to 18-inch stems above great cabbages of leaves up to a foot long. Flower color in the type-species is a light lavender-purple. Superior forms are now available in pure white, clear purple, pink, and rosy red, each blossom with a white eye. Propagation is easy by division after the flowering time, or from the abundant seed. Self-sowing is, in fact, more common in this species than in any other, with the possible exception of *P. japonica.* It must be admitted that after flowering a mass of *P. denticulata* is untidy (and for best effect they should be planted in broad sweeps). An interplanting of deciduous ferns is helpful, since the uncurling fronds appear after the flowering period of the primroses.

P. capitata is rather like a summer-flowering *P. denticulata* in spite of considerable botanical differences. The leaf-rosette is compact and silvery with farina, the individual blunt-tipped, toothed leaves being about 5 inches long. The stout silvery scapes are produced from midsummer to fall, reaching a height of 12 to 18 inches, and carry a circular bonnet of blue or blue-purple bell-shaped flowers that open successively from the rim upward. This hat is a flattened cone of silvery bracts and flower calyces. *P. capitata* wants a good, rich, humus soil, but does not need a great deal of moisture. Many plants die after flowering and setting seed, but new plants from seed flower the summer following sowing.

P. viali on first sight does not look like a primrose at all; it looks more like a miniature, cooler Red-hot Poker. The flowers are produced during the summer in a dense, narrow, cylindrical cone at the top of 15- to 20-inch scapes. In bud they are conspicuous because of the red calyx scales that conceal the immature flowers. As these open, beginning at the bottom of the cone, they form a solid column of rows of lavender frills made up of the small deflexed primroses. This inflorescence creeps up the cone until it is entirely lavender. The silvery, narrow leaves form an erect 8-inch sheaf at the base of the stalks. For best effect this fascinating species should be grown in large closely planted colonies. Easy to grow from seed and flowering the second year, *P. viali* wants considerable moisture but not boggy or watery conditions, especially in winter when the small resting-bud has completely vanished underground. It is very slow to reappear in the spring. A slope of humus-rich soil above a stream or on the edge of woods is excellent.

Primulas for the Woods Garden

Very few primroses can endure really dry sites except during the resting period, and some require really wet sites during the growing season. There are many that succeed best in a humus-rich soil with shade against the sun, at least during the hot part of the day. Special beds made up of 1 part sand or stone chips, 1 part loam, and 3 parts of leaf mold or other humus will furnish the open, spongy, moisture-holding but drained condition favored by the woodland primroses. Some species suggested for bog and waterside will succeed in this type of site, and some here described will succeed in meadow conditions if natural moisture is abundant; but for many the shade and spongy soil encourage husky, healthy plants and copious flowers.

Here, among other woodlanders, is the place to grow sweeps and swatches of the cowslips and polyanthus, those familiar and fabled primroses that everyone knows and loves, belonging to the Vernales Group.

Vernales Group

All the species in the Vernales Group (or Section) are relatively easy to grow and propagate. They will stand a wide variety of soil and exposure but do their best in humus-rich well-drained soil in light shade. Germination of the seed is simple by following the standard procedures. Freezing of the seed, though sometimes advocated, is not essential, yet will do no harm. If the first few waterings of the seed are done with water warmed to about 100° F., germination is speeded. Seedlings will flower the second year. Older plants can be divided easily after the flowering period into as many separate plants as there are leaf-rosettes with roots in the expanding clump. Late-summer root growth assures that even the poorest divisions will soon be rejuvenated. To ensure success, remove the spent flowers and the upper ⅔ of the leaves before replanting the divisions. Old plants benefit from division about every three years.

Primula acaulis (more properly called *P. vulgaris*) is the primrose of English copses, which very early in spring forms tuffets of rough dark green leaves and dark-eyed yellow flowers, each on its own stalk and carried just above the foliage. Modern breeders have modified the plant in many directions—toward more and larger flowers, toward a wide range of colors from pure white through reds to pure blues, and even have produced tiny-leaved, compact plants for pot-culture.

In addition to the wild type of *P. vulgaris* of England and Europe, there are recognized wild varieties of considerable charm. Var. *abschasica,* from the Russian Caucasus, is particularly vigorous and handsome, and probably sufficiently distinct to warrant species status. Very early in spring it produces abundant large flowers of brilliant rosy purple with a golden, white-rimmed eye. Each flower is solitary on a stalk carried just above the bright green clump of smooth, short foliage. The leaves become larger and larger as the spring advances and flush after flush of blossoms open and fade. By July—which is a good time to think about dividing this magnificent primrose—the individual plants assume proportions suggesting a Chinese Cabbage. Unlike those of *P. vulgaris,* the leaves are definitely broadest at the rounded tip, conspicuously but irregularly toothed as they narrow toward the stem (almost like a dandelion leaf), and smooth on the upper surface. Another striking feature of this variety (or species) is that it puts on a real display of second bloom in the late fall, particularly in newly divided plants. Frosts will turn the flowers a deep blue-purple, but they flush back to rosy as the day warms up, and cold does not still the blossoming urge. When the snows of winter are gone, the buds that were ready to burst at the beginning of winter will begin the even more spectacular spring cycle. Though this plant does not set seed readily in the garden, it divides with the greatest of ease. From a single plant it is possible, year after year, to separate off as many as seven vigorous crowns. It will thrive in diverse soils in shade. *P. vulgaris* var. *elatior* carries an umbel of many yellow flowers on stems taller than in the type-species. *P. vulgaris* var. *rubra* (also called *P. sibthorpii*), from eastern Europe, has large pink flowers with a deep yellow eye. The varieties are handled in the same manner as the species.

P. juliae is a species of the Caucasus which has many characteristics in common with *P. vulgaris.* It differs primarily in growth habit, forming an ever-widening carpet of small leaves that lie close to the ground and do not form separate rosettes. The red petiole of the leaf is also distinctive. The blossom color of the solitary short-stalked flowers of the true species is in shades of magenta with a yellow, starry eye. The true species is very little grown, but numerous hybrids have been produced and named, some with solitary flowers on each scape, many with umbellate clusters. The small red-petioled leaf is frequently retained in the hybrids and indicates the parentage. *P. juliae* and its hybrids want rich well-drained soil in light shade. Division is easy after the early-spring flowering and is the only means of propagating named forms, since seed will produce a wide range of color and growth habit.

P. veris is the common Cowslip of grassy slopes and hedgerows throughout western and eastern Europe. It must be admitted that the sweet-scented yellow flowers in their cluster-heads are so pinched and so dominated by the baggy green calyces that they are not showy. But they do have a certain untamed charm, and look at home when grown on an open slope where they have essential drainage but not full sun. Red-flowered forms are also found.

P. polyanthus, Polyanthus, has been a garden plant for hundreds of years and has undergone at the hands of growers innumerable transformations. Most probably it is a development from original hybrids between *P. veris* and *P. vulgaris*. By selection, and possibly by the introduction of genetic influence from other species of the Vernales Group, *P. polyanthus* has become *the* garden primrose. There is an amazing range of flower size and color in the ample, many-blossomed heads, which are carried on stout stalks well above the husky dark green crinkled foliage. *P. polyanthus* wants a rich, deep soil, preferably on a slope or in a bed somewhat raised, to provide the essential drainage at the crown. Some shade is important in summer to prevent attacks of red spider. Division, at least every third year, is necessary to maintain vigor.

Cortusoides Group

Primula cortusoides may be taken as the type for a group of woodland primroses distinguished by thin foliage without farina, with a definite petiole to the leaves, and, in most of them, a leaf shape that is lobed and broad as in *Heuchera*. All this group delight in a shady site in typical woodland soil full of humus. Though species in this group do not set abundant seed, the seeds will germinate readily in spring if given a cool period.

P. cortusoides and the very similar *P. saxatilis* have long-petioled, deeply scalloped leaves in an upstanding cluster around numerous flower scapes. These hairy scapes, produced successively over a long period in early summer, rise to 10 inches and carry umbellate heads of 6 to 20 light magenta flowers, prominently cleft to produce a somewhat starry effect. Like others in this group, the plants prefer ample moisture in spring and early summer but never boggy wetness. They must have good drainage during the winter and will endure considerable dryness after flowering. They are best divided in early spring just before or as growth commences.

P. polyneura as a species name has absorbed both *P. veitchii* and *P. lichiangensis,* which are now classed as varieties under it. Within the species are variations in the hairiness of the leaves and petioles and in the color of the flowers, but the general pattern is a geranium-shaped leaf, white-woolly-haired petiole, and flowers in 1 or 2 tiers on slender stalks about 12 to 18 inches tall. The blossoms are full and round, in shades of rose, crimson, and purple, with an orange-yellow eye. All forms are readily grown from seed and succeed easily in any good soil in shade. The plants disappear to a small resting-bud in early fall and are tardy in appearing in spring.

P. kisoana, from rich woods in Japan, is stoloniferous underground unlike most primroses. The compact hairy clump of geranium-shaped leaves on short, fuzzy petioles does not fully expand until after the flowers have finished in early summer. The 2 to 5 deep rose flowers with widely spaced petals are carried on short dark scapes. In open humus-rich soil, new plants will develop at the ends of underground runners, sometimes as much as a foot from the mother plant. These may be separated from their parent when they have developed their own cluster of feeding roots in late summer.

P. sieboldii, another Japanese woodlander, is one of the easiest

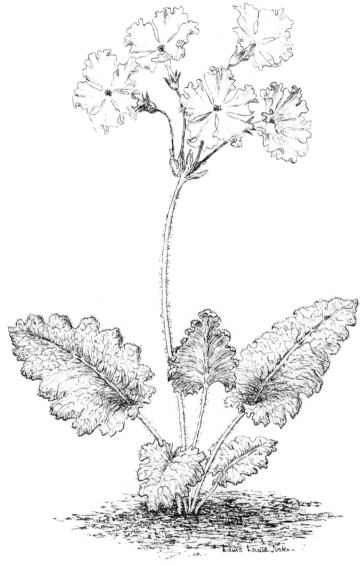

Primula sieboldii
(⅘ life size)

and most permanent of all primroses. In any reasonably good soil, in deep shade, light shade, or part sun, clumps of crinkly oval leaves on long petioles make dense patches, increasing in size year by year as the rhizomes creep just beneath the surface. The open umbels of up to 10 flowers are carried on foot-high stalks and are produced abundantly in late spring above the mat of foliage. The individual flowers are as much as 2 inches across the notched petals, in some forms frilled at the edges. The color of the type-species is a magenta-rose, but there are also pure whites, pale pinks with a deeper reverse, and good, clear reds. The foliage dies down in midsummer, leaving the carpet of rhizomes exposed for easy division. The tardiness of the appearance of the leaves in spring prompts caution about destroying these rhizomes by careless digging. Seed is not produced very freely without hand-pollination, but when available is easy to raise and produces flowers the second year.

Primulas for the Connoisseur

There are a number of lovely and fussy primulas from the Himalayas, which, because of their beauty and cultural difficulty, challenge the enthusiastic gardener. All are found in sites where the early-summer flowering season is wet and cool, the late summer dry and cool, and the winters cold and dry. Success with any of these temperamental Himalayan primulas, and the few North American species outside the Farinosa Group, depends upon efforts to reproduce climatic conditions as nearly as possible like those of their native homes. They can be grown in pots in the alpine-house or frame, where conditions can be more readily controlled, but some success has been achieved in specially prepared sites in the garden.

The ideal is a raised bed near a path with high shade on the south side, so that no sun but plenty of light and air reaches the bed. The north side of the house, if it is not overhung with trees, and the foot of an open north-facing slope in the woods garden provide good places for such a bed. Edged with logs or rocks, the soil can be deeply prepared and sloped gently up toward the `rear. The soil-mix should be at least a foot deep, containing roughly 3 parts of peat, 2 parts of leaf mold, and 2 parts of coarse sharp sand or fine gravel. As the plants are set into the soil a collar of coarse sand or fine gravel should be placed around the neck of the plant. Transplanting is best done right after the flowering period.

Seed of some of these primulas is short-lived and should be sown fresh, and thinly on a surface of a soil mixture similar to the above growing mixture. Sow in a pot or other container with at least an inch of drainage material in the bottom. Cover the seeds lightly with sand, keep moist and shaded. Germination may be delayed until the following spring for those species whose seeds need a cold period. Permit the seedlings to remain in the seed pan until they are of good size, since the roots of these primulas are very delicate and brittle. They are usually best left untransplanted till the second year. Species most likely to succeed are listed below.

Primula cawdoriana is a charming minute plant, forming a compact small rosette of overlapping leaves, somewhat felty in texture. The rosette looks rather like an old-fashioned penwiper. From among the leaves rise a number of 5-inch scapes carrying close heads of nodding flowers. The individual blossoms of pale lavender protrude from densely mealy calyces, each petal deeply notched and pointed to give the appearance of a *Soldanella*. The rosette annually forms a few new rosettes around it, and in late summer dies down to a cluster of resting-buds. Excessive winter dampness among the browned leaves that surround the resting-buds may cause rot. Some protection against this fatality can be obtained by carefully clipping away the dead leaves and working a bit of coarse sand among the crowns.

P. edgeworthii has some of the appearance of a short-stalked elfin polyanthus. It has oval serrate leaves with definite petioles; there is farina on the underside and around the margins. The flowers, produced for well over a month in late spring, are a lovely soft lavender with a yellow eye. They are carried in an upfacing umbel, and each half-inch blossom is finely toothed at the tips of the full petals. Good drainage, especially in late summer and winter, is essential. **P. hyacinthina,** in spite of a tendency to be short-lived, is a worthy candidate for this honored company. The violet-colored flowers are hyacinth-scented, carried in a rather close head on top of 12- to 16-inch silvery, mealy stems. The neat basal foliage-rosette is composed of narrow farinose leaves.

P. nutans, from the high woodlands of Yunnan, carries its smoky blue-violet nodding flowers in dense heads at the end of 8- to 10-inch silvered stems. The packed calyces at the summit form a rounded silver dome from which the bell-like flowers hang. The basal leaves are upstanding, 4 inches long, narrow, and closely covered with fine hairs. Sharp drainage in fall and winter are essential; if prevented from rotting at the crown, these beautiful plants are more perennial than formerly supposed. They come readily from the copious seed and will flower the second year.

P. parryi is one of the few American primroses. Superficially it resembles an Auricula, with its fleshy, erect leaves and many-flowered umbels of reddish-purple, yellow-eyed blossoms. The flowering-stalk rises just about to the top of the erect leaves, which in rich sites may be up to 12 inches long. In the Rocky Mountains it grows where the roots are saturated with meltwater at flowering time in June; then it is dry for the balance of the summer and snow-covered in winter. The special bed proposed for the Himalayan species will meet its cultural needs. Seed germinates easily, but the plants may need three or four years to reach flowering size.

P. reidii is a miniature species with nodding, bowl-shaped blossoms carried in a dense head on stout, mealy, 4-inch scapes. The overlapping silver-edged calyx segments form a neat shingled roof, from which the flowers flare down and out. The blossom color may be a pure ice-white or varying shades of translucent blue or lavender with a white throat. The 3-inch basal leaves are sharply toothed, bristled on the upper surface, and hairy beneath. The whole plant disappears beneath the soil surface in early fall and does not show till late in the spring, when it rushes rapidly into flower.

P. reinii—somewhat like *P. kisoana* and also from Japan and even more delicate and beautiful—should be given a spot close to a shady path where its charms may be readily observed. The rounded heart-shaped leaves are proportionately small and on short, hairy petioles. Well above them are carried on 2- to 3-inch scapes, on widely diverging pedicels, 1 to 4 comparatively large, clear, rich pink flowers with a pale yellow eye. The individual petals are deeply notched and create a neat star. This is a charming primrose for a shady site, with rich, open soil, never parched but not wet. The whole plant disappears to a small resting-bud in late summer. Seed is rarely produced, but the plants increase slowly by offsets and may be divided cautiously right after the early-summer flowering period.

PRUNELLA (Labiatae)

The creeping heal-alls are certainly not plants for the best spots in the rock garden. Though they blossom for a long period in summer and may be used quite fittingly among other ground covers in the alpine lawn, the labiate flowers are rather inconspicuous in the spike because of the large leafy bracts. They are no more brilliant and not as dense as ajuga, which they somewhat resemble. *P. grandiflora* (especially in the horticultural forms *alba, rosea,* and *rubra*) and the purple-flowered *P. webbiana* are far superior to *P. vulgaris,* the naturalized weed of lawns. All are easy of culture in good soil, in sun or light shade, and may be increased readily by seed or division. They all self-sow fiercely.

PRUNUS (Rosaceae)

This very large genus includes peaches, plums, apricots, and cherries, mostly trees with handsome blossoms and edible fruits, but it does include a few dwarf shrubs suitable to various positions in the rock garden. Among the tree forms are some of the best small trees to plant around and within the rock garden for essential shade, furnishing flowers early in the season. Among the dwarf shrubby species are a few like *P. maritima,* the Beach Plum, admirably suited to the large heath garden. *P. glandulosa,* the Flowering Almond, in pink or white, may also be used in the heath or in the mixed planting of the rock garden surround. *P. pumila,* the Sand Cherry, and its smaller relative, *P. besseyi,* are both low enough for inclusion in or near the large rock garden. The variety *P. pumila depressa* can even be completely prostrate, an excellent shrub to creep over the ground and fan out over large rocks. The white blossoms are abundant, but the purple-black fruits are hardly edible. The last-named may be propagated by layers and the rest by soft-wood cuttings or seed.

PSORALEA (Leguminosae)

The summer-blooming scurfy peas are mostly shrubby, but there are a few western Americans of considerable ornamental value. Herbaceous *P. hypogaea* is nearly stemless, with dense spikes of good blue pea flowers among the pinnate foliage. It grows from a heavy tuberous root, in dry sites and in rather heavy clayey soil. Propagate this by seed or spring division of the heavy root.

PTEROCEPHALUS. See *Scabiosa.*

PTILOTRICHUM. See *Alyssum.*

PULMONARIA (Boraginaceae)

The lungworts supply, very early in the season, blue color to the garden in the various strains of *P. angustifolia.* The pubescent green foliage may be short and dense with large sky-blue flowers, or lax and long with pale blue blossoms. There is also a variety *rubra,* with rather muddy color. Quite different both in growth habit and flower color is the plant sold by nurseries as *P. rubra,* probably a form of **P. montana,** which in the type-species has violet funnel-form blossoms, hairy in the throat. The cyme of flowers is terminal on leafy stems that start to flower in the early spring when only a few inches high and keep flowering until they reach 1½ feet and lie out upon the ground in early summer. The color of the nursery-man's *P. rubra* (more properly named **P. montana rubra**) is a glowing, very deep salmon-red, never changing to blue as in **P. saccharata,** the common Bethlehem Sage, or Spotted Dog. This last has spotted leaves and flowers that open an intermediate pink and change to blue. All the lungworts revel in rich soil in either moist sun or shade. They are easily divided after flowering or propagated by seed.

PULSATILLA (Ranunculaceae)

The pasque-flowers are a group of *Anemone* relatives sometimes still listed under that genus, but generally separated from it on the basis of their handsome fluffy seedheads. The genus contains some of the most showy flowers for the early spring season in the rock garden. The blossom in all species is comparatively large, with rather satiny petal-like sepals forming a bowl containing the golden stamens. At flowering time the buds, wrapped in furry, pointed involucral leaves, begin to open on short stems, close to the barely unfurling, much-cut foliage. The flower stems elongate as the season advances and the fluffy seedheads form.

The seeds, which are ripe about a month and a half after the flowers first open, should be gathered and sown immediately, since they rapidly lose viability in storage. Sown in containers of light sandy but nourishing soil, fresh seed will germinate within two weeks and produce neat little plants before winter. It is advisable to sow seed thinly and hold seedlings for transplanting in the spring. The plants should commence to bloom in two years. Old plants have deep thonglike roots and do not transplant easily. Good color forms may be propagated by root-cuttings.

P. alpina is widespread in the alpine meadows and craggy places of the European mountain ranges. The gleaming white flowers are up to 2 inches across and are borne singly on stiff stems that rise above a basal clump of much-cut foliage. The flower stems, which in mature specimens may number as many as 20, elongate as the season progresses, carrying the blossom and the whorl of involucral stem-leaves up to 2 feet at seeding time. *P. alpina* var. *sulphurea,* distributed in Central Europe, is similar, with flowers of a bright deep yellow. Both the species and the variety are slow to attain flowering size and do not transplant easily when large. These beautiful flowers are worth waiting for. When planted in fairly deep, well-drained but rich soil, in sun, seedlings will increase in size and number of stems year by year.

P. halleri, a pasque-flower of great charm, bears deep purple flowers on short stems above silky, hairy foliage. It blooms a bit later than most, and the wide individual blossoms are large, frequently with cleft sepals. *P. montana* is very like this species except that the foliage is smooth and the flowers are nodding.

P. occidentalis is the American counterpart of European *P. alpina.* In the mountains of the West, generally in acid soil, the 2-inch white blossoms begin to open on very short furry stems as soon as the snow departs. The stems rapidly elongate and the grayish, fuzzy seedheads stand as much as 2 feet above the clump of husky, finely cut foliage. This species is not easy to grow in the garden because it requires good drainage in a rocky site but with plenty of moisture at the roots and warm sunshine overhead. A north-facing slope in a gritty, peaty soil promises the greatest chance of success.

P. patens is a very early-blooming pasque-flower whose large pearly-lavender blossoms, richly dressed with silvery fur, appear on very short stems before the leaves unfurl. It is a species of wide distribution with forms in northern Europe and Asia and a beautiful variety, **nuttalliana** (sometimes listed as *P. hirsutissima*), in

America from the Mississippi River westward. All forms are highly desirable because of the large blossoms of diaphanous texture, especially lovely when the spring sun shines through the delicate sepals. They will grow in any well-drained, rich soil, and year by year will increase the number of flowers, each single on a stem, in a mounded cluster.

P. pratensis carries its deep red-purple urns hung downward, with the tips of the sepals curled back. It is a lowland species throughout Europe and easy to grow in good meadow soil. The fluffy seedheads stand erect on elongated stems.

P. vernalis is in the eyes of most growers the absolute queen of

Pulsatilla vernalis
(¾ life size)

the pulsatilla tribe, and ranks among the most prized of rock garden plants. It blooms so early that late snowfall may bury it—but with no harm. It merely closes the opalescent chalice into a tight bud, the outer sheaths of which are densely covered with golden silk. Each 2-inch blossom carries close beneath it on the 3- to 4-inch stem a ruff of golden-haired leaves. The evergreen, deeply cut basal leaves form a close, hard tuft. Though this species comes from lofty places in the mountains of Europe, it will succeed in lowland gardens if given a rich, well-drained soil in a site not utterly parched, such as an open northern slope.

P. vulgaris is the commonest of the pulsatillas, widespread in the lower reaches of the European mountain country. The large, somewhat starry blossoms are carried singly on short stems above the basal rosette of much-cut, stalked leaves. As in the other members of this genus, the flowering-stem elongates as the flowers mature and go to seed. Plants are long-lived and multiply the number of leaf-rosettes until a single individual becomes a sheaf of early spring bloom. The common color in the wild is a rich purple. Pure white, brick-red, and soft pink color-forms have been named and may even come fairly true to seed, especially the white. Plants vary considerably in stature and some become husky creatures with mature leaves 12 inches long and flowering-stems more than a foot high. The named color-forms tend to be less massive.

PUSCHKINIA (Liliaceae)

The small striped squills are dainty bulbs to be grown in groups in the sunny portions of the rock garden or in the light shade of the woods garden. The delicate flowers, held in a close raceme on top of 6-inch stalks, are pale blue with darker blue penciling. Plant these only 3 inches deep in light soil for early spring bloom. They are charming planted among the darker blue scillas in the alpine lawn. The common species is **P. scilloides,** with a slightly huskier variety, **libanotica.**

PYROLA (Pyrolaceae)

These handsome shinleaves are woodland plants of neat proportion, lovely in leaf, beautiful in flower, but difficult to establish. Most species are native to North America and carry their waxy white, green, or purplish flowers in racemes during the summer. The evergreen basal leaves are generally rounded and glossy, in some species marbled. Like the pipsissewas, to which they are related, the shinleaves have creeping subterranean shoots by which they increase to sizable colonies. The feeding-roots are very fine and scattered, which makes transplanting difficult. The best means of establishment is to dig carefully the smallest, most compact clump to be found, shake off the soil, and plant in a pot containing ⅔ sharp sand and ⅓ acid peat. If not permitted to dry out thoroughly, and also not kept too moist, new feeding-roots will be encouraged to form. This will take up to six months. The plant will appear healthy and alive for long periods even without roots, but should not be set in a permanent site in duffy woods soil until new roots are assured.

The dustlike seed is reluctant to germinate, but with patience will produce plants if sown on sphagnum moss. All species are desirable, with the flowering stalks ranging from 6 inches to a foot high. Especially lovely are the following: *P. asarifolia,* with substantial, glossy leaves and pink flowers; *P. minor,* with a dense raceme of pink or white flowers on a 6-inch scape; *P. picta,* with marbled, dentate leaves, purple beneath, and purplish flowers; *P. secunda,* with a one-sided raceme of white flowers; *P. uliginosa,* the Bog Shinleaf for moister soils, with large, shiny leaves, and good-sized pinkish flowers.

PYXIDANTHERA (Diapensiaceae)

The pyxie-mosses are bewitching plants. The mosslike mat of fine foliage is spangled at the tips of the short branches with solitary 5-petaled white flowers in early spring. In the sandy reaches of the

East Coast pine barrens from New Jersey to North Carolina, pyxies make mats up to 2 feet across. In the shade of pines and shrubs the foliage remains a lively green, but in sunny spots the whole mat may be reddish brown. Though the surface sand of its native home may be hot and dry, the roots descend into constantly moist lower layers. The water table in the pine barrens is relatively high, suggesting that in the garden a rather special site of deep acid, fine-grained sandy soil with adequate underground moisture be constructed to accommodate *P. barbulata.* The very similar *P. brevifolia,* distinguished by shorter, hairier leaves and more widely spaced, cuneate rather than roundish flower petals, comes from drier, inland sand barrens of North Carolina. But it too thrives best in a site that suits the more common species.

Small shoots of both may be rooted in early summer by careful treatment in an enclosed pot of sand and peat. Large clumps, well moistened, may be lifted and sliced with a strong knife for increase, but each division must be substantial and must include some of the densely rooted center of the clump. Pyxies do well in a deep pot of pine-barren soil. The genus name is derived from the Greek word *pyxis,* a small box, and the Latin *anthera,* referring to the fact that the anthers open like a lidded box. The fancied relation with pixies is purely fortuitous.

RAMONDA (Gesneriaceae)

These hardy relatives of the popular African Violets are at their best growing in rocky crevices in a cool shady location. In nature they are generally found growing in almost pure humus among limestone rocks, but the limestone is not essential. They are at their best in the vertical face of a shady wall. If they are grown on a shaded slope without rocky crevices, it is important to have a good depth of stone chips for the hairy foliage to rest upon. During droughty spells the leaves may shrivel but they have remarkable powers of rejuvenation following a rain.

With age the rosettes become multicrowned and may be divided. Leaves pulled off the crown in June and July, buried ⅓ their depth in peaty soil, and kept moist, will produce a minute new rosette in about 6 months. The extremely fine seed germinates readily. It should be sown very thinly on a pot of peaty soil and kept constantly moist. Standing the pot in a saucer of water in a shady protected place will effect this. Leave the seedlings in the pot for at least a year before transplanting; it may be necessary to thin them in order to give them sufficient space for developing into the good-sized rosettes prerequisite to beginning life in the garden. It takes three to four years from seed to produce a flowering plant.

R. nathaliae from the Balkans makes a flat rosette of overlapping leaves, oval in outline, deep green above, and hairy along the wavy toothed margins. The stout 4- to 6-inch hairy scapes rise from among the leaves in early summer and carry a cluster of 3 to 4 broad campanulate 4-petaled flowers of lavender-blue, set off handsomely by the golden eye-ring and pointed cluster of golden stamens. White- and pink-flowered forms are sometimes produced. **R. pyrenaica** (properly **R. myconi**) differs in having hairier leaves with a rougher surface and 5-petaled instead of 4-petaled flowers. **R. serbica** has slightly smaller flowers and golden hairs on the leaves. **R. heldreichii** is now listed under *Jankaea*.

RANUNCULUS (Ranunculaceae)

The buttercups are a vast tribe, containing many rather similar meadow plants and a few high alpines of extraordinary beauty. The latter are for the most part uncommon in the wild and challenging in the garden. Established plants of most of the species develop multiple crowns and may be divided for increase. Root-cuttings are generally rather rapid, whereas seed, unless very fresh, is either slow to germinate or fails utterly.

R. adoneus is one of the few really fine American buttercups.

The 1-inch-wide yellow blossoms are carried on 4- to 8-inch scapes above deeply cut foliage. Coming from the high screes in the Rockies, it wants moraine treatment in the garden. *R. alpestris* carries white flowers on stalks of about 6 inches, and like the other white-flowered species has an appeal undimmed by association with the common yellows. The gray-green, 3-part leaves form a pleasing background for the solitary blossoms. Because it grows in wet spots near melting snows in the high Alps, it must be planted in rich soil close to water, or in the primrose bog, or the wettest section of the moraine. *R. amplexicaulis* is another white-flowered species carrying many scapes—9 to 12 inches—each scape with 2 to 3 blossoms an inch wide. The leaves, uncut and lanceolate, are glaucous green and clasp the scape at the base. This species wants rich soil in sun but does not like drought.

R. andersonii, a rare American species, belongs more properly in a separate genus, *Beckwithia,* but its effect is clearly that of a pink-flowered buttercup with much-cut foliage. This is a scree plant that prefers to have some shade against the hot sun. *R. anemonoides* is another beautiful species frequently placed in another genus, *Callianthemum.* The pink or white large blossoms have many narrow petals and stand only about 4 inches above the much-cut fernlike foliage. This fine plant needs rich soil in shade. *R. calandrinioides* is quite unbuttercup-like, having long, narrow, glaucous foliage and large, thin-textured, solitary blossoms of pink or white on 10- to 12-inch scapes. As it comes from rich screes in North Africa and blossoms very early, it is at its best in a deep pot in the alpine-house, but may be grown out-of-doors in a sheltered, rich scree. The whole plant should be allowed to go dormant in summer. *R. crenatus* is one of the easiest of the white-flowered dwarfs, with rounded, wavy leaves and inch-wide white cups on 2- to 4-inch stems. Good drainage in the scree or moraine will suit this alpine of the Caucasus Mountains.

R. glaberrimus sheets the ground with golden flowers very early in spring in the drier intermontane sections of the American Far West. Fall rains bring the shining, fleshy, rounded leaves close above the little knot of roots that lie dormant during the summer. The large golden coins develop quickly in spring, sitting tight upon the tuft of leaves. The flower and leaf stems elongate before the summer rest period, at which time the roots may be divided for increase. When the plants are thriving in a sunny scree, self-sowing will provide a spreading carpet. **R. glacialis** is the delight and the despair of the rock gardener. The large satiny blossoms, opening white and fading through pink to red, are carried on brief stems above the much-divided gray-green leaves. They are carried thus, at least, in the high, wet, earthy screes of the European Alps among the acid rocks. Not difficult to grow from fresh seed, this species generally languishes before blooming in lowland gardens. Give it sun and plenty of moisture in a heavy soil full of broken rock. A special pocket on a streamside or in the wettest part of the moraine offers the likeliest spot for success.

R. gramineus has long, glaucous, grassy foliage and many-flowered, open heads of inch-wide pale yellow blossoms on top of foot-high, slender stalks. Like most of the buttercups, this blooms early in a sunny spot in good rich garden soil. **R. montanus** will grow either in full sun or light shade, in rich, rocky soil. The shining yellow flowers, about an inch across, are solitary just above the dense, dark green, divided foliage. The plant increases by stolons and may be easily divided after the flowering season. In muggy weather the leaves may become mildewed and bedraggled, but this does no permanent harm. Most high peaks in the western American mountains have their complement of dwarf golden buttercups, many of which are yet to be introduced into cultivation. To be sought out are **R. eschscholtzii, R. occidentalis, R. saxicola, R. suksdorfii,** and **R. triternatus.**

RAOULIA (Compositae)

These Australian and New Zealand carpeters, when rather starved in a sunny, well-drained location, form dense sheets or hummocks spattered with almost stemless, tiny, composite flowers. They spread fairly rapidly into solid masses, easily divided for increase, since they root as they run. None are reliably hardy where the temperature drops to zero or below. Give them a gritty soil, preferably acid. *R. australis* forms mats of glistening silver with yellow-bracted flowers. *R. glabra,* probably the hardiest, has minute green leaves and white flowers. *R. lutescens* has almost microscopic yellow-silver leaf-rosettes and very small yellow flowers. All are excellent among rocks in planters and especially in pots in the alpine-house. *R. tenuicaulis* is slightly more open-growing, with silvery foliage and yellow stemless flowers.

RHEXIA (Melastomaceae)

The North American meadow-beauties are found locally in moist acid soils from Maine to Florida. The species carry their showy 4-petaled flowers in an open leafy cyme during the summer. Increase them by seed or by division of the tubers or stoloniferous stems. *R. lanceolata,* of the Blue Ridge Mountains, has small, narrow leaves and large white to pale purple flowers on 18-inch stalks. *R. mariana* may grow to 2 feet, with pubescent foliage and 1-inch, pale purple flowers. *R. virginica,* the commonest species, has 12- to 18-inch, square stems and rosy-purple flowers 1½ inches across. All species do best in constantly moist sandy or peaty soils, with either sun or light shade.

RHODODENDRON (Ericaceae)

There are many dwarf species and hybrids among the rhododendrons admirably suited to growing in the acid rock garden, especially in the heath. Some have small leaves and flowers on tight, twiggy little bushes. Others form mounds of larger leaves and carry ample trusses of proportionately large flowers. Many are true evergreens and their relationship to the massive, showy, large-leaved types is easily recognized. Others are deciduous or semideciduous and carry large open flowers like the plants commonly called azaleas. So varied and so numerous are they, with new and wonderful hybrids being produced annually, that it would take far too many pages to describe even the most desirable. Books devoted to this genus are to be found listed in the Descriptive Bibliography.

Since many of the dwarf species come from high mountain pastures and rocky places, they delight in a peaty, open soil, good air drainage, and a cool aspect. A north-facing slope is excellent. Otherwise they should be planted under high shade to keep them cool in summer and to protect the evergreen sorts from sun-scorch in the winter. They want adequate moisture but must have very good drainage. An acid stone-chip mulch will protect the fine sur-face-roots when rhododendrons are planted in peaty pockets among the rocks on a north-facing slope. In the heath garden a mulch of pine needles will serve the purpose. This genus dislikes cultivation that disturbs the shallow root system, so a ground cover of herbaceous material or smaller shrubs is most suitable. Most of the evergreen and many of the dwarf deciduous rhododendrons may be increased by cuttings of ripened shoot-wood or by layering. Good forms of species and hybrids should be thus propagated. Seedlings are not difficult to grow, though slow to reach flowering size.

RHODOHYPOXIS (Amaryllidaceae)

These South African bulbs, related to the taller American *Hypoxis,* have grassy, pubescent foliage and numerous, enchanting open-faced blossoms of pink or white. They want sandy, acid, well-drained soil in sun or light shade. Winter protection is advisable in cold areas, though they are remarkably hardy if kept dry in winter. Increase these plants by division after they flower in early summer. Seed is possible but slow. **R. baurei** carries solitary 6-petaled flowers of deep rose-red on 3-inch stems among 2-inch grassy foliage. Var. *platypetala* has more pubescent foliage and white flowers.

RHODOTHAMNUS (Ericaceae)

This rare dwarf shrub of moist rocky screes in the limestone Alps of Europe is somewhat like a magnified *Loiseleuria,* and as difficult to handle. The large, generally solitary blossoms on delicate stalks at the tips of the shoots are pure pink. The dense, twiggy, evergreen shrubs, about a foot high, are advantageously planted in the heath garden or in a shaded pocket of rhododendron soil. Because the root system is straggly rather than compact as in rhododendrons, these do not transplant easily. Seed does not germinate unless fresh, and seedlings are very slow-growing. Layers or cuttings are the quickest means of increase. *R. chamaecistus* is the only species.

RIBES (Saxifragaceae)

Some of the flowering currants and gooseberries are handsome both in fruit and blossom. Most of those native to eastern United States are rather dingy, bristly shrubs, but from the Far West come more showy species. *R. sanguineum* has large red flowers and bluish-black currants on shrubs too tall except for the surround of the rock garden or as specimens in the woods garden. *R. erythrocarpum,* the Crater Lake Currant, on the other hand, is an utterly delightful carpeter. On a north slope, clambering over rocks, it makes a dense mat of deciduous scalloped leaves. In early spring, sizable flowers of brick-red and yellow, giving an overall effect of burnt-orange, are produced in 8- to 20-flowered racemes, followed by red fruit. As the rambling branches root down, it may be propagated by layers as well as by seed.

ROMANZOFFIA (Hydrophyllaceae)

The Mist-maiden, *R. sitchensis,* of wide distribution in western North America, is like a delicate saxifrage in appearance. The lovely white or pink blossoms are carried in open racemes above the scalloped, rounded, long-stemmed leaves. This species is sometimes separated into other species or varieties but all are very similar except for height of flower stem, which may be only 3 inches at alpine elevations and up to 8 inches in rich, moist, shady lowlands. A soil abundant in leaf mold and never dry, in either dense or light shade, will provide a congenial home for the somewhat tuberous roots. These roots may be divided during the summer dormancy, or the plant may be propagated easily from seed, which it frequently does by self-sowing.

RUBUS (Rosaceae)

The dwarf and creeping brambles are not all very brambly and, unfortunately, not entirely hardy. The small potentilla-like single blossoms are never abundant, but are pleasant ornaments of the rambling carpets; they are followed by blackberrylike fruits. In spineless, creeping **R. arcticus** the blossoms are pink. **R. chamaemorus,** the Cloudberry, is an erect dwarf with large white flowers. Flat creepers of the far-western evergreen forests, all bearing white strawberry-like blossoms and red fruit are **R. lasicoccus, R. nivalis,** with dark shining leaves, and **R. pedatus.** These make charming if not brilliant ground covers in the woodland garden, beneath and among which other woodlanders may be satisfactorily planted. Propagate them by seed or division of the rooting runners.

SAGINA (Caryophyllaceae)

The mosslike carpets of the pearlworts are very similar to *Arenaria caespitosa,* but often have either muddy-white minute petals to the flowers or none. They are useful as a green ground cover between paving stones or over bulbs in shady locations. They will not grow in parched ground, but should not be admitted to select company in the rock garden—the carpets will thread their way among the saxifrages and androsaces and smother them. The common species, **S. procumbens,** is generally without petals; **S. saginoides** and **S. nodosa** are less invasive and do have small white flowers, quite conspicuous in *nodosa.* These are easy to propagate by division or seed.

SAGITTARIA (Alismaceae)

The arrowheads are suitable only for the shallow water or saturated verges of sizable pools or slow streams, where in the wet mud they increase into dense clumps by underground tuber-bearing rootstocks. The 3-petaled white flowers are set rather close to the stout stalk, rising among arrow-shaped or lance-shaped leaves throughout the summer. The abundant flat seed is gathered in globular seedheads. Of the many American species there are numerous variations, with leaf size and shape depending somewhat on site. Propagation is easy from fresh seed or by division of the roots.

SALIX (Salicaceae)

The dwarf alpine willows, with proportionately small fuzzy catkins, form mats or congested, tiny, erect deciduous shrubs in moist rocky mountain sites. They are suitable for moist spots in the moraine, on the streamside, or among the dwarf shrubs of the heath garden. They may be propagated by division or cuttings, but rarely produce viable seed. *S. herbacea* is a creeping alpine shrub with bright, glossy, rather round, serrate leaves, found in European, Asian, and North American mountains. *S. nivalis,* from the mountains of the American West, is a mat-former with small pointed leaves, dark green above and glaucous beneath. *S. reticulata,* from arctic and antarctic regions, has rough netted leaves, dark green above and whitish beneath. *S. retusa* makes mats of very small round green leaves in the alpine regions of Europe and Asia.

SALVIA (Labiatae)

A few of the salvias from eastern Europe are very useful in the alpine lawn or large rock garden because they provide a show of blossom in that interval between the late spring flush of color and the midsummer resurgence. The tubular 2-lipped flowers are produced in whorls along the upper portion of the arching stems. They are easy to grow from seed and may be divided in spring as the growth commences. *S. bracteata,* from Asia Minor, has a woody shrublike base with woolly cut leaves. The spike of purple flowers forms the upper portion of the 18-inch stems, with small, uncut stem-leaves, purple-colored. *S. jurisicii,* of the Balkan hills, has arching stems about 1-foot tall, set with hairy, divided leaves and long racemes of clear-lavender flowers. A white-flowered form, var. *alba. S. verbascifolia,* of the Caucasus, has thick, wrinkled, broad leaves, woolly gray beneath. The white flowers, with conspicuous blue hairs, are produced in foot-high open panicles.

SANGUINARIA (Papaveraceae)

The Bloodroot, *S. canadensis,* is locally abundant in eastern North America, generally in rich neutral to limy soil, either in sun or light shade. It favors a fairly heavy soil with plenty of spring moisture, but will endure considerable summer drought. In dry sites it is apt to lose its foliage by midsummer, without material loss of vigor. The handsome goblets of white, sometimes faintly tinged with pink, stand solitary on 6- to 9-inch scapes in spring before the large umbrella-leaves have expanded. The lobed leaves later rise on stalks over a foot tall and can be a foot across. The flower petals quickly fall, to be followed by long narrow capsules swollen with many smooth, brown, shining seeds, concealed beneath the canopy of leaves. Fresh seed germinates readily, and frequently self-sows at considerable distance from the parent plant. The stout reddish rhizome, which bleeds orange juice when cut, is very shallow in the soil. It may be divided in summer. The only species of this poppy-relative genus is *S. canadensis.* In forma *multiplex* (frequently misnamed *flore-pleno*) the stamens have been transformed into petals and produce most beautiful, rounded, solid-white globes, longer-lasting than the fertile single form. This form sets no seed and must be propagated by division of the rootstock.

SAPONARIA (Caryophyllaceae)

The soapworts are floriferous, easy plants, doing best in a light gritty soil in full sun. Good forms of species are best propagated by cuttings, because seeds, which are abundant and easy to germinate, will produce plants of considerable variation. They need deep soils and defy division since they are taprooted. *S. caespitosa* forms close pancakes of short linear leaves, above which, in early summer, the 3- to 6-inch flower stalks carry cymes of a few good pink flowers. This plant does its best in sunny limestone scree soils. *S. lutea,* similar in growth habit to *S. caespitosa,* bears rather small pale yellow flowers in dense heads. This wants an acid, well-drained soil, richer and more moist than for the other species. *S. ocymoides* is an easy, sprawly soapwort best grown where it can drape a bank or large stone, there to produce its ample clusters of small, bright rose-pink flowers in early summer. Forms with white flowers, or those of special color and size, should be increased by cuttings. The branching, flopping stems may be cut back severely after flowering to keep the plant neat and compact. Any well-drained deep soil in sun will suit it. More fussy and more beautiful is *S. o. rubra compacta.* The whole plant is reduced in size and tightened, forming a small prostrate mat with brilliant deep pink flowers. Even in ideal conditions—deep, fairly rich well-drained soil with a stone mulch—this form is short-lived and must be renewed by cuttings. It does quite well in a raised bed in light shade. Seed will produce a proportion of plants with good form, but some will be more like the type-species.

SARCOCOCCA (Buxaceae)

These Asiatic shrubs, related to boxwood, have shining, deep green, evergreen foliage, long and tapering to a point. The flowers are inconspicuous; the fruit is a fleshy black berry. It is for the foliage that these plants are grown in acid, peaty soils, even in dense shade. Only *S. hookeriana humilis* is reliably hardy and small enough to be grown in the heath garden or woods garden. Increase it by cuttings.

SARRACENIA (Sarraceniaceae)

The pitcher-plants are curious insect-catchers of boggy situations. The mottled basal leaves are hollow and trumpet-shaped, with a lidlike construction at the summit. Just as strange are the solitary nodding flowers of yellow or crimson with a large umbrella-shaped stigma beneath the 5 large petals. These must be grown only in constantly wet boggy sites. Propagate them by seed sown in sphagnum soup. These American plants are found principally in eastern coastal swamps and bogs. The most widespread and only completely hardy species is *S. purpurea,* with pitcher-leaves up to 12 inches long and with 2-inch red-purple flowers on tall scapes. The water-filled leaves, with erect wavy-edged lids, turn bright red in full sun, but remain green in shady locations. This species and less hardy ones may be grown in pots of sandy peat, kept constantly wet by standing in dishes of water.

SATUREIA, sometimes spelled *Satureja* (Labiatae)

The savories are twiggy little shrubs, valuable for their long and late season of bloom, and for the fine aromatic foliage. Rather like an erect thyme with somewhat larger, labiate flowers, these sunlovers do best and remain most compact in a lean, limy soil. They are easy to propagate by seed or cuttings. *S. alpina* is small of leaf, only about 6 inches high, and bears purple flowers. *S. montana* is a stiffer, more erect shrub up to a foot tall, with white to purplish small flowers.

SAXIFRAGA (Saxifragaceae)

No rock garden, raised bed, or alpine-house would be complete without representatives of this worldwide genus. By very name they are intimately associated with rocks, and in their manifold variety offer beauty of flower and foliage to outshine most other genera. No single set of prescriptions for growing and propagating will fit the vast array of saxifrages. Fortunately they fall into rather clearly defined groups that within themselves do call for much the same treatment. Except in a thorough and scientific description, 4 major divisions cover the genus fairly well so far as garden-worthy species are concerned. There are a few very good ones, however, belonging to other groups and deserving separate treatment.

The Encrusted Saxifrages

The Euaizoon Group includes the ones generally spoken of as "encrusted." They form closely packed rosettes of silvery foliage with white encrustations, generally conspicuous, along the edges of the leaves. To the uninitiated they resemble the hens-and-chicks of the sempervivums unless they are making their summer display of flowers, which are carried in open sprays. Most of the species that fall within this group are not difficult to grow in good, rocky lime soil, in a location where they will not be baked by the summer sun. They do their best and look their best in crevices of rockwork, as on the semishaded face of a raised bed or planted wall. Here the rosettes will multiply, flowing along the joints and over the rocks. The clumps may endlessly be divided into single, rooted rosettes. Even rosettes without roots will produce them quickly in moist sand. The fine seed should be sown very thinly, without covering, on a surface of fine gravel above an open, gritty but fertile soil. Leave the seedlings in the container for about a year, when they will be easy to separate and transplant in spring.

Saxifraga aizoon is the type for the whole group and, since it is found from the Gaspé Peninsula to the Balkans, varies widely in foliage and flower. It has hybridized likewise in the wild and in the garden so that there are limitless variations in leaf shape and size, length of flower scape, and color of flowers. Basically it has rosettes of narrow spatulate leaves, edged with forward-pointing teeth and rimmed with silvery-white encrustations. The flowers are generally white with some minute reddish dots, in open sprays during the early summer. Var. **baldensis** (also called *S. minutifolia)* has small ash-gray rosettes and flower spikes of only 2 to 3 inches. Var. **lagraveana** is also small and compact, with silvery rosettes and especially thick, almost waxy, creamy flowers. Var. **lutea** has good yellow flowers, and var. **rosea** carries plumes of solid pink.

S. cochlearis has heavily encrusted leaves, broadened at the tip to give a narrow spoon shape. The starry white flowers are carried in dense one-sided sprays, bending on the glandular scapes so that all the blossoms are on the upper side. **S. c. minor** has very small, dense leaf-rosettes, each about an inch across.

S. cotyledon is one of the largest of the group with great rosettes of tongue-shaped leaves, beaded but not toothed. The tall panicle of white flowers, frequently branched and pyramidal in outline, may, when well grown, reach 3 feet. To induce flowering it is sometimes necessary to remove and save for propagation all side-rosettes. The flowering-rosette dies after blooming.

S. crustata bears linear leaves in a trim, flat rosette, with hairs at the base of the heavily beaded foliage. The flowers are somewhat dingy, on fairly short stalks. **S. hostii** has large rosettes of strap-shaped, toothed leaves with a blunt tip. The flowers, in tall, rather flat-topped panicles, are white spotted with red. This is generally seen in gardens only in hybrid forms. **S. lingulata** has long, linear, acute leaves that tend to stand erect, and carries an arching inflorescence of white flowers on a dark, leafy stem. There are various forms with more spatulate, blunt leaves which may lie flat on the ground; and, as in all species in the Encrusted Group, are generally seen in hybrid forms.

S. longifolia, from the Pyrenees, grows best in a vertical crevice where it may increase the size of the rosette until it sends out the compact cone-shaped inflorescence, up to 2 feet long. After flowering the rosette dies without offsets, except in the hybrid forms usually seen in gardens. **S. valdensis** gives rise to as many de-

Saxifraga, Encrusted Group
(¾ life size)

scriptions as there are experts. In nature it forms close rosettes of spatulate leaves, very like *S. cochlearis minor,* of which it may be but a variation. The flower spike is glandular and usually under 3 inches.

Mossy Saxifrages

The Mossy Saxifrages, as their name suggests, form sheets of soft foliage, dense, evergreen, and variously divided. Above the mat in early spring, on wiry stems up to 8 inches high, come myriads of flowers in open clusters, mostly pure white but in many of the fine hybrids they are shades of pink and red. These all call for a

Saxifraga, Mossy Group
(life size)

cool semishaded site, in rich, well-drained soil that does not parch
in summer. Along streamsides or in other moist situations they
will endure full sun. Their one common weakness is to die out in
patches, especially during hot, muggy weather. An annual topdressing of equal parts of coarse sand and leaf mold worked into the
carpet of foliage will encourage new roots and help to prevent brown
patches. All are easy to propagate by division after flowering, a
preferred method for the showy hybrids. Seed is very easy to germinate, but is likely to produce a mixed lot of progeny.

Among the best of the species in this group are *Saxifraga
caespitosa* and closely related *S. decipiens,* both with substantial
foliage, each cuneate leaf cleft at the tip into 3 or more segments.
The white blossoms are from ½ to 1 inch across, on stems from
4 to 8 inches high. These two are the base for most of the showy
hybrids. Red color is contributed by *S. muscoides,* which in the
species has yellowish or red flowers on short stems above minute
foliage. There are other species belonging in the Mossy Group
(or Section), some insignificant, some rare. For garden purposes it
is the hybrids that deserve first place in the section, because, though
they retain the character of the wild species, they produce larger
flowers in a range of colors richer and more varied. There is an
endless list of names, such as: **'Kingscote White,' 'Pearly King,'
'Stransfieldii,'** among the whites; **'Apple Blossom,' 'Du Barry,'
'Peter Pan,'** among the pinks; **'Bathoniensis,' 'Mrs. Piper,'
'Pixie,' 'Scarlet Gem,'** and **'Sprite,'** among the reds.

The Engleria Saxifrages

Though the species of this group grade into those of the
Kabschia Group (or Section), they are sufficiently different in leaf
shape and flowering habit to be quite distinctive in the garden.
Since hybrids between the two groups are also numerous, distinc-
tions are not always easy to make. In the extreme form, however,
the englerias have dense rosettes of flattish gray leaves, neatly over-

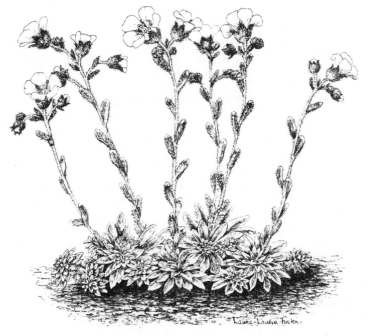

Saxifraga, Engleria Group
(life size)

lapping and becoming smaller in the center of the rosette. From the center of each mature leaf-rosette rises a stout, usually colorful glandular and leafy stalk. The flowers are carried in rather tight nodding panicles. The flowers do not open wide, but are embraced by colorful sepals. All species and hybrids prefer to grow in light shade or on a north slope, in rocky, fairly rich soil (1 part stone chips or coarse sand, 1 part leaf mold). This soil in deep crevices of limestone, provides the optimum growing condition, though they will do in a rich scree mixture in a raised bed if well mulched beneath the rosettes with limestone chips. Hot, muggy weather is trying for the plants; so the planting site should be as airy as possible. These all make excellent pot plants for the alpine-house.

Propagation is most effectively done by rooting rosettes in a pot, which can be enclosed in a plastic bag. Put ample rough drainage material in the bottom and then fill the pot to within an inch of the top with a mixture of half leaf mold and half coarse sharp sand. On the surface put a ½-inch layer of finer sharp sand. Insert the side-rosettes in early summer and water by plunging the pot into a container of water shallow enough so that it does not come over the rim of the pot. When the soil is thoroughly moist, enclose the pot in a plastic bag and set it in a light but shaded position. No further watering should be necessary. Roots ought to form in about a month. When roots have started, remove the plastic bag but leave the rosettes in the pot until the following spring, holding it over the winter in a closed frame or alpine-house. Seed should be handled like that of the Encrusted Group and will produce flowering plants in three years; these require careful handling when small.

Saxifraga grisebachii is perhaps the handsomest species, with large, beautifully symmetrical rosettes composed of spatulate pointed leaves (silvery-edged and reddish beneath) piled up into a tapering mound. In early spring, from the center of the rosette rises a stout crimson stem to 9 inches, brilliant with white hairs and reddish stem-leaves that diminish in size as they go upward, until they mix with the nodding spike of deep red bells. Topdress in spring with sand and leaf mold to encourage the side-rosettes to develop their own roots for anchoring and greater bloom.

S. media has more tightly packed rosettes of somewhat smaller diameter, with sharply pointed silver-gray leaves. The very hairy flowering-stalk is only 3 to 4 inches tall, with rather small nodding pink bells, each enclosed in a purple calyx. The flowers stand out on individual pedicels. Grow this among limestone rocks. *S. porophylla* has small rosettes of fine-pointed silvery leaves, crisp and trim. These grow pile on pile, heaped into humped mounds in the blocky limestone pastures and rockfalls of the Mediterranean world. The species varies from end to end of its range, but mostly in the size of its leaf patterns. The flowering-stalks are very like those of *S. grisebachii,* though not so tall and of a rosier red. It will endure somewhat more torrid sites than the other englerias, especially in var. ***thessalica. S. stribrnyi*** has broad, short, straplike leaves piled into a low column. The 5-inch flower stalk is typically hairy and leafy-bracted, but the purple flower head is rather open and more erect.

The Engleria hybrids are more commonly grown, perhaps, than the species. ***S. × bertolonii,*** which is a cross of *S. stribrnyi* and *S. porophylla thessalica,* makes humped mounds of hard, cartilaginous leaves surmounted by a rather heavy short red flower stalk. ***S. × biasolettii,*** which combines *S. grisebachii* and *S. porophylla thessalica,* has small rosettes of sharp-pointed leaves with blood-red nodding flowers on short reddish stems. ***S. × doerfleri*** *(S. grise-bachii × S. stribrnyi)* has a tendency to mount its columnar rosettes at a horizontal angle on bare stalks. The very hairy bright red calyx encloses a purple hanging flower. The hybrids appear to set no fertile seed. Rooting of rosettes will perpetuate the form. By most botanists and by many horticulturalists the englerias are not separated from the following group, the kabschias.

The Kabschia Saxifrages

For charm of foliage and beauty of flower no other group (or section) of saxifrages can compare with the cushion kabschias. In fact there are few plants in any genus that carry to such perfection the classic features of a rock garden plant. Their only fault in the garden is that they bloom so early that bad weather may batter and tarnish the lovely blossoms. For this reason, and because of their adaptability to pot-culture, they are the plant supreme for the alpine-house or special frame.

Because in nature kabschias are saxatile plants, like the englerias to which they are nearly akin, they should be planted among rocks, in joints and crevices filled with a gritty soil made rich with leaf

mold. Except for one or two, all flourish best with lime chips in
the soil and with their fine roots clinging against porous rock—
limestone or tufa. They want plenty of light to keep foliage clumps
tight and flowers abundant, but they will not endure hot, sunny
sites. The crevices and pockets of a north- or east-facing built-up
ledge offers a good home. It is advisable to give an annual topdressing of sharp sand and leaf mold worked into the tight, ever-
widening clump of compact rosettes. This encourages independent
rooting of the new rosettes, which may be removed and treated
as cuttings after flowering. Unrooted rosettes will form roots in
pots prepared as suggested for the englerias. Seed of the species is
not difficult to grow and should be treated like that of the Encrusted
Group; flowering plants may be produced in three years.

Saxifraga, Kabschia Group
(life size)

Though there are only about 20 recognized species, there are
literally hundreds of named forms and hybrids among the kabschias
and the englerias. The species **Saxifraga aretioides** is densely
tufted with rosettes only about ½ inch in diameter and composed of

tough linear leaves with silvery margins. The golden flowers, ½ inch across, are carried on 2-inch glandular stems. *S. burseriana* for size of flower and neatness of habit is the most popular and cherished of the kabschias. The white flowers, up to 1½ inches across and on short reddish stems, may be so abundantly produced in the earliest days of spring as to conceal the gray rosettes of sharp-pointed stiff little leaves. The irregular rolling hummocks of a mature plant are a delight at all seasons. There are many selected varieties and it has combined with other species to produce outstanding hybrids.

S. caesia is rather like a narrow-leaved dwarf Encrusted Saxifrage; in fact, because of its early summer blooming season and rosette shape, it is by some assigned to the Euaizoon Group. The tiny lime-pitted leaves are linear-oblong in rosettes less than an inch across. The pure-white flowers, ½-inch broad, are carried in few-flowered heads on 3-inch stems. *S. diapensioides* has huddled, hard rosettes of short, narrow, gray leaves that come to a sharp point. The good-sized white flowers, 2 or 3 together, are set on 2-inch stems. There is an excellent yellow-flowered variety, *S. d. lutea.* For success this insists on perfect drainage at the crown and rich, gritty, limy soil.

S. ferdinandi-coburgii, from the Balkans, is another densely tufted species with short, oblong, silvery leaves having a few hairs at the base. The ½-inch yellow flowers in heads do not always open well. It has lent its yellow to some fine hybrids and is itself fairly easy to grow in typical kabschia sites. *S. lilacina* is not an easy species to grow and flower well. Since its introduction from the Himalayas, however, it has played an important role by providing new color-breaks in the Kabschia hybrids. The species itself shuns limestone, calling for a rich, acid, well-drained, never dry soil in semishade. When successful it produces a humped, tight mound of minuscule silver-edged leaves and solitary flowers on 1- to 2-inch stems. The blossoms are a delicate shade of lilac, deepening in the center. It is the strength of the color that has tinged and illuminated so many hybrids, which, it must be admitted, outstrip the species in all aspects: color and size of bloom and, fortunately, willingness to grow.

S. marginata is one of the stalwarts of the Kabschia Group, easy and willing to grow but reluctant to flower except in the kind of site where the summer sun might blight its neat cushions. Give it, nevertheless, a rich gritty soil in a limestone crevice facing east where the morning sun will lure from the lime-pitted rosettes the multiflowered white clusters on 3-inch stalks, which are plainly decked with glandular black hairs. The common variety, *S. m. rocheliana,* is as vigorous but lacks the copious hairiness of the flower scape.

S. sancta varies considerably, in some forms very like its hybrid offspring *S. ✕ apiculata,* in others more compact and grayer in foliage. The leaves of the fairly loose rosettes are dark green and ciliate on the margins, with a sharp point. The head of yellow flowers is carried on a leafy stout stalk about 2 inches tall. The reddening stem and calyx give an overall effect of orange. This species likes a rather rich moist soil with some loam. Large plants tend to die out in patches and should be divided to renew vigor.

There are some other species in this Kabschia Group, all worth growing but either very rare and difficult or quite similar to the ones described: *dalmatica,* white-flowered; *desoulavyi,* close to *S. sancta; erythrantha,* rose-purple-flowered, possibly a natural hybrid *(S. scardica ✕ S. porophylla thessalica); juniperifolia,* a poor grower with small yellow flowers; *scardica,* with large sharp-leaved rosettes and open heads of white flowers; *tombeanensis,* a very rare white-flowered and small-rosetted species; *vahlii,* with small rosettes of almost stemless white flowers; and *vandellii,* like a miniature gray hedgehog with large white flowers on 4-inch stems.

The beautiful hybrids among the Kabschia species and between these and those of the Engleria Group are legion, with new ones being named each year. Few of the new ones are distinctive enough to displace the old standbys, some of which are here briefly described. *S.* × *apiculata (S. marginata* × *S. sancta)* is one of the easiest to grow, forming loose green rosettes of sharp-pointed leaves with clusters of yellow flowers. *S.* × *arco-valleyi (S. burseriana* × *S. lilacina)* forms tight rosettes of pointed gray leaves with almost stemless, large, cherry-red flowers.

S. × *borisii (S. ferdinandi-coburgii* × *S. marginata)* carries clear-yellow flowers on 3-inch stems above a grayish hummock. *S.* × *boydii (S. aretioides* × *S. burseriana)* produces good yellow flowers on short stems above a condensed *burseriana* foliage. *S.* 'Cranbourne' has an obscure ancestry; it provides almost stemless, large flowers of deep rose-pink. *S.* × *elizabethae (S. burseriana* × *S. sancta)* is as easy to grow as *S.* × *apiculata* and is very similar in foliage but has somewhat more open yellow flowers. *S.* 'Faldonside' *(S. aretioides* × *S. burseriana)* is certainly one of the most gorgeous of the hybrids, with very large soft yellow flowers on 3-inch reddish stems.

S. × *haagii (S. ferdinandi-coburgii* × *S. sancta)* is an improvement on the latter parent with good yellow flowers on an easier plant. *S.* × *irvingii (S. burseriana* × *S. lilacina?)* has gray rosettes and fine light pink blossoms deepening in the center. *S.* × *jenkinsae (S. burseriana* × *S. lilacina)* outshines the last with its quicker-growing, hummocky cushion and larger clear-pink flowers on 1-inch stems. *S.* × *paulinae (S. burseriana* × *S. ferdinandi-coburgii)* is an excellent, yellow-flowered hybrid, carrying ample blossoms on 3-inch stems above the silvery cushion.

S. × *petraschii (S. marginata* × *S. tombeanensis)* is about the best of the white hybrids and one of the easiest to grow. It has numerous, good-sized flowers in a head, over tight, grayish mounds. *S.* 'Riverslea' *(S. lilacina* × *S. porophylla)* forms a very dense columnar cushion covered with deep raspberry blossoms on short hairy stems. The whole plant is slow to increase. *S.* × *sundermanii purpurea (S. burseriana* × *S. stribrnyi)* has Engleria-like reddish-purple blossoms on a bun of pointed gray leaves. *S.* 'Valerie Keevil' *(S. godroniana* × *S. lilacina)* has erect deep pink flowers, 2 or 3 together on hairy reddish stems above a hard, compact tuffet of gray foliage.

Other Saxifrages

There are some garden-worthy saxifrages that do not fit into the groups (sections) already discussed, besides, to be sure, many which are of interest only to specialists. **Saxifraga aizoides** is found growing along rocky streams and in other moist spots in northern Europe and America. The summer-blooming, starry yellow flowers, speckled with red, are carried on branching stalks about 6 inches above the open mats of narrow, green, succulent leaves. Easy to propagate, either from seed or by division, it does not always grow well except where root moisture is abundant. It needs some shade in rocky soil near a stream or bog. Similar to the above but with hairy leaves, is **S. bronchialis,** frequently found in the mountains of the American West. At high elevation on north faces of rocky cliffs and screes, or by shady brooksides at lower elevations, it colors its trailing mats with white, starry, red-dotted flowers.

From the Orient come a few distinctive autumn-flowering species with orbicular leaves and irregular white blossoms in large open panicles on 6- to 10-inch stalks. Because of the uneven length of the narrow flower petals these are placed in the Diptera Group (or Section.) They are best grown in rich woodsy soil in semishade. **S. cortusaefolia** is the type-species of this group, with a number of recognized varieties in Japan. Good forms of the variety *fortunei* are handsome in leaf and abundant in flower.

A very beautiful, though difficult saxifrage is **S. oppositifolia,** which grows in moist, rocky sections in Europe, North America, and Asia, generally on limestone. In nature it will form vast carpets of tiny rosettes. The leaves are rounded and hairy-edged, only about ¼ inch long. The fuchsia-pink cuplike flowers sit close to the mat of foliage. The size and color of the blossoms vary considerably; even pure whites and reds are known. Grow this on a north-facing rocky slope in gritty soil full of humus. It will not endure drying out, especially in spring. Seedlings are slow to get established. Summer-cuttings root satisfactorily in a moist, cool medium and should be carried along in a pot until firmly rooted before attempting to establish in the garden. A well-grown carpet of this species is worth all effort. Closely related but with smaller, smooth leaves and small reddish flowers is *S. retusa,* even slower to increase.

The eastern American *S. virginiensis* is the type of various American species. The basal leaves are generally roundish, scalloped, and reddish beneath. The small white flowers are carried in dense heads on thick, viscid, hairy stalks. Selected forms of the eastern species and the western *S. erosa, S. integrifolia,* and *S. nivalis* are worth growing in gritty leaf-mold soil in light shade.

S. umbrosa, the London Pride of English gardens, is an easy and delightful saxifrage for shady sites. In woodsy soil it forms dense clumps composed of overlapping, smooth, dark green scalloped leaves arranged in neat rosettes. Above these in summer are carried airy sprays of numerous small, starry pink flowers on foot-high wiry stems. There are smaller forms with shorter flower stems and deeper-colored flowers, easily propagated by division of the clump or from the abundant, fine seed. Of quite different effect are the saxifrages of the Megasea Group (or Section), which in this book are put in a separate genus, *Bergenia.*

SCABIOSA (Dipsaceae)

Most of the pincushion flowers are border plants, but there are a few smaller dwarf species that look their best growing among sunny rocks in ordinary garden soil, where they give late summer bloom on 1- to 2-foot stems. They may be propagated by seed or division in early spring. *S. columbaria* has good blue flowers above grayish, much-cut foliage. Give it a lean soil to make it compact and floriferous. *S. graminifolia* has light blue flowers and linear, uncut silvery leaves. *S. lucida* has cut leaves and rose-lilac blossoms. *S. ochroleuca* has very silvery cut leaves and yellow blossoms. These and other desirable dwarf species are sometimes listed under the genera *Knautia* and *Pterocephalus.*

SCHIVERECKIA (Cruciferae)

These crucifers are rather like husky drabas. They will make good clumps of narrow gray leaves and carry dense racemes of clear-white flowers. *S. bornmuelleri* grows about 2½ inches high, with somewhat more pubescent leaves than *S. podolica,* which will grow to 4 inches tall. Treat these as alyssum for growing and propagation.

SCHIZOCODON (Diapensiaceae)

These gorgeous woodlanders from Japan are not at all common in American gardens, nor anywhere outside their mountain homes. There, beneath thickets of rhododendron and azalea, in rocky, acid soil that is rich with peaty leaf mold, thick clumps of the shining evergreen foliage are bedecked in early summer with most beautiful, lacy, fringed bells of pink, nodding on 6- to 9-inch stems. Plant these in a cool shady site in a gritty soil with at least half the mixture made up of acid leaf mold and peat. Give them a cover of pine needles during the winter to prevent browning of the leaves, which turn to coppery reds in autumn. Fresh seed will germinate if sown on chopped sphagnum over a typical rhododendron soil and never permitted to dry out. The seedlings are slow to develop an adequate root system and should be grown on in the seeding-container for at least a year. Side-rosettes of established plants may be rooted as cuttings.

S. macrophyllus is the larger round-leaved species, with galax-like leaves in dense fairly erect clumps, among which are produced the clustered heads of pure-pink fringed bells. This is easier to grow and propagate than the more beautiful *S. soldanelloides.* This

soldanella-like species carries its larger, deeply fringed and lacy
bells well above the rounded evergreen foliage. The whole plant is
very like a delicate *Shortia,* to which genus, indeed, it is closely
related and sometimes assigned. The bells, in clusters of 4 to 6,
grade most charmingly from deep pink at the base to a pale flush at
the fringed edges. This species and its variety ***ilicifolius,*** which has
a holly-like leaf outline, call for the kind of site that suits the American Oconee-bells, but it is even more demanding and appears to
need more protection against the violent changes of winter weather
and summer drought.

SCILLA (Liliaceae)

The early spring-flowering squills, which should be planted in
dense drifts, are of easy culture in any reasonably good soil in full
sun or light shade. Plant the bulbs in the fall about 3 inches deep.
Catalogues of bulb-growers will give descriptions of the commonly
grown species and varieties. Some are listed under the genus
Endymion, including the English Bluebell, *S. **non-scripta,*** and the
summer-flowering *S. **campanulata.*** These two require some shade
in the woodland garden.

SCUTELLARIA (Labiatae)

The skullcaps are not a showy race, but have the advantage of
producing their hooded, 2-lipped flowers in summer, either among
leafy bracts or in terminal spikes. They want rich soil in a position
that does not dry out. Propagate by seed or division. *S. **alpina***
forms its purple and white flowers in dense terminal racemes on
10-inch stems. There are pink and yellow color-forms. *S. **angustifolia,*** from northwestern America, has 1-inch violet-blue flowers in
the axils of the narrow leaves on the 6-inch plants. *S. **indica*** var.
japonica forms trim little shrubby plants with gray-green leaves and
blue-flowered spikes. Propagate this variety by cuttings. *S. **orientalis*** carries small grayish leaves on a flat, spreading plant, above
which sit yellow flowers in a 3-inch spike.

SEDUM (Crassulaceae)

There are few stonecrops that can rank among the aristocrats of the rock garden, but many of them have architectural beauty and a few are brilliantly flowered. All are, however, utility plants. The majority flourish in the most difficult sites and in the most meager of soils. For this very reason, they are generally relegated by gardeners to positions where little else will grow and where the sedums themselves never have a chance to develop their full potential. To be sure, when grown in favorable soil, many have an aggressive way of running and rooting, self-sowing, and, in some cases, rejuvenating themselves by fallen leaves that root with ease. Most, therefore, are readily propagated by these methods.

S. acre is the common small ground-covering, yellow-flowered stonecrop that will flourish in any sunny situation, even in the thinnest layer of soil over rock. The variety *minus* is tighter, smaller, and not quite so ramping. *S. album,* from Europe, has become established as a roadside plant on rocky banks in the eastern United States. It forms dense bushy clumps up to 8 inches high, with somewhat flattened sausage-shaped leaves, frequently reddish-tinged. The white flowers are produced in abundant flat-topped clusters in early summer. There are many named variations, all quick-spreading.

S. anacampseros has trailing stems set with alternate, round, succulent leaves. The small purple flowers are carried about 6 inches above the mat in summer. *S. anglicum* is a tiny creeping evergreen plant with short thick leaves and starry white flowers topping the 2- to 3-inch-high carpet. The foliage is often reddish-tinted. *S. brevifolium* is like a very small *S. dasyphyllum* with especially mealy leaves arranged in 4 rows around the 2-inch-high stems crowned with small white stars. This species needs particularly good drainage. *S. caeruleum* is only of annual duration but quick to grow from seed sown where wanted, there to produce its branching stems set with sparse green leaves. The pale blue flowers will open in summer and scatter seeds in the fall for perpetuation.

S. cauticola is an excellent plant for growing on a dry cliff-face or wall. From the deciduous root crown spring up multiple trailing stems about 8 inches long, set with opposite, roundish leaves. In late summer and early autumn the tips of each branch erupt into a large head of brilliant rose-red blossoms. *S. dasyphyllum* makes a stunning close mat of powdery gray-blue, small, ovoid leaves on 1- to 2-inch stems. The summer flowers are pale pink or white. Give this plant very good drainage. *S. divergens,* from the western mountains of the United States, forms creeping open mats of reddish stems beaded with shining, reddish, globular leaves. The flowers are bright yellow in summer.

S. ellacombianum is a Japanese species growing about 6 inches high. The arching stems carry broad, glossy, scalloped leaves and good heads of yellow flowers in August. *S. ewersii* varies from 4 inches to 1 foot in the trailing stems. The opposite leaves are broad and rounded, blue-gray in color and the late summer flowers are pink or red. *S. gracile* is like a miniature *S. album* with white flowers frequently dotted with red, as are the thin leaves. In nature this is found in moist rocky places in the Caucasus. *S. hobsonii* produces numerous prostrate 6-inch stems from a heavy rootstock. These are decked with narrow, dark green, fleshy leaves and carry open heads of good-sized, rose-red flowers in summer. The plant dies down in winter, and is most successfully propagated by seed or root-cuttings.

S. kamtschaticum is an erect plant, up to 9 inches, with large toothed leaves, sometimes edged with white. The summer flowers are an undistinguished orange-yellow. *S. leibergii,* in the mountains of the western United States, forms clustered rosettes of small, fleshy, spatulate leaves, frequently glowing with pink, orange, or red tints, depending on soil and exposure. The fleshy sparsely leaved flowering-stalks carry a small cluster of starry yellow flowers.

This is best grown in dry, acid, rocky soil in light shade. *S. lydium* forms mats only 2 to 3 inches high, with small cylindrical leaves that are reddish in summer. The white flowers are held in red calyces. *S. middendorffianum* has green needle-leaves up to 2 inches long on 10-inch stems that root down to make a large dense clump, topped in summer with golden flowers.

S. nevii inhabits the southeastern American states on shaded rocks, where it forms tuffets of spatulate leaves. It is completely hardy and in early summer, white flowers with purple anthers star the 4-inch erect stems. *S. oreganum* comes from shaded rock-walls and cliffs in its native state. There it forms flat rosettes of crenate leaves from which in summer rise 6-inch stems of very starry yellow flowers that fade to a quaint pink. *S. populifolium,* in well-drained soil in a sunny site, will form a dense shrubby bush up to 18 inches high. The stems are well clothed with toothed, succulent leaves and crowned in late summer by an open head of pale pink or white flowers. In severe winters this plant may be cut to the ground, but it will spring anew from the roots. *S. pulchellum,* unlike most sedums, wants a moist semishady site where it can run to form broad mats of rooting-stems. The inch-long needlelike leaves are dense along the stems and make handsome lycopodium-like growth even without the lovely, sparse, rosy-purple flowers in late summer. This is a rare eastern American native.

S. purdyi forms flat button-rosettes of overlapping leaves and increases by forming new buttons at the end of succulent red runners. The white flowers are carried on 4-inch stems. This rare Siskiyou Mountain sedum grows on shaded cliffs. *S. reflexum* grows in mats of foot-high stems densely set with linear leaves and carries bright yellow flowers in summer. There is a smaller, coxcomb form, var. *cristatum.* In moist rocky places of the Rocky Mountains *S. rhodanthum* forms an erect plant up to 18 inches tall. The rose-colored flowers are carried in a dense elongated head, mixed with oblong fleshy leaves. *S. sexangulare* is similar to *S. acre,* except for the spiral, 6-ranked arrangement of the bronze-green leaves.

S. sieboldii should be grown where the arching stems, set with glaucous pink-edged leaves, may be viewed at close hand and where the late-autumn pink blossoms will not be concealed by windblown leaves. *S. spathulifolium* varies widely in leaf color and texture as it grows in rocky ground in sun or light shade in the Cascade Mountains and Coast Ranges of western North America. The red-purple rosettes of thick, fleshy leaves in some forms may become green when grown in shadier sites. The variety '**Capa Blanca**' has almost white-silver foliage. All forms are desirable for their leaf pattern and color, much more than for the early yellow flowers on 5-inch leafy stems, but they are not always hardy in exposed locations.

S. spinosum is a handsome species from China that masquerades as a *Sempervivum* and is sometimes incorrectly listed by nurserymen under that genus. It has also been assigned to the genera *Cotyledon* and *Umbilicus.* The hard spatulate leaves, each tipped with a conspicuous cartilaginous spine, form a large dense rosette which curls into a tight ball in winter but opens to a flattened artichoke in summer. The tall—sometimes up to 18 inches—flower spike of thickly packed yellowish-white blossoms rises from the center of this basal rosette. Side rosettes are sparingly produced for increase.

S. spurium is a most useful carpeter, forming tangled mats of succulent rooting-stems with oval, wavy-edged leaves. The flowers of the several named forms vary from deep red to white. The species will grow in almost any site and is one of the few plants that will thrive beneath maple trees. *S. ternatum* is an early white-flowering native of the eastern United States, distinguished by the arrangement of the broadly oval leaves in 3's. It should be grown on shady rocks, especially limestone. There are literally hundreds of other species of sedums suited for garden culture. Specialist nurseries offer a vast assortment, but none, perhaps, very different from those listed above.

SELAGINELLA (Selaginellaceae)

The dwarf spike-mosses are not showy plants, but the dense tuffets of foliage, in appearance rather like a stiff enlarged moss or diminished lycopodium, are neat enough to grow among delicate plants in the raised bed or planter. They prefer a rather moist gritty soil and may be propagated by scattering pieces of the leafy stems on damp sandy soil in a closed frame or plastic-enclosed pot. Many species are not hardy except in the alpine-house. For outdoor growing are *S. douglasii, S. helvetica, S. rupestris* (which will endure real drought and sun on limestone rocks), *S. uncinata,* and *S. wallacei.*

SEMPERVIVUM (Crassulaceae)

The houseleeks are true alpine plants, growing in crevices and pockets of the high mountains in Europe and the Middle East. They are admirably suited to growing on or between rocks in sunny sites, demanding only a fairly thin layer of good, loamy soil. They look especially fine lacing the joints of a wall, forming an ever-increasing colony of rosettes. Though the flowers of some are large and brightly colored, they are not abundantly produced. It is for the texture, form, and color of the rosettes that these plants earn their deserved popularity. All are easy to propagate by separation of the rosettes, which, even after being dry for a year, have been known to make roots and grow when placed on moist sandy soil. The flowering-rosette dies after setting seed but an established colony has many young offsets to keep it going. Seed will germinate readily and will frequently produce a mixed progeny, since much of the material grown in gardens is of hybrid origin. Named forms are offered by many nurseries, all of which are variations on the 20 or so species of the familiar hens-and-chicks.

S. arachnoideum is the cobwebbed species of differing dimensions, with gray threads woven across the rosette from leaf to leaf. Full sun encourages denser webbing. The large flowers are bright rose-red on a stout stalk. *S. ciliosum* is a Bulgarian species with incurved leaves, reddish on the back, in a 1- to 2-inch flattened rosette that is gray with long stiff hairs. The flowers are greenish yellow. *S. erythraeum* is another Bulgarian species with hairy leaves. Here the flowers are red-purple with white lines and are carried on 8-inch leafy stalks above the open, wide-spreading rosettes. The leaves are gray-green, tinged with purple. *S. heuffelii* has only short, fine hairs on the edges of the pointed leaves, which form red-brown tips to the 2-inch rosettes. Instead of increasing by offsets, the rosettes split symmetrically to produce 2 new rosettes. The flowers are straw-yellow. *S. montanum* is widespread and variable in the Alps, and is the parent of many garden hybrids. It has rather small rosettes of leaves in compact clumps. The narrow leaves are deep green and hairy. The reddish-purple flowers are carried in a hairy panicle, 2 inches across.

S. octopodes has small, upright, downy rosettes, dark brown at the tips. The distinctive feature is the radiating, leafy stolons that may be up to 3 inches long. The flowers are greenish yellow. *S. pumilum* may be only a miniature of *S. montanum* found in the Caucasus. The rosettes are less than an inch across. *S. soboliferum* makes very dense mats of globular rosettes with bright green, smooth leaves. The numerous offsets are attached to weak short stolons and are easily detached, rolling off to form new colonies. Hence, this is the species originally called Hen-and-chickens. *S. tectorum* is the common species of Europe, once planted on house roofs to ward off witches, the original Houseleek. The rosettes are large and rather open, with wide, smooth, pointed leaves, generally colored in tones of red and especially at the tips. The flowers of pinkish red on tall, hairy, branching stalks are infrequently produced. There are many named forms and hybrids. *S. wulfenii* has fairly tall conical rosettes, 2 to 3 inches across, glaucous and ciliate, red-toned at the base. The flowers are yellow in a dense hairy panicle.

SENECIO (Compositae)

Many of the groundsels are weedy and have small daisy-like flowers. There are, however, a few mountain dwellers with handsome foliage and proportionate golden flowers. They are easy to grow from seed or root-cuttings, prospering in rocky, acid soil. *S. abrotanifolius* carries its heads of orange-yellow flowers on foothigh stems above the much-cut glossy-green foliage. This is a summer-flowering species that wants a moist peaty soil. The variety known as *S. a. tyroliensis* is smaller, with larger, ragged flowers of orange-red. *S. canus* comes from well-drained rocky sites in the Rockies and the western American Coast Ranges, where the mounds of narrow, oblong leaves are silvery white. The heads of yellow flowers are carried on 10- to 12-inch stems in early summer. *S. incanus* has variously cut foliage of silvery, hairy, oval leaves. The small yellow flowers are carried on 6-inch stems. *S. uniflorus* is a high-alpine plant in moist acid screes, where it forms tuffets of deeply lobed, woolly white leaves. The solitary yellow flowers are produced on 6-inch stems in early summer. *S. websteri* is a rare plant in the high screes of the Olympic Mountains of Washington. Above a husky rosette of broad, oblong, woolly leaves come large, solitary, ragged yellow flowers on short hairy stems.

SERRATULA (Compositae)

There is one horticultural form of these generally tall thistle-like plants very useful for its autumn flowers—*S.* 'Shawii.' The purple-red cornflower-like heads are carried on 8- to 9-inch stems above the clump of much-divided foliage. It does well in ordinary garden soil in sun or light shade, and may be increased by division.

SHORTIA (Diapensiaceae)

The rare American Oconee-bells, *S. galacifolia,* and the Japanese Nippon-bells, *S. uniflora,* stand in the forefront of plants for the acid, shady garden. Both make dense evergreen carpets and produce in early spring magnificent crenulated white flowers. The woody creeping rootstocks carry rather sparse hairlike roots and are slow to become established. Once growing happily in either fairly deep or light shade and in acid leaf-mold soil, they will make clumps up to a yard across. Large mats may be lifted and divided into many plants, each with an individual or multiple leaf cluster, a section of root-stock and a few feeding-roots. Such divisions should be handled as cuttings until well rooted in an acid sandy-peaty mixture and never permitted to dry out. Larger divisions, carefully made, may be re-planted immediately in proper situations kept well watered and shaded. Fresh seed, which is ripe by July, may be sown on chopped sphagnum as one would grow rhododendrons from seed. It takes many years, however, to produce flowering plants in this manner.

S. galacifolia, native to a small part of the southern Appalachian Mountains where it grows in dense rhododendron thickets, is perfectly hardy north and will even endure heavy spring snows and frosts while in flower. The hard, shining green leaves with promi-nent veins and slightly wavy margins are about 3 inches long; the oval blades are on stiff petioles. In sites where sun may reach them, the leaves turn dark red in fall. The solitary bell-like white flowers on 6- to 8-inch stems are an inch across and wavy-margined. The pair of red sepals show pink through the flower and form the glow-ing capsule of the abundant, minute, brown seed.

S. uniflora, the Japanese representative, is very similar. The leaves are slightly more rounded, somewhat larger, and more densely produced. The flowers, especially in var. *grandiflora,* are larger, somewhat more open, and frequently tinged with pink, the petals being wavy and slightly fringed at the margins. This species is either less hardy than the American or requires denser shade and more moisture. It never seems as easy, even in sites where Oconee-bells thrive. The Japanese *S. soldanelloides* is described under the genus *Schizocodon.*

SIDERANTHUS. See *Haplopappus.*

SIEVERSIA. See *Geum.*

SILENE (Caryophyllaceae)

Among the catchfly or campion tribe are found a few desirable summer-blooming plants for the sunny rock garden, with some carrying on into the fall. They generally tend to make many flowering-stems from a deep, fleshy rootstock. The opposite leaves are mostly narrow and pointed, generally with a swelling on the stem where they are attached. The 5-petaled flowers in white, pink, or red are frequently much notched and cut. Though some are of easy culture in any deep garden soil, others demand rather careful handling to make them grow, persist, and flower. Seed is the surest way of propagation. Some may be divided in early spring, others increased by root-cuttings.

S. acaulis, the Moss Campion, makes sizable mossy cushions studded with almost stemless vivid-pink flowers in rocky places of the high mountains throughout the Northern Hemisphere. It rarely flowers well under cultivation. To encourage production of blossom, give it gravelly soil in a rather tight deep pocket between rocks, in full sun, and feed with liquid manure as growth commences. It is well to carry seedlings or rooted cuttings along in pots until they have made a cushion an inch or more in diameter before setting in the garden. Even when well settled, plants in the garden have a tendency to show only a spatter of bloom on and off during the summer. Plants from seed vary in their inclination to bloom, in their size and color of blossom, and in length of flowering-stem. Good floriferous forms should be increased by stem-cuttings or division in summer.

S. alpestris is also listed as *Heliosperma alpestre.* Under either name it is a fine, easy plant, thriving most happily in deep but well-drained limy soil. In its best forms it makes a dense erect clump about 6 inches high, with narrow pointed leaves, slightly sticky to the touch. For a long period in early summer, on wiry stems are carried thick showers of pure-white ½-inch flowers, each petal being 4-lobed. It is simple to grow from seed and to divide. Division of course is to be used for the showy long-lasting variety *flore-pleno.*

S. californica is a stunning plant with flopping tomentose stems up to 1 foot long that rise from slender carrot-like roots. The stems carry oval, pointed light green leaves up to 3 inches long. The terminal flowers are a brilliant scarlet, 1½ inches across, each petal deeply 4-cleft. Propagate this from seed and plant in deep, rocky, acid soil in light shade. It likes summer drought, and for winter protection in cold sections a cushion of pine needles over the crown.

S. caroliniana is the Wild Pink of the eastern United States, sometimes listed as *S. pensylvanica.* In sandy or rocky acid soil, in either sun or light shade, this plant produces a neat compact tuffet of sticky, hairy, lanceolate leaves 3 to 4 inches long. The heads of deep pink to white 1-inch flowers are abundantly produced in early summer. Each petal is slightly notched. Var. *pensylvanica* and var. *wherryi* differ in technical detail, but some forms of the latter are large-flowered and of a particularly good rich pink. These are all easy to grow from seed and bloom the second year. Good forms may be propagated by careful division of the taproot or by root-cuttings.

S. elizabethae (frequently listed under *Melandrium* as are others of this genus) forms flat rosettes of narrow, shining green leaves from among which in summer come downy pink stems up to 6 inches long, topped by an open cluster of large cut flowers of brilliant rose-red. Many impostors are sent out as seed for this plant. When the true beauty is procured, grow it in deep, rocky, limy soil in a cool site, out of the hottest sun but with plenty of light.

S. hookeri is a real challenge in the garden, though to see large patches of it growing in many different sites and soils in south-central Oregon and northern California would make one think it

Silene hookeri
(life size)

easy to grow. It appears to flourish in a fairly heavy clay soil well mixed with rock particles, either in sun or light shade. The sprawling, clustered stems (up to 6 inches long) rise from slender rootstocks, which in turn rise from a deeply buried heavy taproot. The furry gray leaves, spatulate and pointed, with a winged petiole, are about 2 inches long. The flowers, 2 inches across, are produced at the tip, either singly or up to 3 in a cyme and ranging in color from a salmon-pink to white. Each petal is deeply cleft into 4 lobes, the middle two slightly longer. Because in nature it dries out completely by midsummer, it is best grown in a deep rocky soil with the top of the heavy root about 1 inch below the surface on a dry slope in light shade. Seed is the preferred method of propagation, the seedlings set in permanent location when fairly young because the roots soon go very deep. There is a suspicion that it should have some winter protection in severe climates, but most important of all is a good dry resting period. *S. ingramii* differs from *S. hookeri* in being more compact, with slightly larger leaves, and blossoms of cherry-red. This wants growing conditions similar to those for *S. hookeri* and is probably somewhat easier to grow.

Japanese *S. keiskei* varies from a tight clump of thin stems set with narrow pale green leaves (only 3 inches high) and carrying heads of ample, much-divided bright pink flowers in late summer to a 6- to 8-inch clump with pale pink to white flowers in midsummer. Both forms want rich scree treatment but appear to be either short-lived or tender in cold areas. Good forms are desirable enough for pot-culture in the alpine-house. *S. maritima* is of the bladder campion group and has a prim tuft of blue-gray foliage and arching stems with heads of fringy, small blossoms having inflated, striped calyces. Unless grown in poor, lean soil it becomes disproportionately leggy.

S. schafta makes handsome tuffets of branching 6-inch stems set with narrow hairy leaves. The shallowly notched petals form pinwheel-like blossoms of magenta-pink carried in abundance at the tips of the stems and in the axils over a long period in late summer. It will grow in almost any soil in sun or light shade and is easily propagated by seed, division, or cuttings. *S. virginica* is the Fire Pink of the eastern United States. In summer a succession of stems sparsely set with narrow leaves rise to 2 feet from the flat evergreen rosette of long sticky leaves. Each stem is topped by a loose, somewhat nodding head of crimson to scarlet flowers, each an inch or more across and with petals notched and 2-cleft. This is a stunning plant for the woods garden in a sandy leaf-mold soil. It is to be propagated by seed, division in early spring, or by root-cuttings.

SISYRINCHIUM (Iridaceae)

There are many rather similar species of blue-eyed grass, and a few distinctive ones. All, in growth, have the general appearance of a dwarfed Siberian Iris. Among the grassy clumps appear the leafy stalks which carry, near the summit, clusters of satiny, 6-petaled flowers on thin pedicels, surmounted usually by leaflike spathes. The fibrous root clumps are easily divided for increase, and they all come readily, if not quickly, from seed. *S. angustifolium* may be taken as the type of eastern American species which make clumps of foliage up to 18 inches tall and carry, for a long season in summer, rather disappointingly small, blue to lavender flowers. *S. arenicola, S. campestre, S. montanum,* and *S. mucronatum* are similar. They will grow in any good soil in sun or light shade and can become a nuisance through self-sowing. *S. californicum* is really what its name Golden-eyed Grass implies, with stiff grassy foliage and ½-inch yellow blossoms. It prefers a moist site and is somewhat tender. *S. douglasii,* the Grass-widow of far-western America, is the real beauty of the genus, with comparatively large satiny-purple nodding flowers in groups up to 3 among rushlike foliage. This is a dry-land plant, completely dying down in summer. Give it a well-drained, acid, rocky soil, with some clay or loam. The seed takes two years to germinate. Large plants may be divided while dormant. This species is frequently listed as *S. grandiflorum.*

SMELOWSKIA (Cruciferae)

These western American crucifers are fairly common in the high mountain screes and look rather like gray-leaved hutchinsias. The blossoms, it must be confessed, are disappointingly sparse and small, and generally white, though occasionally purple. Plant them in clumps in scree soil in a sunny site for their handsome cushions of foliage. Because they grow from a stout taproot, they are best propagated by seed. The common alpine *Smelowskia* is *S. calycina.*

SMILACINA (Liliaceae)

The false Solomon's-seals are husky woodland plants of considerable beauty—in foliage, flower, and fruit. From thick rootstocks, which run rather close to the soil surface, rise the stiff arching stems with large alternate leaves close-set along the undivided stems. The small white flowers are carried in large terminal racemes or panicles, in some species handsomely plume-like. All are easy to propagate by division of the running roots, and by seed. All enjoy typical humus-rich woods soil, but are not fussy about site. *S. amplexicaulis* of the Far West and *S. racemosa* of widespread distribution in North America are about 3 feet tall, with 6-inch strongly-ribbed leaves. In *amplexicaulis* the flower plume is up to 6 inches long and the red berries are spotted with purple. In *racemosa* the plume is shorter and the berries pure red. *S. sessilifolia* grows only 2 feet tall, with a few-flowered, short raceme, and produces purple berries. *S. stellata* will quickly make a thicket of erect 18-inch stems clad with glaucous green leaves, each topped with an open raceme of starry white flowers. The handsome shining berries are green, with dark brown, almost black stripes that make them like old-fashioned bull's-eye candies. *S. trifolia* is the dwarf bog species of northern regions. It is not as showy as the others, and has few flowers in the 2-inch raceme.

SOLDANELLA (Primulaceae)

These high-alpine plants, which spring to bloom even before the melting snow has completely uncovered the foliage, are so bewitching that no pains are too great to induce them to flourish and flower. Select for them a site that will never become dry and parched, either in light shade or on a north slope. Mix with a sandy, humus-rich soil some limestone chips and make a bed close to running water or with artificial underground watering. In such a situation they are not difficult to grow into sizable patches; their underground-running stems are thickly adorned with round leathery leaves. To coax them to flower is another matter. They set the flower buds in fall close to the ground beneath the leaves, but only when snow cover has been constant and slugs have been kept away, will the fringed lavender cups appear on the 6- to 10-inch stems. That they will flower regularly in the alpine-house or when constantly protected by deep snow suggests susceptibility of the curled brown buds to destruction by freezing. Give them a covering of glass-wool in winter where the snow is inconstant. Once established, they may easily be increased by division after the flowering period. Fresh seed germinates readily, old seed tardily or not at all.

S. alpina carries 1 to 3 lavender-blue fringed bells on each 3- to 6-inch stem. *S. minima* has tiny circular leaves and solitary pale lilac, narrow funnel-shaped flowers on 2- to 3-inch hairy stems. *S. montana* is the biggest and easiest, with leaves up to 2½ inches across. This plant inhabits the thin woodlands of the European Alps, where it produces, on stout stems 8 to 10 inches high, many-flowered umbels. The individual, wide funnel-form, fringed blossoms are a rich blue, ¾ inch across. Other species are recognized by botanists, but all are quite similar to the three basic species just described.

SOLIDAGO (Compositae)

The goldenrods are mostly tall and rather weedy plants and have never been popular in America in any type of garden. There are some, however, which because of their late season of bloom and neat proportions should be more generally used in the rock garden. If grown in lean soil and full sun, they rarely become aggressive, frequently becoming handsomer in cultivation than in the wild. They may be propagated easily from divisions, shoot-cuttings, or by seed. Because most species are exclusively American, they have perhaps been ignored as common wildflowers; they are, however, grown extensively in British gardens. To be sought out are: (1) mountain species of Washington and Oregon like *S. algida* (with globose heads on 1-foot stems), *S. bellidifolia* (with small, oval, toothed leaves and dense flower heads on plants under 1 foot), and *S. spathulata nana* (similar to the last); (2) species of the Rockies like *S. ciliosa* (a 6- to 8-inch plant with small, narrow, hairy leaves and flowers in dense one-sided heads), *S. decumbens* (dwarf and creeping, with erect, dense, flower heads), *S. multiradiata* (from 3 to 12 inches high, with hairy, spatulate leaves and small tight flower heads), and *S. scopulorum* (with long, narrow, toothed leaves and flowers in a broad, flat head); (3) eastern American species like *S. cutleri* (with erect flower heads on dwarf plants), and *S. tenuifolia* (with narrow linear leaves and dense flat blossom heads).

SORBUS (Rosaceae)

The mountain-ashes are handsome flowering and fruiting trees in various American and European species, suitable for the woods garden or the surround of the rock garden to give light shade. Two species, easily propagated from seed, are especially desirable for their bushlike habit of growth, and have small dense heads of white flowers followed by crimson berries. *S. occidentalis,* of the American Cascade Mountains, will grow slowly up to 3 feet. *S. reducta,* from China, is even smaller, generally under 18 inches.

SPHAERALCEA (Malvaceae)

The globe-mallows of western America are plants of the dry lands, producing for long periods in summer colorful blossoms on rather tall, floppy plants, with lobed leaves. These are easy to grow from seed or summer cuttings of nonflowering shoots. *S. coccinea* (also known as *Malvastrum coccineum*) sends up from a woody taproot branching, silvery, hairy stems to about 10 inches. The silvery leaves are much divided and the glowing orange-red 1-inch blossoms are carried in close spikes at the tips of the numerous branches. Grow this species in deep, well-drained soil in full sun. Propagate it by seed or cuttings of young shoots. *S. munroana* makes taller stems, with broad and coarsely toothed leaves carrying 1-inch bright pink flowers in axillary clusters all summer. This wants a dry, hard soil among large rocks, where its 2-foot silvery white stems may splay out and keep dry in the sun.

SPIRAEA (Rosaceae)

Besides the wide variety of spring- and summer-blooming, taller spireas, there are some smaller species admirably adapted to growing in the rock garden itself. All want a good soil in sun, but do not take kindly to drought conditions. They are slow but possible to grow from seed, and are generally increased by layering and summer cuttings. *S. bullata* makes a twiggy upright shrub about 1 foot high. The rusty-brown stems are densely clothed with small dark green puckered leaves, and with flat heads of rose-red flowers in late summer. This species and the next are improved by spring pruning of some of the heavier stems right to the ground and by removal of all old flower heads. *S. bumalda nana* is a miniature, almost prostrate form of the species that also provides the common raspberry-colored '**Anthony Waterer**.' *S. decumbens* sprawls in a carpet about 10 inches thick, with many heads of white flowers in early summer. *S. densiflora* of the Rockies produces in early summer very dense flat heads of rich pink blossoms. It may reach 2 feet in rich soil. *S. normandii* is a sprawly dwarf form of *S. bumalda,* insignificant in flower but valuable for its crimson autumn foliage. Three western mat-forming spireas are described under *Petrophytum.*

SPIRANTHES (Orchidaceae)

The ladies'-tresses, with their spiraling spikes of white blossoms, are among the easiest of the orchids to transplant into the garden. Given a moist rich soil in sun or light shade, they soon settle down and will frequently self-sow. They will succeed in the unmown bulb lawn if it is not too dry. *S. gracilis* produces its 8- to 12-inch stems and green-lipped white flowers as early as June. *S. cernua* and most other species of America and Europe do not blossom until late summer and autumn. One of the largest-flowered of these late bloomers is **S. romanzoffiana,** with a dense spike of ½-inch creamy-white flowers.

SPRAGUEA (Portulacaceae)

The pussy-paws of the Cascade and Siskiyou Mountains are a conspicuous and beautiful component of the alpine flora, in some rocky exposed areas carpeting the ground with pure stands or mixed with dwarf lupine and calochortus. They form pancakes of shining, spatulate, evergreen leaves, frequently tinged with reddish brown. Radiating out and generally quite flat to the ground are many stems, each producing—out beyond the succulent leaf-rosette—a dense pompon head of small flowers, ranging in color from white and cream to pink and rose. Fresh seed provides the best means of propagation, since the plant grows from a deep taproot and appears short-lived even in nature. It must have excellent drainage in a rocky soil well supplied with clayey loam. Related as it is to lewisia, it will succeed under the same conditions as *Lewisia rediviva.* **S. umbellata** is the type-species of wide distribution in its native haunts. Botanists recognize the smaller, more alpine, and more perennial form either as var. **caudicifera** or as a separate species, **S. multiceps.**

STACHYS (Labiatae)

This genus produces the Lamb's-ears used as a foliage bedding-plant, and some border-plants. One species, **S. lavandulaefolia,** is well-suited to a sunny, well-drained site in the rock garden. It carries spikes of rose-purple labiate flowers on the 12-inch, rather woody, branching stems. The stems and gray leaves are velvety with soft hairs and strongly aromatic when crushed. The plant may be increased by spring division, layers, or seed.

STATICE. See *Limonium.*

STOKESIA (Compositae)

S. laevis, the Stokes Aster, is native to the southeastern United States, growing in well-drained, sandy loam. It is not reliably hardy without protection north of Maryland. The species has many named color-forms: blue, creamy yellow, and pink. The flower heads, up to 4 inches across, have enlarged marginal flowers around a centaurea-like center, on stiff, leafy stems, 8 to 10 inches high. This late-summer bloomer may be increased by seed or by division in the spring.

STREPTOPUS (Liliaceae)

The twisted-stalks of North America and Japan are woodland plants of considerable beauty, especially when the brilliant, shining, scarlet berries dangle beneath the canopy of lily-like leaves. The alternate leaves are arranged elegantly and close to the arching stems, which generally divide into 3 branches. The small lily-like blossoms with recurving lobes, hung on curiously bent pedicels, are not con-spicuous but are charming on close inspection. All species grow in rather rich humus soil in dense shade, but are easy to grow and not difficult to propagate by division of the rootstock. Seed is slow to germinate, tending to mildew unless released early from the pulpy fruit. *S. amplexifolius* is up to 3 feet tall, with large, glaucous, clasping leaves and greenish-white flowers. *S. curvipes* of western Canada is only 1 foot tall, with rose-pink campanulate flowers and sessile leaves. *S. roseus,* the commonest eastern American species, has sessile leaves, 4 inches long and 1½ inches wide. The recurving flowers are purple or rose, usually solitary on thin, bent pedicels. *S. streptopoides,* from Japan, looks rather like Solomon's-seal in foliage and stature. The flowers, however, are solitary and deep red, with recurving yellow tips. The globose berries are brilliant red.

STYLOPHORUM (Papaveraceae)

The Celandine Poppy, *S. diphyllum,* is rarely seen in woodland gardens, though it is a charming early-spring perennial in the rich woodlands from western Pennsylvania to Wisconsin and Missouri. It has a pair of deeply cut leaves beneath the flower cluster of 2 to 4 deep yellow 4-petaled blossoms, each 2 inches across. After flowering, the plant may reach 18 inches, but it begins to flower in early spring when only a few inches high. It is easy to establish in humus-rich soil, in light shade, and may be increased by seed, or root divisions after the flowering period.

SYMPHYANDRA (Campanulaceae)

These differ only technically from the campanulas, which they resemble in foliage, flower, and in culture. The bell-shaped flowers of good proportion tend to nod on long wiry stems. They succeed best in rich well-drained but not dry soil, in sun or light shade, where they bloom from midsummer to late summer. All species may be propagated from the abundant dustlike seed, or by division in the early spring as growth commences. Older plants lose vigor and should be renewed.

S. armena has rounded, toothed basal leaves with long petioles, from among which rise on 1-foot stems the clusters of ¾-inch blue-violet nodding bell flowers. *S. hoffmannii* has similar leaves and many arching stems up to 2 feet long, each carrying leafy panicles of numerous 1½-inch white bells. This species will self-sow generously in good soil. *S. pendula* has hairy, coarsely-toothed leaves and racemes of 1¼-inch creamy-yellow bells on foot-high stems. *S. wanneri* is the dwarf beauty of the genus, with narrower, sharply serrate leaves and many 6-inch branched stems. The nodding purple bells, up to 1½ inches long, are produced in late summer. This is a coveted plant for the raised bed or planted wall.

SYMPLOCARPUS (Araceae)

Where there is plenty of room in a boggy situation, the common Skunk-cabbage, *S. foetidus,* may be introduced for its massive leaf effect and its curious hooded blossoms of earliest spring. It is not easy to eradicate once it is established.

SYNTHYRIS (Scrophulariaceae)

These delightful western American plants usher in the spring with dense spikes of small bell flowers of blue or violet just above the foliage. Most are woodland plants with tough, roundish, evergreen leaves that form neat basal clumps. The woodland species are of the easiest culture, enduring even poor soil beneath maple trees. They respond with richer foliage and more abundant flower spikes when grown in rocky soil enriched with good leaf mold. Propagation is not difficult from seed, nor is division after the flowering period. Only a few species are in general cultivation and even these not so frequently as their beauty deserves.

S. alpina (also known as *Besseya alpina*) has small, wavy-toothed, oval leaves and 6-inch spikes of purple flowers. Other *Besseya* species are not worth growing. *S. reniformis* has large, round, variously toothed leaves on stout pedicels. The leaves are beautifully textured and are evergreen like the foliage of galax. The dense flower spikes carry sharp-petaled blossoms of blue or purple. There are many variations of this species, some of which have been given specific standing, such as *S. missurica,* with large leaves and larger flowers, and handsome *S. stellata* of the Columbia River Gorge. *S. rotundifolia* has small cordate leaves and produces light-colored, sometimes white flowers, except in var. *sweetseri,* which has clear-blue blossoms. There are many recognized species or geographical variants of the woodland *Synthyris,* and botanists frequently reclassify the whole lot. Quite different, more difficult to grow but truly bewitching are the alpine species, which inhabit lofty, rich, wet screes. These have variously cut and divided foliage, frequently silvered with dense pubescence. The flower spikes are proportionately dwarfed and range in color from pink to bright blue. In this group are *S. canbyi, S. cymopteroides, S. dissecta, S. lanuginosa,* and *S. pinnatifida.*

SYRINGA (Oleaceae)

The lilacs offer two species from the Orient which are comparatively small and of such neat and wild-looking proportions as to fit them into the rock garden company. Young plants will bloom when only a foot or so high, but if not restrained will eventually grow into large twiggy bushes. It is possible to keep them low by a meager diet in sun and by encouraging multiple shoots from the base by annual pruning of the oldest wood. They may be propagated by soft- or hardwood cuttings, and most readily by layers. *S. microphylla,* from northern China, has small round leaves, pubescent beneath, and bears in early summer numerous small pale lilac panicles. *S. velutina* is often listed as *S. palibiniana.* It is a slightly larger plant than the last, though some forms of recent introduction are of slow growth. The oval pointed leaves and the larger panicles of violet flowers are both generally pubescent.

TALINUM (Portulacaceae)

These relatives of the lewisias have flowers suggestive of *Lewisia leana* and *L. columbiana,* except that here the blossoms open in the afternoon and fall by morning, day by day in summer, after the manner of portulaca. They thrive in poor sandy soil and flourish in the sun; quick and easy to grow from seed, they bloom the first year. *T. calycinum* carries cherry-colored blossoms 1 inch or more across on much-branched, wiry, 8-inch stems with sparse, fleshy leaves. Self-sown seedlings will carry on if the old plants succumb to a hard winter. *T. okanoganense* forms dense low clumps of short, gray-green, fleshy leaves. On 1½-inch stems comes a succession of evanescent ¾-inch white flowers with golden stamens. Because this species demands perfect drainage and endures long drought, it is a good subject for pot-culture, which affords protection from wet and cold in winter. *T. spinescens* is like a small linear-leaved cactus, with soft spines on the tubby sprawling branches. On wiry 5- to 6-inch stems are borne day by day rose-red saucers full of golden stamens. Give this a droughty, sunny spot or grow it in a pot in the alpine-house or frame; it is not reliably hardy in a snowless winter.

TANACETUM (Compositae)

The feathery foliage and heads of golden button-blossoms of the tansy tribe are combined in a few compact dwarf western American species. These are rarely seen in rock gardens, but are as fine for foliage effect as any yarrow or artemisia. They are of easy culture in well-drained sunny sites, and may be increased by fresh seed or division of the clumps. These are summer bloomers. *T. canum,* from southern Oregon and California, is a silvery-gray, hummocky bush about 10 inches high, with narrow leaves and dense yellow flower heads. *T. capitatum,* of the Rocky Mountains, makes a small compact mound of feathery, aromatic foliage topped by small spherical heads of yellow blossom, the whole plant less than 6 inches high. *T. potentilloides* is covered with white wool on decumbent stems and fine, feathery foliage. The golden flower heads are held in open clusters. Grow in well-drained limy soil.

TANAKAEA (Saxifragaceae)

The spirea-like subshrub from Japan, *T. radicans,* forms a 4-inch-high carpet of dark green serrate leaves. The plumes of white blossoms rise about 8 inches in summer. This is a woodland plant for acid soils, well suited to the lightly shaded heath. Rooting runners may be separated from the parent plant for increase.

TAXUS (Taxaceae)

The yews have become so commonplace as foundation shrubs and subjects for topiary work that they rarely fit into the essential wildness of the rock garden. A few forms, however, will retain character without pruning and have their use for their substantial, deep green needles. Propagate these by cuttings. *T. baccata repandens* makes a swirling mat of almost prostrate stems with rather long dark green needles. It will eventually grow broad and about 1 foot high. Our native *T. canadensis nana* is the dwarf creeping form of Ground-hemlock. It will endure considerable shade and becomes denser if sheared. *T. cuspidata minima* remains less than a foot high, but is rarely available from nurseries.

TELLIMA (Saxifragaceae)

The fringecups of the American Northwest are woodlanders

rather like the bishop's-caps and heucheras. Hairy stems up to 18 inches tall, with small fringed bells in a close, long spike, rise in early summer from the tuft of rounded, heart-shaped, serrate leaves. These plants grow in moist, rocky, shaded sites. Increase them by seed or division. *T. grandiflora* has greenish flowers that turn dark red. *T. odorata* carries fragrant red flowers. Other closely related species are listed under *Lithophragma.*

TEUCRIUM (Labiatae)

The bushy germanders form low, twiggy, aromatic shrubs, set in late summer with small hooded flowers among the upper leaves. These are mostly native to the Mediterranean region in rocky, sunny sites, and hence require the warmest positions in the garden. The tops may be damaged in severe winters, but winter-killed twigs may be clipped back to live wood in the spring and the plant will break quickly from the roots. Increase them by seed, or summer-cuttings. *T. chamaedrys* has shining, small, oaklike leaves and pink flowers; it is evergreen if protected. *T. montanum* has narrow rolled leaves and heads of white and yellow flowers on 6-inch decumbent stems. *T. pyrenaicum* carries yellow flowers on trailing stems that are set with small round woolly leaves.

THALICTRUM (Ranunculaceae)

Among the meadow rues are some excellent foliage plants with unpretentious and attractive feathery blossoms. Many of the tall species are handsome in the woods garden, where the fernlike foliage is most appropriate. Of the smaller species there are two especially desirable for growing in good, rich soil. The dwarf, stoloniferous species are easy to propagate by division. *T. alpinum* is valuable chiefly for its foliage, which is like that of a dwarf blue-green Maidenhair Fern. The petalless flowers, with prominent yellow stamens, make tassels at the top of wiry 6- to 8-inch stems in summer. This likes a fairly moist rocky soil, where it will make easily divided sizable clumps. *T. dioicum* makes thick clumps of ferny foliage on

Thalictrum kiusianum
(life size)

18-inch stems in rich soil of openings in the woods of the north-eastern United States. The long-stamened tassels of blossom are produced among and above the leaves in late spring. Increase this species by division or seed, which is produced only on the less conspicuous pistillate plants. *T. kiusianum* is the gem of the tribe, forming ever-increasing carpets of divided foliage on 3-inch stoloniferous stems. The pinkish-lavender mist of stamens with small sepals of a deeper tone is produced for a long period in summer. The whole plant is slow to leaf out in the spring and must be guarded against careless digging. Grow it in light shade in humus-rich soil and divide for increase in the spring.

THERMOPSIS (Leguminosae)

These summer-blooming plants of rich, well-drained soils in woodland openings produce close racemes of yellow pea blossoms. They are best grown from seed and transplanted when young. *T. caroliniana* forms tall sheaves of 5-foot stems clad with 3-part hairy leaves and erect terminal spikes of bright yellow. Of 3-foot stature are *T. fabacea, T. fraxinifolia, T. mollis,* and *T. montana.* In the 1-foot class are *T. argentata, T. gracilis, T. lanceolata,* and *T. rhombifolia.*

THLASPI (Cruciferae)

The alpine penny-cress in its many species produces sweet-scented crucifers of lavender or white on short stems above a mound of packed rosettes. The species with well-proportioned flower heads on very short stems are prized members of the elect and should be grown in the moist moraine. Some, however, are weedy and not worth considering. They are easy to grow from seed but are not long-lived in cultivation. In a favorable spot self-sowing will generally maintain the colony. *T. coloradense* forms low mounds of spatulate-leaved rosettes, with dense heads of white flowers on 4- to 6-inch stems. This is an uncommon and admirable plant from the Rockies. *T. bellidifolium* is probably a long-leaved geographical

variation in Macedonia of the classic *T. rotundifolium*. **T. rotundifolium** (often listed as **T. limosellifolium**) is a satisfactory name to
encompass the many variants, even to white-flowering forms, that
inhabit alpine screes and moraines, and create domes of closely held,
smooth, more or less succulent, rounded leaves. The sweet-scented
flowers are produced in very early spring on stems so short as to rise
barely above the leaves. The color of the 4 petals ranges from flushed
white to deep violet. A succession of flowering stems may appear as
the clump increases, but meager growing conditions ensure longer
life, if smaller clusters. A gnarling virus affects plants too richly
grown. There are other species—either worthless annuals or postur-
ing perennials of lumpy, serrate leafage with minuscule white or pale
washed blossoms on gawky stems—that are mostly given to bold
self-sowing. It is difficult to warn against these specifically because
they hide in seed lists under royal pseudonyms and must be un-
masked through frustrating experience.

THUJA (Pinaceae)

The arbor-vitae trees of North America and eastern Asia have
produced many interesting dwarf forms, generally looking rather
dumpish because the broad, fanlike small branches are disproportionate to the stature of the plants. The dwarfs belong mostly to the
species **T. occidentalis** or **T. orientalis** of eastern America and the
China-Korea region, respectively. Names in nurseries are very mis-
leading, and stocks have been jumbled. It is advisable to select a
specimen at first hand with a guarantee that it is not a juvenile
deceptively trimmed. In addition to the dwarf forms, there are those
with varied leaf coloration. To add to the confusion is the separate,
similar genus, *Thujopsis,* which has its own dwarf forms. All are easy
to grow in any reasonable soil.

THYMUS (Labiatae)

The thymes are perfect plants for the joints of walks and pavements of stone or for clothing the alpine lawn. If introduced among

cherished alpines, however, they have a way of insinuating a long inconspicuous runner to colonize and eventually overrun precious plants. Or the seed washes into the edge of some cushioning plant and goes unnoticed until well established. When dug out, these seedlings and rooted runners are useful for increasing the wanted carpets where thyme may be safely grown. Young plants establish quickly and more surely than larger sods and, when established, will endure drought and even heavy foot traffic in almost any soil. Plants recently set should be kept watered until new growth is evident. For general purposes there are two types of thyme, the prostrate creepers and the erect bushes. The carpeting forms, widespread in nature throughout Europe, North Africa, and Asia, vary in size and woolliness of leaf, in color and size of flower, and in rapidity of spread. Many geographical forms are given specific standing and do breed true from seed, whereas others appear to be but gradients in the whole series under *T. serpyllum*.

T. adamovicii from Serbia has velvety leaves with conspicuous glandular red hairs. *T. caespititius* is a particularly tight, slow-growing carpeter with small shining leaves. *T. × citriodorus* forms 6-inch bushes with golden foliage in the horticultural variety 'Aureus' and silvery leaves in 'Silver Queen.' *T. membranaceus* is unique in having large white flower heads backed by papery white bracts on dwarf bushes. This Spanish species is not reliably hardy and requires especially good drainage in a limy scree. *T. serpyllum* is the Mother-of-thyme and the mother of a great many named varieties. Flower colors range from white through pink and lavender to a good red in var. 'Coccineus.' Foliage may also be variegated, smooth and dark or pale green, or gray-woolly as in var. *lanuginosus*. Plants may be husky or minute as in var. 'Minus.' All are close-creeping.

TIARELLA (Saxifragaceae)
The foamflowers are very beautiful, easy woodland plants of

North America and Asia. The cordate basal leaves form dense clumps, in some species increasing by runners to make sizable mats, mostly coloring handsomely in autumn to shades of pink or reddish brown. The small, individual, starry flowers of white or light pink are carried in well-proportioned fluffy racemes or panicles well above the foliage. All species are quick to grow from seed and easy to increase by division, either in early spring or after flowering. They thrive best in light shade with a rich leaf-moldy soil. *T. collina* is a neat, clumpy plant of moist shady sites in the southeastern United States, producing for a long period in summer a succession of 10-inch flowering plumes. It does not produce runners. *T. cordifolia* is the stoloniferous, showy Foamflower of the eastern United States, with broadly cordate leaves variously lobed and toothed. Given rich soil under light shade, it produces in late spring a foaming sea of white flowers about a foot high. Pink and even wine-red flowering forms have been described but are not generally in the nursery trade. A vigorous glossy-leaved form in the southern part of the range is known as var. *austrina. T. polyphylla,* the Asiatic representative, has smaller, wavy-toothed leaves, and flowers that rise to 1½ feet. *T. trifoliata,* from the western United States, has 3-part, toothed leaves and narrow panicles of white flowers. *T. unifoliata* differs from the last in having the leaves only lobed. *T. wherryi* is a clumpy plant without runners, distinguished from *T. collina* by having the leaves more clearly 3- to 5-lobed, with fewer, broader dentations.

TOFIELDIA (Liliaceae)

The bog asphodels make trim plants for the bog or other wet sites in the sun. The spike-like cluster of small flowers rises well above the narrow lily-like leaves at the base. A small clump of these is a charming, if not brilliant, picture in summer. *T. glabra* has white flowers in a 4-inch spike at the top of a 2-foot stalk. *T. racemosa* is quite similar. Both are from the southeastern United

States. *T. intermedia* and *T. glutinosa* are West Coast Americans with spikes of yellowish flowers on stems of a foot or less. *T. calyculata,* from Europe, is smaller still, with 6-inch stems and yellowish flowers.

TOWNSENDIA (Compositae)

These condensed aster relatives are sometimes called Easter daisies, because they bloom early in the spring. Large, solitary, aster-like flowers of white, pink, or lavender are carried in crowded abundance among the low mounds of linear or spatulate leaves, which are frequently silvery with fine hairs. The hummocks rise from a stout root, not easily transplanted. Some species are short-lived in the garden. The abundant seed will germinate quickly if sown as soon as it is ripe in early summer. All species are to be grown with excellent drainage, in full sun, and if possible in a site that will dry thoroughly in summer, a condition they are accustomed to in the drier sections of western North America. *T. exscapa* (sometimes separated into other species, including *T. sericea*) has almost stemless 2-inch blossoms huddled in the linear green leaves. *T. florifer* is definitely biennial, with 1½-inch lavender or pink rayed flowers on 4-inch stems among broadly spatulate, hairy leaves. *T. grandiflora,* from the Southwest, has large violet flowers on 8-inch stems above linear grayish leaves. *T. parryi* has large purple flowers on 8-inch stems among spatulate leaves. This species is definitely perennial wherever it can remain dry in summer.

TRADESCANTIA (Commelinaceae)

The spiderworts are almost exclusively eastern American plants, growing in openings in the woods, in sandy, open waste places or along the roadside. The ephemeral 3-petaled flowers are produced daily for a considerable period in early summer. The commonest species in cultivation is *T. virginiana,* which spreads by underground stolons and is best grown in openings in the woods garden where it will have room to spread and will look more at home.

Color-forms from white through pink and blue to purple are all available. There are other species in the same 2- to 3-foot height range. *T. longipes,* however, is a dwarf plant of considerable appeal, with late-spring flowers in pink or blue on 3- to 4-inch stalks that elongate as the foliage develops. Grow in sandy, rocky soil only slightly enriched with humus.

TRICYRTIS (Liliaceae)

These oriental toad-lilies have a quaint charm to add to their value of being among the last to bloom in the season. They do their best in a humus-rich soil in light shade, where the erect or arching stems (set with alternate, clasping lily-like leaves, glistening with short hairs) will rise to 2 feet. *T. flava* produces unspotted, large, soft yellow blossoms in an open raceme at the tips of the branches, so heavy that the stems arch over. It is therefore best planted where the stems may lie over a rock or log above a woodland path. *T. hirta* blooms in October, the flowers being of a crystalline texture and grouped in the leaf axils. The 6 divisions of each erect blossom splay outward, revealing the prominent flattened style and the spots of purple and black that freckle the petals. In var. *alba* the waxen blossoms are the purest white throughout. Severe frost will damage late flowers of this species, but the plants are hardy and long-lived. The toad-lilies will flower the second year from seed, or may be divided in early spring.

TRIENTALIS (Primulaceae)

The starflowers are not spectacular but do have a dainty attractiveness in the woodland garden. There, in good leaf-mold soil, in either light or deep shade, they will form colonies by underground stolons. At the top of the 6-inch stem is a spoke-like whorl of narrow, pointed, 4-inch leaves, varying in number from 5 to 10 and unequal in length. From the whorl a few starry white flowers with 5 to 9 petals rise on fine wiry pedicels in early summer. Plants are easily established by division of the stolons at any season. *T. bore-*

alis is the eastern American species. *T. europaea,* of Europe and Asia, has shorter, broader leaves and slightly larger flowers. Pink-flowered forms have been discovered.

TRIFOLIUM (Leguminosae)

The better colorful perennial clovers are so similar in general effect to the common but dull species of lawns and meadows that they need no description. Though many are truly brilliant dwarf plants of high mountain screes and pastures, they are rarely brought into the rock garden. They are probably shunned because rock gardeners are all too familiar with the way the common lawn clovers sneak into and root deeply among the finest plants. The alpine species, however, are not aggressive, and in fact are sometimes difficult to grow. The surest chance of success is to plant them in a scree mixture with some clayey loam admixed. Increase these by seed, by division of those that make layering shoots, or by cuttings. They look especially appropriate in the homelike setting of the rocky pasture, where they will contribute not only a long season of summer bloom but a rich perfume and food for bees.

T. alpinum produces fairly large flowers of pale pink on 3- to 6-inch stems above a carpet of bright green trifoliate leaves in the European Alps. *T. beckwithii,* of the western United States, has glabrous leaves and large, showy, solitary heads of bright purple. This is one for moister sites. *T. macrocephalum,* of dry lands in the American West, has hairy leaves composed of 5 to 7 leaflets in a low mound. The large solitary heads carry flowers of rose-purple with a yellow standard. Other desirable western American mountain species are: *T. nanum,* very small in leaf and flat in growth, with reddish-purple flowers; and *T. parryi,* with sharply toothed leaves and conspicuously bracted purple flowers.

TRILLIUM (Liliaceae)

America has contributed many lovely plants to the woodland garden, and among the best are the trilliums. Many species come from the rich, moist, wooded hillsides of the southeastern United States and a few extend their range up into New England and westward. All are hardy and long-lived when given a good, deep soil, rich with leaf mold and in a shaded position. The tuberous rhizomes should be planted in late summer, 2 to 6 inches beneath the surface; the larger the rhizome, the deeper the planting. All look best in drifts and masses, with ground-covering plants beneath them, or among ferns. Seed extracted from the pulpy fruit in early autumn should be planted immediately about 1½ inches deep in sandy leaf mold. Older seed may not germinate for two to three years, and seedlings do not flower for three years. Most plants in gardens are from collected rhizomes. Some woodlands in nature hold thousands of plants, and conservative collecting has not reduced the stands wherever conditions for increase are ideal. Some species make offsets that may be removed and replanted in late summer. Special double or multiplex forms may be increased by careful nicking of the edges of the rhizome to encourage offsets. This operation may be performed after the flowering period by removing soil without digging the rhizome. After the rhizome is nicked the excavation should be filled with sand.

   T. cernuum has 3 broad leaves on the 1½-foot stalk with white flowers on a nodding peduncle that frequently conceals the blossom beneath the leaves. *T. chloropetalum* of the Far West has mottled leaves on the 1½-foot stalk with a 4-inch flower, erect and sessile, ranging in color from dark red through yellowish green to white. *T. erectum* is the early eastern wake-robin, with brownish-red or greenish-purple evil-smelling flowers held erect well above the collar of leaves on the 1-foot stems. White and creamy forms are not infrequent in some regions. *T. grandiflorum* is indeed the grandest and one of the easiest of the genus. Here the large, pure-white, 3-inch flowers stand considerably higher than the broad rhombic leaves. The blossoms as they fade blush with pink, until they appear like a new species, transformed and wonderful. This is a widespread species, ranging from Quebec to North Carolina and westward to Missouri, frequently in glistening sweeps in rich hardwood forests. Variations toward green striping, multiple petals, and all sorts of odd floral and leaf patterns makes this a collector's species. One technical botany says, "Our handsomest, most fickle and sporting species, with many scores of aberrant forms, belonging more to the field of teratology than to taxonomy!"

T. nivale is the earliest and a pygmy of the genus. Like a miniature issue of *T. grandiflorum,* this produces its delightful white cups well above the fan of leaves only 6 inches from the still-brown floor of the early spring woods. Never common in the wild, it is found in rich woods or on shady ledges from western Pennsylvania to Minnesota and southward to Missouri. *T. ovatum* is the West Coast replica of *T. grandiflorum,* the flower slightly smaller and closer to the overlapping foliage. *T. petiolatum,* though even more shrunken in stature than *T. nivale,* is not worth growing except as a curiosity, or, for an adventuresome gardener, as a hybrid parent. The small dingy purple flower sits close to the ground where the 3 long-stalked leaves separate. *T. rivale,* from the Siskiyou Mountains, mimics eastern *T. nivale,* but the white blossoms, frequently etched with purple, are smaller and on proportionately taller stems. Grown in the moraine, it may be kept neatly dwarf in stature. *T. sessile,* in many color-forms of red, yellow, or white, has erect pinched blossoms, sessile at the whorl of leaves 1 foot above the ground.

T. stylosum is a beautiful pink-flowered species rather similar to *T. grandiflorum* on the wane. *T. undulatum* is rightly called the Painted Trillium. The margins of the thin white petals are wavy, and each petal is elegantly stenciled with a central marking and radiating stripe of red. The swollen seed capsule is a scarlet berry. This is unfortunately one of the most difficult of the genus to grow. The rhizome is found deep in acid, moist, almost boggy conditions, frequently around mountain ponds beneath hemlock trees. Unless supplied with ideal conditions when moved into the woodland garden, it dwindles in size from its 1 to 2 feet in nature till it pines utterly away. There are other species, mostly rare or inferior to those listed above. Rare *T. vaseyi,* with 6-inch red-purple flowers, is the giant of the tribe.

TROLLIUS (Ranunculaceae)

The globe-flowers, in appearance very like magnified buttercups, all inhabit moist meadows and streamsides or swampy pockets. The thick, fibrous roots give rise to palmately lobed and divided basal foliage and flowering-stalks of varying heights which bear generally solitary, showy flowers of yellow or white. The blossoms, either open cup-shaped or globe-form, are composed of 5 or more petal-like sepals, and within these are many inconspicuous actual petals and numerous stamens. Fresh seed germinates speedily, while older seed may lie unsprouted for two or three years. Large clumps are easily divided after the flowering season. All enjoy a rich soil that never becomes parched or dry. Flowering is more abundant in sunny sites, but light shade helps keep the plants cool.

T. acaulis bears solitary, lemon-yellow, wide-open, 2-inch flowers on 6-inch stems. *T. albiflorus* of western America has 1½ inch cuplike white blossoms on 1-foot stems. *T. europaeus* carries its globe-shaped yellow blossoms on stems up to 2 feet. *T. japonicus* has buttercup-like flowers on 8-inch stems. A double-flowered form is known. *T. laxus,* a rare native of the eastern United States, produces in early spring, in brushy swamps, 2-inch open cups of pale greenish yellow, which become creamy as they mature. The solitary flowers are on stems that are at first close among the dark, palmate leaves but elongate as the season advances, sometimes to 2 feet. *T. ledebouri,* from Siberia, is a summer-flowering species with orangey-yellow open flowers on 2- to 3-foot stems. *T. patulus,* from the Caucasus, and *T. pumilus,* from the Himalayas, both carry bright yellow wide-open platters, 1 to 2 inches across on stems from 6 inches to 1 foot.

TSUGA (Pinaceae)

The Canadian Hemlock has produced some very distinctive dwarf forms suited to the rock garden proper and best located where they are not parched in summer or wind-scorched in winter. Among the best and slowest-growing are *T. canadensis* 'Bennett's,' 'Cole's Prostrate,' 'Horsford,' 'Jervis,' 'Minuta.' Others, such as 'Sargent's Weeping,' grow large in time but are excellent in the shrubby fringes of the rock and woods gardens. The aberrant forms are easier to root from cuttings than the species.

TSUSIOPHYLLUM (Ericaceae)

Never over 10 inches tall, *T. tanakae,* from Japan, forms a twiggy miniature shrub with minute oval pointed leaves. Small paired flowers, like much reduced azalea blossoms, erupt in late spring from the tips of the branches. This rare and enchanting pygmy should be given a select spot among other treasured plants in the heath or in company with such plants as *Schizocodon.* The fine seed can be germinated on chopped sphagnum, or the short twiggy growth rooted in early summer. It is one of the few shrubs small and interesting enough to be grown in the alpine-house or special planter of acid soil.

TULIPA (Liliaceae)

Among the species tulips are many of dwarf stature which flower in the spring. Some are so flamboyantly colored, especially among the scarlet reds, that they need careful placing in the rock garden where many plants are blooming concurrently. As many of them come from baked and rocky fields and pastures of the Middle East, they are suited to such sites in the garden. To ensure long life, and to help foil rodents, plant them 6 inches or more deep in well-drained soil. Bulb catalogues generally offer a wide variety with adequate descriptions. It takes about four years to produce a flowering plant from seed.

TUNICA (Caryophyllaceae)

The common species, *T. saxifraga,* blooms all summer long in a sunny, well-drained site. From the grassy-leaved tuffet the wiry stems, up to 10 inches long, carry heads of small pink dianthus-like blossoms, the individual flowers inconspicuous but producing a misty effect. There are forms with white flowers, varying shades of pink, and one—especially lovely—with double flowers. Easy and quick to grow from seed, particular forms may be propagated by cuttings taken close to the taproot.

UMBILICUS. See *Cotyledon* and *Sedum.*

UVULARIA (Liliaceae)

The bellworts of the eastern United States add considerably to the spring display in the woods garden. From the running rootstocks rise stiff green stems up to 1½ feet with alternate lily-like leaves, either sessile at the base or surrounding the stem. The hanging flowers are produced at the tips of thin branches at the top of the stem. Division of the rootstocks is the simplest method of increase, though seeds are quite easy also. *U. grandiflora* has perfoliate leaves on the 18-inch stalks with dangling lemon-yellow blossoms, 1½ inches long. *U. perfoliata* is smaller throughout, with paler yellow and slightly smaller flowers. *U. sessilifolia* is smaller still— only reaching a height of about 10 inches—and has pale greenish-yellow flowers.

VACCINIUM (Ericaceae)

The blueberries, bilberries, lingenberries, and cranberries all belong to this genus. Though generally valued as crops for their edible fruits, many species are wonderfully suited to growing with other ericaceous shrubs in the heath garden or with woodlanders in acid soil. A sunny or semishaded position in sandy-peaty soil suits them all. Mat-formers may be increased by early-spring or late-summer division of the clumps. Cuttings of half-ripened wood will root slowly.

V. angustifolium is the variable Lowbush Blueberry of old pastures and openings in rocky woods in the eastern United States. It forms a dense twiggy carpet from 6 to 18 inches high, with terminal clusters of small white bell flowers in spring, followed by sweet, plump berries that are generally light blue and bloomy but occasionally red or even white. The fall leaf color is brilliant scarlet and the bare winter twigs may be either red or green. *V. caespitosum,* the Dwarf Bilberry, inhabits rocky, peaty soils from sea level to high-alpine regions from Labrador across Canada and the northeastern United States to the Rockies and Coast Ranges. It has shining membranaceous leaves on 3- to 12-inch tufted shrubs. The solitary deep pink to red flowers nod on short pedicels in the leaf axils. The berries are light blue and bloomy. *V. deliciosum* of the Cascades is similar but has thicker, distinctly glaucous leaves.

V. oxycoccos and the larger-leaved and larger-fruited *V. macrocarpon* are the cranberries, the latter widely cultivated for the large, tangy red fruits. The trailing vines are set with small evergreen leaves and in early summer with flights of pink flowers, the reflexed petals resembling those of a Shooting-star. The fruit ripens in late fall and persists throughout the winter. Though generally growing in boggy sites, the vines make dense mats in drier, acid soil in light shade. They provide good ground covers for the heath garden. Rooted runners may be detached for easy increase. Cuttings and seed may also be used.

V. scoparium, of the Rockies and westward, forms mats of stiff, erect green stems about 6 inches high. The light green leaves are small and sparse, as are the urn-shaped white flowers and red berries. *V. uliginosum* is a widespread dwarf shrub with shredding brown bark, glaucous leaves, and blue-black glaucous berries, found in Europe, America, and Asia. *V. vitis-idaea* is a stoloniferous dwarf evergreen with shining oval leaves, clusters of nodding pink or white bells and brilliant red berries. These are the lingenberries. The European form will grow to 8 inches in height, but the North

American variety *minus* forms dense mats only half the height and with smaller leaves. Increase by division is easy. This is a handsome ground cover, flowering and fruiting best in rocky, peaty soil in full sun.

VALERIANA (Valerianaceae)

The sweet-scented valerians are common plants in many mountain ranges of the world. They may be tall species with heavy flat heads of white blossoms or condensed mounds with ample pink flowers on short stems. They are generally found in moist meadow sites but will endure considerable drought when established. They are quick to grow from seed and easy to divide. *V. arizonica* has heads of white flowers 6 inches above the creeping carpet of round leaves. *V. celtica* of the European Alps carries spiky heads of reddish-yellow blossoms on 3-inch stems above tufts of spatulate leaves. *V. supina* makes a dense clump of oval leaves, hairy on the edges. Good-sized heads of pink flowers are carried for a long season in early summer on 4- to 6-inch stems. This will grow in considerable shade or in a good, heavy soil in sun.

VANCOUVERIA (Berberidaceae)

These woodland plants of western North America are rather similar to epimediums, making carpets of compound ferny foliage and erect, leafless flower stalks about 1 foot tall. The panicle of nodding flowers is produced during the early summer. Increase these by division of the creeping rootstocks. To ensure dense growth, plant in rich leaf-mold soil in shade. *V. chrysantha* has a rather narrow range in the Siskiyou Mountains. In rocky, acid soil it generally locates on the north side of a rock or ledge or beneath a shrub out of the blaze of the sun, but does not seek dense shade or very moist sites. The yellow blossoms are carried above rather thick evergreen foliage, somewhat tender to extreme low temperatures. *V. hexandra* is a far easier and hardier plant, making wide carpets in acid woodsy soil in shade. The thin foliage is deciduous. The small white flowers with reflexed sepals give it the name Inside-out Flower. *V. planipetala* has small white flowers and hard evergreen leaves. It wants shady sites in very acid soil, with pine-needle protection in winter.

VERBASCUM (Scrophulariaceae)

The Mediterranean mulleins have escaped to roadsides and waste places in America—chiefly as tall biennials with handsome woolly leaves—but these are quite unsuited to the rock garden. There are a few dwarf perennial species, however, with attractive foliage and good yellow summer flowers. All mulleins are easy to grow from seed and flourish in poor stony soil in full sun. *V. dumulosum,* from Asia Minor, makes a compact plant 12 to 18 inches tall, with masses of yellow mullein flowers darkening at the center. These, produced for a long period in summer, are arranged in dense spikes above oval foliage of dark green, lightly frosted with woolly hairs.

VERBENA (Verbenaceae)

Most of the showy verbenas are tender perennials from South America, grown as annual bedding-plants. Some of the prostrate species, such as the scarlet everblooming *V. peruviana,* are worth carrying over in the closed frame or alpine-house as fall cuttings to provide young plants to set out in sunny sites the next spring. Thus they can supply steady summer bloom for the rock garden. The North American species, known as vervains, have spikes of flowers disappointingly small and opening a few at a time up the stem. *V. bipinnatifida* is the best of these, with divided leaves and ½-inch purple flowers in heads that elongate to form a spike on rather prostrate stems. It is easy to propagate from seed or by division.

VERONICA (Scrophulariaceae)

There are many species of speedwell adapted to and easy to grow in the rock garden in either full sun or light shade. Some form sprawling mats; others carry their blossoms in steeple-like spires. The predominant colors are lavender and blue, though there are pinks and whites. It must be admitted that the individual flowers in most species are rather fleeting, and that only those with good foliage are decorative over a long period. All are easy to grow from seed and, because they make good matted roots, are readily divided. Nor do they have whims as to soil.

V. alpina forms a low creeping bush of about 6 inches, with dark green leaves and dense evanescent racemes of small blue flowers at the erect tips of the sprawling branches. *V. armena* forms a tangled mat of prostrate stems with gray-green leaves cut into thin segments. The racemes of rather large bright blue flowers in summer make this, with the beautiful foliage, one of the notable species. Give it a warm rock to sprawl on. *V. bonarota* forms a procumbent dense clump with glossy, round, toothed leaves and dense 4-inch spikes of purple-blue flowers with prominent stamens, in midsummer. *V. cinerea,* from Asia Minor, carries axillary racemes of pink flowers on creeping stems, all clothed with woolly gray leaves. This needs a scree condition and may suffer in cold climates. *V. filiformis,* a rampant runner with tiny blue-white flowers, should be kept out of the rock garden.

V. fruticans makes a little shrub of about 6 inches, the many branches decked with ½-inch oval leaves and short racemes of clear-blue flowers, reddish purple in the center. *V. gentianoides* has basal leaves like those of Spring Gentian and an open spire of large light blue blossoms veined with darker blue. This wants a rich soil. *V.* × *guthrieana* makes a tight evergreen shrub about 5 inches high with sizable dark blue flowers in early summer. It may burn badly in a severe winter but will usually recover. This plant is best grown in well-drained soil. *V. incana* has silvery basal leaves and dense spires of lavender-blue flowers, 12 to 18 inches in height. *V. pectinata* makes large mats of woolly foliage with short racemes of white-centered blue flowers. It is most commonly seen as var.

rosea, with pink flowers. Give it a well-drained soil and a rock to sprawl on.

V. rupestris is an easy but excellent plant, making a thick round pancake of prostrate stems with small dark green leaves and abundant terminal clusters of flowers in various shades of pink, blue, or white. The blossoms come early in summer in a brief but brilliant burst. This is also known as *V. prostrata. V. satureioides* is a flat creeper with very dense short racemes of clear-blue flowers. *V. serpyllifolia* is an improved *V. alpina,* with better habit and larger, dark, striped blue flowers. *V. spicata nana* is a 6-inch version of the common border veronica with dense small spikes of lavender-blue that last well in summer. Some species are classified under *Hebe.*

VINCA (Apocynaceae)

As an evergreen ground cover in light to dense shade and even in full sun, there is no surer plant than the cheerful Periwinkle, *V. minor,* whose blue flowers in the type-species have given their name to this particular shade of blue. Aggressive and easy to grow, it will maintain an area beneath shrubs and trees almost entirely free of weeds without robbing the soil for taller sturdy plants. To establish a thick and permanent carpet, it pays to prepare the soil and plant thickly the rooted runners so generously supplied by established plants. Besides division, easily rooted cuttings are a method for increase. In addition to the periwinkle-blue form, there are other colors of *V. minor:* white and wine-red, single and double blossoms, and forms with variegated foliage. *V. herbacea* is another and somewhat different species. The genus likeness is there in the trailing stems and 1-inch-wide blue flowers; but here the plant is quite herbaceous, dying-back in winter to the perennial root and beginning again in early spring the production of long runners with narrow, opposite leaves and a succession of summer flowers. This, from Asia Minor, will stand a sunny well-drained site, and in severe climates may not persist.

VIOLA (Violaceae)

Vast and varied is the race of violets, flourishing as they do from one end to the other of both the northern and southern temperate zones. They grow in marshlands, in woods, in the plains, and in rocky mountain screes; in sun, in shade; in rich, leafy, acid soil, in sandy gravels, in limestone crevices. Some carry their flowers on stems directly from the rootstock, others from the axils of leafy stems. Many have unopening, self-fertile flowers late in the season. Most are prone to hybridizing both in the wild and in the garden. Plants grown from seed cannot always be counted on to come true, but most violets are easy to propagate by division of the rootstock, and most root quickly from cuttings. A few call for special handling, both in growing and propagating.

V. adunca is a common western American species with round, slightly toothed leaves and violet to deep purple flowers growing on pedicels from the leaf axils. It is a variable species that has a particularly large blossomed dwarf variety in the Olympics, *V. flettii,* purple with yellow markings. *V. beckwithii* is a cut-leaved dwarf from the dry, gravelly soils of the Cascades and lowlands to the south and east. The flowers, on 4-inch stems, are deep purple on the upper two petals and pale violet on the three lower. Quite similar but with the three lower petals a soft creamy yellow is *V. hallii.* Both go dormant in the summer in their dry gravelly sites. They may be moved most easily then and propagated by careful division of the rootstock. *V. biflora* is the tiny plant that carries narrow yellow blossoms streaked with black-purple lines among small, roundish, smooth leaves for a long season in the European alpine woods and high rocky meadows.

V. blanda is the Sweet White Violet of moist woods in eastern North America. The stoloniferous plants, with rounded, acute leaves, carry in spring short-stemmed white, purple-veined, rather narrow-petaled flowers. *V. incognita* and *V. pallens* are quite similar. *V. calcarata* is a charming species of the French and Swiss

Alps, which paints the high meadows and pastures with sheets of blue or purple or yellow. The blossoms, which begin to open in early spring, are large and pansy-like on 3- to 4-inch stems above increasing mats of light green, rather thin foliage. Individual plants seem short-lived in the garden and are best maintained by cuttings. Seed collected in the garden is generally hybridized with Johnny-jump-ups. For best success grow this species in a sunny, rich, moraine mixture that does not become parched.

V. canadensis is an easy and delightful species for the woodland, where in rich leafy soil it produces foot-high plants with heart-shaped leaves, pointed at the tip, and large axillary flowers, white on the face and tinged with lavender on the reverse of the petals. After the flush of early-summer bloom, there will be scattered blossoms all summer and a good show in the fall before the plant retreats to the husky shallow rootstock. The western American *V. rugulosa* is very similar in effect, somewhat huskier and with hairs on the underside of the leaves. *V. cornuta* is the ancestor of some of the handsome bedding-violets and pansies. In its native Pyrenees it is a variable plant, with a wide range of colors from clear blue to white.

V. cuneata, from wet pockets of gravelly clay which dry in summer, in the Siskiyou Mountains, has long, cuneate, toothed leaves and long-stemmed large flowers. The upper petals may be purple or purple-patched and the lower ones white or pale lavender, veined and spotted. *V. delphinantha* is a real challenge. From the rocky screes in Greece and Bulgaria comes this un-pansy-like plant with narrowly divided leaves and pink blossoms with narrow petals and long spurs. *V. enzanensis* is a large-flowered Japanese woodlander. It is frequently listed as *V. dissecta,* describing the long-stemmed leaves, which are 3-parted and then cut into linear divisions. The blossoms are purple, white, or rose-colored.

V. fimbriatula is one of many eastern American violets, very similar in effect and inhabiting woods, openings, meadows, and old pastures. This is an intermarrying group with leaves of various outline (scalloped but not cut) and, on stems rising from the roots, with single flowers mostly violet-blue, though occasionally pure white or white with purple markings. Here belong these species of *Viola: cucullata,* a highly variable wetland woods violet with incurled young leaves and invasive habits; *papilionacea,* the common moist-woods and dooryard violet, probably the ancestor of the aggressive Confederate Violet *(V. priceana);* also *affinis, hirsutula, missouriensis, nephrophylla, septentrionalis,* and *sororia*—distinguished from each other mostly by leaf outline and hairiness. These are all suited to the wilder sections of the woods garden, where they may ramp and run, scatter their seeds, intermarry, and produce a delightful, variable progeny of just plain violets. Of much the same garden value are those species with leaves sagittate or fingered, like *V. palmata, V. pedatifida, V. sagittata, V. septemloba,* and *V. triloba.*

V. glabella, a western American woodlander, has shining, cordate leaves and axillary flowers of yellow on the 1-foot, branching stems. It has much the same garden effect as the eastern *V. hastata, V. pensylvanica,* and *V. pubescens. V. jooi,* from southeastern Europe, forms tidy little clumps of upstanding smooth leaves and open-faced flowers of pinkish violet. *V. lanceolata* is a narrow erect plant of marshes and swamps, with long-stemmed white flowers above slender leaves. Of similar effect is *V. primulifolia,* also to be grown in wettish sites. *V. nuttallii* is an early-blossoming clear-yellow flower from the western United States, having much the effect of the common eastern woods violets.

V. pedata is certainly one of the most desirable of the whole violet genus. The Birdsfoot Violet has a few special demands for successful cultivation quite different from those of most violets. It wants sandy or rocky acid soil and either sun or very light shade. This species has the two upper petals dark violet and the three lower ones pale lilac. This form is sometimes distinguished by the name *bicolor,* whereas the form with the petals uniformly lilac is designated *concolor.* White- and pink-blossomed forms are also known, especially in var. *lineariloba,* a more widespread variety in the eastern United States, having leaves much cut into fine segments. From fresh seed, plants will flower in two years. Root-cuttings are the most satisfactory method of increase for particularly good color-forms. Mature plants may be lifted and cut longitudinally through the crown of the rootstock with feeding-roots attached to each segment and treated as cuttings in the sand bed.

V. rostrata, the Beaked or Long-spurred Violet of rich woods in the eastern United States, is the handsomest of the group of stemmed violets. It has flowers on fine pedicels from the axils of the upper leaves on the branching stems. These leafy stems lie out from the noncreeping root and form a neat plant with the long-spurred, rather flat blossoms looking upward. The color of the flowers varies in shades of violet to deep purple with darkened veins and eye-ring. A pure-white form is known. This is a noninvasive fine plant for rich but well-drained soil in shade. *V. rotundifolia,* the earliest eastern violet to bloom, has butter-yellow sweet-scented flowers on short stems clustered among the not yet unfolded leaves. The blossoms appear just as the snow melts in acid upland woods of the eastern United States. By summer the large, shining, rounded, heart-shaped leaves lie out flat on the ground in a handsome pattern.

V. tricolor, one of the parents of garden pansies, violas, and Johnny-jump-ups, needs no introduction or cultural directions. Sooner or later it will appear, as though spontaneously, carried in on some other plant or as a reversion of some hybrid, to self-sow in the moister, richer sections of the rock garden. It is short-lived but is immortal through self-sowing. *V. yakusimanum,* from Japan, is perhaps the tiniest violet of all. It forms very fine mats of ¼-inch heart-shaped leaves and just above them produces many ⅓-inch white blossoms, penciled with purple. It is so inconspicuous in the natural habitat of mossy woods—where it is not very permanent but does self-sow—that it is most aptly grown in pots or other containers.

WAHLENBERGIA. See *Edraianthus.*

WALDSTEINIA (Rosaceae)

The barren-strawberries have strawberry-like, 3-part leaves and yellow strawberry flowers in summer. These make good ground-covering plants in light, humus-rich, acid soil in semishade. Increase these by division. *W. fragarioides* comes from the eastern United States and the slightly smaller *W. sibirica* (also called *W. ternata*) from eastern Europe and Japan.

WULFENIA (Scrophulariaceae)

The only species generally grown is *W. carinthiaca,* from moist meadows in the mountains of eastern Europe. It forms flat rosettes of thick, oval, scalloped leaves, from which in summer rise sturdy 10- to 18-inch stems with dense spikes of deep purple tubular flowers at the summit. Grow this in a well-drained sunny site. Seed will produce flowering plants the second year, which may be divided for increase.

XEROPHYLLUM (Liliaceae)

The Turkey-beard *(X. asphodeloides)* of the eastern and the Bear-grass *(X. tenax)* of the western United States are handsome tall plants with great plumes of ivory-white flowers above dense clumps of coarse grassy foliage. These are plants of special sites and are difficult to establish, but because of their great beauty in nature, it is worth the effort to bring them into cultivation. Though it is more true of the Beargrass, neither is easy to transplant from the wild because of the enormously deep woody rootstocks and easily injured roots. Choose really small plants (even these are deeply rooted) and dig carefully so as not to skin the thin bark from the roots. Keep them watered until established. *X. asphodeloides* is found in dry sandy pinelands from New Jersey to North Carolina and does climb into the mountain woods of Virginia and Tennessee. It will reach 4 feet in height and has a 6-inch cluster of blossoms at the summit of the grassy-leaved stout stem. It is slow to reach flowering size from seed; established plants may be divided with care in the spring. *X. tenax* is a huskier plant, making a magnificent display in forests and meadows at high elevations in the Rockies and westward. Only mature clumps, with a huge tousled basal hummock of tough grass, will bloom—and these erratically; but the great, domed, dense heads of ivory blossoms are spectacular. This species is best grown in deep rocky soil in openings in the woods where the drainage is rapid.

ZAUSCHNERIA (Onagraceae)

The California Fuchsia, **Z. *californica,*** which is not a true fuchsia, forms a decumbent, spreading, gray-leaved plant that carries throughout the summer a succession of brilliant scarlet tubular flowers about 2 inches long. Not reliably hardy except in warmer gardens, it wants full sun in very gritty well-drained soil. *Z. californica* is the commonest species of *Zauschneria* but not as hardy as the very similar **Z. *latifolia,*** which comes from higher mountain sites in northern California and southern Oregon. Propagate these by seed, division, or cuttings.

ZYGADENUS, sometimes spelled *Zigadenus* (Liliaceae)

The death-camasses of both eastern and western North America have wandlike clusters of flowers frequently only on one side of the arching stems among the narrow, iris-like foliage. The summer flowers, though about ½ inch across, are not brightly colored and are generally greenish-tinted. Some species grow from bulbs, others from fibrous roots. They are most successfully grown in moist meadows or in rich woods. The best species, all about 2 feet tall, are **Z. *elegans, Z. fremontii, Z. glaucus,*** and **Z. *paniculatus.***

Ferns

The flowering plants and shrubs have, in addition to the color and structure of their blossoms, patterns and textures of leaf and design of growth habit. So do the dwarf evergreen trees; and for their architectural form and beauty of foliage we bring them into the garden to complement the flowering plants. For the same reason we place among the flowering herbs and shrubs the delicately textured ferns. It is generally in praise that we speak of a plant as having ferny foliage. How much more intensely and properly does a fern have such foliage.

Ferns are plants of an ancient heritage, primitive still in their sexual reproduction but eternal and modern in the pure architecture of leaf form. To many people all ferns look alike. That may be because in almost every natural site there is a fern that looks like a fern, in company with the flowering plants that catch the eye and pique the curiosity. It is simple to dismiss a fern. But to introduce into the garden the same natural mixture of fern form and flower interest, we must see that there are a number of different genera and species of ferns adapted to a variety of sites, with a variety of effects. The first part of this section lists those ferns most suitably grown in shaded woodsy sites. Those that do better in crevices among rocks are listed in a second part.

Ferns for the Woodland Garden

It is in the cool shade of the forest that we are perhaps most conscious of ferns. There, in all parts of the world, they flourish at their handsomest. The best assurance of success is to make use of those species native to your own region. Yet once you have discovered their variety and charm, it is likely that you will wish to try species from other areas. But not all woodland ferns are of equal elegance or usefulness in the woods garden. Some are too aggressive, and therefore it is well to learn to differentiate among them.

All ferns should be transplanted in early spring before new growth commences; nevertheless, most can be moved safely at any season if carefully handled. Woodland ferns want deep, well-drained, leaf-mold soil and—until established—ample moisture. Once growing well, they will endure long periods of drought. Many have running rootstocks that can be divided easily in early spring or late summer for increase. Some have a single enlarging crown that can be sliced through longitudinally for propagation. Growing them from spores is a fascinating challenge. Methods of doing so can be found in specialized fern books.

ADIANTUM (Polypodiaceae)

The maidenhair ferns are delicate and graceful in leaf and stem. They increase slowly by creeping at the roots but are easily restrained by cutting back the root clump with a sharp spade. These are ferns for rich soil and a shady site. *A. pedatum,* of the eastern United States, is handsome at all stages, from the late-spring uncurling of the rosy "watch spring" crosier to the full rich swirl of overlapping, delicate leaves on top of the 2-foot, blackish, shiny stem in summer. *A. aleuticum* is the western American species, very similar except for tending to be slightly smaller. It has some interesting forms: a fastigate form with a swirl of leaflets in a dense erect pattern; and a very small Alaskan dwarf form only a few inches high, with crisp overlapping leaflets in the frond.

ATHYRIUM (Polypodiaceae)

These woodland ferns, when in fresh new growth, are among the loveliest of the medium-tall species. But they tend to become untidy and ragged by midsummer. Moreover, they advance rather rapidly by elongating densely packed rootstocks and should be used only where there is plenty of room. *A. filix-femina,* the Lady Fern, is widespread in nature and is highly variable. Subspecies, varieties, and forms are numerous, all unfortunately marked by the two disadvantages mentioned above. *A. goeringianum,* from Japan, is neither as untidy nor as invasive as the Lady Fern. It is generally seen in gardens in the handsome variety *pictum,* which has purplish stems and a central gray band to the fronds. This prefers moist rich soil in shade. *A. pycnocarpon,* the Glade Fern or Narrow-leaved Spleenwort, of the eastern United States, is not so rapidly invasive as the Lady Fern but does tend to develop untidy fronds by late summer. It wants considerable moisture and rich soil. *A. thelypteroides* is the common Silvery Spleenwort of woods and roadsides of the eastern United States. Though a solid-textured and handsome fern when in prime condition, it may become weedy.

BLECHNUM (Polypodiaceae)

These tough, leathery, evergreen ferns are mostly not hardy except in the greenhouse. *B. penna-marina* is a dwarf carpeting hard fern from the colder parts of the Southern Hemisphere. It wants moisture beneath but good drainage for the creeping, scaly rhizomes. *B. spicant* is the Hard Fern of Europe and Asia and the Deer Fern of western America. It wants deep rich soil in shade. There are many forms and sizes, not all reliably hardy in northern gardens.

CYSTOPTERIS (Polypodiaceae)

Here are delicate ferns for the rocky woodland in pockets of rich, moist, neutral to limy soil. *C. bulbifera,* the Bulblet Bladder Fern of rock ledges and shady streamsides of the eastern United States, forms curtains of narrow fronds, tapering to a long, graceful tip. In moist, limy soil this may become invasive by self-sowing of bulblets from the underside of the frond. *C. fragilis* is the widespread dwarf Fragile Fern of shady, rocky pockets. One of the first to show up in spring, it tends to shrivel up during drought and disappear in late summer.

DENNSTAEDTIA (Polypodiaceae)

The Hay-scented or Boulder Fern, **D. punctiloba,** is the common lacy fern growing about a foot tall around boulders in northeastern American pastures and in dense, extensive stands in dry woodlands. It is of such rapid spread that it should be excluded from all but a large woodland garden or be restrained around a clump of large rocks.

DRYOPTERIS (Polypodiaceae)

The woodferns, or shield ferns, are of worldwide distribution and include some of the most desirable species for the woodland garden though one species inhabits rocky ledges and is therefore described under "The Rock and Cliff Ferns." Many are evergreen—or nearly so—have sturdy, handsome leaves 18 inches to 4 feet long from a central crown, and do not ever become invasive. Most inhabit forest sites of humus-rich soil that retains adequate moisture. **D. arguta** of western America is a tall husky species with neatly toothed subleaflets. **D. bootii** is an erect lacy-looking fern of good substance—a rare natural hybrid between D. *spinulosa* and D. *cristata.* This species is for a prominent spot in rich, moist woodland soil. **D. clintoniana** is a large handsome species with erect fronds, narrow for their stature. **D. cristata** is very similar to the last in texture and habit, but is shorter and narrower, with leaflets arranged venetian blind fashion. It needs a moist site. **D. filix-mas,** the Male Fern, is more common in Europe than in America. It is a thick-textured and handsome semi-evergreen species with tall, elegant, deep green fronds. **D. goldiana,** of rich moist woods in the eastern United States, is the real giant of the genus, with broad, long-stalked fronds up to 4 feet tall. The yellow-green leaf blades lean out from the crown, forming a striking pattern above the dark scaly stalks. **D. marginalis** has handsome glaucous-green fronds of leathery texture and is the most permanently evergreen species of the genus. It prefers to grow in deep rocky pockets of leaf mold, but will endure more dryness than the others. **D. spinulosa** is the typical Lacy Woodfern, the fronds of which are gathered in the wild for use by florists. It has many varieties and forms in America and Europe.

GYMNOCARPIUM (Polypodiaceae)

The dwarf Oak Fern, **G. dryopteris,** has the shape of a small Bracken and the delicacy of a maidenhair fern. It will form a charming 4- to 6-inch-high carpet of cool green in rich acid soil in deep shade.

LYGODIUM (Schizaeaceae)

The Climbing Fern, **L. palmatum** (also known as the Hartford Fern), is a rare vine-like plant of the eastern United States with palmate, sterile leaves and a cluster of narrowed fruiting-leaves at the tips of the clambering stems. Grown in light shade in rich acid soil, constantly moist but not actually boggy, it will festoon low shrubs or mount a steeply sloping bank. This is not easy to transplant.

MATTEUCCIA (Polypodiaceae)

The statuesque Ostrich Fern, **M. struthiopteris,** with its massive vase of tall, upsweeping fronds and the central ostrich plumes of shorter fertile fronds, needs space in which to develop and requires a strong back for digging. It will make impressive, practically indestructible groves in good, rich, somewhat moist neutral soil. This is an excellent fern beside a woodland stream where there is space for its rapid spread and grand beauty.

ONOCLEA (Polypodiaceae)

The Sensitive Fern, **O. sensibilis,** decorative as it is with its broadly cut fronds of about 1 foot and beady fruiting-stalks, is an invasive, weedy species. Except in remote moist corners of the woods, it is best excluded from the garden.

OSMUNDA (Osmundaceae)

The osmundas are stalwart and stately, and in humus-rich soil will grow to be more than 5 feet tall. Because of their great size and deep-rooting hummocks of fibrous rootstocks, they require extensive room and a massive setting. Both *O. cinnamomea,* the Cinnamon Fern (with woolly fiddleheads and tawny furred fruiting-plumes), and *O. claytoniana,* the Interrupted Fern, are very similar except when in fruit. *O. claytoniana* produces interesting fertile leaflets partway up the stalk of some of the sterile fronds. Both are easily grown in deep soils in sun or shade as long as there is some moisture. The Royal Fern, *O. regalis,* with fertile panicles topping the handsomely divided fronds, enjoys a really moist site.

POLYPODIUM (Polypodiaceae)

The Common or Rock Polypody, *P. vulgare,* forms dense carpets of evergreen fronds, generally less than a foot high. The common form has rounded, deeply indented segments, but there are interesting crested and toothed forms. It thrives best in a shady site, in shallow, preferably acid soil, over rocks or logs.

POLYSTICHUM (Polypodiaceae)

The evergreen holly ferns form upright clumps of leathery fronds, mostly 1 to 2 feet tall, with sharply toothed leaflets. All are admirably suited to humus-rich soil in a shady situation, especially among rocks. *P. acrostichoides,* the widely distributed Christmas Fern, occurs in many interesting forms, all very easily grown. Old fronds may be clipped off in the spring as the new ones uncoil. *P. braunii* is a northern fern of distinctive cutting, with tall arching fronds of a spiny, scaly effect. It wants a cool, moist, rich site where the soil does not become powder-dry in summer. *P. lonchitis* is the Mountain Holly Fern of northern North America, Europe, and Asia, rather similar to the Christmas Fern. *P. munitum,* the Sword Fern, is the giant of the genus (up to 5 feet) and grows in rich, moist, shady locations. Of smaller dimensions and prudently kept where the roots may run between and under large rocks are *P. andersonii,* *P. lemmonii,* and *P. scopulinum,* all rather rare but beautiful ferns of the northwestern United States and Canada. The European *P. aculeatum* is very dark green, with leathery, sharply serrate leaflets.

THELYPTERIS (Polypodiaceae)

These lacy, delicate ferns form sizable patches in moist rich woods or swampy pockets. They all increase fairly rapidly by running rootstocks, the fronds rising singly but rather closely spaced as the rootstocks branch. All are fairly small, averaging about a foot in height. Though they may increase fairly rapidly once established, they run shallowly and are easily controlled. *T. noveboracensis,* the New York Fern, will endure drier sites. *T. palustris,* the Marsh Fern, needs wet soil in sun or shade. *T. simulata,* the rare Massachusetts Fern, is found in cool northern sphagnum swamps, generally in Red Maple shade. The two beech ferns—*T. hexagonoptera,* the Broad Beech Fern, and *T. phegopteris,* the Narrow Beech Fern—like rich woodsy soil.

WOODWARDIA (Polypodiaceae)

The chain ferns are both definitely suited only to very moist, acid soils. The tall Virginia Chain Fern, *W. virginica,* is erect, from 2 to 4 feet, and frequently grows in shallow water at the edge of swampy ponds. The smaller, dark-stemmed *W. areolata* might be mistaken for a Sensitive Fern from the sterile fronds, but is easily identified by the narrow fertile leaves. This is an East Coast species found commonly in wet pockets of acid, sandy soil.

The Rock and Cliff Ferns

For the rock garden proper there are many beautiful small ferns that grow naturally in the humus-filled cracks and crevices of cliffs and ledges. Some demand acid conditions, some limy, and some are indifferent to soil acidity. Some will grow in full sun, others only in shady positions. What they all demand is rock among which to spread their fine roots. The crevices between the stones of a planted wall or raised bed offer ideal situations. Most of the small rock ferns are excellent for container-growing, for terrace planters, or for pots in the alpine-house. Drainage must be good, and it is wise to plant between pieces of rock or brick inserted in the container. None will endure stagnant moisture at the roots.

ASPLENIUM (Polypodiaceae)

The true spleenworts are all compact, dwarf, graceful ferns of exquisite proportion. They lace the cliffs with delicate wiry stems elegantly set with small leaflets. *A. montanum* hangs from shaded shale or schist ledges, forming a curtain of small, rather blunt, firm, segmented leaflets on triangular fronds about 4 inches long. It wants shade and acid soil. *A. pinnatifidum,* the Lobed Spleenwort, is a rare plant, inhabiting fine cracks in shaded sandstone cliffs from New Jersey south and west. The stiff lobed leaves taper to a long uncut point, in appearance rather like a deeply indented Walking Fern, though it never roots at the tip. *A. platyneuron,* the Ebony Spleenwort, is the easiest of the group to grow, even enduring house-plant conditions, and is the commonest in nature. It will grow in limy or neutral well-drained rocky soil, selecting by preference a position either in a rock crack or clustering at the base of a partly buried stone. Half-shade suits it best. *A. ruta-muraria,* the Wall Rue of both the Old World and the eastern United States, is found locally in the shaded cracks of limestone cliffs and boulders. The fleshy, fan-shaped leaflets form a triangular stemmed frond about 3 inches tall. *A. trichomanes* is a delicate rock fern forming a swirl of black-stemmed fronds set closely with tiny roundish leaflets. This Maidenhair Spleenwort clings to the moist mossy surfaces of shaded limestone crags. *A. viride,* the Green Spleenwort, is similar in appearance to the Maidenhair Spleenwort, except that the stems are green and the whole plant is somewhat fleshier. It grows under conditions favored by the Maidenhair Spleenwort. In addition to the above species, there are fascinating natural hybrids among them.

ASPLENOSORUS. See *Camptosorus.*

CAMPTOSORUS (Polypodiaceae)

The Walking Fern, *C. rhizophyllus,* with its long, tapering, decumbent, undivided fronds, is most unfernlike in appearance. It makes extensive colonies on shaded limestone rocks, spreading by forming a new plant at the tip of the frond where it touches the mossy stone. The fine roots cling to the rocky surface and rarely extend into free soil at the base of the crag. It is frequently found growing in association with the Ebony Spleenwort, and occasionally, the rare hybrid *Asplenosorus ebenoides* may result. This plant will not naturally root at the tip unless the leaf is severed from the plant and inserted point-first into sandy leaf-moldy soil kept constantly damp.

CETERACH (Polypodiaceae)

The Rustyback Fern, *C. officinarum,* is a common rock fern in Europe, absent from America but quite adaptable in narrow limestone crevices. It is best placed where it receives some shade, though it will endure considerable drought, shriveling thoroughly and recovering rapidly. The rather silvery fronds, rusty brown on the back, are compact and only 2 to 3 inches long.

CHEILANTHES (Polypodiaceae)

The lipferns are all plants of dry rocky situations, mostly in the southern and western parts of the United States. They want plenty of light but not a southern exposure and require good drainage at the crown, either in rocky pockets or in a vertical wall. The eastern species favor acid rocks and the westerners appear indifferent. These are small graceful ferns with dense, generally hairy or woolly leaves. *C. feei,* a dense, hairy fern growing about 4 inches high, is one of the hardiest species. It is widespread throughout the western United States. *C. gracillima,* the Lace Fern, has close-set, dark green, rolled leaflets, hairy on the reverse. It forms tight clumps about 6 inches tall in the mountain ledges of the Northwest. *C. tomentosa,* the Woolly Lipfern, will grow up to 12 inches, but is not reliably hardy outdoors above its southern range from Mexico to West Virginia. *C. lanosa,* the Hairy Lipfern, about 8 inches tall, has scattered hairs on stems and leaflets. This will endure all but the severest winters, growing best in semishaded but dry rocky crevices, preferably in acid rocks.

CRYPTOGRAMMA (Polypodiaceae)

The rock brake ferns are distinguished by having fertile fronds with narrow, incurved leaflets, quite different from the leafy sterile fronds. *C. crispa,* the Parsley Fern, about 4 to 5 inches tall, is found among acid rocks in the mountains of the western United States, and in a slightly different form in Europe. *C. stelleri,* a widely distributed but local fern, forms patches about 4 inches high in moist, muddy soils on limestone rocks. It tends to shrivel up and disappear completely in summer.

DRYOPTERIS (Polypodiaceae)

Most of the dryopteris are described under the listing of "Ferns for the Woods Garden." The only dwarf species of the woodferns is *D. fragrans,* a rare and local species, mostly far north. On dry rock ledges and talus slopes, generally north-facing, it forms aromatic clumps of finely cut dense fronds up to 1 foot tall, with the old, browned leaves clustered at the base.

PELLAEA (Polypodiaceae)

The cliffbrake ferns have distinctive blue-green foliage with the well-spaced leaflets curled back along the edges. These are neatly arranged on lustrous wiry stems that range from a few inches to 2 feet in height. All want excellent drainage among limestone rocks and will endure considerable sun and drought. *P. andromedae-folia,* the Coffee Fern of California and Oregon, forms upstanding, narrow fronds about 1 foot tall with rounded leaflets on flesh-colored stems. It is not hardy in very cold areas. *P. atropurpurea* and the smaller, smooth-stemmed *P. glabella* form erect clumps to 1 foot in height on limestone ledges, frequently fully exposed to the sun; *atropurpurea* has somewhat hairy, almost black stems; in *glabella* the stems are smooth and chestnut-brown. *P. brachyptera* has narrow, linear, blue-green leaflets on purplish-brown stems up to 8 inches tall. This is a fern for sunny limestone crevices. *P. breweri* has ample blue-green fronds in tight clumps. This is a rare fern of western limestone cliffs. *P. densa* has crowded, wiry, short fronds at the top of 6-inch naked black stems. It prefers semishaded or shaded pockets among rocks. *P. ornithopus,* the Birdsfoot Fern, has needlelike leaflets on the 1-foot-high purple-stemmed fronds.

PHYLLITIS (Polypodiaceae)

The Hart's-tongue Fern, *P. scolopendrium,* has unique broad strap-shaped fronds of lustrous green, which are up to 2 feet long. There are frilled and crested forms, commonly grown in England. This fern needs a moist, shady, protected, limy site.

PITYROGRAMMA (Polypodiaceae)

The Goldback Fern, *P. triangularis,* carries short triangular fronds with a golden, mealy reverse at the tip of foot-long stems. This grows in semishaded pockets of broken rock and humus (generally acid), but is not easy to transplant.

WOODSIA (Polypodiaceae)

The woodsias are small, tufted, lacy ferns growing among rocks and in crevices. Some want acid soils, others limy or neutral conditions. They will stand considerable drought and some sun, but do best in light shade with adequate moisture, as long as the drainage is good. *W. alpina* forms an erect clump of narrow fronds only about 4 inches tall. It is a rare fern in moist limestone crevices, northward in Europe, Asia, and North America. *W. glabella* has small fan-shaped leaflets widely spaced on narrow 5-inch fronds growing on moist shaded limestone. *W. ilvensis,* the Rusty Woodsia, is a dwarf, dense, compact fern, with thick hair on the backs of the fronds which turns rusty brown in fall. This species wants acid soil among rocks and will endure rather dry sites. *W. obtusa* is the commonest eastern American Woodsia, adaptable to a variety of rocky sites and soils, preferably not acid. In shade it will form a finely cut clump up to 15 inches tall, becoming yellow-green and less tall in sun. Rather similar but with narrower and shorter fronds are *W. oregana* and *W. scopulina.*

Selective List
of Common Names

Selective List
of Common Names

THE PURPOSE of this selective list is to help the reader who knows a plant only by its common name to find it under its correct scientific name in the Descriptive Catalogue of Plants. I have therefore included in this list common names in general usage even though these are not always mentioned in the text. I have, however, omitted those that are employed only locally and those invented specifically for the nursery trade or for popularized wildflower books.

Many of the genera and species in the Descriptive Catalogue of Plants have no common names. The common names for some species of plants are descriptive modifiers attached to a generic common name shared by all the species within that genus. These have not been given separate listings and will be found only under the generic common name. For example: Yellow Lady's-slipper, Pink Lady's-slipper, and Showy Lady's-slipper are listed only under "Lady's-slippers." Where the common generic name closely resembles the scientific generic name (i.e., *Iris, Gentiana*), these have not been included in the following list except where ambiguity might result. In a few cases common generic names are applied to more than one true genus. To illustrate some: the common generic name "heather" is applied to *Calluna, Erica,* and *Bruckenthalia;* it is also used in the name "mountain heather," which can be either *Phyllodoce* or *Cassiope,* and in "beach heather," meaning *Hudsonia.* Where this occurs the full common name is listed in the interest of clarity.

It is perhaps obvious, considering the above, that common names, though more popular and less frightening than scientific names, are almost useless when it comes to acquiring a desired plant. The common name "Bluebell," for example, is used for any one of 50 plants in 3 different genera, and the chance of your getting the particular bluebell you admire, when ordering it by that name, is consequently slim. It is therefore advisable to accustom yourself to using both the scientific generic and specific names even if at first they seem difficult to remember and pronounce.

Flowering Perennials, Bulbs, Trees, and Shrubs

Almonds – *Prunus*
Andromedas – *Andromeda, Pieris*
Anemones – *Anemone, Pulsatilla*
Arbor-vitaes – *Thuja*
Arrowheads – *Sagittaria*
Atlas daisies – *Anacyclus*
Aubrietias – *Aubrieta*
Auricula – *Primula auricula*
Autumn crocuses – *Colchicum, Crocus*
Avalanche Lily – *Erythronium montanum*
Avens – *Geum*

Bachelor's buttons – *Centaurea*
Balloon flowers – *Platycodon*
Baneberries – *Actaea*
Barberries – *Berberis*
Barren-strawberries – *Waldsteinia*
Basket-of-gold – *Alyssum saxatile*
Beach heathers – *Hudsonia*
Bearberry – *Arctostaphylos uva-ursi*
Beargrass – *Xerophyllum tenax*
Bellflowers – *Adenophora, Campanula*
Bellworts – *Uvularia*

Bethlehem Sage – *Pulmonaria saccharata*
Bilberries – *Vaccinium*
Birches – *Betula*
Birdseye primroses – *Primula* (Farinosa Group)
Bishop's-caps – *Mitella*
Bitter-root – *Lewisia rediviva*
Blackberries – *Rubus*
Bladder campions – *Silene*
Bladderpods – *Lesquerella, Physaria*
Blazing-stars – *Liatris*
Bleeding-hearts – *Dicentra*
Bloodroot – *Sanguinaria canadensis*
Bluebead-lily – *Clintonia borealis*
Bluebells – *Campanula, Mertensia, Scilla*
Blueberries – *Vaccinium*
Blue Cohosh – *Caulophyllum thalictroides*
Blue-eyed grasses – *Sisyrinchium*
Blue-eyed Mary – *Omphalodes verna*
Bluets – *Houstonia*
Bog asphodels – *Tofieldia*
Bog rosemaries – *Andromeda*
Box, boxwoods – *Buxus*
Brambles – *Rubus*

Broom-crowberry – *Corema conradii*

Brooms – *Cytisus, Genista*

Buckbean – *Menyanthes trifoliata*

Buffalo-robe – *Callirhoe involucrata*

Bugbanes – *Cimicifuga*

Bugleweeds – *Ajuga*

Bunchberry – *Cornus canadensis*

Buttercups – *Ranunculus*

Butterfly-weed – *Asclepias tuberosa*

Butterworts – *Pinguicula*

Cacti – *Neobesseya, Opuntia*

California Fuchsia – *Zauschneria californica*

Camass lilies – *Camassia*

Camomiles – *Anthemis*

Campions – *Lychnis, Silene*

Candelabra primroses – *Primula* (Candelabra Group)

Candytufts – *Iberis*

Cardinal Flower – *Lobelia cardinalis*

Catchflies – *Lychnis, Silene*

Catmints – *Nepeta*

Cat's-ears – *Calochortus*

Cedars – *Juniperus*

Celandine Poppy – *Stylophorum diphyllum*

Checkerberry – *Gaultheria procumbens*

Cherries – *Prunus*

Chickweeds – *Cerastium*

Christmas Rose – *Helleborus niger*

Cinquefoils – *Potentilla*

Cloudberry – *Rubus chamaemorus*

Clovers – *Trifolium*

Columbines – *Aquilegia*

Coral-bells – *Heuchera*

Cornflowers – *Centaurea*

Cowslip(s) – *Caltha palustris, Dodecatheon, Mertensia virginica, Primula veris*

Cranberries – *Vaccinium*

Cranesbills – *Geranium*

Creeping Snowberry – *Gaultheria hispidula*

Cresses – *Lepidium*

Crowberry – *Empetrum nigrum*

Crown Imperial – *Fritillaria imperialis*

Crown-vetches – *Coronilla*

Cucumber-root – *Medeola virginiana*

Cupflowers – *Nierembergia*

Currants – *Ribes*

Daffodils – *Narcissus*

Daisies – *Chrysanthemum*

Death-camasses – *Zygadenus*

Devil's-bit – *Chamaelirium luteum*

Dogtooth violets – *Erythronium*

Dogwoods – *Cornus*

Doll's-eyes – *Actaea pachypoda*

Dragonheads – *Dracocephalum*

Dragon-mouth – *Arethusa bulbosa*

Dragonroot – *Arisaema dracontium*

Dutchman's-breeches – *Dicentra cucullaria*

Easter daisies – *Townsendia*

Edelweiss – *Leontopodium*

English Bluebell – *Scilla non-scripta*
English Turfing Daisy – *Bellis perennis*
Evening-primroses – *Oenothera*
Everlastings – *Antennaria, Helichrysum*

Fairy bells – *Disporum*
Fairy Slipper – *Calypso bulbosa*
False cypresses – *Chamaecyparis*
False indigos – *Baptisia*
False Solomon's-seals – *Smilacina*
Fescues – *Festuca*
Figworts – *Ourisia*
Fire Pink – *Silene virginica*
Fireweed – *Epilobium angustifolium*
Flaxes – *Linum*
Fleabanes – *Erigeron*
Flowering shamrocks – *Oxalis*
Foamflowers – *Tiarella*
Forget-me-nots – *Eritrichium, Myosotis*
Foxgloves – *Digitalis*
Fringecups – *Lithophragma, Tellima*
Fringed orchids, fringed orchises – *Habenaria*

Garland Flower – *Daphne cneorum*
Garlics – *Allium*
Gayfeathers – *Liatris*
Gaywings – *Polygala paucifolia*
Germanders – *Teucrium*
Ginsengs – *Panax*
Glacier-lilies – *Erythronium*

Globe-flowers – *Trollius*
Globe-mallows – *Sphaeralcea*
Gold-drops – *Onosma*
Golden asters – *Chrysopsis*
Golden-eyed Grass – *Sisyrinchium californicum*
Goldenrods – *Solidago*
Goldenseal – *Hydrastis canadensis*
Goldthreads – *Coptis*
Gooseberries – *Ribes*
Grape-hollies – *Mahonia*
Grape-hyacinths – *Muscari*
Grass-of-Parnassus – *Parnassia*
Grass-pink – *Calopogon pulchellus*
Grass-widow – *Sisyrinchium douglasii*
Ground-hemlock – *Taxus canadensis*
Groundnut – *Panax trifolium*
Groundsels – *Senecio*
Guinea-hen Flower – *Fritillaria meleagris*

Harebell – *Campanula rotundifolia*
Hawkweeds – *Hieracium*
Heal-alls – *Prunella*
Heaths – *Bruckenthalia, Daboecia, Erica*
Heathers – *Bruckenthalia, Calluna, Erica*
Hemlocks – *Tsuga*
Hens-and-chicks – *Sempervivum*
Heronsbills – *Erodium*
Hollies – *Ilex*
Horned rampions – *Phyteuma*

Horsemints – *Monardella*
Hound's-tonque – *Cynoglossum grande*
Houseleeks – *Sempervivum*
Huckleberries – *Gaylussacia*

Indian paintbrushes – *Castilleja*
Indian tobaccos – *Antennaria*
Innocence – *Houstonia caerulea*
Inside-out Flower – *Vancouveria hexandra*
Irish Heath – *Daboecia cantabrica*
Ivies – *Hedera*

Jack-in-the-pulpits – *Arisaema*
Jacob's-ladders – *Polemonium*
Johnny-jump-up – *Viola tricolor*

Kinnikinnicks – *Arctostaphylos*
Knotweeds – *Polygonum*

Labrador teas – *Ledum*
Ladies'-tresses – *Spiranthes*
Lady's-slippers – *Cypripedium*
Lady's-mantle – *Alchemilla alpina*
Lamb's-ears – *Stachys lanata*
Larkspurs – *Delphinium*
Laurels – *Kalmia*
Lavenders – *Lavandula*
Leatherleaf – *Chamaedaphne calyculata*
Leeks – *Allium*
Lenten Rose – *Helleborus orientalis*
Lily-turfs – *Liriope*
Lilacs – *Syringa*

Lingenberry – *Vaccinium vitis-idaea*
Liverleaves – *Hepatica*
London Pride – *Saxifraga umbrosa*
Lords-and-ladies – *Arum maculatum*
Loosestrifes – *Lysimachia*
Louseworts – *Pedicularis*
Lungworts – *Mertensia, Pulmonaria*

Madworts – *Alyssum*
Mahala Mat – *Ceanothus prostratus, C. pumilus*
Mallows – *Callirhoe, Malva*
Mandrake – *Podophyllum peltatum*
Manzanitas – *Arctostaphylos*
Mariposa-lilies – *Calochortus*
Marsh Marigold – *Caltha palustris*
Masterworts – *Astrantia*
Mayapples – *Podophyllum*
Mayflower – *Epigaea repens*
Meadow-beauties – *Rhexia*
Meadow rues – *Thalictrum*
Milk-vetches – *Astragalus*
Milkweeds – *Asclepias*
Milkworts – *Polygala*
Mist-maiden – *Romanzoffia sitchensis*
Moneywort – *Lysimachia nummularia*
Monkeyflowers – *Mimulus*
Monkshoods – *Aconitum*
Moss-pink – *Phlox subulata, Silene acaulis*
Mountain-ashes – *Sorbus*
Mountain heathers – *Cassiope, Phyllodoce*
Mountain-sorrel – *Oxyria digyna*

Mulleins – *Verbascum*
Myrtle – *Vinca minor*

Nailworts – *Paronychia*
Navelworts – *Omphalodes*
New Jersey Tea – *Ceanothus americanus*
Nippon-bells – *Shortia uniflora*

Oconee-bells – *Shortia galacifolia*
Old-maid's Bonnet – *Clematis douglasii*
Onions – *Allium*
Oregon grapes – *Mahonia*
Oregon sunshines – *Eriophyllum*

Paintbrushes – *Castilleja*
Partridgeberry – *Mitchella repens*
Pasque-flowers – *Pulsatilla*
Pearlworts – *Sagina*
Penny-cresses – *Thlaspi*
Peonies – *Paeonia*
Perennial peas – *Lathyrus*
Periwinkle – *Vinca minor*
Persian candytufts – *Aethionema*
Pickerelweed – *Pontederia cordata*
Pincushion flowers – *Scabiosa*
Pines – *Pinus*
Pinks – *Dianthus*
Pipsissewas – *Chimaphila*
Pitcher-plants – *Darlingtonia, Sarracenia*
Plantain-lilies – *Hosta*
Plums – *Prunus*
Plumbago – *Ceratostigma plumbaginoides*

Polyanthus – *Primula polyanthus*
Poppies – *Meconopsis, Papaver*
Poppy mallows – *Callirhoe*
Prickly-pears – *Opuntia*
Primroses – *Primula*
Pussy-paws – *Spraguea*
Pussytoes – *Antennaria*
Pyxie-mosses – *Pyxidanthera*

Quaker ladies – *Houstonia*

Ragworts – *Senecio*
Rattlesnake plantains – *Goodyera*
Restharrows – *Ononis*
Rock cresses – *Aethionema, Arabis, Aubrieta*
Rock-jasmines – *Androsace*
Rock-roses – *Helianthemum*
Rose Pogonia – *Pogonia ophioglossoides*
Rue Anemone – *Anemonella thalictroides*

Sagebrushes – *Artemisia*
Sages – *Salvia*
St. Bernard's Lily – *Anthericum liliago*
St. Bruno's Lily – *Paradisea liliastrum*
St. Johnsworts – *Hypericum*
Sand Lily – *Leucocrinum montanum*
Sand-myrtles – *Leiophyllum*
Sandworts – *Arenaria*
Savories – *Satureia*
Saxifrages – *Bergenia, Saxifraga*

Scurfy peas – *Psoralea*
Sea-lavenders – *Limonium*
Sea-pinks – *Armeria*
Sedges – *Carex*
Sheep's-bits – *Jasione*
Shinleaves – *Moneses, Pyrola*
Shooting-stars – *Dodecatheon*
Showy Orchis – *Orchis spectabilis*
Silverback – *Luina hypoleuca*
Silverweed – *Potentilla anserina*
Skullcaps – *Scutellaria*
Skunk-cabbages – *Lysichitum,*
   Symplocarpus
Snakeroots – *Cimicifuga*
Snapdragons – *Antirrhinum*
Snowdrops – *Galanthus*
Snowflakes – *Leucojum*
Snow-in-summer – *Cerastium*
   tomentosum
Soapworts – *Saponaria*
Solomon's-seals – *Polygonatum*
Sorrels – *Oxalis, Oxyria*
Speedwells – *Veronica*
Spiderworts – *Tradescantia*
Spike-mosses – *Selaginella*
Spiny thrifts – *Acantholimon*
Spotted Dog – *Pulmonaria sac-*
   charata
Spring-beauties – *Claytonia, Montia*
Spruces – *Picea*
Spurges – *Euphorbia, Pachysandra*
Squills – *Scilla*
Squirrel-corn – *Dicentra canadensis*
Starflowers – *Trientalis*
Stargrasses – *Hypoxis*

Star-of-Bethlehem – *Ornithogalum*
   umbellatum
Statices – *Limonium*
Stokes Aster – *Stokesia laevis*
Stone-cresses – *Aethionema*
Stonecrops – *Sedum*
Strawberries – *Fragaria*
Striped squills – *Puschkinia*
Sundews – *Drosera*
Sunflowers – *Balsamorhiza*
Sun-roses – *Helianthemum*
Swamp-pink – *Helonias bullata*
Sweet-vetches – *Hedysarum*

Tansies – *Tanacetum*
Thrifts – *Armeria*
Toadflaxes – *Linaria*
Toad-lilies – *Tricyrtis*
Toothworts – *Dentaria*
Trailing Arbutus – *Epigaea repens*
Trout lilies – *Erythronium*
Turkey-beard – *Xerophyllum*
   asphodeloides
Turtleheads – *Chelone*
Twinflower – *Linnaea borealis*
Twisted-stalks – *Streptopus*

Umbrella-leaf – *Diphylleia cymosa*

Valerians – *Patrinia, Valeriana*
Vervains – *Verbena*
Vetches – *Anthyllis*
Violets – *Viola*
Virgin's-bowers – *Clematis*

Wake-robins – *Trillium*
Wallflowers – *Erysimum*
Wandflower – *Galax aphylla*
Waterleaves – *Hydrophyllum*
Welch Poppy – *Meconopsis cambrica*
Wheel-bells – *Edraianthus*
Whitlow-worts – *Paronychia*
Wild buckwheats – *Eriogonum*
Wild Calla – *Calla palustris*
Wild gingers – *Asarum*
Wild lilies-of-the-valley – *Maianthemum*
Wild Pink – *Silene caroliniana*
Willow-herbs – *Epilobium*

Willows – *Salix*
Windflowers – *Anemone, Pulsatilla*
Wine-cups – *Callirhoe*
Winter Aconite – *Eranthis hyemalis*
Wintergreen – *Gaultheria procumbens*
Wood betonies – *Pedicularis*
Woodruffs – *Asperula*
Wormwoods – *Artemisia*

Yarrows – *Achillea*
Yellow-eyed Grass – *Hypoxis hirsuta*
Yews – *Taxus*

Ferns

Beech ferns – *Thelypteris*
Birdsfoot Fern – *Pellaea ornithopus*
Boulder Fern – *Dennstaedtia punctiloba*
Bulblet Bladder Fern – *Cystopteris bulbifera*

Chain ferns – *Woodwardia*
Christmas Fern – *Polystichum acrostichoides*
Cinnamon Fern – *Osmunda cinnamomea*
Cliffbrakes – *Pellaea*
Climbing Fern – *Lygodium palmatum*
Coffee Fern – *Pellaea andromedaefolia*

Deer Fern – *Blechnum spicant*

Fragile Fern – *Cystopteris fragilis*

Glade Fern – *Athyrium pycnocarpon*
Goldback Fern – *Pityrogramma triangularis*

Hard ferns – *Blechnum*
Hartford Fern – *Lygodium palmatum*
Hart's-tongue Fern – *Phyllitus scolopendrium*
Hay-scented Fern – *Dennstaedtia punctiloba*
Holly ferns – *Polystichum*

Interrupted Fern – *Osmunda claytoniana*

Lace Fern – *Cheilanthes gracillima*
Lady Fern – *Athyrium filix-femina*
Lipferns – *Cheilanthes*

Maidenhair ferns – *Adiantum*
Male Fern – *Dryopteris filix-mas*
Marsh Fern – *Thelypteris palustris*
Massachusetts Fern – *Thelypteris simulata*

New York Fern – *Thelypteris noveboracensis*

Oak Fern – *Gymnocarpium dryopteris*
Ostrich Fern – *Matteuccia struthiopteris*

Parsley Fern – *Cryptogramma crispa*
Polypodies – *Polypodium*

Rock brakes – *Cryptogramma*
Royal Fern – *Osmunda regalis*
Rustyback Fern – *Ceterach officinarum*

Sensitive Fern – *Onoclea sensibilis*
Shield ferns – *Dryopteris*
Spleenworts – *Asplenium, Athyrium*
Sword Fern – *Polystichum munitum*

Walking Fern – *Camptosorus rhizophyllus*
Wall Rue – *Asplenium ruta-muraria*
Woodferns – *Dryopteris*

Descriptive Bibliography
Other Sources of Information

Descriptive Bibliography

All About Rock Gardens and Plants by Walter A. Kolaga. New York: Doubleday and Co., Inc., 1966.

Chapters devoted to construction and maintenance of a variety of types of rock gardens are written clearly. Description of basic plants for the rock garden, including separate chapters on bulbs, annuals, and conifers make the book fairly comprehensive, if not as complete as the immoderate title suggests.

Alpine and Rock Gardening by W. E. Shewell-Cooper and Others. Vol. II in the Ullswater Library of Gardening. London: Seeley Service and Co., Ltd., 1961.

This contains chapters on all aspects of construction and maintenance of the rock garden proper, and includes special features such as moraines, wall gardens, peat beds, alpine-house. Each section is written by a well-known modern British authority. Well illustrated and indexed.

Alpine Gardening by Roy Elliot. London: Vista Books, 1963.

This is a charmingly written book about the author's personal experience with alpine plants in his garden and alpine-house. There is both inspiration and instruction.

The Azalea Book by Frederic P. Lee. 2nd Ed. Princeton, N.J.: Van Nostrand, 1965.

Mr. Lee has brought to this book many years of study and practical experience in growing deciduous and evergreen azaleas. Valuable as a reference for descriptions of species and hybrids and sound cultural information.

California Mountain Wildflowers by Philip A. Munz. Berkeley: University of California Press, 1963.

A handy field guide, with 276 species pictured, some in color. By no means complete. No cultural directions but some clues about habitat.

Campanulas by H. Clifford Crook. London: Country Life, 1951.

A scholarly yet readable book describing all species of campanulas likely to be available to gardeners; most species illustrated in black and white photographs.

Collectors' Alpines by Royton E. Heath. London: Collingridge, 1964.

This thick, beautifully illustrated book is devoted to the growing of rock garden plants in pots. The directions are explicit and thorough, frequently of value in giving sound hints for success not only in pot-culture but in the garden. Many rare and recently introduced plants are described.

Collins Guide to Alpines by Anna N. Griffith. London: Collins, 1964. The American edition is titled *A Guide to Rock Garden Plants*. New York: Dutton, 1965.

A thorough book, very useful as a reference for identification and growing instructions, including easy and difficult plants. 1900 plants described, 200 pictured in color photographs by Valerie Finnis.

Collins Guide to Bulbs by Patrick M. Synge. London: Collins, 1961. The American edition is titled *The Complete Guide to Bulbs*. New York: Dutton, 1962.

Excellent cultural information and very thorough description of most species of all important genera. Hundreds of handsome color illustrations. An essential reference work.

Dwarf Conifers: A Complete Guide by H. J. Welch. London: Faber, 1966.

This comes close to living up to the title, since there are described almost every known dwarf and slow-growing conifer, at least as they exist in England. Many are illustrated. There is also much highly readable information on how to grow these increasingly popular plants.

Dwarf Conifers: A Handbook on Low and Slow-growing Evergreens Vol. 21 (1965), No. 1 of *Plants and Gardens*. Brooklyn, N.Y.: Brooklyn Botanic Garden.

This 65-page handbook is the best American reference work for the dwarf conifers suitable for the rock garden. Besides articles of general information on the subject, including advice on propagation and culture, the heart of the book is a description of 300 kinds arranged alphabetically by genus. Many are illustrated in black and white photographs of superior quality.

The English Rock-Garden by Reginald Farrer. 2 vols. London and New York: Nelson, 1918.

This is the classic reference work, indispensable for its vast fund of knowledge and inimitable style. A delight to read and use.

A Field Guide to the Ferns by Boughton Cobb. Boston: Houghton Mifflin, 1956.

A true guide to identification of northeastern United States ferns, horsetails, and lycopodiums. Excellent illustrations plus easy-to-follow, nontechnical keys make this a handy and useful book. Some cultural information included.

A Field Guide to Rocky Mountain Wildflowers by John J. Craighead, Frank C. Craighead, Jr., and Ray J. Davis. Boston: Houghton Mifflin, 1963.

Though by no means complete, this describes 590 of the commoner and showier species of the flowering plants in the Rockies. Of great value are the 209 color photographs.

Gentians by David Wilkie. 2nd Ed. London: Country Life, 1950. New York: Scribner, 1936 (1st Ed.).

A complete guide to identification and culture of an important genus by the world's acknowledged expert.

Hardy Heaths by Arthur T. Johnson. London: Blanford Press, 1956.

A compact book covering all aspects of the heath garden: species and varieties of heaths, heathers, and allied plants, cultural directions, propagation, and companion plants.

How to Plan, Establish, and Maintain Rock Gardens by George Schenk. Menlo Park, Calif.: Lane Book Co., 1964. A Sunset Book.

A sound approach to construction and landscape effects. Many fine photographs truly illuminate the brief, well-written text. A clear point of view about rock gardening somewhat slanted to the north-western United States but adaptable elsewhere.

The Present-Day Rock Garden by Sampson Clay. London and New York: Nelson, 1937.

This is to supplement the classic Farrer work, essential for its description of plants not known at the time Farrer wrote. It also corrects some errors of the earlier work.

Primulas in the Garden by Kenneth C. Corsar. 2nd Ed. London: Geoffrey Bles, 1952. New York: Macmillan, 1949 (1st Ed.).

A clearly written guide, with fine black and white photographs; descriptions with cultural directions for the common and rare species.

The Propagation of Alpines by Lawrence D. Hills. New York: Pellegrini and Cudahy, 1950.

Packed with sound information on the propagation of rock garden plants. Covers all methods for 2500 species, ranging from the very easy to the very difficult.

Rhododendrons of the World by David G. Leach. New York: Scribner, 1961.

This is the authoritative work on the whole range of rhododendrons (excluding those commonly called azaleas) and how to grow them. An expensive book, but essential for reference.

Rock Garden Plants by Doretta Klaber. New York: Holt, 1959.

This is a concise and sensible guide to growing a wide assortment of rock garden plants in the average home landscape. Sketches by the author illustrate cultural advice and suggested plants.

Wild Flowers by Homer D. House. New York: Macmillan, 1961.

An excellent nontechnical book for wildflowers of the northeastern United States. Excellent color photographs and clear text, with ample information on habitat and blooming season. No cultural directions.

Wild Flowers of the United States, Vol. I (in two parts), The Northeastern States, by Harold W. Rickett. New York: McGraw-Hill for The New York Botanical Garden, 1966.

This is the long awaited first volume of the projected pictorial guide to the wildflowers of the whole country. About 1700 species are described in layman's language and all but a few are illustrated by color photographs, mostly of good quality. An expensive but useful reference for the gardener's library. Vol. II (also in two parts), The Southeastern States, was published in 1967.

Other Sources of Information

MEMBERSHIP in rock garden societies and others that specialize in plants associated with the rock garden is rewarding. The publications are full of information, and the seed exchanges furnish a source of seeds frequently difficult to acquire commercially.

Because the Society secretaries change from time to time, none are listed here. Your horticultural society, botanical garden, state university, or nurseryman generally can supply current addresses for the following:

> Alpine Garden Society (England)
> American Penstemon Society
> American Primrose Society
> American Rhododendron Society
> American Rock Garden Society
> Scottish Rock Garden Club

No list of nurseries is included because they come and go. Reference to advertisements in the publications of the societies listed above will furnish names and addresses of currently operating nurseries.

Index

Index to
Part I

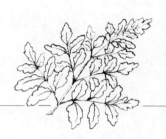